Psychology and the Bible

**Recent Titles in
Psychology, Religion, and Spirituality**
J. Harold Ellens, Series Editor

Married to an Opposite:
Making Personality Differences Work for You
Ron Shackelford

Sin against the Innocents:
Sexual Abuse by Priests and the Role of the Catholic Church
Thomas G. Plante, Editor

Seeking the Compassionate Life:
The Moral Crisis for Psychotherapy and Society
Carl Goldberg and Virginia Crespo

PSYCHOLOGY AND THE BIBLE

A New Way to Read the Scriptures

VOLUME 1

From Freud to Kohut

Edited by

J. Harold Ellens and Wayne G. Rollins

Foreword by Donald Capps

PRAEGER PERSPECTIVES

Psychology, Religion, and Spirituality

Westport, Connecticut
London

Library of Congress Cataloging-in-Publication Data

Psychology and the Bible: a new way to read the Scriptures / edited by J. Harold Ellens
and Wayne G. Rollins; foreword by Donald Capps.
    p. cm.—(Psychology, religion, and spirituality, ISSN 1546–8070)
    Includes bibliographical references and index.
    Contents: v. 1. From Freud to Kohut—v. 2. From Genesis to apocalyptic vision—v. 3.
From Gospel to Gnostics—v. 4. From Christ to Jesus.
    ISBN 0-275-98347-1 (set : alk paper)—ISBN 0-275-98348-X (v. 1 : alk paper)—
ISBN 0-275-98349-8 (v. 2 : alk paper)—ISBN 0-275-98350-1 (v. 3 : alk paper)—
ISBN 0-275-98462-1 (v. 4 : alk paper)
    1. Bible—Psychology.   2. Psychoanalysis and religion.   I. Ellens, J. Harold, 1932–
II. Rollins, Wayne G.   III. Series.
BS645.P89 2004
220.6′01′9—dc22   2004050863

British Library Cataloguing in Publication Data is available.

Library of Congress Catalog Card Number: 2004050863

ISBN: 0–275–98347–1 (set)
        0–275–98348–X (vol. I)
        0–275–98349–8 (vol. II)
        0–275–98350–1 (vol. III)
        0–275–98462–1 (vol. IV)
ISSN: 1546-8070

First published in 2004

Praeger Publishers, 88 Post Road West, Westport, CT 06881
An imprint of Greenwood Publishing Group, Inc.
www.praeger.com

Printed in the United States of America

The paper used in this book complies with the
Permanent Paper Standard issued by the
National Information Standards Organization (Z39.48–1984).

10 9 8 7 6 5 4 3 2 1

CONTENTS

Foreword

Donald Capps

I learned about the psychological study of the Bible as a PhD student, when, in a psychology of religion course taught by David Bakan, I was introduced to an essentially psychoanalytic approach to the Bible. Before that, despite two years of intensive graduate study, not one of my professors had ever breathed a word about the psychological study of the Bible. Even in Bakan's course, the idea that the Bible could be approached psychologically seemed idiosyncratic and odd, yet strangely compelling. At the time, Bakan was mostly interested in what he called the "infanticidal impulse," the desire of adults to kill children, and he viewed the story of Abraham and Isaac in Genesis 22 as illustrative not only of the infanticidal impulse itself but also of its displacement through animal sacrifice (see Bakan, 1968).

I might not have gotten hooked by this field of study had my introduction to it involved merely abstract theorizing, or had I not been introduced to it when young men were being sent by their political fathers to fight in a controversial war in Vietnam. In any case, I did get hooked, and the psychological study of the Bible has been the primary, perhaps the sole, means by which I have remained faithful to the religious legacy that was imparted to me as a child. I am sure that many others whose work is presented in these four volumes could make similar testimonies to the personal value and importance of the psychological study of the Bible and would subscribe to the view that the way to renewed faith and trust is not around but through psychology.

The field of the psychological study of the Bible has come a very long way since my introduction to it in the mid-1960s. As Wayne G. Rollins documents in *Soul and Psyche: The Bible in Psychological Perspective*, a "sheaf of articles and books in the late 1960s and early 1970s appeared from within the orbit of biblical scholarship," calling "for a fresh look at the contributions psychological and psychoanalytic research might bring to the task of biblical interpretation" (1999, 68). Many scholars both within biblical studies and in fields such as the psychology of religion, which had manifested considerable but erratic interest in the Bible in previous decades, responded to this call. Over the next two decades, so much interest had been generated that in 1991 the Society of Biblical Literature approved a proposal to establish a program unit on Psychology and Biblical Studies. This program unit would assess the significance of the approaches employed to date and would provide a forum for developing the future agenda of psychological criticism as a subdiscipline within biblical studies. The faithfulness with which these responsibilities have been carried out accounts to a large extent for the fact that, some thirteen years later, J. Harold Ellens and Wayne G. Rollins had little difficulty finding willing contributors to this four-volume collection titled *Psychology and the Bible*.

Both editors of these volumes have offered their own characterizations of the field. In a special issue on psychology and the Bible in *Pastoral Psychology*, a journal whose editor, Lewis R. Rambo, has been unusually receptive to psychological studies of biblical texts, J. Harold Ellens, who guest edited the issue, assessed the state of the field and clarified its focus. In his guest editorial, "Psychology and the Bible: The Interface of Corollary Disciplines" (1997a), he pointed out that, beginning in the early 1960s, a consciously crafted critique of the positivist assumptions of the Enlightenment had given rise to interest in interdisciplinary studies, and that one of the most significant of these was the application of interdisciplinary approaches using scientific models and methods for investigation of religious traditions, practices, and experiences. As one such scientific discipline, psychology has played an increasingly important role in these interdisciplinary approaches. As Ellens notes, "we found ourselves teaching courses and doing research in the sociology of religion, the psychology of religion, the Bible in Western literary traditions, psychotheology, psychospirituality, transcendental psychology, and the like. This undertaking was influenced, as well, by the birth of sturdy concerns to investigate the interface of many of the great religions of the world, particularly the encounter between Eastern and Western psychology and spirituality" (1997a, 159–160).

In his essay "The Bible and Psychology: An Interdisciplinary Pilgrimage" in the same issue of *Pastoral Psychology*, Ellens noted that one of the fruitful products of this new interest in interdisciplinary studies was the publication of many significant books and articles on the interface between the disciplines of psychology, theology, and biblical studies, and suggested that the focus of interdisciplinary work in psychology and biblical studies is that of bringing "the insights and models of psychology to bear upon a biblical text, assessing the nature and function of the author, of the implied or stated intended audience, of the real audiences in the church's history which interpreted the text, together with their interpretations, and thus assess the reasons, healthy or pathological, for the constructs that were expressed in the text and in subsequent uses of it" (1997b, 206). Note, here, the assumption that biblical texts have not only been used—misused—to legitimate pathological ideas and behaviors, but that the original texts themselves may also reflect pathological as well as healthy ways of thinking and behaving.

A very tangible reflection of this understanding of what psychology may contribute to biblical studies is the recent publication of four volumes titled *The Destructive Power of Religion: Violence in Judaism, Christianity, and Islam* (2004), edited by Ellens. One of the four volumes is devoted exclusively to sacred scriptures. In his own essay "Toxic Texts," Ellens notes that "sacred scriptures motivate ordinary people to amazing achievements in spirituality, religion, and cultural creativity." By the same token, "the inspiration of sacred scriptures can also be devastatingly destructive, spiritually, psychologically, and culturally" (2004, 3:1–2). To illustrate their destructive side, he explores the story in John 9 about Jesus' healing of a man who was born blind, noting that this text "is generally prized by Bible scholars and religious devotees," yet it "has a dangerous subtext or underside that has been ignored," a subtext that "can have a destructive effect on persons, communities, and cultures by the negative archetypes that it may generate at the unconscious psychological level" (2).

In "Rationale and Agenda for a Psychological-Critical Approach to the Bible and Its Interpretation, Biblical and Humane" (1996), published at nearly the same time as Ellens's two *Pastoral Psychology* articles, Wayne G. Rollins identified what he termed "a psychological-critical approach" to the Bible. The goal of this approach "is to examine texts (including their origination, authorship, and modes of expression,

their construction, transmission, translation, reading, and interpretation, their transposition into kindred and alien art forms, and the history of their personal and cultural effect) as expressions of the structure, processes, and habits of the human psyche, both in individual and
collective manifestations, past and present" (1996, 160). Key here is
the understanding that the original texts, their transmission, and
their transposition into other forms are all expressions of the human
psyche, its cognitive and emotional structures and processes, its habits
of mind and heart.

Three years later, in *Soul and Psyche*, which comprehensively reviews
both past and present work in this burgeoning interdisciplinary field,
Rollins cited a third effort to characterize the field and commended it
for its accuracy and succinctness. This is Antoine Vergote's proposal
that the purpose of psychological biblical criticism is "to understand
the mental universe of the biblical tradition" (1999, 78). Building on the
idea that the "mental universe" of the biblical tradition is its appropriate focus, Rollins went on to suggest that the fundamental premise that
informs research in the field of psychological biblical criticism and that
constitutes the insight that gave birth to the discipline can be stated as
follows: "From a biblical-critical perspective, the Bible is to be seen as
part and product, not only of a historical, literary, and socioanthropological process, but also of a psychological process. In this process, conscious and unconscious factors are at work in the biblical authors and
their communities, in the texts they have produced, in readers and
interpreters of these texts and in their communities, and in the individual, communal, and cultural effects of these interpretations" (1999, 92).

This premise not only includes the view that the Bible is part and
product of "a psychological process" but also introduces the idea,
emphasized by psychodynamic theorists such as Freud, Jung, and their
followers, that both conscious and unconscious factors are at work in
this process. Thus, one of the primary purposes of the "psychological-
critical approach" is to make that which is unconscious conscious.
Rollins goes on, however, to emphasize that what is especially under
examination in a psychological-critical approach "is the *psychological
context* and *psychological content* of the Bible and its interpretation"
(1999, 93). Together, these two prongs of critical examination have
the larger objective of enhancing the repertory of critical perspectives
on the Bible (historical, literary, socioanthropological) "by adding to it
a vision of the text as itself a psychic product, reality, symptom, and
event, and as a source of commentary on the nature, life, habits,
pathology, health, and purpose of the psyche/soul" (1999, 94). Thus,

endorsing Ellens's view that a central focus of interdisciplinary work in psychology and biblical studies is to "assess the reasons, healthy or pathological, for the constructs that were expressed in the text and in subsequent uses of it," Rollins suggests that in addition to being "a source of commentary" on matters of pathology and health, the Bible, as itself a psychic product, may reveal both healthy and pathological mental and emotional structures and processes.

Because one of my own special interests is the pathogenic character-istic of some biblical texts, I am both impressed and encouraged by the fact that whether explicitly or implicitly, the essays included in these four volumes are concerned with the pathology and health of the psy-chological process at work in the biblical authors and their communi-ties and in their subsequent interpreters. For Rollins, as for Ellens, this concern is part of the second of two agendas in the psychological study of the Bible, the exegetical and the hermeneutical. In a section of his chapter "The Hermeneutical Agenda" in *Soul and Psyche,* bear-ing the heading "The History of Biblical Effects in Psychological Per-spective: Pathogenic and Therapeutic Effects," Rollins notes: "It is no longer a secret in scholarly and even ecclesiastical literature that the Bible and its interpretation can have pathogenic effects on individuals and cultures—an acknowledgment that has been both liberating and dismaying for those who treasure the text" (1999, 175).

By the same token, the very recognition of the pathogenic effects of the Bible and its interpretation has reawakened interest in its thera-peutic effects:

> Scholarly interest in the pathogenic aspects of the Bible has been matched at the end of the twentieth century with renewed interest in its therapeutic dimension. As much as the Bible provides evidence of patho-genic potential, even more does it provide evidence that it can transform consciousness, change behavior patterns, and open up a new cognition of reality in ways that have affected individuals and shaped entire cul-tures for generations. (Rollins, 1999, 177)

Rollins concludes that a major undertaking for psychological biblical criticism in the future

> will be to develop a critical method for identifying, measuring, and assessing the degree to which the text presents itself as the mediator of a therapeutic agenda, to come to an understanding of the strategies it recommends for achieving this agenda, to compare it with contempo-rary therapeutic models, and to consider what insight it can add to col-lective scholarship and thought on the *cura animarum* in our own time. (1999, 179)

Although the psychological-critical approach to the Bible has much in common with other critical approaches, these other approaches are not as likely to give sustained or systematic attention to the fact that the Bible has both pathogenic and therapeutic aspects. The psychological-critical method bears a special responsibility for recognizing and pointing out the difference. Attempts throughout history to make the case that certain biblical texts have priority over other biblical texts because they are more central to the Bible's own intentionality—the so-called canon within the canon—have been exposed as misleading and self-serving. However, those who endorse (as I myself do) the view of the editors of these four volumes that the psychological study of the Bible entails the assessment of the pathogenic and therapeutic aspects of biblical texts may well accord the healing stories in the New Testament Gospels a special status as a "source of commentary" on matters of health and pathology, and thus as valuable in their own right for assessing the healthy and pathological constructs in other biblical texts and interpretations thereof. This means that it is not merely a matter of bringing twenty-first-century understandings of health and pathology to bear on biblical texts—after all, these understandings are implicated in the very constructs that they intend to assess—but also of using the biblical tradition's own understandings of what makes for health and pathology to assess its own psychological processes. Perhaps this is why Erik H. Erikson could both endorse the spirit of Thomas Jefferson's attempt to provide Native Americans an abridged version of "the philosophy of Jesus of Nazareth" extracted from the four Gospels and critique his decision to eliminate "all references to Jesus' healing mission" (Erikson, 1974, 40–50).

Finally, the very fact that the Bible continues to have an emotional as well as intellectual attraction even for those of us who acknowledge its pathogenic features is itself a question that invites and warrants psychological examination and assessment. Three or four years before I was introduced to the psychological study of the Bible, I read Erik H. Erikson's *Young Man Luther: A Study in Psychoanalysis and History* (1958). This book—which, with its advocacy of a psychohistorical method attuned to religious themes, was itself an indirect contributor to the development of the psychological study of the Bible field—advances a psychological theory of the attraction that the Bible held for Luther. I suggest that this theory may have wide application and that it may be one of several emotional links creating a bond between all of the essays (and essayists) in these four volumes. The theory occurs in the midst of a discussion of Luther's "passivity," which

Erikson emphasizes is not mere indifference but the activation of perceptions and their emotional counterparts that existed before Luther's—and other children's—development of will and willfulness. Thus, it is the "passivity" of active reception, the kind of reception that occurs when readers allow a biblical text to "speak" to them. Erikson asks:

> Is it coincidence that Luther, now that he was explicitly teaching passivity, should come to the conclusion that a lecturer should feed his audience as a mother suckles her child? Intrinsic to the kind of passivity we speak of is not only the memory of having been given, but also the identification with the maternal giver: "the glory of a good thing is that it flows out to others." *I think that in the Bible Luther at last found a mother whom he could acknowledge: he could attribute to the Bible a generosity to which he could open himself, and which he could pass on to others, at last a mother's son.* (1958, 208, my emphasis)

Noting that Luther spoke of being reborn "out of the matrix of the scriptures," Erikson adds, "matrix is as close as such a man's man will come to saying 'mater'" (208).

As we have seen, for editors Ellens and Rollins, the psychological process to which the psychological-critical approach attends occurs in the biblical authors and their communities, in the texts they have produced, in the readers and interpreters of these texts and in their communities, and in the individual, communal, and cultural effects of these interpretations. This psychological process *is* the very matrix of the Scriptures. Thus, the essays included in these four volumes attest to the generosity of the Bible, to the fact that it is, indeed, the "good book" (although by no means perfect book) that richly rewards those who come to examine it, assess it, and take its measure. Undoubtedly, its greatest rewards are reserved for those who are unabashedly—perhaps hopelessly—in love with it. In the course of reading these essays, the reader will find, however, that examination, assessment, and love—all three together—are integral to the psychological process to which the Bible itself gives testimony.

Decades from now, our successors will surely wonder how such a monumental undertaking as these four volumes on psychology and the Bible could ever have come about. This undertaking is a reflection of the organizational and administrative acumen that the two editors have also displayed in their work on behalf of the Psychology and Biblical Studies program unit of the Society of Biblical Literature. It is also a tribute to the respect in which they are held by their colleagues. But these four volumes also testify to the editors' exquisite sense of timing. As Jesus' own illustration of the children in the marketplace attests (Matt. 11:16–17), one can pipe a tune, but if no one is either willing or able to dance, nothing much happens. According to my count, aside from the editors themselves, thirty-two responded to their invitation to write essays, and some more than once. Had Abraham done even half as well, the city of Sodom would have been spared. Ellens and Rollins clearly discerned that there are scholars out there who, if asked, are not only willing but able to set aside their inhibitions and fear of self-embarrassment and to venture out on the dance floor, secure in the knowledge that there is safety in numbers. May this monumental undertaking inspire others to make a similar venture.

References

Bakan, D. (1966). *The Duality of Human Existence: An Essay on Psychology and Religion.* Chicago: Rand McNally.

Bakan, D. (1968). *Disease, Pain, and Sacrifice: Toward a Psychology of Suffering.* Chicago: University of Chicago Press.

Ellens, J. H. (1997a). Psychology and the Bible: The Interface of Corollary Disciplines. *Pastoral Psychology, 45,* 159–162.

Ellens, J. H. (1997b). The Bible and Psychology: An Interdisciplinary Pilgrimage. *Pastoral Psychology, 45,* 193–209.

Ellens, J. H., ed. (2004). *The Destructive Power of Religion: Violence in Judaism, Christianity, and Islam* (4 vols.). Westport: Praeger Publishers.

Erikson, E. H. (1958). *Young Man Luther: A Study in Psychoanalysis and History.* New York: Norton.

Erikson, E. H. (1974). *Dimensions of a New Identity.* New York: Norton.

Rollins, W. G. (1996). *Rationale and Agenda for a Psychological-Critical Approach to the Bible and Its Interpretation, Biblical and Humane,* D. Barr, L. B. Elder, & E. S. Malbon, eds. Atlanta: Scholars Press, 153–172.

Rollins, W. G. (1999). *Soul and Psyche: The Bible in Psychological Perspective.* Minneapolis: Fortress.

Series Foreword

J. Harold Ellens, PhD

The interface between psychology, religion, and spirituality has been of great interest to scholars for a century. In the last three decades a broad popular appetite has developed for books that make practical sense out of the sophisticated research on these three subjects. Freud expressed an essentially deconstructive perspective on this matter and indicated that he saw the relationship between human psychology and religion to be a destructive interaction. Jung, on the other hand, was quite sure that these three aspects of the human spirit—psychology, religion, and spirituality—were constructively and inextricably linked. Anton Boisen and Seward Hiltner derived much insight from both Freud and Jung, as well as from Adler and Reik, while pressing the matter forward with gratifying skill and illumination. Boisen and Hiltner fashioned a framework within which the quest for a sound and sensible definition of the interface between psychology, religion, and spirituality might best be described or expressed (Aden & Ellens, 1990). We are in their debt.

This set of general interest books, so wisely urged by Greenwood Press, and particularly by its editor Debbie Carvalko, defines the terms and explores the interface of psychology, religion, and spirituality at the operational level of daily human experience. Each volume in the set identifies, analyzes, describes, and evaluates the full range of issues, of both popular and professional interest, that deal with the psychological factors at play in the way religion takes shape and is expressed, in the way spirituality functions within human persons and shapes both religious formation and expression, and in the ways that spirituality is shaped and expressed by religion. The primary interest is psychological. In terms of the rubrics of the discipline and the science of psychology, this set of superb volumes investigates the operational dynamics of religion and spirituality.

The verbs *shape* and *express* in the previous paragraph refer to the forces that prompt and form religion in persons and communities, as well as to the manifestations of religious behavior in personal forms of spirituality, in acts of spiritually motivated care for society, and in ritual behaviors such as liturgies of worship. In these various aspects of human function, the psychological drivers are identified, isolated, and described in terms of the way they unconsciously and consciously operate in religion and spirituality.

The books in this set are written for the general reader, the local library, and the undergraduate university student. They are also of significant interest to the informed professional, particularly in corollary fields. The volumes in this set have great value for clinical settings and treatment models as well.

This series editor has spent an entire professional lifetime focused specifically on research into the interface of psychology, religion, and spirituality. These matters are of the highest urgency in human affairs today, when religious motivation seems to be playing an increasing role, constructively and destructively, in the arena of social ethics, national politics, and world affairs. It is imperative that we find out immediately what the psychopathological factors are that shape a religion that can launch deadly assaults on the World Trade Center in New York and murder 3,500 people, or a religion that motivates suicide bombers to kill themselves and murder dozens of their neighbors weekly, or a religion that prompts such unjust national policies as preemptive defense—all of which are wreaking havoc on the social fabric, the democratic processes, the domestic tranquility, the economic stability and productivity, and the legitimate right to freedom from fear in every nation in the world today.

Of course not all of the influences of religion now or throughout history have been negative. Indeed, most of the impact of the great religions upon human life and culture has been profoundly redemptive and generative of great good. It is just as urgent, therefore, that we discover and understand better what the psychological forces are that empower people of faith and genuine spirituality to give themselves to all the creative and constructive enterprises that, throughout the centuries, have made of human life the humane, ordered, prosperous, and aesthetic experience it can be at its best. Surely the forces for good in both psychology and spirituality far exceed the powers and proclivities toward the evil that we see so prominently in our world today.

This set of Greenwood Press volumes is dedicated to the greater understanding of psychology, religion, and spirituality, and thus to the profound understanding and empowerment of those psycho-spiritual drivers that can help us transcend the malignancy of our pilgrimage and enormously enhance the humaneness and majesty of the human spirit, indeed, the potential for magnificence in human life.

Reference

Aden, L., & Ellens, J. H. (1990). *Turning Points in Pastoral Care: The Legacy of Anton Boisen and Seward Hiltner*. Grand Rapids: Baker.

CHAPTER 1

INTRODUCTION

J. Harold Ellens and Wayne G. Rollins

Carl Jung once observed that "everything to do with psychology, everything it essentially is and asserts, touches the human psyche so closely that religion least of all can afford to overlook it" (1953–1978, 11:72). We might add a corollary, equally true, that everything to do with religion, everything it essentially is and asserts, touches the human psyche so closely that psychology least of all can afford to overlook it.

Psychology and biblical studies, and religion in general, are beginning to warm up to one another after decades of cool distrust. They are beginning to recognize certain objectives in common, with a faint suspicion that, in history and in fact, they might even be soul mates. In biblical terms, they are discovering they might be mates in the womb, like Jacob and Esau, who for years were estranged and antagonistic but eventually reconciled in the realization of a common bond (Gen. 25:21–26, 33:1–11). For Jacob and Esau, the bond was one of blood and destiny. For psychology and biblical studies, the bond is in the rediscovery of a shared history of commitment to the *cura animarum*: to the study, care, and cure of the human soul or psyche; to the healing of persons, every one of which is a living human document.

The relationship between psychology and biblical studies has not always been cordial. For a period of fifty years or more, from the 1920s to the 1970s, relations between the two disciplines were poisonous. Albert Schweitzer started the downhill attitude toward psychology among biblical scholars with his volume *The Psychiatric Study of Jesus* (1913). Schweitzer, a medical doctor and established biblical scholar, repudiated the psychoanalytic judgment of four psychological theorists who had come to the psychological conclusion that Jesus of Nazareth was "mentally diseased." Schweitzer objected less to their conclusion than to the reductionist and unscholarly methods by which they had arrived at it. On both medical and biblical, historical-critical grounds, Schweitzer declared their work to be worth "exactly zero."[1]

On the psychological side of things, attitudes toward religion began to dim largely as a result of the ascendancy of behaviorist psychology. Before the 1920s it had been commonplace to read about religious topics in psychological journals, but gradually these journals refused to accept articles that had anything to do with religion. In addition, some in the psychoanalytic tradition had the predilection to reduce religion, as well as art and poetry, to a neurosis. Jung himself had added his own denunciation of reductionism: "If a work of art is explained in the same way as a neurosis, then either the work of art is a neurosis or a neurosis is a work of art" (1953–1978, 15:98–100). Even so, many shared disdain for the unthinking dogmatism, the literalism, and the antagonism to secular learning among so many religionists and Bible-toting proponents of religion who dismissed "secular" learning. The result was silence and, more truthfully, hostile alienation.

By the 1960s and 1970s, however, the ill will between the two camps began to dissipate as the result of three developments. The first was the appearance of new schools of psychological theory and method, for example, humanistic psychology, cognitive psychology, learning theory, and developmental psychology, all of which challenged the reductionist, materialist, and positivist approach of behaviorist psychology.

A second development within biblical studies was the emergence of new types of biblical criticism that undermined the sovereignty of historical-literary studies. In 1977 John Dominic Crossan foresaw that "biblical study will no longer be conducted under the exclusive hegemony" of one or two disciplines but rather "through a multitude of disciplines interacting mutually as a field criticism" (41). These new approaches would include social-scientific, rhetorical, ideological, canonical, contextual, feminist, structural, deconstructionist, and psychological criticism, among others, all raising new questions about the Bible that traditional historical criticism was unequipped to ask or answer.

The third development was the general "psychologization" of Western culture. Most everyone, from TV commentators to novelists, theologians, and cabbies, found themselves speaking with a psychological accent, making commonplace references to "unconscious motives," "repressed desires," "complexes," "neuroses," and "Freudian slips." Largely the legacy of Freud and Jung, the new language voiced a changing popular consciousness about the nature of the self. One of the more striking pieces of evidence that psychology and biblical studies are moving into the reconciled Jacob and Esau stage is a remarkable report published in 1993 by the Pontifical Biblical Commission. Titled "The Interpretation of the Bible in the Church," the report identified fifteen major approaches to biblical studies in the twentieth century, one of which was "psychological and psychoanalytic approaches." Joseph Fitzmyer, one of the authors, offered the following elaboration:

> The psychological and psychoanalytical analyses of human experience have proven their worth in the area of religion and enable one to detect multidimensional aspects of the biblical message. In particular, this approach has been invaluable in the analytical explanation of biblical symbols, cultic rituals, sacrifice, legal prohibitions, and biblical taboos. Yet once again, there is no one psychological or psychoanalytic exegesis that can substitute for the properly oriented historical-critical method, whereas the aid that can come from this approach to that method cannot be underestimated. (1994, 51–52)

The present volume, the first title in the set *Psychology and the Bible: A New Way to Read the Scriptures*, demonstrates the range of psychological approaches, methods, or schools that have been applied to biblical interpretation "from Freud to Kohut." Included are approaches of Freudian psychology, Jungian psychology, developmental psychology, social psychology, cognitive psychology, object relations theory, post-Freudian psychoanalytic theory, post-traumatic stress disorder theory, family systems theory, psychosymbolic approaches, the psychology of language, and Heinz Kohut's Self Psychology. Also included is a special chapter on the approach of Eugen Drewermann, a Roman Catholic priest, psychologist, and theologian who has caused a stir in European ecclesiastical circles since the beginning of the 1980s. This group of psychological approaches has been selected from the more than fifty specialized divisions of psychological studies cited by the American Psychological Association.

The chapters in this volume have in common their authors' desire to gain insight into the texts and readers of the Bible from the standpoint of the perennial habits and experiences of the human psyche. The chapters explore how those habits contribute to or detract from human wholeness. The biblical subjects enlisted in this enterprise range widely; they include the creation stories in Genesis, the remarkable labyrinth of laws on sexuality in the Hebrew Bible, the archetypal birth stories in the Gospels, stories of family and jealousy within the historical tribal tradition of 1 and 2 Samuel, the psychology of the Hebrew prophets in meeting the traumas of national disaster, and the autonomous spawning of messianic images across the Judaic and Christian worlds.

The foreword introduces all four volumes in this set and is written by Donald Capps, the William Hart Felmeth Professor of Pastoral Theology at Princeton Theological Seminary. His own prodigious writing has covered a wide range of topics bridging the fields of psychology, religion, Scripture, and counseling. He has long been associated with the work of the Psychology and Biblical Studies group of the Society of Biblical Literature. In the foreword, Capps describes the development of his interest in reading the Bible through the lens of psychology and cites the introductory work to the field found in Wayne Rollins's book *Soul and Psyche: The Bible in Psychological Perspective* (1999), Erikson's *Young Man Luther: A Study in Psychoanalysis and History* (1958), and J. Harold Ellens's *God's Grace and Human Health* (1982), as well as other related works.

D. Andrew Kille's "Reading the Bible in Three Dimensions" (Chapter 2), provides a fitting entree into this four-volume set on psychology and the Bible. Beginning with a thumbnail sketch of the historical and current state of psychological and biblical scholarship, Kille clarifies the natural link that has developed between these two fields in the past thirty years. He attributes this new relationship to historic changes in both psychology and biblical studies and in the culture at large. For example, the field of psychology has become increasingly broadened and diversified, with an interest not only in the "neurotic" but in behavioral, developmental, and cognitive aspects of the Bible and its interpretation. The field of biblical studies has added new methods to its repertory of historical and literary studies, including rhetorical, ideological, and feminist approaches, all of which regard psychological concepts as foundational to a proper understanding of Scripture. In the culture at large, psychological terms and concepts have become part of the vernacular.

Against this background, Kille reviews the three main arenas of biblical research and suggests which psychological approaches might best apply to each: the world behind the text (the historical and cultural background out of which the Bible emerged); the world of the text (its literary forms and expressions); and the world in front of the text (the encounter between the Bible and the reader). Kille concludes that although the psychological approach to the Bible is not the only approach, it is nonetheless an essential resource for a fuller understanding of the text, of the unmistakable effects that texts have on people, and of ourselves as readers. He would have us remember that "whenever a human being is involved with the Bible, in every aspect from its origins to some distant future when it is interpreted for the last time, psychological dynamics of perception, thought, learning, and socialization are at work."

Ilona Rashkow's contribution, "Sexuality in the Hebrew Bible: Freud's Lens" (Chapter 3), begins with the observation that both Freud and the Bible address issues of human sexuality. Rashkow focuses on what the Hebrew Bible renders as "acceptable" or "unacceptable" sexual practice, with special interest in the nuances of incest laws. Rashkow describes her approach as influenced but not dominated by psychoanalytic theory. Rather than submitting the Bible to the "authority" of psychoanalysis, Rashkow prefers a tactic of "coordination," reading Freud and the Bible side by side, or as she puts it, "reading the Bible while reading Freud," and using his approach (not his biblical interpretive writing) as a tool for exegesis.

After reviewing recent books on psychology and the Bible, Rashkow gives an encyclopedic itemization of sexual law and convention in the Hebrew Bible. She begins with a section on "sin and sex as defined in the Hebrew Bible," in which she contends that it was a phallocentric society that created much of biblical literature and law, as evidenced, for example, in circumcision being identified as the primary identity marker for a member of the covenant people. In a section on "the laws," she catalogues lists of sexual transgressions, prohibitions, and forbidden females. One of the surprising discoveries she makes is that there are no brother–sister or father–daughter incest prohibitions, despite the detailed prohibitions of other relationships. In similar fashion, she notes that the laws against homosexuality applied only to males.

Rashkow concludes her discussion of Freud and the Hebrew Bible with two case histories "while reading Freud." In the first—the story of Noah and his son Ham in Genesis 10—she cites a range of commentators, from the rabbis to church fathers, to English mystery pageants. In the second—the story of Lot's intercourse with his daughters in Genesis 19—she cites the tepid criticism of Lot by a string of commentators ranging from John Calvin to current biblical scholars, and

the "reading" of the story in three Renaissance paintings. In her closing section, "Phallocentrism and Logocentrism," Rashkow contends
that in the Hebrew Bible, particularly in the patriarchal stories and
legal materials, male characters have defined *woman, man,* and sexual
experience, and their opinions have been "cast in stone" by two thousand years of biblical interpretation.

In Chapter 4, "Jung, Analytical Psychology, and the Bible," Wayne
Rollins opens his presentation with a quotation from Jung that will
probably surprise both psychologists and biblical scholars: "We must
read our Bible or we shall not understand psychology. Our psychology, whole lives, our language and imagery are built upon the Bible."
Although not commonly acknowledged, it cannot be denied that biblical allusions constitute a lion's share of Jung's reflection on the
meaning of symbols and archetypes, the process of individuation, and
archetypal images of the Self. The first half of Rollins's essay brings to
light data on Jung and the Bible unfamiliar even to Jungians. Rollins
documents the role of the Bible in the formation of Jung's childhood
and professional adult consciousness and notes Jung's psychologically
oriented understanding of texts and readers, in tension with the Swiss
Reformed approach of his pastor father and six clergy uncles.

The second part formulates a Jungian agenda for reading the Bible
through a psychological lens by focusing on Jung's interpretation of
biblical symbols, dreams, the psychology of biblical personalities, biblical religious experiential phenomena (rites and practices), the pathogenic and psychotherapeutic elements and effects of the Bible, biblical
hermeneutics, and biblical psychology (the biblical concept of the self).
The chapter concludes with a description of the two interpretive modes
Jung endorses in dream and literary interpretation, amplification and
active imagination, both of which have been in use within Jewish,
Christian, and Muslim practice for centuries under different guises.

In Chapter 5, Dieter Mitternacht, in "Theissen's Integration of Psychology and New Testament Studies," reports on a landmark publication in the history of psychology and biblical studies. New Testament
scholar Gerd Theissen's *Psychological Aspects of Pauline Theology*
(1987) was the first major attempt in decades by an internationally
known biblical scholar to bring contemporary psychological insight
to bear on biblical interpretation. Without sacrificing his commitment
to conventional historical scholarship, Theissen stressed the importance of another dimension of biblical studies that would bring the discussion of human life and experience back into the circle of critical
research. His goal was to "make texts intelligible on the basis of their

context in life," and that context, he insisted, would include psychic factors related to the new patterns of experience and behavior that explain and define the emergence of early Christianity. Theissen's most famous observation in the book is the acknowledgment that "we do not yet grasp what historical forces brought forth and determined early Christianity. But beside and within this external history there is an inner history. . . . Anyone who thinks that this religion can be illumined historically and factually without psychological reflection is just as much in error as one who pretends that everything about this religion can be said in this fashion"(1987, 398). Mitternacht rightfully calls it a "therapeutic contribution to New Testament studies."

Mitternacht reports that because of a long-standing resistance to psychology within the guild of biblical scholars, Theissen, a New Testament professor at Heidelberg, realizes he must construct a tight-knit defense for his approach. He does so with a tour-de-force introduction of three psychological fields, showing the light each casts on a reading of five major passages in Paul. The three psychological fields are learning theory, derived from behaviorist insights on how behavior is changed through learning; psychodynamic theory, about the unconscious primordial conflicts (Freud) and powerful archetypal themes (Jung) residual in the text; and cognitive psychology, which explores the early Christian phenomenon of changed cognitions that led to the restructuring of perceptions about the world. Theissen would insist that no one field has an absolute claim on truth but that each complements the other with valuable insights on the role of the text in the inner life of Paul, of the communities he addressed, and of the modern reader.

The five passages Theissen selects for refracting through each of the three psychological models highlight five themes: first-century awareness of the dimension of the "unconscious" (1 Cor. 4:1–5, Rom. 2:16; 1 Cor. 14:20–25); Paul's unconscious projections on Old Testament legal texts (2 Cor. 3:4–4:6); Paul's classical psychological-autobiographical statement in Romans 7–8; the New Testament phenomenon of speaking in tongues (glossolalia) (1 Cor. 12–14); and the concept of a higher wisdom and consciousness (1 Cor. 2:6–16). Mitternacht takes one example from the list of five, giving readers a tour of Theissen's thought on Romans 7–8 as "the most intense presentation in Paul of a transformation in human life." Mitternacht concludes with a brief critical response to Theissen and words of appreciation for the way Theissen makes plain "the luminous psychological beauty of Pauline theology."

Lyn Bechtel's chapter, "Developmental Psychology in Biblical Studies" (Chapter 6), demonstrates how a well-articulated psychological model can "open the eyes of interpreters to elements of the text that previously have been overlooked." Bechtel begins with the ABCs of psychological developmental theory. At the same time, she justifies its application to an ancient text like the Bible on the grounds that developmental psychology describes a process indigenous to the human condition. Bechtel proposes that developmental theory traces a path taken by all of us as we move from infancy to early and middle childhood, adolescence, and adulthood and manifest the social and cognitive learning curve native to each stage. Applying this model to the story of the "genesis" of Adam and Eve awakens us to a subtext of human development that is not immediately apparent in the thick of the story in its mythic form. Bechtel takes us on a journey, moving from Adam's "infancy" as a naked newborn in the dreaming innocence of Eden ("pleasure"); through the maturational stages of identity formation, the development of naming and language skills, differentiation from one's parents, union with the "mother of the living"; followed by the growing consciousness of good and evil, a self-defining act of disobedience, and eviction to a land east of Eden, where work, childbirth, and death are the ultimate state of "the human being" made in the image of God. Bechtel's chapter brings new life to an old story—through the use of a new story hidden in the old, which resolves itself before our eyes when read through the lens of developmental psychological insight.

Ralph Underwood opens Chapter 7, "Winnicott's Squiggle Game and Biblical Interpretation," with an observation by Harvard's chaplain, Peter Gomes, that readers of the Bible may have the problem that they trust neither the texts nor themselves. This insight is at the heart of Underwood's "object relations" reflections on what happens when we read the Bible: namely, that the basic fact about the process from an object relations perspective is not the issue of getting information but of establishing a relationship of trust. Object relations theory as a psychoanalytic approach begins with Freud; the theory describes how we introject the primary persons in our lives through mental images that represent those persons in our psyches, even when the persons are actually absent. "Blankies" and teddy bears express that need early in life; later on, photographs or mementos serve the purpose. Called "transitional objects," they keep the relationship stable even in the absence of the relationship they represent. Thus, at the heart of object relations theory is the psychoanalytic affirmation that we are quintessentially social beings, an affirmation that takes exception to Freud's primary emphasis on the psychology of the individual.

Underwood compares the stabilizing effect that transitional objects have in personal development to the relationship an individual has to the Bible. The role the Bible plays in the lives of readers is analogous to what object relations theorist Don Winnicott demonstrates with his squiggle game at the Squiggle Foundation in London. The game takes place when Winnicott draws a squiggle, line, or doodle with no particular meaning and asks a child to make something of it, to add something. In return the child asks the "doctor" to add his squiggle to what he or she has done. What transpires is the forging of a relationship built on the progressive empathy that comes out of this encounter. The squiggles themselves obviously come out of the unconscious in the sense that they are spontaneous and unplanned. This does not mean, however, that they do not represent deep and even profound feelings on the part of the participants. Biblical interpretation is seen as a "transitional space" in which the Bible provides squiggles of imaginal transitional objects—for example, images of the prodigal son, the good Samaritan, Psalm 23—which bespeak an energizing sense of trust and relationship developing between text and reader. Underwood concludes with a provocative discourse on the "illusion-making" process in the human psyche (from Latin *illudere*, "to play with"), namely, the "playful" "suspension of disbelief" that bespeaks a growing trust-filled symbiosis between text and reader. In the end, "the meaning of Scripture is not only what it says but also what happens to us as we study Scripture."

In Chapter 8, "Gospel Narrative and Psychoanalytic Criticism: Peter Brooks, Norman Holland, and Jacques Lacan," Petri Merenlahti proposes that psychoanalytic theory can contribute to the new discipline of narrative criticism by providing insight into the dynamic between text and reader. In the first section, Merenlahti delineates two models derived from Freud for understanding narrative. The first, from Freud's *Beyond the Pleasure Principle*, deals with the psychology of the compulsion to repeat, common both to narrative/neurosis. The second is the psychoanalytic concept of transference that occurs between text and reader. Merenlahti proposes that these two principles, repetition and transference, are at work in both writing and reading narrative whose purpose is to understand the present by "repeating" its origin in the past. This function also appears operative in the Gospel tradition.

In the second section, Merenlahti explores the ego psychology of

Norman Holland, in which reading a narrative is considered a form of identity processing. Every transaction with a text is an expression of the highly personal history and style of the reader, who subsequently uses a literary work to reinforce (or modify) his or her identity. All of us, according to Holland, read a text through the lens of our own "characteristic patterns of desire and adaptation," as a mirror for sculpting our personal identities. Merenlahti, in broader social perspective, sees this same dynamic at work in the Deuteronomic rewriting of Israelite history in Exile and the shaping of the oral narrative about Jesus by the Gospel writers. He identifies the dynamic as a process of "textual socialization," which adapts sources to current norms, needs, and expectations.

The third section reviews the Lacanian theory that the advent of language in the life of the individual is the onset of the realization that language always falls short of what one wants to say and that, at best, language might be seen as a way of signaling the absence of what it stands for. Merenlahti finds in the Bible this same realization of the function of language to signal absence. As an example he mentions the Markan parable theory, which suggests that parables are riddles whose meanings are past finding out. Another is the Johannine leit-motif of "misunderstanding," in which the "absent" spiritual meaning constantly eludes the key figures in the story, who fail to "see" that "the Real resides beyond the letter" and "is of necessity unspeakable."

William Morrow, in Chapter 9, "Post-Traumatic Stress Disorder and Vicarious Atonement in the Second Isaiah," focuses on the crisis of second-generation, exiled Judeans living in Mesopotamia in the late sixth century BCE. The problem they lived with was anger and grief over the injustice inflicted on their exiled forebears, and subsequently on themselves. At a deeper level they had also come to distrust the God of Israel and the religious tradition their forebears had trusted. Morrow presents evidence for judging their state as one of post-traumatic stress disorder, and he sees the servant songs of Isaiah, especially Isaiah 52:13–53:12, as an antidote to this state of alienation. The remarkable achievement of Isaiah 53 was to model "a process of rationalization that enabled the exiled community to overcome a psychological and theological impasse created by grief and anger." The spiritual strategy of Isaiah 53 was to attempt to get the exiles to see their "suffering as a vicarious sacrifice for coming generations," thus resolving "the conflict between angrily turning blame for the violence inward (self-hatred) or outward (toward God and Israel's religious heritage)."

Morrow develops his thesis in five stages. The first, "The Effects of Violence on Exiled Israel," catalogues the initial catastrophe and the obliteration of national identity. The second section, "The Servant Songs and the Sufferings of Israel," picks up on post-traumatic stress disorder (PTSD) symptoms hinted at in Isaiah: the injury to self-esteem among the exiles, the loss of meaning, a sense of abandonment, lack of affect, and dissociation (the exclusion of traumatic experience from language and memory). The third section, "Isaiah 53 as a Therapeutic Response to Israel's PTSD," chronicles the prophet's effort to provide a reconstructed worldview that can find hope beyond the revulsion and collective identity of a people who have come to think of themselves as despised by God. The fourth section, "Vicarious Atonement and Empathy," observes that Isaiah's mythic image of the suffering servant succeeds as effective communication with the exiles because of its implied empathy for their despair, shame, guilt, grief, and rage. It is precisely that empathy that provides the psychological basis for the community's trust in Isaiah's vision for them. The fifth section, "Vicarious Processes in Isaiah 53," touches the nerve of Isaiah 53 by citing its image of vicarious atonement as a "culturally validated means for the community to reconnect with a disowned identity" and to claim Isaiah's vision of the future.

In Chapter 10, "Family Systems Psychology as Hermeneutic," Kamila Blessing introduces us to the work of psychiatrist Murray Bowen. She finds in Bowen's family systems theory an illuminating hermeneutical device for understanding the psychodynamics not only within religious congregations and "families of faith" but also within familiar family stories in the Bible. The foundational observation of family systems theory is that individuals are connected to one another by an invisible web in which the movement of one person affects everyone else within the web. Needless to say, we are all parts of innumerable such systems. Bowen defines a system as "any relationship with balancing forces and counterforces in constant operation." In a departure from Freud, Bowen further holds that the source of mental illness can be traced not only to the inner psychological history of the individual but to psychodynamics within "families," and even histories of families, in which destructive patterns develop over generations.

In this chapter, Blessing focuses on the special role of the triangle within family systems theory. Bowen observes that families tend to form three-way relationships that become emotional/cognitive sites in which the differentiation or breakdown of individuals takes place. Differentiation refers to the ability of an individual within a triangular relationship to fuse or balance emotional and intellectual functioning, as opposed to becoming overwhelmed by the anxiety-producing factors in the mix. The therapeutic goal within the triangle is to reach the state of the solid self, displacing the pseudo-self generated by super-ego constraints of the other members of the triangle. Blessing demonstrates how a triangular family systems template can illumine a biblical text. She constructs three biblical case studies: the triangular relationship of God, Adam, and Eve in the Garden, and of the three-some of God, Eve, and the serpent, in Genesis 3–4; the dynamics between Elkanah, the father-to-be of the prophet Samuel, and his two wives, Hannah, who begins as a barren woman, and Peninnah, who is fertile and as a consequence exercises emotional control over Hannah; and the psychologically intriguing story in John 9 of the man born blind and the progressive triangulations among different members of the cast, including a triangle that includes the reader. Blessing concludes that systems theory is a "powerful tool for understanding not only the content of the text, but the very nature of the message and of the reader's relationship with it."

In a sturdy chapter titled "A Romantic Psychologist Reads the Bible: Eugen Drewermann," Bernhard Lang introduces an English-speaking audience to a German psychologist-theologian-priest whose name has enjoyed instant recognition in European intellectual and ecclesiastical circles since the early 1990s. Like his confrere Hans Küng, Drewermann is a prodigious writer. One need only survey the table of contents of his two-volume *Depth Psychology and Exegesis* (1984–1985, yet to be translated), to appreciate his encyclopedic perspective on world literature and its significance in the life of the human psyche. Of his seventy books, one-quarter are devoted to psychological commentary on biblical texts. Lang starts off with a characteristic Drewermannian approach to the Bible—his interpretation of Luke's infancy narratives in his 1994 work, *Discovering the God Child Within*, one of the few books by Drewermann translated into English. Lang spells out the three levels of the story that Drewermann explores: the historical or surface level, the symbolic or mythic level, and the anthropological or human-relevance level. Although Drewermann acknowledges remnants of historical memory in the birth stories, he focuses on the archetypal mythical pattern in the story of the birth of the hero and its relevance for the individuation process in anyone's life. Lang adds his own Drewermann-like analysis of the four rivers of Paradise depicted in Genesis 2:10–14.

The main thrust of Lang's chapter is to identify the three sources that inspired Drewermann's psychological reading of the Bible: the Freudian "inspiration" with its emphasis on the interpretation of the dreamlike fantasies found in biblical myths; the Eliadean and Jungian inspiration, with its interest in symbol and story, and specifically its reclamation of the wisdom of cyclical views of history, as opposed to the classical linear view of biblical tradition; and the inspiration of two Romantic era writers, Friedrich Schleiermacher and Novalis (Friedrich von Hardenburg), an early nineteenth-century philosopher and a late eighteenth-century poet, respectively. Drewermann was drawn to their conviction that poetry and symbol, more than prose and ecclesiastical dogma, provide the route to the heart of reality. Lang provides ample bibliography on Drewermann and his Promethean application of psychological insight to the interpretation of the Bible.

Robert Neuwoehner's Chapter 12, "The Psychosymbolic Approach to Biblical Interpretation," opens with a sketch of the three-stage interpretive process Carl Jung finds at work in every reading experience: reading the text, amplifying its images, and interpreting the text. Each stage involves a fundamental construction (and reconstruction) as the text progressively interprets the reader and the reader progressively interprets the text, a process in which unconscious as well as conscious factors are always at work.

Neuwoehner next explores the psychology of inspiration, unpacking the mystery of the creative factor that seizes poet, prophet, playwright, or painter with archetypal force. Jungian ethicist Erich Neumann describes the creative event as a "breakthrough in which the dimension of the purely personal opens out into that realm of the intrinsic essence of things which constitutes the suprapersonal background of reality" (1989, 160). From a psychological perspective, ordinary inspiration and divine inspiration are indistinguishable: "the Muses . . . are sisters of the Paraclete."

Finally Neuwoehner takes us to postmodern hermeneutics. He offers a helpful definition of the term *postmodern* and links it to those mid-twentieth-century hermeneutical geniuses, New Testament scholar Rudolf Bultmann and philosopher, psychologist, and theologian Paul Ricoeur, whose goals were "to bring out the spiritual essence from within or behind the historically conditioned [biblical] text." What is "interpretation" made of? It is the event that occurs when the symbols of the text and the unconscious and conscious depths of the reader encounter one another in a discourse, with profound effect on both.

Ithamar Gruenwald, in Chapter 13, "Jewish and Christian Messianism: The Psychoanalytic Approach of Heinz Kohut," takes a new approach to the history and development of messianism. Rather than itemizing the many messianisms within the Judeo-Christian tradition, he chooses to take the measure of messianism in general against the background of a psychoanalytic paradigm. The paradigm he employs is that of Heinz Kohut and his school of Self Psychology. His goal is to discuss the historical development of the messianic archetype in its main manifestation from the standpoint of the psychological needs it expresses and fulfills. Gruenwald begins with a quick survey of the contrasting messianisms found in the New Testament and the early church, noting also the dual messianism at Qumran and inter-testamental Judaism, a royal monarchic messiah and a priestly messiah. Gruenwald raises the question of what kind of position these Christian forms of messianism took in comparison to their counterparts in Judaism. He also notes that although the term *mashiah* is Hebrew, the messianic archetypal image is not uniquely Judaic.

Gruenwald's psychoanalytic analysis begins with an introduction to the self/self-object psychology of Kohut. It rests on the observation that from childhood the self is involved in the identification of empathetic self-objects, like the breast of the mother and ultimately of God, that are taken into oneself as sources of affirmation, empathy, security, and creativity. Kohut identifies three stages in the evolution of a self/self-object relation: mirroring, idealization, and twinship, the latter being a state of total psychic identification with the self-object. At the heart of Gruenwald's argument is the contention that the second temple period and the centuries immediately surrounding the rise of Christianity experienced a "silencing of the voice of God" and a withdrawal of the empathy associated with the God self-object. It was a crisis in the God concept, which was further confounded by the infusion of Iranian, Babylonian, and Hellenistic ideas into the Judaic world. Gruenwald spends the last part of the chapter identifying how Christian piety and Rabbinic and Qabbalistic Judaism were able to resolve the problem of the "silence of God" in the form of new messianic modalities.

In "The Bible and Psychology: An Interdisciplinary Pilgrimage" (Chapter 14), J. Harold Ellens speaks out of his experience of having worked forty years on the critical edge between psychology and Scripture, as the first executive director of the Christian Association for Psychological Studies and the founding editor of the *Journal of Psychology and Christianity*. His work here forms an appropriate and lucid concluding assessment of the central burden of this volume. It was in the context of his lifelong work on psychology and religion that the question arose of how the two relate. Should the relationship between psychology and the Bible be one of integration or of interfacing mutual illumination? Ellens held to the latter, maintaining that the goal of the conversation between the two is not mutual absorption but rather dialogue on a topic of common interest, namely, the living human document, or human being. Ellens writes that the "more we know about human psychology, the more we can understand the real story in our religious texts," and the more we know about Scripture, the wider our perception of the heights and depths of the human psyche. Also out of the dialogue between psychology and the Bible comes the realization that there are no saints in the process: religion can be therapeutic but also pathogenic; psychology can enlighten or distort.

Ellens proposes three principles as the model for mutual illumination between the two. The first is the recognition that biblical studies and psychology are both sciences in their own right and have truths independent though not unrelated to one another. Second, the criterion of "soundness" in their relationship is not how they fit one another but how they enlarge, illumine, and challenge one another. Third, both camps must see themselves not as possessors of the truth but as midwives of the truth. Ellens concludes, as a theologian speaking appreciatively of psychology, that psychology provides a worthy lens for understanding how a text like the Bible "reflects the living human documents behind it," offering insight into "how humans function, what they tend to say, why they say what they say the way they say it, and what messages mean as seen through standardized psychological paradigms."

It is our conviction that anyone who is serious about the quest for meaning in human life will need to pay close attention to the Bible and to the biblical tradition of understanding both the human and the transcendent world. Furthermore, anyone who is serious about understanding the Bible and its impact on the human quest and human history must look carefully at the biblical text through the lenses of literary analysis, historical analysis, other relevant forms of critical analysis, and psychological analysis. These four volumes are about looking at the Bible through the lens of careful and responsible psychological perspectives in the hope that such a lens will produce more light and truth regarding who we are as human beings and what we are about. As Gerd Theissen observed in his application of psychological insight to the Bible: "Anyone who thinks that this religion can be illumined historically and factually without psychological reflection is just as much in error as one who pretends that everything about this religion can be said in this [psychological] fashion" (1987, 398).

Note

1. For a brief account of the history of the distrust and eventual rapprochement, see Rollins (1999, 63–65).

References

Crossan, J. D. (1977). Perspectives and Methods in Contemporary Biblical Criticism. *Biblical Research, 22,* 41.

Ellens, J. H. (1982). *God's Grace and Human Health.* Nashville: Abingdon.

Erikson, E. (1958). *Young Man Luther: A Study in Psychoanalysis and History.* New York: Norton.

Fitzmyer, J. A. (1994). *Scripture: The Soul of Theology.* New York: Paulist.

Jung, C. G. (1953–1978). *The Collected Works of C. G. Jung,* R. F. C. Hull, trans. Princeton: Princeton University Press.

Neumann, E. (1989). *The Place of Creation: Six Essays,* Hildegard Nagel, Eugene Rolfe, Jan van Heurck, & Krishna Winston, trans., *Essays of Erich Neumann,* vol. 3. Bollingen Series. Princeton: Princeton University Press.

Rollins, W. G. (1999). *Soul and Psyche: The Bible in Psychological Perspective.* Minneapolis: Fortress.

Schweitzer, A. (1913). *Die psychiatrische Beurteilung Jesu: Darstellung und Kritik.* [*The Psychiatric Study of Jesus: Exposition and Criticism*]. (Doctoral dissertation, University of Strassbourg, 1913). Tübingen: J.C.B. Mohr.

Theissen, G. (1987). *Psychological Aspects of Pauline Theology,* John P. Galvin, trans. Philadelphia: Fortress.

CHAPTER 2

READING THE BIBLE IN THREE DIMENSIONS: PSYCHOLOGICAL BIBLICAL INTERPRETATION

D. Andrew Kille

More than simply a sourcebook for theology and doctrine, the Bible has always served as a resource for people's lives. Countless multitudes have looked to it as a guide for behavior and ethical conduct and as a support for personal growth and insight. People in the pew have known that the images of Scripture—be they inspirational characters from Bible stories, accounts of religious experience, or powerful religious symbols—have the ability to shape us, to confront us, and to lead us to greater wholeness and fuller life. In our increasingly psychological age, the language used to describe that process of growth and transformation usually draws on the terms and concepts of psychology. Thus, those who work with Scripture and with people have seen clearly how the Bible is a richly psychological document.

Formal biblical scholars, however, have often been far more skeptical of psychological approaches to interpreting the Bible. Much has been written about the Bible from psychological perspectives, but often the authors lacked systematic grounding in the accepted methods of critical biblical study. Pastors and pastoral counselors, after all, have not been interested primarily in the fine points of biblical scholarship; their concern is with the lives of those with whom they work. How can these people be encouraged toward personal growth and maturity, and what role might the Bible play in that encouragement?

Although there has been more written about psychological biblical interpretation than most people know, such writings often do not spend much time reflecting on methods or theory. They frequently do not exhibit current biblical scholarship and, in many cases, are the result of an author's single insight or intuition, so they remain disconnected not only from the field of biblical studies as a whole but even from other works by the same author.

Until recently, psychological biblical criticism was mostly unknown within the field of biblical studies. Hundreds of articles, books, and commentaries have been published only to languish on the fringes of scholarship, ignored by the mainstream. However, significant shifts of attitude and expectation in psychology, biblical studies, and the wider culture have opened new doors to psychological approaches to Scripture.

A Shift of Attitude: Psychology

Since its origins in Wilhelm Wundt's laboratory in the late nineteenth century, modern psychology has grown significantly, deepening its methods and broadening its theories. There has been a shift from nearly exclusive attention to the (often neurotic) individual toward more foundational explorations of cognition, behavior, and a social psychology that deals with interactions between people.

Furthermore, in some corners of psychology there is an increasing awareness that in its search for models for understanding human behavior, psychology is as much a theory of interpretation as it is a science. Early psychologists had hoped that their studies might produce a unified scientific field similar to the natural sciences, but as time went on, psychology diversified into a wide array of subdisciplines. Not only did these subdisciplines focus on different aspects of behavior and mental processes—sensory processes and perception, cognition, physiology, development, learning theory, and the like—but they offered different and often conflicting explanations of the phenomena. For example, there have been bitter disputes between the advocates of behaviorism and depth psychology over the objects and methods of research. Even the definition of the term *psychology* is up for grabs; a former president of the American Psychological Association commented that it might be more accurate to speak of the "psychological sciences" (Koch, 1992).

What a psychologist chooses to study, how he or she determines what "counts" as significant in examining behavior, and how the findings are related to each other and ultimately integrated into conclusions all reflect the psychologist's own theoretical preconceptions.

When describing psychological structures and dynamics, particularly when they cannot be observed directly but only inferred from outward behavior, psychologists are forced into metaphorical language. Because they attach great importance to the unconscious, which by its very nature is not directly visible, depth psychologies in particular represent sophisticated interpretational systems (Wulff, 1985).

If we understand that interpretation is unavoidable in psychological theory, we begin to understand why there are so many often-conflicting psychological perspectives. Rather than reflecting some failure of the scientific method, the diversity of theories demonstrates clearly what Paul Ricoeur (1974) called an unavoidable "conflict of interpretations" inherent in the very nature of language itself. In his introduction to *Psychological Aspects of Pauline Thought*, New Testament scholar Gerd Theissen alluded to the reality in this way: "For a hermeneutical consciousness, precisely the plurality of psychologies competing successfully with one another is an indication that there are no psychic processes in themselves but only interpreted processes that run differently in accordance with historically variable human self-understanding" (1987, 43).

A Shift of Attitude: Biblical Studies

For most of the twentieth century, biblical studies have been dominated by the historical-critical method, which relies on analysis of the Bible's historical origins. Careful attention was given to the language, literary structures, and presumed historical context of a passage in order to tease out clues to its original form and meaning and its shaping by editorial processes into the present-day text. Historical-critical approaches, which had their origin in the Enlightenment, presumed it was possible to bring an objective eye to the interpretation of texts. Personal attachments or community interpretations of texts were considered irrelevant, or at best secondary, to the "true" meaning—the meaning intended by the historical author.

Preachers and students struggled to find ways to bridge the gap between what they were being taught in seminaries and the needs of preaching, teaching, and counseling in the religious communities that honored the Bible. If the true meaning of the text was in the past, what possible meaning could it have for today? Sermons needed to be more than history lectures. This general feeling was given stark voice by Walter Wink when he wrote in *The Bible in Human Transformation: Toward a New Paradigm for Biblical Study* that "historical biblical criticism is bankrupt" (1973, 1). He meant the term precisely. Historical criticism was not without value; it was simply unable to deliver on what it had promised for biblical interpretation.

Historical-critical methods remain important in studying the Bible, but the past thirty years have seen a blossoming of new methods in biblical studies. These new methods focus attention on the literary structures, linguistic features, and narrative and oratorical strategies of the Bible. They pay attention to how readers read, how ideologies are supported, and how cultural norms are preserved. Many of these methods have their roots in ways of reading the Bible that predated the historical-critical method, and among them, psychological perspectives have found a new lease on life. In fact, many of the newer approaches that have emerged out of contemporary perspectives carry with them the psychological dimension that characterizes our contemporary culture.

A Shift of Attitude: The Psychologized Culture

Without a doubt, psychological language, concepts, and categories have become the everyday vocabulary of Western culture. Terms such as *Freudian slip, Oedipus complex*, the *unconscious, projection*, and *free association* were once only used as the specialized vocabulary of psychologists. Nowadays, these words and references can be found on the comics page, in the movie theater, and on television. In bookstores, the shelves of self-help and "pop-psychology" books grow larger, and Dr. Phil, the popular psychologist, is on nightly. "We [modern Westerners] think psychologically; we evaluate our feelings psychologically," wrote Robin Scroggs. "We are not aware of the specific content of the deep and hidden dimensions of our psyches, because we know that they are most often repressed and inaccessible to our consciousness; but we are aware that such dimensions exist and that they control our lives and actions more than do our conscious egos" (1982, 335). Peter Homans observes that psychoanalytic ideas in particular have become in America "a guiding set of ideas woven into the fabric of its institutional life." So extensively has psychology shaped our personal and social awareness, Homans maintains, that it is appropriate to describe a new social being—the "psychological [hu]man" (1979, 1, 3).

The combination of these three shifts—the movement toward more developed psychological theory, an openness to new methods and perspectives in biblical studies, and the psychological culture in which we find ourselves—has created an environment in the current setting that has stimulated a new interest and excitement in psychological biblical studies.

Psychology and Biblical Interpretation

What happens when the psychological human meets the biblical text? The Bible did not originate in this psychological age, nor do Freudian terms appear in its pages. The Bible is not a psychological book in itself, but modern interpreters live in this psychologized era, and the task of interpretation is to make the ancient text understandable to an audience that is profoundly affected by psychological perspectives. Some understanding of psychological concepts and dynamics is needed if one can ever hope to connect with the modern reader, the person in the pew.

So inescapable are psychological perspectives that they have already found their way, often quite unnoticed, into other forms of biblical interpretation. Writers seeking to highlight the structures or meaning of the Bible from feminist or literary points of view, or to understand the process of reading and the interaction of the reader and the text, often elaborate their arguments within a framework of assumptions about how people think, learn, and act that are essentially psychological. Others have come to recognize that psychology offers important tools for biblical study and have sought to be more forthright and clear about how they use psychological insights to understand the Bible.

In recent years, Wayne G. Rollins's *Soul and Psyche: The Bible in Psychological Perspective* (1999) and my own *Psychological Biblical Criticism* (2001) have sought to place psychological methods squarely in the mainstream of biblical studies, whereas the book you are now reading seeks to make this approach more accessible beyond academic circles.

Rollins's book is a comprehensive and wide-ranging exploration of the field. He notes that psychological themes and reflection began as far back as the early church fathers and have been a part of the history of biblical interpretation up through today. His bibliography, which runs some thirty-three pages, evidences the richness and diversity of this approach.

Rollins's summary of the goals of psychological biblical criticism is deceptively brief: "to examine texts, their origination, authorship, modes of expression, their construction, transmission, translation, reading, interpretation, their transposition into kindred and alien art forms, and the history of their personal and cultural effect, as expressions of the structure, processes, and habits of the human psyche, both in individual and collective manifestations, past and present" (1999, 77–78).

In short, whenever a human being is involved with the Bible, in every aspect from its origins to some distant future when it is interpreted for the last time, psychological dynamics of perception, thought, learning, and socialization are at work. Rollins has space in his book only to suggest how attention to psychological issues may shape the task of explaining what the Bible says (exegesis) and understanding what the Bible means (hermeneutics).

The Bible in Three Dimensions

Psychology and the Bible: what could be simpler? That they are closely interconnected is plain. It is only when we begin to look more clearly and carefully at our task that we discover that what seemed so simple is, indeed, tremendously complex. I wrote above of how there are so many branches and subdisciplines of psychology, often mutually contradictory. We may be compelled to understand our task as psychologies and the Bible.

Yet even though the Bible in one sense is a single book that can be held in my hand, that book represents layers and layers of activities and levels. Who wrote it? How were they inspired to do it? Who gathered all these writings from many times and places and put them into a particular order? Who decided which writings should be included and which left out? What happened when it was translated from Hebrew, Aramaic, and Greek into nearly all the languages on earth? What happens when someone reads it? What happens when someone preaches a sermon, teaches a lesson, paints a ceiling, carves a block of marble, writes a poem, issues a manifesto, stands up to a militia, or feeds the hungry because of what they have read and understood in these pages?

I believe it is helpful to look at the Bible in three dimensions, three broad areas for consideration. One dimension can be called the world behind the text, a second the world of the text, and a third, the world in front of the text. What do these areas include? The world behind the text has to do with the origins and development of the biblical text. It includes that original referential context—the culture, customs, history, and attitudes prevalent in the time of the first speakers, writers, editors, and their communities—that has been obscured or lost over the years. The world of the text is expressed in the Bible's literary structures, narratives, poetry and prose, descriptions, characters, and oratory. And finally, the world in front of the text comes into being in the encounter between a reader and the text. It is that imaginative dialogue between the words of the text and the imagination, personality, attitudes, and experiences of a person seeking to understand it.

As with the three dimensions of length, breadth, and depth, these three dimensions are inextricably intertwined. However, even as we might acknowledge that an object has depth and breadth while focusing our attention on measuring its height, we can also set out to focus, for example, on the world of the text and let the other two fade into the background. Likewise, although the tools for measuring length, breadth, and height are similar, we will use them somewhat differently in approaching different dimensions. What works to measure length may not serve well to measure height.

As we consider how psychology can approach the Bible fruitfully, it is important always to be aware of the tools we are using (that is, which psychological theories) and what we are trying to apply them to (that is, which world of the Bible). The skepticism that greeted earlier psychological approaches was sometimes justifiable, given that the scholars were using psychological categories and dynamics that simply were not appropriate for the dimension they were studying. For example, a favorite early form of investigation involved psychoanalyzing biblical characters, who were taken at face value without regard for historical context or literary shaping. Many such efforts were, at base, an attack on the Bible itself and on those who took it seriously, and thus some authors delighted in highlighting multitudes of "pathological" symptoms in the apostle Paul, the Hebrew prophets, or Jesus himself. In response to such ham-handed efforts, Albert Schweitzer wrote *The Psychiatric Study of Jesus: Exposition and Criticism* in 1913, in which he stated that those who described Jesus as a pathological personality had distorted both the biblical and the psychological evidence. On the one hand, they had ignored the historical context of the Gospel writings and their literary development; on the other, they had modified the clinical descriptions of psychopathology to suit their own purposes and conclusions (Schweitzer, 1948).

The World behind the Text

Perhaps it was the lingering effects of historical-critical study that led so many writers in the late nineteenth and early twentieth century to attempt a kind of psychohistory, that is, analyzing individuals from the past on the basis of written materials or other accounts. Historical-critical study was focused precisely on the world behind the text, seeking to recover the referential aspect of the conversation as described by Ricoeur. By examining the earliest manuscripts available, the conventional forms of speech and writing in the ancient world, the modes of oral transmission, archaeological evidence, and historical reconstruction, historical criticism tried to reconstruct the origins, context, and setting of biblical passages.

Some scholars sought to employ psychological insights as yet one more tool in historical inquiry, one that would enable us to get inside the minds of the writers and biblical characters to understand better their thinking, motivations, and quirks. However, psychology has very limited value as a tool for studying history, especially ancient history. The materials we have on which to base such an individual analysis are limited to a tiny handful of biblical texts, and these are even more compromised because of the processes of literary composition and transmission. There is skepticism enough about psychohistory in relation to more recent individuals, about whom we have more complete biographical records, eyewitness descriptions, or even personal journals and other writings.

With care, however, it is still possible to suggest insights into biblical figures that can aid our understanding of them. The prophet Ezekiel has attracted much attention, given the seemingly more autobiographical nature of the book attributed to him and the unusual experiences and activities described therein. David Halperin, in *Seeking Ezekiel: Text and Psychology* (1993), took great care to acknowledge the issues of textual development, and yet he develops a psychological portrait of the prophet that offers a possible solution to some longstanding difficulties with understanding not only Ezekiel's personality but some of the more obscure passages in his book. Two more recent psychological approaches to Jesus also reflect the authors' care to recognize the difficulties inherent in the Gospel texts as biographical sources. Both John Miller's *Jesus at Thirty: A Psychohistorical Inquiry* (1997) and Donald Capps's *Jesus: A Psychological Biography* (2000) avoid the excesses of earlier works and draw on other disciplines to put their psychological portraits of Jesus into a broader context appropriate to the first century.

Descriptive psychology plays a much more useful role in the world behind the text. Klaus Berger's recent book *Identity and Experience in the New Testament* (2003) helps to bridge the distance between contemporary psychology and the ancient world by exploring just how identity, emotion, behavior, and demon possession were understood in the New

Testament world. His is the most comprehensive work to date to illuminate scriptural experiences that might include such phenomena as speaking in tongues or conversion, and he does so by use of analogy to contemporary experience and understanding. Studies of cognition and memory in relationship to oral tradition or the psychological dynamics of family life may also serve to explain the world behind the text.

The World of the Text

Although psychological portraits of biblical figures are popular, they are not so much historical inquiries as they are analyses of a character in a story, analogous to a character in a contemporary novel. As such, these portraits belong more properly to the world of the text. We remain cautious about how much we can see into the mind of a historical figure, but when we notice that what we know of that figure comes to us through written description, we can turn our attention to how that person is revealed in the writing itself. The characters in biblical tales, or the presumed authors who speak to us out of the letters, sermons, and stories of the Bible, certainly have a life of their own. No matter how that literary life may or may not be linked to historical fact, these figures nonetheless live and move and have their being in ways that reflect recognizable human thought, emotion, and behavior. We can assuredly describe these biblical characters and imagine what may have moved them in the depths of their souls, but we must be careful not to presume we are doing historical research.

Nor can we assume more about the character than is presented in the text itself. With such a small body of material to work with, we may be tempted to fill in the details of a story. This "filling in" is evident in many psychological analyses of biblical figures and often represents not much more than an imaginative justification of the interpreter's own pet theory. When we see phrases like "it is possible (or likely, or certain) that . . . ," "we may assume that . . . ," "this may indicate that . . . ," or "this is nothing other than . . . , " we must ask whether the writer is conscious of the fact that he or she is offering an elaboration of the text or is covertly trying to beef up the argument.

It is not necessary to fill in the blanks in order to find ample evidence of psychological dynamic of all kinds in the Bible. In relationships within families, in conflicts between people, and in the social dynamics of the community we find examples of psychological development and defenses. The Bible is not a self-consciously psychological book; it was written long before the language and categories of contemporary psychology were developed. Nevertheless, in its own way it speaks of thought, will, intention, suffering, emotions, and human behavior. Furthermore, it expresses itself in the language of images and symbols, which touches the deepest levels of the psyche. Again, with care not to obliterate the differences between the ancient world and our own, we can discover commonalities and connections rooted in archetypal images such as the tree of life, the purifying fire, or the heavenly city. Historical-critical methods have long recognized that biblical symbols can be understood more fully by comparing them with symbols in other ancient Near Eastern texts, artwork, and cultures. Psychological sensitivity might serve to broaden such comparisons to similar manifestations worldwide. Symbols by their very nature both communicate and continue culture, as well as serve a balance in the human psyche. In so doing, they manifest themselves in diverse ways across time and space. Rollins reminds us that along with the conscious activities of the biblical tradition, there exists the "possibility of unconscious factors at work in the cultural inheritance, transmission, and adaptation of religious motifs and cultural practices in the Bible" (1999, 121).

Psychological models of the dynamics of cognition and meaning making have deeply influenced some literary and linguistic approaches to biblical interpretation. Structural critics, for example, draw consciously on such psychological concepts as archetypal images and the recurring motif of the bringing together of opposites to analyze the "deep structures" of the text. The cognitive and symbolic frameworks that together make up a written work, they argue, reflect the structure of the psyche itself. Other critics, deeply influenced by Freud's observation that our conscious thoughts and actions often mask powerful unconscious motivations, have taken the path of deconstructionist and other postmodern strategies of interpretation that question the very foundations of language and meaning (Aichele et al., 1995).

Still other critics have been deeply influenced by psychological theory, even when they seem unaware of the fact. Rhetorical criticism seeks to analyze how a particular message is connected to a desired response. To do so requires some model of human thinking and motivation, a model that is, by its very nature, psychological. Any author, ancient or modern, who wishes to prompt some specific behavior in his or her readers needs some idea of how to go about doing so. Even when the author uses conventional forms provided by the historical context and culture, those forms are derived from a theory of human behavior.

The World in Front of the Text

Rhetorical criticism begins to fade from the world of the text into our third world, the world in front of the text. We need always to recognize that even in seeking to get at the worlds behind the text and of the text, we cannot escape the fact that there is always an interpreter present in front of the text. This is the inherent paradox and uniqueness of psychological investigation. As Jung himself once observed, the unique challenge is that "in psychology, the means by which you study the psyche is the psyche itself . . . the observer is the observed. The psyche is not only the object, but also the subject of our science" (1976, 126). When we begin to pay special attention to the reader and the process of reading, we enter the world in front of the text. Here psychological biblical criticism is the most useful as we deal with present readers and how they interact with what they read.

Paul Ricoeur understood the world in front of the text to be the arena in which a reader comes to understand himself or herself through the reading and interpretation of a text. The world in front of the text is an imaginative space created between the experiential world of the reader and the possible world (or world of possibilities) that the text creates through language, story, symbol, imagery, and so on. The world in front of the text is not controlled by the text itself—there is no "objective" meaning exclusive of all others. Nor is it controlled simply by the subjectivity of the reader; texts do mean some things and not others. The world of the text represents a negotiation between reader and text, between objective and subjective.

The world in front of the text represents a psychological space described by Paul Pruyser, who extended D. W. Winnicott's concept of the childhood transitional object to explain adult behavior. Winicott described the psychological function of a child's treasured object, such as a teddy bear or blanket, as seeming to exist simultaneously as a concrete object and as a precious entity in the subjective world of the child. Yet it is not only the child who sees the object as special; family members and other adults will "play along" with the child's perception, treating the object with unusual reverence, care, and appreciation for its imaginative liveliness.

Pruyser suggested that this "playing along" created a middle space of experience, one in which there is tension between the "realistic" world of the relatively objective environment and the "autistic" world of subjective perception. This third world, which he named the illusionistic world, is characterized by shared and orderly imagination that can be communicated to others. Experience and facts in the realistic world are based on objects that one can see, hear, touch, or point to. Experience in the wholly interior autistic world consists of images and symbols beyond expression and communication. The illusionistic world allows expressible images, shared symbols, and meaningful stories. The realistic world is a world of work; the autistic world one of dreams. In between lies the illusionistic world of play, of art, of religion and culture (Pruyser, 1991; Underwood, 1997).

Because the reader is always a factor in the process of reading, psychological criticism reminds us to be attentive to both the conscious and unconscious factors that may shape an individual's (or community's) interpretation of the text. Schleiermacher was one of the first to point out how significant a reader's beginning presuppositions are in the process of interpretation. In hermeneutics—the systematic study of how interpretation unfolds—it is a given that each interpreter brings his or her own concepts, capabilities, context, attitudes, and prejudices to the reading of a text. One of the vital tasks of interpretation is to become conscious of these presuppositions and how they affect one's interpretation.

That consciousness is not easily achieved. As Freud noted emphatically, there are powerful unconscious forces that affect our conscious thoughts and actions. It is precisely on the basis of this observation that contemporary critics have urged a "hermeneutic of suspicion," which takes no text or assertion at face value. Ideological criticism starts with this suspicion to uncover the ways that sacred texts serve a community or culture by establishing or maintaining a particular view of the world and the ways subsequent interpretations of those texts enforce certain attitudes or behaviors. Although ideological critics seldom make reference to psychological theories (and indeed have turned their critical idea on those theories themselves), nevertheless their analyses involve questions of how people take in and organize information, think about what they know, act on their convictions, and influence each other. All of these factors rely on psychological models and expectations.

Readers bring yet more psychological factors to the task of reading. Along with conscious biases or presuppositions and socially conditioned perspectives and categories, an interpreter takes in and evaluates evidence in individually characteristic ways. In C. G. Jung's model of personality there are four fundamental personality types derived from two sets of polarities. Some people, when taking in information, prefer to rely on sensory input—what they see, hear, taste, feel, and so forth—whereas others prefer intuitions, hunches, and "gut feelings." In evaluating information, some rely on logical and systematic organization, whereas others may be more concerned about relationships and how ideas or conclusions may affect others. Clearly, scholars of differing personality types focus on different aspects of the text and may be drawn to one theory or method over another because of their fundamental psychological orientation. In three books based on the weekly readings for worship from the Christian Gospels, British psychologist Leslie Francis has explored how one might approach these texts differently in order to connect more fully with people of diverse personality types (Francis, 1997; Francis & Atkins, 2000, 2001).

The Bible provides important resources for pastoral counseling, offering guidance for living, characters that can serve as models for action, and images and symbols that can help clients to express their own inner lives (Capps, 1981, 1984; Clinebell, 1984). A person's choice of favorite Bible stories may also give insight into his or her own psychic life. Pastoral counselor Wayne Oates remarks that the Bible can be seen as "a mirror into which a person projects his own concept of himself, and which in turn reflects it back with accuracy" (1950, 43).

The Bible has had, and continues to have, an effect on every reader who comes to it. Extending far beyond the original "setting-in-life" sought by historical criticism, this "afterlife" offers us clues about how the Bible functions psychologically. As we pay close attention to how people actually read the Bible, and how their thinking and actions are (or are not) shaped by that reading, we find another point of intersection between this text and the psychic lives of its readers. It is no wonder that much of the work in psychological biblical criticism has been done by psychologists and pastoral counselors. Such people often see the unmistakable effects that sacred texts, stories, and interpretations have on the people with whom they work. These effects can be healthy and unhealthy, both therapeutic and pathological.

Conclusions

If it is misleading to speak of psychology as if it were a single, unified science, it is fair to ask whether we can talk about psychological biblical criticism as a single approach or method. With so many different psychological theories to choose from as we read the Bible in three dimensions, we surely must conclude that psychological criticism is more a way of reading than it is a method or technique. No single method or approach will be universally applicable to all dimensions of a text, nor can any single theory exhaust the possibilities for under-standing the text.

As a way of reading, psychological criticism is similar to feminist criticism, which draws on many tools—historical, contextual, literary, and ideological—for its work. What binds these all together is the sensitivity to women's experience that is behind, in, and in front of the text. Psychological criticism also draws on a full tool kit for inter-pretation, but the method uses its tools always with an eye toward psychological interactions in and beyond the text.

This current multivolume work is a vivid illustration of the range of methods, theories, issues, and observations emerging from psycholog-ical approaches. From Freud to family systems, from Genesis to Rev-elation, from ancient patriarch to contemporary reader, from healing to pathology, the essays here represent just a few of the possibilities in the biblical text that are opened by a psychological sensibility.

The key to fruitful interpretation is found in a good fit between the-ory and text. We need to be clear that we are working with texts, not persons, and therefore interpretation must proceed cautiously. The text (or its author) is not lying on the couch, free-associating so that we can achieve a diagnosis. It is a text generated in a historical context and influenced by the culture, language, and literary conventions of another time. The fact that the Bible does not self-consciously present itself as a psychological record also requires a greater level of gener-alization as we seek to apply psychological theory. We do not have sufficient information or data for a detailed explication, nor is it pos-sible to check our intuitions by asking the "patient."

At the same time it is important to deal accurately with psycholog-ical theory and not to generalize beyond recognition. There is some-thing valuable to be learned from the differences between theories, giving us a kind of parallax view that can serve to highlight hidden aspects of the text as well as clarify the strengths and weaknesses of any given approach.

Although the Bible is full of psychological insight and examples, it is not only psychological. Freud spoke of overdetermination, that is, the fact that any single phenomenon, such as a dream image, results from the interaction of more than one cause. Along with the tools of psychology, we need to be willing and able to draw on the whole range of historical, literary, and cultural tools for teasing out the meaning of a text.

Beyond all cautions, warnings, and advice, one fact remains—psy-chological criticism is a significant tool in the task of interpretation.

Every step of the way from sacred experience to sacred story to sacred text, every group that gathered, evaluated, and canonized the Bible, and every act of interpretation have involved and been shaped by the human psyche. We take our place in the long line of those who seek to understand this fascinating text and, standing before it, seek to understand ourselves.

References

Aichele, G., Burnett, F. W., Castelli, E. A., Fowler, R. M., Jobling, D., Moore, S. D., et al., eds. (1995). *The Postmodern Bible*. New Haven: Yale University Press.

Berger, K. (2003). *Identity and Experience in the New Testament*, C. Muenchow, trans. Minneapolis: Fortress.

Capps, D. (1981). *Biblical Approaches to Pastoral Counseling*. Philadelphia: Westminster.

Capps, D. (1984). The Bible's Role in Pastoral Care and Counseling: Four Basic Principles. *Journal of Psychology and Christianity*, 3(4), 5–15.

Capps, D. (2000). *Jesus: A Psychological Biography*. St. Louis: Chalice Press.

Clinebell, H. (1984). *Basic Types of Pastoral Care and Counseling: Resources for the Ministry of Healing and Growth* (Rev. ed.). Nashville: Abingdon.

Francis, L. J. (1997). *Personality Type and Scripture: Exploring Mark's Gospel*. London: Mowbray.

Francis, L. J., & Atkins, P. (2000). *Exploring Luke's Gospel: A Guide to the Gospel Readings in the Revised Common Lectionary*. London and New York: Mowbray.

Francis, L. J., & Atkins, P. (2001). *Exploring Matthew's Gospel: A Guide to the Gospel Readings in the Revised Common Lectionary*. London: Mowbray.

Halperin, D. J. (1993). *Seeking Ezekiel: Text and Psychology*. University Park: Pennsylvania State University Press.

Homans, P. (1979). *Jung in Context: Modernity and the Making of a Psychology*. Chicago: University of Chicago Press.

Jung, C. G. (1976). *The Tavistock Lectures, The Collected Works of C. G. Jung*, H. Read, M. Fordham, & G. Adler, eds. (Vol. 18). Princeton: Princeton University Press, 5–182.

Kille, D. A. (2001). *Psychological Biblical Criticism*. Minneapolis: Fortress Press.

Koch, S. (1992). The Nature and Limits of Psychological Knowledge, *A Century of Psychology as Science*, S. Koch & D. E. Leary, eds. Washington, DC: American Psychological Association, 75–97.

Miller, J. W. (1997). *Jesus at Thirty: A Psychohistorical Inquiry*. Minneapolis: Fortress.

Oates, W. E. (1950). The Diagnostic Use of the Bible: What a Man Sees in the Bible Is a Projection of His Inner Self. *Pastoral Psychology*, *1*, 43–46.

Pruyser, P. (1991). The Tutored Imagination in Religion, *Religion in Psychodynamic Perspective: The Contributions of Paul W. Pruyser*, H. N. Maloney & B. Spilka, eds. New York: Oxford University Press, 101–115.

Ricoeur, P. (1974). *The Conflict of Interpretations: Essays in Hermeneutics*. Evanston: Northwestern University Press.

Rollins, W. G. (1999). *Soul and Psyche: The Bible in Psychological Perspective*. Minneapolis: Augsburg Fortress.

Schweitzer, A. (1948). *The Psychiatric Study of Jesus: Exposition and Criticism*, C. R. Joy, trans. Boston: Beacon Press.

Scroggs, R. (1982, March 24). Psychology as a Tool to Interpret the Text. *Christian Century*, 335–338.

Theissen, G. (1987). *Psychological Aspects of Pauline Theology*. Philadelphia: Fortress.

Underwood, R. (1997). Primordial Texts: An Object Relations Approach to Biblical Hermeneutics. *Pastoral Psychology*, 45(3), 181–192.

Wink, W. (1973). *The Bible in Human Transformation: Toward a New Paradigm for Biblical Study*. Philadelphia: Fortress.

Wulff, D. M. (1985). Psychological Approaches, *Contemporary Approaches to the Study of Religion*, F. Whaling, ed., vol. 2, *The Social Sciences*. Berlin: Mouton, 21–88.

CHAPTER 3

SEXUALITY IN THE HEBREW BIBLE: FREUD'S LENS

Ilona Rashkow

It is almost a commonplace to state that Freud *and* the Hebrew Bible deal with many aspects of human sexuality.[1] In this chapter I examine the sexual practices the Hebrew Bible deems "acceptable" and "unacceptable" (focusing in particular on the biblical laws against incest) and explore the relationship between these biblical incest laws and two incest narratives that seem almost anachronistically Freudian: the father–son narrative of Noah and Ham, and the father–daughter narrative of Lot and his two unnamed female children.

My theoretical approach is literary, albeit *influenced* by psychoanalytic theory. Unfortunately, the phrase "literature and psychoanalysis" usually implies a relationship of subordination rather than coordination. Literature is submitted to the "authority" or the "prestige" of psychoanalysis (Felman, 1980, 5). The literary text is considered as a body of language to *be* interpreted, whereas psychoanalysis is a body of knowledge used *to* interpret. I have tried to read Freud and the Bible concurrently rather than to provide a hierarchical positioning. That is, I have not been reading the Bible *in light* of Freud but rather *while* reading him. Certainly I do not consider Freud a biblical scholar. Rather, I appropriate his approach as a tool for biblical interpretation.

A significant amount of work has been done recently, in various disciplines, on psychology and the Hebrew Bible. However, most of what has been written by sociologists and psychoanalysts is of a highly theoretical nature generally not accessible to those not already steeped in the field. Within the area of biblical studies, books and articles are beginning to appear. More general studies include Rollins's *Soul and Psyche: The Bible in Psychological Perspective* (1999), perhaps the most definitive survey of the field of psychological biblical criticism to date, which includes a comprehensive examination of the past, present, and future of the field and provides an extensive bibliography; Kille's *Psychological Biblical Criticism* (2001), which provides an introduction to psychological biblical criticism in general and also examines Genesis 3 from the perspectives of Freudian, Jungian, and developmental psychologies; and Polka's *Depth Psychological Interpretation and the Bible: An Ontological Essay on Freud* (2001), which is a critique of Freud's metapsychology and focuses primarily on the explanatory function of the father complex, the castration complex, and the pleasure principle as internally contradictory to the presuppositions of Freud's analytic practice.

Recent studies devoted to individual texts include Edinger's *Ego and Self: The Old Testament Prophets from Isaiah to Malachi* (2000), a psychological commentary on the prophetic books; Kluger and Kluger-Nash's *A Psychological Interpretation of Ruth* (1999), in which they claim that the book represents a return of the feminine to Israelite religion after it had been displaced by the cult of YHWH; Cohen's *Voices from Genesis: Guiding Us through the Stages of Life* (1998), which is an application of the developmental theory of Erik Erikson to an interpretation of the patriarchal narratives—from Adam and Eve as illustrations of infancy to Cain and Abel as illustrations of early childhood; and Halperin's *Seeking Ezekiel: Text and Psychology* (1993), the centerpiece of his argument being a reexamination of Edwin C. Broome's article "Ezekiel's Abnormal Personality" (1946).

Another recent book, Carmichael's *Law, Legend, and Incest in the Bible: Leviticus 18–20* (1997), deals specifically with incest. His assumption is that the biblical lawgivers (that is, the writers of Lev. 18–20) "set out to tackle the ethical and legal problems they encountered in their reading of these tales" and that the biblical laws "constitute a commentary upon matters arising in the national folklore" (1997, 5).

In addition to these book-length studies there have been a few shorter articles by biblical scholars who use Lacanian theory in examining the Genesis 1–3 narrative. Both Piskorowski's "In Search of Her Father: A Lacanian Approach to Genesis 2–3" (1992) and Fodor's "The Fall of Man in the Book of Genesis" (1954), for example, discuss the prohibition against eating from the tree of knowledge of good and evil as "the law of the Name-of-the-Father" or the "phallus." In addition, Parker's "Mirror, Mirror on the Wall, Must We Leave Eden, Once and for All?" (1999) suggests that the maturation theme as discerned in the Eden narrative has certain affinities with modern psychoanalytical theory, and in particular with the work of Lacan. He sees the expulsion from Eden as necessary and just as painful as a child's maturation and socialization through Lacan's Oedipal stage.

Sin and Sex as Defined in the Hebrew Bible

Biblical references to male and female erogenous zones, both primary and secondary, are generally euphemistic, and the culture reflected in the Bible protects the penis and its physical environs with vigor. The phallocentric society that created biblical literature posits the human penis as the explicit characteristic of religious identity. The penis is the special link between its god and the members of the community. As I discuss more fully elsewhere, circumcision, imported from other cultures and reinterpreted, defines males as members of the community (Rashkow, 1993, 65–84). By this token, women are excluded a priori from that symbolic order, and bonding with the (male) god is stamped on the (male) body.

Sex-determined biological difference, gender difference, and difference in sexual orientation and/or sexual practice are characteristics of patriarchal societies in which power lies in the hands of heterosexual males. Heterosexual males in such societies reinforce their authority by defining themselves as the "norm" and marking all others as different. Sexual practices viewed as "deviations" from the accepted biblical sociosexual mores include, in addition to homosexuality, incest, bestiality, adultery, rape, and prostitution. With the exception of bestiality, the descriptions, prohibitions, and penalties for participating in these acts differ for males and females.[2]

The Laws

Biblical sexual prohibitions are significant because they have had a major effect on Western law. The Levitical sexual prohibitions (with the addition of rules from Roman law in some instances) became the law governing incestuous relations in those countries in which the church was most influential. For centuries, not only were the prohibitions of Leviticus 18 and 20 in force but a great many other prohibitions derived from them.[3]

In the Hebrew Bible, Leviticus (chaps. 12ff.) is primarily a code of moral and ritual laws whose motivation is holiness. (In this context, holiness refers to the entire people, not just to the priestly tribe.) Because a major concern of the writers of the Levitical and Deuteronomical texts seems to have been the creation of rules that would shape the identity of the emerging nation, these passages state over and over again a claim that the Israelites are "different" from peoples of the surrounding cultures. As a result, they established incest rules by which Israelites could and should define themselves. It is possible, however, that the Israelites were not as "different" as they proclaimed themselves to be. According to the Rabbis,[4] the Israelites' attitudes toward sexuality were similar to those of the Persians. Indeed, the Babylonian Talmud notes that the Zoroastrians were equally chaste in sexual matters:

> It has been taught: R. Akiba says: "For three things I like the Medes [Persians]: When they cut meat, they cut it only on the table; when they kiss, they kiss only the hand; and when they hold counsel, they do so only in the field." . . . R. Gamaliel says: "For three things do I like the Persians: They are temperate in their eating, modest in the privy, and chaste in another matter [in sexual matters]." (Berakhoth 8b)

Certain cultural similarities with their surrounding neighbors notwithstanding, the Israelites, within the biblical construct, regarded the segregation of both persons *and* things a primary consideration. For instance, Leviticus 19:19 and Deuteronomy 22:11 prohibit the wearing of *sha'atnez*, cloth combining wool and linen. (The Levitical passage defines the prohibition as cloth made from a mixture of two kinds of material; the Deuteronomical text is more specific and prohibits wearing wool and linen together.) The clothing of the priests was notably exempt from the prohibition of *sha'atnez*. Exodus 28:6, 8, 15, and 39:29 prescribe various pieces to be made of linen and colored wool interwoven. Although seemingly irrelevant to the discussion at hand, this prohibition is considered a prime example of a divine statute that has no *rational* explanation, and Jewish philosophers have attempted to rationalize its intent in ways that are reminiscent of their explanations of both *incest* prohibitions and dietary laws. Maimonides, in *The Guide for the Perplexed*, explains that the wearing of mixed garments was forbidden because heathen priests wore such garments (1904, 3:37), and Nahmanides suggests that the person mixing diverse kinds was guilty of displaying that he was improving upon the species created by God.

In other words, because biblical writings emphasize the differences between the Israelite community and all others, prohibitions against and penalties for illicit relations, homicidal cult practices, and magic probably exist for the same reason as do the *sha'atnez* and food prohibitions: separation and distinction from the neighboring tribes, whose perceived idolatrous and immoral practices were to be avoided. The Levitical verses that deal with illicit sexual relations, for example, are encased by an introduction that castigates the Egyptians and Canaanites for the depravity of their sexual practices:

> You shall not do as they do in the land of Egypt, where you dwelt, and you shall not do as they do in the land of Canaan, to which I am bringing you. You shall not walk in their statutes. (Lev. 18:3)

Total destruction and exile is threatened if these laws are not followed:

> Lest the land vomit you out, when you defile it, as it vomited out the nation that was before you. For whoever shall do any of these abominations, the persons that do them shall be cut off from among their people. (Lev. 18:28–29)

In this chapter I concentrate on those aspects of "holiness" that refer to human sexuality, and within this context, I define sexuality according to the laws in the three juridical texts (Lev. 18, 20; and Deut. 27:20, 22–23).

Of the lists of prohibitions of sexual relations in Leviticus, that of Chapter 18 is the most unified. After an introduction attributing abhorrent sexual practices to Egypt and Canaan (vv. 1–5), a superscription (v. 6), and the prohibition against a man "uncovering the nakedness" of his father, a list of twelve categories of forbidden females is presented (vv. 7b–18):

- Mother (v. 7)
- Father's wife (v. 8)
- Maternal and/or paternal sister, from the household or outside it (v. 9)
- Son's or daughter's daughter (v. 10)
- Stepmother's daughter by the same father (v. 11)
- Paternal aunt (v. 12)
- Maternal aunt (v. 13)
- Uncle's wife (v. 14)
- Daughter-in-law (v. 15)
- Brother's wife (v. 16)
- Woman and her daughter, and their female descendants (v. 17)
- Woman and her sister (v. 18)

Other sexual prohibitions follow (vv. 19–23):

- Intercourse with a menstruating woman (v. 19)
- Adultery (v. 20)
- Sacrifice of "seed" to Moloch (v. 21)
- Male homosexuality (v. 22)
- Bestiality of male and female (v. 23)

The list of Leviticus 20 is of a somewhat different nature, although males (again) are addressed. In addition, the terminology differs slightly, as do the punishments. Seven categories of forbidden females are included within other categories of sexual transgressions:

- Father's wife (v. 11)
- Daughter-in-law (v. 12)
- Woman and daughter (v. 14)
- Maternal and/or paternal sister (v. 17)
- Maternal or paternal aunt (v. 19)
- Uncle's wife (v. 20)
- Brother's wife (v. 21)

Other sexual prohibitions are interspersed:

- Male homosexuality (v. 13)
- Bestiality of male and female (vv. 15–16)
- Intercourse with a menstruating woman (v. 18)

Unlisted here (by comparison to Lev. 18) are

- Adultery
- Sacrifice of "seed" to Moloch
- Man's granddaughter
- Stepmother's daughter by the same father
- Woman and her sister

Incest

Incest taboos in the ancient world were not universal.[5] Indeed, sexual relations among blood relatives were directly encouraged in many ancient cultures and often based on divine example. Most of these societies were tribal, and sibling marriages formed the simplest types of kinship systems. That the historical works and literature of the ancients are filled with tales of incest and that the practice occurred among ancient people is validated further by the especially strict customs, taboos, and punishments that eventually evolved to prohibit continuance of the practice.

Incest rules have fascinated scholars of various disciplines—anthropologists, ethnographers, historians, philosophers, sociologists, psychologists, and theologians, among others—and attempts to explain the prohibitions are associated with writers as diverse as Philo, Plutarch, Augustine, Maimonides, Jeremy Taylor, Hugo Grotius, David Hume, Charles Montesquieu, Jeremy Bentham, Lewis Morgan, Émile Durkheim, James Frazer, Sigmund Freud, Bronislaw Malinowski, and Claude Lévi-Strauss (Carmichael, 1997, 3). Yet despite all of the scholarly attention, there is little agreement about the *origin* of the incest taboo. According to some behavioral psychologists, for example, prohibitions against incest are "uniquely human," an instinctive safeguard against the consequences of inbreeding. Behavioral psychologists who argue otherwise, however, note the lack of universality in attitudes toward incest. That is, different societies have different taboos concerning paternal versus maternal sisters as well as extensions of the taboo from blood to marital kin.

Some sociological theories form a correlation between sex and power and posit incest prohibitions as exogamy/endogamy rules that help regulate socioeconomic forces. This school of thought holds that woman is the basic social currency. As such, she establishes and regulates both the economy and the hierarchy, and therefore all male members of the clan must out-breed. In other words, incest prohibitions provide a collective male sanction against aggressive males who might attempt to seize power over society's basic commodity (women), beginning with their own female relatives. This explanation might apply to the biblical taboos discussed later in the chapter. As is well recognized, biblical society was by and large patriarchal, and the "father's house" was the basic family unit. Because typically the nuclear unit encompassed two or three generations of blood kin, marital kin, and dependents, incest laws helped set boundaries.

Lévi-Strauss's well-known analysis of kinship systems seems particularly relevant to biblical literature. Lévi-Strauss argues that the most significant rule governing any family structure is the ubiquitous existence of the incest taboo, which imposes the social aim of exogamy and alliance on the biological events of sex and procreation. Indeed, Genesis alone nearly constitutes a meditation on the questions that concern the patriarchy: where wives should come from, how closely they should be related to "us," or how "other" they should be (Pitt-Rivers, 1977, 128, 165). Is there a pattern here? Certainly, the numerous examples of incestuous unions indicate that at least among the major characters of the Hebrew Bible, the incest prohibitions seem to be observed more in the breach than in the maintenance. Indeed, the Hebrew Bible is replete with consanguineous sex. Abraham twice acknowledges his wife to be his sister, and his son, Isaac, marries his father's brother's daughter. Isaac's son, Jacob, acquires two wives, sisters who constitute a lineal double of each other. That is to say, Jacob marries two of his father's father's brother's son's son's daughters, who are simultaneously his mother's brother's daughters and thereby are connected back to Abraham. In the next generation, Reuben sleeps with his father's second wife's maid, symbolically violating family purity laws, and Judah sleeps with his daughter-in-law. Certainly Jacob views Reuben's act as a violation of family purity laws. In Genesis 49:4, Jacob censures Reuben for "going up to" his father's bed and "defiling" it. (The verb Jacob uses is from the stem "pollute, defile, profane" and is used in connection with sexual depravity; see, for example, Lev. 19:29, 21:9.) The list of prohibited yet consummated sexual relations is impressive: Adam–Eve, Noah–Ham, Lot–his daughters, Ruben–Bilhah, and Jacob–Tamar all involve parent–child incestuous congress or exposure, whereas Adam–Eve and Abraham–Sarah are brother–sister unions (as is Amnon–Tamar in 2 Sam.), and Isaac–Rebecca and Jacob–Leah–Rachel are cousin marriages. And the theme of forbidden relationships does not end with Genesis. The Hebrew Bible is replete with banned sexual behavior. Significantly, this same text has been used as a paradigm of righteous behavior, and throughout history the Bible has also been used as a justification for various societal abuses such as slavery, misogyny, and child abuse. Hmmmm.

In *Totem and Taboo*, Freud argues that totemic religion and exogamy, the incest taboo, originated in response to Oedipal guilt. The son's desire to kill the father was enacted, Freud theorizes, by the primitive horde of sons who collectively murdered their primal father in order to gain possession of the women he had monopolized. The primitive prohibitions against sexual relations with women of the same clan and against the killing of the totem animal (the representative of the father) derived from the sons' remorse at the murder of a loved object. The ritual sacrifice of the totem animal once a year, however, "not only comprised expressions of remorse and an attempt at atonement, it also served as a remembrance of the triumph over the father" (1913, 145).

Another theory is that incest prohibitions might have evolved from a concern with procreation, not in terms of the birth of defective children but rather in terms of the inability of certain unions to produce children. For example, the (observed) difficulty of postmenopausal conception may have led to a prohibition against sexual relations between a man and a *female* relative of an older generation but not between a woman and an older *male* relative (as in the case of Isaac and Sarah). Certainly the astonishment expressed by Sarah and Abraham when she becomes pregnant in her old age points in this direction. In Genesis 17:17, Abraham fell upon his face and laughed when he heard that Sarah was to have a child. Later, the narrator emphasizes the absurdity of that prediction: "Abraham and Sarah are old and coming in years. For Sarah, it had ceased to be after the manner of women" (Gen. 18:11). Not surprisingly, the postmenopausal Sarah, hearing of the prediction, does not believe it: "Sarah laughed inwardly and said, 'After I am shriveled! I shall have pleasure? My Lord is old!'" (Gen. 18:12).

As is apparent from the lists quoted earlier in the chapter, the Levitical and Deuteronomical incest laws are quite specific, and some of the prohibitions differ from those of today. For example, although biblical notions of incest *include* marital restrictions, biblical concepts of incest are broader than specific marital prohibitions. In fact, marital ties are seldom mentioned explicitly.

It should be noted that the law of levirate marriage (Deut. 25:5–10) contradicts the incest prohibition of sexual intercourse with a sister-in-law. According to the Deuteronomical requirement, if a married man dies childless, his brother *must* marry the widow, and their first-born child will be the heir of the deceased man (any subsequent children will be heirs of the second husband). If the brother refuses his obligation, the widow must humiliate him publicly.

In addition, the Levitical list contains no express prohibition against intercourse with a full sister (as compared with a maternal or paternal sister). Nor is there a prohibition against a father having intercourse with a son or a daughter. By contrast, both the Hittite Code[6] and the Code of Hammurabi[7] prohibited a son from having intercourse with his mother and a father from having intercourse with his daughter and/or son. (Cf. article 199 of the Hittite Code, which says that a citizen may not have sexual intercourse with his mother, his daughter, or his son. Cf. also article 154 of the Code of Hammurabi, which says that if a citizen has sexual intercourse with his daughter, he will be exiled from the city; and article 157, which says that if a citizen has intercourse with his mother after the death of his father, then both are to be burned at the stake [Pritchard, 1958, 196].) The lack of biblical prohibition of brother–sister incest and father–daughter incest is particularly curious because the sexual abuse of a son or daughter (or a sister by a brother) is the most prevalent in the world of experience (Herman and Hirschman, 1981).

Homosexuality

For a patriarchal system to be sustained, not only must men endeavor to control women's sexual behavior, but they must police and (preferably) prohibit all forms of sexual expression that fall outside the binary world of heterosexuality (and which therefore do not maintain the status quo), specifically (male) homosexuality. For example, article 20 of the Middle Assyrian Code says that if one citizen has homosexual intercourse with another, then, following due process, the defendant will be castrated. The Hebrew Bible has a similar prohibition: "You shall not lie with a male as with a woman; it is an abomination" (Lev. 18:22).

The punishment for this transgression is found in Deuteronomy 24:7, which says that if a man kidnaps and "abuses" a fellow Israelite, he must receive the death penalty. Because the reflexive tense of this verb (hit`ammer) can involve sexual possession and domination (as is clear from an analogous usage in the case of a captured foreign woman [Deut. 21:14], where the punishment in the Hebrew Bible is death), it can be argued that the penalty here is perhaps even worse than that of the Middle Assyrian Code.

David Daub has argued that the curious formulation of this rule may be an invective against anal intercourse, because the language is not "to uncover the nakedness" (as in the incest prohibitions) or "to lie," but "to lie with a male [as it were] the lying with a woman"—and the only way a man can penetrate another man as he might a woman is by anal intercourse (1986, 447–448). Thus, Daub suggests that the view of male homosexuality in Israelite society may have been similar to that of the Greeks, who condemned anal intercourse but not other homosexual activity.[8]

Like incest prohibitions, the prohibition against homosexuality applies only to men; there is no corresponding prohibition against female homosexuality. To be sure, if anal intercourse is the issue, the practice envisaged is obviously *inapplicable* to women. Of course, there are probably additional reasons why we find no proscriptions of lesbian sex. (Because article 20 of the Code of Hammurabi specifically restricts homosexual activities to "citizens," by implication the Babylonian Code does not address lesbian relationships either.) For example, it is virtually inconceivable that a woman would have been asked about her sexual preference when the issue of her marital arrangement arose between a prospective husband and her father or guardian. Perhaps another reason we find no rule about lesbian sex in the Hebrew Bible is that the traditions with which the lawgivers worked simply did not discuss the topic.[9] Significantly, in the Talmud lesbian conduct is compared with adultery by the rabbis (Talmud, Mas. Sotah, 26b), and to women's joining in when men sing (Talmud, Mas. Sotah, 48a).

Lack of overt prohibition notwithstanding, proscription of lesbianism is assumed by many modern authors to be implied in Leviticus, chapters 18 and 20. The eighteenth chapter is introduced by a general prohibition against subscribing to the practices of Egypt and Canaan (Lev. 18:2–3): "Say to the people of Israel, 'I am the lord your God. You shall not do as they do in the land of Egypt, where you dwelt, and you shall not do as they do in the land of Canaan, to which I am bringing you. You shall not walk in their statutes'" (Lev. 18:2–3).

Most of the exegetical material on these verses tries to recover the reasons Egypt and Canaan are addressed in this section and the curious verse against following "their laws." A midrash in Sifra Aharei Mot offers one solution—it is the practices of the ancestors of Egypt and Canaan that lie behind this phrase. According to the midrash, "And what did they do? One man marries another man, a woman marries a woman, and a man marries a woman and her daughter, and a woman marries two [men]" (Sifra Aharei Mot 8:9).

Similarly, the Jerusalem Talmud includes a debate between the schools of Hillel and Shammai over whether female homosexual intercourse invalidates virginity and thus disqualifies such women from marrying priests: Shammai disqualifies them, but Hillel permits them to marry priests. (Note the bisexual assumption underlying this controversy.)

Baruch Levine writes that "in due course, Rabbinic interpretation added this prohibition [of lesbianism] as well [as that against homosexuality in this verse]" (1989, 123), although Maimonides claims that the punishment for lesbianism is neither biblical nor Rabbinic (commentary to Mishnah Sanhendrim 7:4). Maimonides addresses the topic more fully in the Mishnah Torah:

> Women are forbidden to be *mesolelot* with one another. This is the practice of the Land of Egypt, against which we have been warned, as it is said: "Like the practice of the Land of Egypt etc. you shall not do." The Sages said: "What did they do? A man marries a man, a woman marries a woman, and a woman marries two men." Although this practice is

forbidden, no flogging is imposed, since there is no specific negative commandment against it, nor is there any intercourse at all. Consequently, [such women] are not forbidden to the priesthood on account of harlotry, nor is a woman prohibited to her husband on account of it, since there is no harlotry in it. However, a flogging for disobedience (*mardut*) should be given, since they have performed a forbidden act. A man should be strict with his wife in this matter, and should prevent women who are known to engage in this practice from visiting her, and prevent her from going to them.

Freud and the Hebrew Bible

Freud and the Oedipal Complex

The Oedipal complex is so central to the issue of Freud and sexuality in the Hebrew Bible that I provide a bit of background material. The theory, however, is not easy to summarize clearly. It is complicated and arguably confused; Freud himself never gave a systematic account of it (Laplanche & Pontalis, 1983, 283). As Dollimore describes, essentially it is a theory of how the human being becomes positioned within the existing system of social and sexual difference as a result of a critical and fraught relationship with his or her parents (1991, 223). According to Laplanche and Pontalis,

> in its so-called positive form, the complex appears as in the theory of Oedipus Rex: a desire for the death of the rival—the parent of the same sex—and a sexual desire for the parent of the opposite sex. In its negative form, we find the reverse picture: love for the parent of the same sex, and jealous hatred for the parent of the opposite sex. In fact, the two versions are to be found in varying degrees in what is known as the complete form of the complex. (1983, 282–283)

In the resolution of the complex, elements of the psychic and sexual life of the child that are incompatible with its social/sexual positioning within the polarities of sexual difference are repressed and sublimated, especially its incestuous desires, but also the perversions more generally. In John Fletcher's formulation, the law of the Oedipal polarity commands, in effect: "you cannot *be* what you desire; you cannot *desire* what you wish to be" (1989, 101).

Freud's first recorded mention of the Oedipal complex is in his letter of October 15, 1897, to Fleiss in which he refers also to memory distortion. Freud describes his own early love for his mother and his awareness of his father's jealousy, recognizing that it accounted for "the riveting power of *Oedipus Rex*" by Sophocles.[10] According to Freud, "each member of the audience was once, in germ and in phantasy, just such an Oedipus, and each one recoils in horror from the dream-fulfillment here transplanted into reality, with the whole quota of repression which separate his infantile state from his present one" (1897, 256).

Beginning with this reference, Freud apparently considered the Oedipal complex as the nucleus of every neurosis, and he continued to write on the subject for more than thirty years. The first insights seemed to come during his self-analysis by way of parallels with Sophocles' tragedy and Shakespeare's *Hamlet*. Hamlet, according to Freud, is "the hysteric" who delays because he is paralyzed by guilt over Claudius's enactment of his own unconscious wishes (1916–1917, 235). In the course of clinical analyses of men, women, and children, Freud connected the Oedipal complex and dreams, symptoms, jokes, primitive cultures, religion, and literature.

By 1916–1917, Freud had formulated the relationship of pre-Oedipal material to the complex itself. For Freud, pre-Oedipal events—including loss of love or abandonment, the period of toilet training, and the sight of the female genitals—can contribute to Oedipal castration fear. The child's first love object, the mother's breast, supplies food and erotic pleasure. From the attachment to the breast, the child progresses to the mother herself; both breast and mother are absorbed into the Oedipus complex and influence its development.

In the so-called positive Oedipal constellation of a boy from two and a half years to six years,[11] the child desires his mother and is hostile to his father as the obstacle to his wishes. He fears his father's retaliation in the form of castration, which corresponds to the talion law of the unconscious. The Hebrew Bible law of an "eye for an eye" expresses, for Freud, the literal character of the unconscious thinking that motivated Oedipus's self-blinding as upwardly displaced self-castration. In the so-called negative constellation, the boy identifies with his mother and becomes, in fantasy, his father's passive love object.

By 1923, in *The Ego and the Id*, Freud wrote that the Oedipus complex operates bisexually—that is to say, the negative *and* positive constellations interact in every case. In other words, although the boy is hostile to his father, he also loves him—an ambivalent relationship. In the 1928 essay "Dostoevsky and Parricide," Freud describes the bisexuality of the Oedipus complex as heightened in neurosis and in certain creative individuals. However, regardless of whether the positive or negative constellation predominates, the boy fears castration—either as punishment or as a prerequisite for his feminine identification.

With the dissolution of the Oedipus complex, the boy's ego adopts the father's values, by the process of identification, and becomes the nucleus of the superego. The superego, in turn, prohibits incest and murder, which sublimates the libidinal and aggressive forces of the Oedipus complex. The aim of those forces is thereby inhibited, and in ideal circumstances they are transformed into affection.

As for the Oedipus complex of a girl, it appears that Freud did not finalize his theory until 1931. Although originally Freud seemed to consider male and female development to be parallel, he later wrote that a girl's dynamics differ from those of a boy, comparing this insight to unearthing the Minoan civilization, which had only been hinted at in myths and legends during the Greek era (1931, 231)

The girl, like the boy, takes her mother as her first love object, but there is less hostility in the girl's relationship to her father. In contrast to the boy, the girl's positive Oedipus complex requires a change in object from mother to father that corresponds to the girl's renouncing of the clitoris as the primary genital zone in favor of the vagina. According to Freud, the fantasy in girls that castration has already taken place precedes and paves the way for the Oedipus complex, whereas in boys it is the *fear* of castration that destroys the Oedipus complex. These writings seemed to shed a new light on the importance of the girl's pre-Oedipal stage and explain her tendency to remain attached to her mother. They also clarified the complexity of female development, the likelihood of a prolonged Oedipus complex, and the greater flexibility of the female superego as compared with the male.

Freud seems to have taken great pains to point out that his formulation of the Oedipus complex is a *construct* and that all people are bisexual (Freud, 1925, 251ff.). However, the interplay of Oedipal forces and their variations form a cornerstone of his psychoanalytic theory, particularly in relation to sexuality and family.

As Brenkman discusses, the dissolution of the Oedipus complex—as opposed to its merely more or less unsuccessful repression—requires, first, that it be initially formed along the lines of the "simple positive Oedipus complex," that is, in the heterosexual form in which the little boy has an erotic attachment to his mother and a (desexualized) identification with his father (1993, 24). Freud had in fact come to the conclusion that "a strong innate bisexual disposition becomes one of the preconditions or reinforcements of neurosis" (Freud, 1928, 184). Once the Oedipus complex is appropriately formed, it can then be utterly dissolved, without any repressed residue, only if the son's rivalrous hatred of his father and his erotic attachment to his mother each end

in a particular way. As regards the father, the route for the son to follow is laid down by the heterosexual imperative. "What makes hatred
of the father unacceptable is *fear* of the father; castration is terrible,
whether as a punishment or as the price of love. Of the two factors
which repress hatred of the father, the first, the direct fear of punishment and castration, may be called the normal one; its pathogenic
intensification seems to come only with the addition of the second factor, the fear of the feminine attitude" (Freud, 1928, 184). As regards
the mother in the simple positive Oedipus complex, the son's fear of
castration is the motive for abandoning his erotic attachment. But
what then is the fate of this love? According to Freud, "its place may
be filled by one of two things: either an identification with his mother
or an intensification of his identification with his father. We are accustomed to regard the latter outcome as the more normal; it permits the
affectionate relation to the mother to be in a measure retained. In this
way the dissolution of the Oedipus complex would consolidate the
masculinity in a boy's character" (1923, 32).

The Biblical Context

One salient feature of all of the biblical laws cited earlier is that the
juridical texts are addressed exclusively to *males*: males are subjects of
the incest prohibitions, and for the most part females are objects. That
is to say, specific blood-kindred and marriage-kindred females are
cited as forbidden to the relevant *males*. The prohibitions that refer to
a marriage kinship are often referred to as "exposing the nakedness" of
some male relative (Lev. 18:7–8, 14, 16). For example, in the list of forbidden relations, sex with one's father's wife is referred to as "exposing the nakedness of one's father." The implication is that when a son
has relations with his father's wife, a woman who may or may not be
his biological mother, he is trespassing on the spot where the nakedness of his father has already been exposed. G. Wenham arrives at a
similar analysis: "Foreign to our way of thinking is the idea that a wife's
nakedness is her husband's nakedness and vice versa. In other words,
marriage or more precisely marital intercourse, makes the man and
wife as closely related as parents and children. In the words of Genesis
2:24, 'they become one flesh'" (1979, 255).

Similarly, when incest occurs with a father's brother's wife or a
brother's wife, the "nakedness" of these men is exposed because the
kinship tie through marriage is metaphorically a "*man's* nakedness." In
other words, it is the nakedness of a male relative that has made these
women kin.

Despite a definition of incest based on the term *nakedness*, the Hebrew
Bible by and large seems to lack evidence of either a social understanding of nakedness or its more common uses. For example, when Tamar
dresses as a prostitute to seduce Judah, she covers herself *completely*:
"She put off her widow's garments, and put on a veil, wrapping herself
up, and sat at the entrance to Enaim, which is on the road to Timnah;
for she saw that Shelah was grown up, and she had not been given to
him in marriage" (Gen. 38:14).

Similarly, Joseph is attractive to Potiphar's wife, although he always
remained clothed: "She caught him by his garment, saying, 'Lie with
me.' But he left his garment in her hand, and fled and got out of the
house" (Gen. 39:12). Tamar is dressed in a tunic (the narrative is careful to tell us) when Amnon rapes her: "Now she was wearing a long
robe with sleeves; for thus were the virgin daughters of the king clad
of old. So his servant put her out, and bolted the door after her" (2
Sam. 13:18). It is only Bat-Sheba's nakedness that is portrayed as sexually tempting to a male: "It happened, late one afternoon, when
David arose from his couch and was walking upon the roof of the
king's house, that he saw from the roof a woman bathing; and the
woman was very beautiful" (2 Sam. 11:2).[12]

Significantly, the Hebrew Bible does not seem to use nakedness as a
marker of either character or marital status, but nakedness does indicate vulnerability, as the exchange between Michal and David upon
his success in bringing the ark into Jerusalem indicates: "And David
returned to bless his household. But Michal the daughter of Saul came
out to meet David, and said, 'How the king of Israel honored himself
today, uncovering himself today before the eyes of his servants' maids,
as one of the vulgar fellows shamelessly uncovers himself!'" (2 Sam.
6:20).

In this narrative, as David's procession enters the city, Michal
watches the proceedings from a window and observes her husband
"leaping and dancing before YHWH." Michal speaks with authority,
with an assumed voice of strength, and her speech concerns honor.
Her sarcastic comment indicates clearly that she regards David's
behavior as inappropriate—instead of conducting himself as a king,
David shamelessly frolics before his servants' maids, and the weight of
her criticism lies entirely in the fact that David has "uncovered" himself. (Because David is wearing only a loincloth [2 Sam. 6:14], it is
more than likely that David is exposing himself, and not just "some
part of his thighs or legs.")

This aversion to male nakedness in antiquity appears to have been to a large degree unique to the Israelites (the ancient Persians' apparently chaste sexual practices notwithstanding). From the ancient Near East to Greek and Roman cultures, there was little squeamishness about the display of the phallus in sacred contexts or in the representation or description of the genitalia of the gods. Sumerian art, for example, regularly portrayed naked male divinities, and their literature did not refrain from description of their genitalia.[13] Much later representations in Greek and Roman art of naked male divinities, especially Pan, are of course quite common, and Greek and Roman art depicts soldiers going into battle wearing only a loincloth as well as priests of mystery cults performing their duties while naked, in further attempts to ward off evil.

Surprisingly, there are very few Rabbinic comments on Greek and Roman portrayals of the genitalia of their male gods. One exception is a reference in the Babylonian Talmud, which describes how a queen used the phallus on a statue of a god to satisfy herself sexually:

> But has it not been stated, "And also Maacah the mother of Asa the king, he removed her from being queen, because she had made an abominable image . . ." What means abominable image?—Rab Judah said: "[An object which] intensifies licentiousness as R. Joseph taught: 'It was a kind of phallus with which she had daily connection.'" (Abod. Zar. 44a)

Despite the paucity of evidence, however, there can be little doubt that the rabbis would have seen the statues of Hermes and Priapus as ridiculous. According to Abod. Zar. 33.8, 43a, for example: "Baal: His head was a penis, and it was like a pea." In other words, the Rabbis mock the biblical Baal not only because he was represented as a penis, but a small one at that!

Two Case Histories: Freud and the Hebrew Bible

The book of Genesis relates two episodes of a father drinking wine to excess, having a sexual encounter with his offspring, and subsequently condemning not his offspring but his grandchildren. Genesis 9:18–27 narrates the tale of an inebriated Noah, and Genesis 19 relates the story of Lot. Although most commentators have excused the fathers' behavior and censured the children, I see an alternative reading—one in which neither father is blameless. That is to say, under the influence of alcohol, Lot and Noah acted on repressed desires or frustrations.

The Lot story exemplifies the commonest type of incest and has many similarities to clinical reports of father–daughter incestuous relationships: the disintegrated family, the father who has lost his patriarchal role, the abuse of alcohol, the mother who looks away, and the involvement of more than one daughter. The usually unconscious desire of the father toward the daughter is, in this instance, consciously acted out. Similarly, psychoanalytic literary theory, other literary representations of the incest motif, and clinical situations involving father–son incest allow the Noah narrative to be read as involving either Noah's *fantasizing* about a homosexual activity or, possibly, even actually *initiating* such a liaison with his son Ham.

In addition, literary representations of this primary incest scene abound. For example, as a by-product of incest with the mother, many myths contain a theme of jealous hatred toward the father that stems from sexual rivalry (see, for example, Hesiod's *Theogony*). Often, however, the son's animosity is focused only indirectly toward the father's life and instead is directed toward his father's genitals. In addition, there are many myths in which the father attempts to castrate his son (again, as in Hesiod's *Theogony*). In many cases, the actual castration, sometimes carried out upon the father by the jealous son and sometimes carried out upon the son by the jealous father, is replaced either by mutilation of body parts other than the genitalia (blinding, for example) or by a symbolic castration, that is, the loss of power. The story of Samson is particularly interesting in this regard because not only is the cutting of his hair a *symbol* of castration, but simultaneously Samson's loss of physical prowess is stated explicitly. Further, from the perspective of psychoanalytic literary theory, the Oedipal significance of Samson's blindness as upwardly displaced castration can be associated with Icarus's fall in that hubris requires a failure to "see" intelligently and in*sight*fully and therefore is punished accordingly. In other words, it is as grandiose for a blind man to lead others as it is for Icarus to disobey Dædalus and for the citizens of Babel to build a tower reaching to the heavens.

Significantly, there are many myths in which the symbolic castration of the son by the father is an incestuous homosexual relationship (Rank, 1912). That is to say, from a psychoanalytic perspective, this homosexual incest in effect "feminizes" the son (Freud, 1909, 138) and thereby the father diminishes his son's status and power. Generally speaking, in these myths the father's actions occur either because the father wants to prevent his son's attack on him or, according to Freud, because the father has not successfully resolved his own homosexual fantasies/desires (1909, 139).

Just as the Oedipal relationship is represented frequently in general literature and is particularly prevalent in mythology, so too is the analogous relationship of fathers and daughters. One difference, however, is the *perspective* of the narrative. The mother–son relationship is generally presented from the point of view of the son. On the other hand, the father–daughter relationship is rarely presented from the point of view of the child but instead mainly from the *father's* perspective (as in the Lot narrative, discussed later). Often the father, after having an incestuous relationship with his daughter(s), condemns the offspring (again, as in Lot's case).

Noah and Ham

Genesis 9:18–27 narrates the "unconventional" behavior of an inebriated Noah and his sons Shem, Ham, and Japheth. This short episode, which constitutes a link between the story of the Flood and the Table of Nations, is puzzling. Because of its brevity and textual inconsistencies, a number of scholars have suggested that this narrative is merely a "splinter from a more substantial tale" (Speiser, 1964, 62). If so, it might account for some of the many unanswered questions. A fuller account, for example, might address why Ham is spoken of as the youngest son in verse 24 and listed as the second of three sons in verse 18; or exactly what Ham "had done to" Noah that incurred such wrath; or how Noah "learned" what occurred; or why, if it was Ham who was guilty of some significant misdeed, Noah's curse is directed at Canaan; or why this particular punishment was selected; or why Japheth is allied with Shem; or why a threefold emphasis is on Ham's paternity of Canaan; or why there are many other obvious elements of critical importance that need clarification. Have two different stories been merged? Is a part of the text missing? Although text critics (scholars who "correct" one text in light of another) and source critics (scholars who do not view the Masoretic Text as a unified entity but rather examine narratives as disparate units) have much to say about the linguistic and literary development of the Hebrew Bible, I prefer the approach of literary scholars, who view this text as a puzzling but unified whole. As such, I assume that even *this* narrative in its present state is intended to "make sense." That is, there is a coherence in the narrative that various "readings" help explicate.

The narrator of this enigmatic tale begins with a seemingly inconsequential piece of information in presenting the genealogy of Noah: Genesis 9:18 tells us the names of Noah's sons, reasonable enough, and then casually mentions that Ham is the father of Canaan. Typical of biblical narrative, this offhand comment is an example of a frequently used literary technique of the biblical writer—introducing information presumably irrelevant to the immediate context yet crucial to the understanding of subsequent developments. Without it, we would be as ignorant of the identity of the *object* of Noah's curse as we are of its *cause*.

Then the story begins. After the Deluge, Noah was "the" tiller of the soil. (According to Tanxuma Gen. 11, Noah invented the plow, that is, Noah was the initiator of true agriculture as opposed to hoe agriculture or horticulture.) The article *the* implies something well known about Noah, possibly a tradition as a folk hero; or perhaps by initiating viticulture, Noah was the first to discover the soothing, consoling, and enlivening effects of wine. Indeed, many commentators who discuss this passage excuse Noah's excessive drinking exactly because he *was* the first wine drinker. For example, John Chrysostom, a church father, writes that Noah's behavior is defensible: as the first human being to taste wine, he would not know its aftereffects. According to Chrysostom, Noah, "through ignorance and inexperience of the proper amount to drink, fell into a drunken stupor" (Hamilton, 1990, 202–203). Philo, a Hellenistic Jewish philosopher, goes even further in exonerating Noah. He notes that one can drink in two different manners: "For there is a twofold and double way of becoming drunken: one is to drink wine to excess, which is a sin peculiar to the vicious and evil man; the other is to partake of wine, which always happens to the wise man. Accordingly, it is in the second signification that the virtuous and wise man is said to be drunken, not by drinking wine to excess, but merely by partaking of wine" (1971, 160). Philo goes on to explain that Noah was not "drinking to excess" but "merely . . . partaking of wine."

The Rabbis place Noah in a somewhat more ambiguous light:

> Satan thereupon slaughtered a lamb and then, in succession, a lion, a pig, and a monkey. As he killed each, he made its blood to flow under the vine. Thus Satan conveyed to Noah what the qualities of wine are: before a man drinks of it, he is innocent as a lamb; if he drinks of it moderately, he feels as strong as a lion; if he drinks more of it than he can bear, he resembles a pig; and if he drinks to the point of intoxication, then he behaves like a monkey, he dances around, sings, talks obscenely, and knows not what he is doing. (Gen. Rabbah 36:3)

It was not only the ancients who felt it necessary to exonerate Noah, at least partially. Indeed, this kind of apologetic permeates the work of most contemporary scholars. For example, when Nahum Sarna discusses Noah's drinking, he says that "no blame attaches to Noah since he was oblivious to the intoxicating effects of his discovery" (1989, 65). Similarly, G. Knight writes that

> under no circumstances are we to bring a moral judgment to bear upon Noah as he falls drunken in his tent. Man learns only from experience. In our day, every material discovery brings its compensatory disadvantages, road deaths from the development of the internal combusion [*sic*] engine, unspeakable devastation from the discovery of nuclear fission. Noah is the "guinea-pig," so to speak, from whom all mankind has been able to learn that along with drunkenness goes moral laxity, and that the drugging of the higher powers of human consciousness leads to sexual license. (1981, 105)

Back to the story. The narrator relates two facts: first, having become inebriated, Noah "uncovered himself within his tent"; and second, Ham "saw his father's nakedness." At this point, the text takes on several additional layers of ambiguity, all of which revolve around sexuality.

There appears to be little doubt that Noah's "uncovering himself" means exposure of his genitalia. In fact, Habakkuk 2:15 and Lamentations 4:21 mention such exposure by the inebriated and associate it with shame and loss of human dignity: "Woe to him who makes his neighbors drink of the cup of his wrath, and makes them drunk, to gaze on their shame!" (Hab. 2:15); "Rejoice and be glad, O daughter of Edom, dweller in the land of Uz; but to you also the cup shall pass; you shall become drunk and strip yourself bare" (Lam. 4:21).

Further, there is little doubt that Ham saw his father's exposed genitalia. Not surprisingly, there have been several interpretations of this anecdote. However, there has been little unanimity as to what actually occurred within the confines of Noah's tent. For example, the Babylonian Talmud, tractate Sanhedrin, has an interesting "dialogue" on the episode, and Rabbinic sources are divided on whether Ham castrated his father or engaged in a homosexual act, the former interpretation relying upon the fact Noah has no children after the flood. Rav maintains that Ham castrated his father, whereas Samuel claims that he sexually abused him:

> [With respect to the last verse] Rav and Samuel [differ,] one maintaining that he castrated him, whilst the other says that he sexually abused him. He who maintains that he castrated him, [reasons thus:] Since he cursed him by his fourth son, he must have injured him with respect to his fourth son. But he who says that he sexually abused him, draws an analogy between "*and he saw*" written twice. Here it is written, *And Ham*

the father of Canaan saw the nakedness of his father, whilst elsewhere it is written, *And when Shechem the son of Hamor saw her [he took her and lay with her and defiled her]*. Now, on the view that he emasculated him, it is right that he curse him by his fourth son; but on the view that he abused him, why did he curse his fourth son: he should have cursed him himself?
—Both indignities were perpetrated. (Sanhedrin 70a)

More recently, W. G. Cole suggests that although Genesis 9:22 cites "looking" as Ham's only crime,[14] Ham did more than mere looking, and Cole thinks the words "what his younger son had done to him" reveal a sexual attack on the father (1959, 43). Along these lines, J. M. Robertson draws attention to the similarity of this story to that of the castration of Uranus by Kronos (1900, 44). F. W. Bassett suggests that the idiomatic expression "saw his father's nakedness" could mean that Ham "had sexual intercourse with his father's *wife*" (1971, 236, my emphasis). However, other scholars disagree. E. A. Speiser notes that although the phrase "saw his father's nakedness" relates to genital exposure (contrast Gen. 42:9 and 12), it does not necessarily imply sexual offenses (cf. Gen. 2:25 and Exod. 20:26) (Speiser, 1964, 61).

Nahum Sarna takes Ham's actions quite literally—that Ham is "guilty" of having seen Noah's genitalia and then compounds his crime (lack of modesty and filial respect) by leaving his father uncovered and "shamelessly bruiting about what he had seen" (1989, 66). Sarna seems to backtrack, however, by adding that verse 24 ("Noah knew what his younger son *had done to him*" [my emphasis]) and the severity of Noah's reaction suggest that the Torah has "suppressed the sordid details of some repugnant act" (1989, 66).[15]

But whose "repugnant act"? As I stated earlier, on the basis of psychoanalytic literary theory, other literary representations of the incest motif, and clinical situations involving father–son incest, the act could have involved either Noah *fantasizing* about the homosexual activity or possibly actually *initiating* such a liaison with his son Ham.

Although the narrator is silent about what actually occurred between Noah and Ham, the text reports that Ham told his brothers about the encounter. Having "learned what [?] his youngest son had 'done to him,'" Noah curses Canaan (?), condemning him to the status of "slave of slaves," a grammatical construction that expresses the extreme degree of servitude—and blesses Shem and Japheth.[16] The text is silent about how Noah became aware of the situation and why Canaan, not Ham, is cursed. Saadia and Ibn Janah construe the curse to mean "cursed be [the father of] Canaan," a phrase that has already appeared twice in this brief narrative. Ibn Ezra has an interesting reading of this verse. He claims that "his youngest son" does not refer to Ham as *Noah's* youngest son but rather to Canaan as *Ham's* youngest son (quoted in Sarna, 1989, 66). Thus, Ham is the offended party and *his* son Canaan the perpetrator of some base deed. Accordingly, Noah, as grandfather, blames Canaan for "defiling" Ham. All that can be said with any surety about Ibn Ezra's reading is that Noah remains "pure," the righteous man saved from the deluge by the deity and from condemnation by most commentators.

Although source critics might argue that in the fuller story, Canaan, son of Ham, was a participant in the offense against Noah, there are so many questions and ambiguities relating to this narrative that perhaps we may find explanations within the text itself by using the approach of psychoanalytic literary theory. As in the psychoanalytic process, one way to arrive at possible answers is to raise (perhaps obvious) questions.

Question 1: How did Noah "uncover himself within his tent"? Did he intentionally remove his clothing and *then* lie down, or did he accidentally expose himself while sleeping?

Question 2: If Noah intentionally removed his clothing (rather than accidentally kicking off his garment while asleep), can we assume that he was relatively sober (as Philo maintains, as quoted earlier), at least sober enough to disrobe? Or, in the words of Genesis Rabbah, was Noah a lamb, lion, pig, or monkey?

Question 3: When did Ham enter the tent? That is, was Ham *already* in the tent when Noah arrived or did Ham wander in sometime later?

Although these questions may seem meaningless, bear with me and hopefully they will become more relevant and ultimately lead to the most germane question: If Ham entered the tent first and Noah intentionally removed his clothing in Ham's presence, was Noah initiating (either consciously or unconsciously) an incestuous encounter?

Because the text does not state explicitly that Noah lost consciousness and because it requires at least some coordination to remove clothing, I am assuming that Noah was probably not drunk enough to pass out. If Noah disrobed, *aware* that Ham was in the tent, again, there are (at least) three possible scenarios, each of which could be said to rely on Noah's reduced inhibitions resulting from the effects of the wine. All three of these readings are based on the premise that under the influence of alcohol, Noah was more likely to act on repressed desires or frustrations. Or, as Joseph Conrad wrote, "it is a maudlin

and indecent verity that comes out through the strength of wine"
(1912, 194).

Option 1: Noah undressed before his son arrived, and when Ham
arrived Noah initiated a forbidden fantasy—an incestuous liaison with
his son.

Option 2: Noah disrobed in his son's presence, and by doing so,
Noah's heretofore repressed fantasy of an incestuous, homosexual
encounter with his son was brought to the surface of his consciousness
but *not* acted upon.

Option 3: Ham, seeing his naked father, is the one who initiated a
sexual encounter (as most commentators suggest).

The third scenario, one that most Rabbinic authorities seem to
favor, appears to be the *least* reasonable. If Ham had either castrated
his father or initiated a homosexual act, it seems unlikely that he
would then run outside looking for his brothers Shem and Japheth as
witnesses. Indeed, clinicians report that in most cases, children who
have had incestuous homosexual relations do not report the incident
until many years later (Medlicott, 1967, 135). More likely, therefore,
are either of the first two readings, options that help explain the
extreme nature of Noah's curse: his guilt and his shame.

Although many elements of the conventional vocabulary of moral
deliberation (such as *ethical, virtuous, righteous*, and their opposites) are
largely alien to the psychoanalytic lexicon, the concepts of guilt and
shame do appear, albeit in technical (and essentially nonmoral) contexts (Smith, 1986, 52). Guilt and shame are described as different emotional responses, stemming from different stimuli, reflecting different
patterns of behavior, and functioning in different social constructions—
although the two are often related. Their primary distinction lies in the
norm that is violated and the expected consequences.

Guilt relates to internalized, societal, and parental *prohibitions*,
whose transgression creates feelings of wrongdoing and the fear of
punishment (Piers & Singer, 1953). Shame, on the other hand, relates
to the anxiety caused by inadequacy or failure to live up to internalized societal and parental *goals and ideals* (as opposed to internalized
prohibitions), expectations of what a person "should" do, be, know,
or feel. These feelings of failure often lead to a fear of psychological
or physical rejection, abandonment, expulsion (separation anxiety), or
loss of social position (Alexander, 1948, 43). The person shamed often
feels the need to take revenge for his or her humiliation, to save face.
By "shaming the shamer," the situation is reversed, and the shamed
person feels triumphant (Horney, 1950, 103).

If we apply to this narrative the Freudian theory that the primary incest scene (the Oedipal relationship) must be successfully resolved for the "healthy" mental development of every individual or else the repressed desire may return in another setting, the result may read as follows: When Noah "awoke from his wine," apparently he realized that either an *actual* incestuous, homosexual encounter with his son Ham had occurred, or he recognized his *repressed* desire for such a relationship. Presumably as a result, Noah understandably felt guilt (for having violated the societal norms that prohibit homosexuality) and shame. Hence, Noah's need for revenge in order to maintain his dignity and self-esteem. In other words, Noah shamed the shamer. In what reads anachronistically like classical Freudian defense mechanisms, Noah attempted to alleviate his own anxiety by using methods that would deny, falsify, or otherwise distort his heretofore repressed fantasy. First, Noah sublimated the obviously dangerous memory or idea—his desire for Ham. Next, Noah rejected *himself* as the source of his uncomfortable feelings and attributed the origin of these emotions to Ham. That is, instead of saying "I wanted Ham," Noah said, "Ham wanted me." Essential here is that by displacing his emotions, Noah, the *subject* of unresolved incestuous, homosexual desires, changes himself into the *object* of these desires. By doing so, Noah is able to provide a rationalization for his curse. As a result, Ham is forced into the position of shouldering Noah's displaced guilt and shame.

But why curse Canaan and not Ham? Looking at artistic and literary representations of this narrative in light of psychoanalytic literary theory may provide a different insight into Noah's actions than that of traditional biblical scholars. Renaissance painters appear to display a somewhat playful approach to this biblical episode, one that seems also to echo Freudian thought and recent clinical data. Generally speaking, the pictures portray the obviously masculine naked patriarchal figure lying in a drunken state. However, significant from the perspective of psychoanalytic literary theory and actual reported incest cases, there is considerable sexual confusion in the representation of the three brothers, Japheth, Shem, and Ham. A twelfth-century mosaic, for example, shows Ham without a beard beside his two bearded brothers, perhaps suggesting the often-used theme equating beards and masculinity, as in the well-known Samson narrative of Judges 13–16. Jacopo della Quercia (ca. 1430) shows only two brothers, one with his eyes averted and carrying a cloak, and behind him (presumably) Ham with his garments drawn up to expose his own genitalia. Hiding in the vines is a mysterious feminine figure. (Might she represent a feminized portrayal of Ham?) Giovanni Bellini portrays a nude, heavily bearded Noah cavorting about. Ham, smooth skinned, is pictured in the middle of the scene.

For purposes of this chapter, I am most interested in Michelangelo's reading of the text. Michelangelo shows all three brothers with feminine hair arrangements. The brother nearest Noah, however, is the most masculine, with clearly identifiable male genitalia; the second brother has male genitalia but a rather protuberant feminine-like abdomen and is being embraced from behind by a dark Ham, who has no male genitals to clearly identify his sex.

The decreasingly masculine representations of each of the brothers suggest that Michelangelo's reading of the narrative portrays the first brother as sufficiently secure in his own masculinity not to hurry to look at his father's genitals, the second brother as confused, and Ham *as* a female. Why would Ham be portrayed in such a feminized style? Significant for purposes of my reading is that clinically it has been generally accepted that homosexual seduction by the father threatens the son's masculinity and overwhelms him with a passive feminine identification (Medlicott, 1967). That is, the father who makes sexual approaches to his son symbolically castrates him by "making a woman" of him, which is consistent with my interpretation of the representations by Michelangelo and other Renaissance artists. In other words, these painters are portraying Ham from *Noah's* perspective— as feminized.

Surprisingly the Noah narrative has not had much of a literary influence, perhaps because we know so little of the family dynamics. Notwithstanding, the few instances of the Noah motif could also be said to support Noah rather than Ham as the initiator of the sexual encounter. For example, English mystery plays generally portray Noah as the convivial drunkard and his wife as an ill-tempered shrew who makes his life on the ark intolerable.[17] Similarly, Clifford Odets's 1954 play *The Flowering Peach* turns the story of Noah and the Flood into a Jewish family sitcom.[18] Noah tipples, calls Esther, his wife, "girlie" and says things like "What am I, a loaf of bread? Don't butter me" whenever someone tries to flatter him. Esther complains, weeps, and complains some more. Sibling rivalries divide the grown sons: Shem, the wheeler-dealer; Ham, the rake; and Japheth, the misfit and mother's favorite, affectionately known as Jafey. (Then there's this whole mad business of having to build an ark just because Noah hears divine orders in rolling thunderclaps—but that is another issue.) Again, of interest because of their Freudian nature, both of these literary representations portray Noah as feeling inadequate in his masculinity and having difficulty mastering women; thus he is vulnerable to engaging in a homosexual relationship, as well as emasculating his male partner (in this case, Ham) in the process.

But this still does not explain fully why Canaan, and not Ham, is cursed. Psychoanalytic literary theory suggests that by consigning Ham's son and further progeny to abject slavery, Noah *symbolically* castrates Ham. Although the word *phallus* is interchangeable with *penis* in ordinary usage, this is not the case in the branch of psychoanalysis that concerns itself with psychosexual development. In the discourse of psychoanalysis, the word *phallus* does not denote the anatomical organ *penis* but rather the signifier or symbol of what we desire but lack, and it is most often associated with the concept of power. By making Canaan the "slave of slaves," Canaan becomes powerless, lacking a phallus, in effect having the same standing as females. Ham, although not *physically* castrated, is *symbolically* castrated by the enslaving of Canaan and his progeny. Noah, on the other hand, is exonerated and can maintain his status as "righteous."

Lot and His Daughters

Noah is not the only father who imbibes with tragic results. The story of Lot and his two daughters is disturbing, complicated, and (probably, therefore) one of the most often-discussed incestuous relationships in the Hebrew Bible. Genesis 19 relates that two angels in (male) human form come as visitors to Lot's house in Sodom to warn him of its impending destruction. Lot makes a lavish drinking feast for them and invites them to stay overnight.[19] All the men of Sodom, young and old, surround the house and demand that he surrender the "men" to them. The details of this scene are chilling, and the narrator emphatically notes the number and strength of the mob: "Before they lay down, the men of the city, the men of Sodom, surrounded the house—from young to old, *all the people, entirely*" (Gen. 19:4, my emphasis). Lot's response is strange and shrouded in secrecy: "Lot went out of the entrance-way to the men, and shut the door after him" (Gen. 19:6).

This narrative, like that of Noah, practically begs for questions to be asked. The most obvious are these: Why does Lot deliberately depart from the protection of his house in order to present his alternative in secret? Why doesn't Lot elicit the assistance of the angels to thwart the plan of the townsmen? I have seen few answers that satisfy me.

Lack of explanations notwithstanding, Lot for whatever reasons becomes a procurer rather than protector: "Please, my brothers, do not so wickedly. Look, I have two daughters who have not known man. Please, I shall bring them out to you. Do to them as is good in your eyes. Only to these men do nothing because they came under the shadow of my roof" (Gen. 19:7–8).

Lot speaks to the men of the town as though they were comrades. Indeed, he even addresses them as "brothers" (Gen. 19:7). Inexplicably, even though Lot recognizes that their proposal is evil, he tries to substitute an equally abhorrent act. The men of Sodom want the angels, but Lot offers his daughters, who, he stresses, have not "known man"—their virginity being a necessary aspect to the last part of the narrative. Indeed, Lot *volunteers* to hand them over to be abused by the crowd. Further, because the daughters are betrothed (Gen. 19:14), and because the rape of a betrothed woman is a crime punishable by death (Deut. 22: 23–27), Lot's actions could have implicated him as an accomplice.

Lot's offer to the mob is incredible. The willingness of a father to hand over his own daughters to be raped rather than allow the homosexual rape of a stranger who happens to be a guest in his home is baffling; more remarkable still, the narrator's views about the potential violence to the daughters is not revealed directly. Nevertheless, the narrative itself presents a powerful portrait of the effects of threatened sexual violence. Most curious of all, however, is that although commentators recognize that the proposed sodomy against the (male) angels is portrayed as reprehensible, they have been *sympathetic* to Lot's actions toward his daughters. Instead of condemning the offer of his daughters as rape victims, they point to the "mitigating circumstances," the demands of "hospitality," which excuse his behavior. For example, as Leah Bronner has observed, nowhere in classical Rabbinic literature is there a discussion of the daughters' feelings about the matter, nor is there a condemnation of Lot (1994, 113–114). This is unusual because classical Rabbinic literature tends to discuss all aspects of life and normally is not reticent regarding sexual matters. Yet it remains silent on this important issue.[20] John Calvin writes that "Lot's great virtue was sprinkled with some imperfection. . . . Although he does not hesitate to prostitute his daughters . . . Lot, indeed is urged by extreme necessity" (quoted in Lerner, 1986, 172). And modern commentators have essentially followed this line of reasoning. Their pro-Lot position is illustrated by this statement of Bruce Vawter:

Certainly to our tastes he [Lot] proves himself to be more sensitive to the duties of hospitality than those of fatherhood . . . the spectacle of a father offering his virgin daughters to the will and pleasure of a mob that was seeking to despoil his household would not have seemed as shocking to the ancient sense of proprieties as it may seem to us. . . . Really, there is no need to make excuses for him, as far as the biblical perspective is concerned. In all the stories about him the soundness of Lot's judgment is never the point at issue. . . . He is a good and not a bad man. (1977, 235–236)

John Skinner's assessment of Lot's character is similar. He states that "Lot's readiness to sacrifice the honor of his daughters . . . shows him as a courageous champion of the obligations of hospitality in a situation of extreme embarrassment, and is recorded to his credit" (1930, 307). So too Nahum Sarna, who comments that "Lot is true to his code of honor. Hospitality was a sacred duty, according the guest the right of asylum" (1989, 135). Surprisingly, E. A. Speiser, who otherwise annotates Genesis line by line, has no comment here. His only hint of a gloss on the incident with the daughters is this sentence: "True to the unwritten code, Lot will stop at nothing in his effort to protect his guests" (1964, 123). Lest I be accused of viewing these readings as cases of exegetical mal[e]-practice, Nehama Leibowitz's comments are as favorable toward Lot as the male scholars quoted above: "Lot tried to maintain Abraham's way of life even in the heart of Sodom striving to preserve, at the risk to his life, the elementary obligations of hospitality to strangers . . . resulting in his throwing his daughters to the mercy of the populace, in exchange for his guests" (1981, 176).

Although Susan Niditch correctly points out that the potential rape of the divine messengers is "a doubly potent symbol of a cultural, non-civilized behavior from the Israelite point of view" (1982, 369), she ignores the threat of sexual brutality to the daughters. Why would this not be equally reprehensible in the Israelite perspective? Could it be that Freud's theory about the role of mythology is tacitly expressed by the—*narrator?* That is, this myth serves the same function for an entire *people* that dreams and literature provide for the *individual*—psychological release for the impulses repressed in the course of development, impulses that have become unconscious and brought to the surface only in narrative form. Phrased differently, were Lot's actions a simple strategy to protect the visitors or were they an accurate precursor to the incest both Lot and the narrator (acting as a substitute for an entire *people*) unconsciously desire, incest that Lot actually commits at the end of the chapter? At the very least, I read this incident as

Lot's repressing his own desire to "know" his daughters and displacing this desire onto the townsmen.[21]

In any event, after having offered to have his daughters gang-raped, Lot in an interesting reversal is saved by the angels, and almost as an afterthought the two daughters are saved from a brutal crime. The mob storms the house and is about to break the door when the angels strike blind all the men of Sodom, warn Lot of the imminent destruction of the city, and prophetically tell him that he and his "family" will be saved.

At this point, the narrative needs an available Eve to pluck fruit and offer it to the father. Conveniently, the only other survivors of Sodom are Lot's two daughters, with whom he escapes to the city of Zoar, Lot's wife having been turned into a pillar of salt. But Lot is afraid to stay in Zoar and flees once more with his daughters, this time to the rocky hill-country above the Dead Sea plain. And where do they take refuge? In a cave. The image of the cave is quite potent: generally speaking it signifies descent to a lower world. The cave is referred to as *sheol* in various places in the Hebrew Bible: it is where the spirit of Samuel is conjured by the Witch of Endor; it is the belly of Jonah's whale; and it is the pit into which the speaker of the penitential psalms has been cast. The cave/underworld is generally dark, and its inhabitants are stripped of all clothing by death the leveler. On the other hand, the cave is also a place where lost treasure is found, threatening monsters are confronted, and help is enlisted for the accomplishment of a goal. Psychologically, the underworld of the cave is synonymous with the subconscious, from which we wake "up" every morning. It is the home of dreams, intuitions, hidden desires, and suppressed energies. Most important, however, is that the sexual connotation of the cave is obvious both psychoanalytically (Freud, 1916–1917, 156) and linguistically. To quote David Gunn, "[cave] associates easily with words such as, a bare place, to be naked, exposed, to strip oneself, and nakedness, genitals" (1980, 94).

Once in the cave, the despairing daughters, who were betrothed in Sodom, conclude that not just Sodom but the whole earth has been laid waste and that there are no men left. On two successive nights they give Lot wine, "lie with" him in a cave (the place where one "sleeps" with one's father), and "seduce" him into impregnating them. The narrative suggests that the father did not knowingly participate in this incestuous act. Although it is unclear just who he thought had stopped by the cave on the two sequential nights of his seduction, twice we are told that "he knew not when *she* lay down and got up."

Unlike Noah, who could at least plead ignorance of the effects of wine, Lot becomes inebriated on two successive evenings, with the result that the man who offered his betrothed daughters to gang-rape deflowers them himself.

It is significant that when Freud writes about female virginity, he does not consider the young woman's position but that of the man about to deflower her. Indeed, the value Freud attaches to virginity is phrased in a discourse of scientific logic and subjective justification: "The demand that a girl shall not bring to her marriage with a particular man any memory of sexual relations with another is, indeed, nothing other than the logical continuation of the right to exclusive possession of a woman, which forms the essence of monogamy, the extension of the monopoly over the past" (Freud, 1905, 136).[22]

Freud's logic presents a mixture of legal monopoly, right, and cognitive concerns (memory). The crux of his essay is a circular argument that moves from the woman's feeling via the male act to the man's feeling that inspires his guilt, its projection on the woman, and thus, ultimately, her hostility. As Mieke Bal notes, from a value, virginity becomes a danger (1988, 15). Certainly this is the case with Lot and his daughters.

Patriarchal law decrees that the "product" of sexual union, the child, belongs exclusively to the father (Gallop, 1989, 109). In the case of Lot and his daughters, it appears that this maxim is followed to the extreme. Describing his daughters as virgins, Lot tells the Sodomites that they "had not 'known' a man" (Gen. 19:8). These daughters "belong" exclusively to Lot. At the end of the narrative, the wombs that bear Lot's sons are those of his two daughters, repossessed by Lot as a means of reproduction.

As in the case of Noah, Lot's offer to sacrifice his daughters and his incestuous relationship with them are not treated in the text as "wrong." Indeed, both go unpunished and without further narrative comment.[23] Perhaps because this story is disturbing it is not surprising that biblical scholars have studied the Lot narrative. What is interesting to me, however, is that there has also been considerable clinical psychiatric interest in the Lot narrative because it seems to be the prototype of parent–child incest, in part because it is more directly related to actual clinical incest than is the Oedipus story.[24] When clinical practitioners examine parent–child incest, the questions frequently considered include, among others, the following: What was the setting and family structure in which it occurred? What was the frequency of the behavior in question? What were the respective personalities and roles of the parent and the "victim"? What was the personality and role of the other parent in the incest case? What was the effect on the participants? These are the same questions asked by psychoanalytic literary theorists as well.

With regard to the questions of setting and family structure, the setting is a catastrophic situation wherein the daughters believe the world was destroyed. Medlicott notes that the cave's lack of privacy is quite similar to the primitive housing situation found in many cases of clinical incest (1967, 135). And although the daughters in this instance appear to be the active initiators of the incestuous behavior, the fact that more than one daughter is involved brings the story closer into line with clinical incest in which the incestuous father commonly moves from older to younger daughters.

The personalities and roles of the parents and "victims" also seem to fall into the classical incestuous paradigm. Lot, the incestuous father, has lost his status as the all-powerful patriarchal father who holds his family together. (Indeed, Lot is saved from the mad[ding] crowd by the very visitors whom he felt it necessary to protect.) By blinding the would-be attackers, the visitors in effect render both Lot and the townsmen symbolically castrated. That is to say, by blinding the townsmen, the narrator uses the frequent substitution of eyes for the dismemberment of genitalia. And like many incestuous fathers, Lot appears to have had a problem with alcohol, allowing himself to become inebriated on two consecutive nights.

In addition, the role of Lot's wife is not out of keeping with clinical incest stories. Ernest Jones writes of the remarkably close association between the ideas of salt and fecundity and points out that salt, both in absence and excess, prevents fruitfulness and sexuality (1938, 72). Therefore, from a psychoanalytic perspective it is particularly appropriate that Lot's wife was turned into a pillar of salt

Once again, artists seem to have interesting "readings" of Mrs. Lot. For example, Albrecht Dürer's *Lot and His Daughters* seems almost clinical. This scene (painted on the reverse side of his *Madonna and Child*—anything Freudian there, do you suppose?) portrays Lot and his two children fleeing from the destruction of Sodom and Gomorrah, which are erupting in blinding explosions of fire in the background. Significantly for purposes of this chapter, Lot's wife, visible but clearly from a distance, is on the path at the upper left.

By "looking back," Mrs. Lot could be viewed, in effect, as having "looked away" from what was going on between father and daughters, a behavior common in clinical incest. The only information we have about the last question—the general effect of the incestuous behavior on the victims, Lot's daughters—is that they both became pregnant and their sons fathered two tribes that were persistent thorns in Israel's flesh. In other words, Lot's grandsons, like Noah's, are damned because of grandpa's actions.

Interestingly, various paintings on this theme are less forgiving of Lot than are the biblical commentators. Carracci, for example, portrays an unrestrained and erotic Lot, significantly depicted as the aggressor. Here, a sexually aroused Lot grasps a voluptuous daughter, while the other daughter waits in the background. Noteworthy from a clinical perspective, the figure of Mrs. Lot is seen in the distance, as in the Dürer painting. In Bonifazio de'Pitati's colorful painting *Lot and His Daughters*, one of the women is seen plying Lot with wine, a beverage he is obviously enjoying. Her bright red dress is disheveled, and she is barefoot as she apparently tries to excite her father. Two putti,[25] one of them wearing a mask, appear behind the other daughter, who is fully dressed and holding a mirror. Given that in Renaissance iconography the mirror is a symbol of prudence, wisdom, and ideas of truth, whereas falsehood is alluded to by the mask, the daughters of Lot could be viewed as acting out the struggle between *voluptas* (carnal pleasures) and *virtus* (goodness and virtue). But perhaps the mirror and mask had an additional meaning to Bonifazio's fellow Venetians, who were accustomed to donning elaborate facial ornamentation during their annual *carnevale* festivities, events known for their license and drunkenness.

Most damning to Lot's reputation, however, is Albrecht Altdorfer's *Lot and His Daughter*. Clearly, Altdorfer did not accept that Lot played a totally passive role. For some reason, it seems as though artists may be more Freudian readers of the biblical text than are biblical commentators, and perhaps at least as creditable. It appears that on the basis of clinical reports and the readings of Renaissance artists, the unconscious desires of Lot seem to have surfaced.

Variations

Although the following examples are not actual cases of "true" father–daughter incest, I mention them briefly. The first case, that of Judah and Tamar, involves an equally forbidden father-*in-law*/daughter incestuous relationship. The second incident, between Boaz and Ruth, consists of a father-*figure*/daughter-*figure* liaison. I have included these two narratives because the stories of Lot's daughters, Tamar, and Ruth have been read as three installments in a series that supplies

King David with a genealogy. That is, the first story narrates the birth of the maternal forefather, Moab; the second narrates the birth of the paternal forefather, Perez; and the third story brings together Ruth the Moabite and Boaz of Perez's lineage.

In the first story, Tamar, like Lot's daughters, uses incest to solve a serious domestic problem (Gen. 38). At the beginning of the story, Tamar is married to 'Er,[26] one of Judah's sons. The death of 'Er without a son made Onan subject to the levirate law. Although marriage between a man and his brother's wife is strictly forbidden in the Pentateuchal legislation of Leviticus 18:16 and 20:21, the only exception to the prohibition occurs when the brother dies without a son. According to Deuteronomy 25:5, a man has an *obligation* to marry his widowed sister-in-law: "When brothers dwell together and one of them dies and leaves no son, the wife of the deceased shall not be married to a stranger, outside the family. Her husband's brother shall unite with her [literally "go in to her"], take her as his wife and perform the levir's duty" (Deut. 25:5).

This institution is known in Hebrew as *yibbum* or "levirate marriage."[27] The second son, Onan, refusing to follow the laws of the levirate marriage, lets his seed "go to spoil" on the ground. (Although Targum Jonathan and Gen. Rabbah 8:5 connect the name with the Hebrew *'on,* or "grief," it could also be understood to mean "vigorous," perhaps a piece of biblical humor? How this contraceptive device of coitus interruptus evolved into a synonym for masturbation— onanism—is a semantic enigma.)[28] What he did was "displeasing to YHWH," and God slays him as well. Although the text does not make clear specifically why Onan incurs divine wrath, the development of the narrative seems to indicate that Onan's failure to impregnate Tamar is considered an unpardonable crime because the provision for voluntary renunciation of the levirate duty found in Deuteronomy 25:7–9 did not apply at this time. However, it could also be argued that by frustrating the purpose of the levirate marriage, that is, by perpetuating the line of his brother for purposes of inheritance, Onan has placed his sexual relationship with Tamar in the forbidden category of incest, a capital offense.

Judah, fearful that his youngest son upon whom the levirate responsibility now lies might follow in the ill-fated footsteps of his two older brothers, banishes his daughter-in-law, Tamar, to widowhood in her father's house. In this state, she is not free to remarry, she is still subject to the authority of her father-in-law, and she now must live with and be provided for by her parents. Tamar, in effect, has been purchased through marriage by Judah, the head of the family, and thus she is part of the estate of her dead husband, 'Er. As such, she remains the property of the clan after his death.

When the widowed Tamar realizes that her claim for a husband is unlikely to be satisfied even through the third son of Judah and that she will remain childless, relegated to live in her father's house, Tamar becomes desperate. She deceives her father-in-law by disguising herself as a prostitute. Oblivious to her identity, Judah has intercourse with her (the incestuous relationship forbidden in Lev. 18:15). The text does not tell us why Tamar felt she had to keep this matter within the family, nor why she believed that disguised as a harlot, she would have a better chance at Judah, but the ruse works: she conceives, the problem is solved, and David's lineage is further established.

In the second narrative, Ruth, a daughter *figure*, delivers a demand for marriage to a father *figure* related to her by marriage.[29] Indeed, Boaz addresses Ruth as "my daughter" (Ruth 2:8, 3:10), and as Athalya Brenner notes, even if this address implies a recognition of her inferior social status or younger age (most readers tend to read Boaz as older), the similarity of this story to the other two is striking (1997, 103 n. 36). The motifs of wine and drinking, fatherly cooperation, family survival, and the daughter's desire for a son are present in various measures in all three stories.

The Righteous Father Syndrome

It is not entirely unreasonable to wonder if there are more correspondences between the Noah narrative and the well-known stories of Lot, Judah, and Boaz than at first appearance. The stories of Noah and Lot are, of course, in many ways similar: both Lot and Noah are saved as righteous men from destruction, and the seed of Judah and the seed of Boaz are saved from destruction as well. However, all four are involved in creation myths and all four are sexually involved with their children.

More importantly, the patriarchs Noah, Lot, Judah, and Boaz are absolved from any guilt and are free to maintain their status as righteous—in their own minds, in the viewpoint of the narrator, as well as in the writings of most commentators. Accordingly, perhaps the most significant similarity between the stories of Lot's incestuous relationship(s) and Noah's is that within the patriarchal world of the Hebrew Bible, fathers commit incest with their children and remain unpunished, whereas the children and grandchildren involved are damned forever.

Conclusion: Phallocentrism and Logocentrism

Throughout this chapter I have been examining biblical sexual prohibitions. My approach has been to read psychoanalytic literary theory and the Bible concurrently. Reading the biblical laws regarding
human sexuality and the work of Freud simultaneously, I find it can
seem difficult to distinguish their respective ideas: "We might lay it
down," writes Freud, "that . . . sexuality . . . is of a wholly masculine
character" (1905, 217–218). In biblical narratives, as in Freud, female
sexuality is explicitly subordinated to and subsumed by the male.[30] As
Simone de Beauvoir argues, heterosexual men have established an
absolute human type, the heterosexual male, against which all others
are measured. Men are always the definers, women the defined (1961,
xv–xvii). Likewise, the Hebrew Bible makes phallocentrism synonymous with logocentrism. Within the Scriptures, it is primarily the
male characters who have defined woman and man, and in the two
thousand–some years of biblical interpretation, it is male-dominated
discourse that has "cast in stone" these constructs. The laws of Leviticus and Deuteronomy, symbolized by the circumcised heterosexual
penis, have resulted in the "erection" of a paternal logos through the
denial, or misnaming, of alternative sexual experience(s). Reconstructing biblical sexuality reveals the textual struggle within and
against this patriarchy.

Notes

1. Freud's principal works on the sexual life of human beings are his
Three Essays on the Theory of Sexuality (1905, 135–243) and "Some Psychical
Consequences of the Anatomical Distinction between the Sexes" (1925). For
recent representative neo-Freudian reviews and critiques of Freud's ideas,
see Mitchell (1975, 1–131) and Irigaray (1985, 34–67).

2. It is questionable whether masturbation is considered a category of
"negative" sexual activity in the Hebrew Bible; I do not discuss masturbation in this chapter. The sin of Onan (Gen. 38) is not necessarily that of
masturbation; otherwise, oblique references to seminal emission, such as "a
man, when an emission of semen comes out of him" (Lev. 15:16), refers to
the emission rather than its circumstances; female masturbation is never
mentioned in the Hebrew Bible.

3. See Carmichael (1997, 1–3).

4. In this chapter the word *Rabbis* refers to the particular group of Jewish
religious leaders known technically as "the Rabbis." The Rabbis flourished
from the second until approximately the end of the sixth century in Pales-

tine and Babylonia. Growing out of a particular sect of first-century Judaism, the Rabbis, whose cultural hegemony over the masses of Jews grew during this period, produced the major literary works of rabbinic Judaism—the midrashim and Talmuds. Their closest historical cognates are, therefore, the church fathers.

5. Incest within this context consists of acts of sexual intercourse performed by consent, rape, or trickery between persons related either through blood or marriage.

6. The Hittite Code represents legal thinking in Hatti between 1450 and 1200 BCE. Parallels to the Hittite Code in ancient Israel appear mainly in Lev. 17–26 and Deut. 12–26. These parallels are especially clear in the code's use of similar technical terms. For example, the terms *brother* and *brother-in-law* identify citizens who are covenant partners rather than simply individuals who are kin to one another by birth. So too in Deut. 25:5–10, where the term *brother-in-law* refers to a legal guardian.

7. The Code of Hammurabi is a treatise on legal theory, political science, and social organization. Hammurabi, king of Babylon from 1792 to 1750 BCE, published this document to endorse legal thinking and moral values of his government. In the Hebrew Bible, the covenant code (Exod. 21–23), the holiness code (Lev. 17–26), and the Deuteronomic code (Deut. 12–26) are parallel to the Code of Hammurabi.

8. For views on homosexuality in ancient Greece, see Dover (1989, 60–68, 81–109); and Cohen (1987, 6–21).

9. See also Bailey, 1955.

10. The Oedipus myth, which Sophocles followed closely in his dramatization, relates that Oedipus—the son of Laius, king of Thebes, and his wife Jocasta—was left to die immediately after birth because an oracle had revealed to the father, eager for offspring, that he was destined to be killed by his son. The infant is rescued by shepherds and grows up as a prince in another court until, unsure of his origin, he consults the oracle and is advised to avoid his homeland lest he become his father's murderer and his mother's husband. Upon leaving his new home, he encounters King Laius, his unrecognized father, and kills him. He arrives in Thebes, solves the riddle of the sphinx that is bringing doom to the city, and is rewarded by the Thebans with the remuneration reserved for the liberator of the city: he is made king and receives the hand of the queen, his mother Jocasta, in marriage. For a long time, he reigns peacefully and with honor; he has two sons and two daughters by his mother. A plague breaks out in the city, and the Thebans, inquiring of the oracle how they can be freed from the plague, are informed by the messengers that the plague will cease as soon as Laius's murderer is banished from the land. Eventually, it is revealed that Oedipus himself is the murderer of Laius but is also his son and the son of Jocasta. Overwhelmed by the terrible act he has unwittingly committed, Oedipus blinds himself and leaves his homeland.

11. The terms *positive* and *negative* are used here, as they are by Freud, in the sense of reversal, as in negative film and positive print, and not in the sense of good and bad.

12. A modern Arab village near Hebron might shed some light on the story of David and Bat-Sheba. In the mountain villages, it is customary even today to spend hot summer nights on a round, open verandah built on the rooftops. The king's palace was probably located in the highest place in the city, allowing him to see what was happening on the rooftops below.

13. For portrayals of cultic functions carried out by naked priests, see Pritchard (1958, plates 597, 600, 603, 605). Among the representations of male Canaanite gods catalogued in Negbi (1976), however, very few have visible genitalia.

14. The Levitical prohibitions involve "uncovering" one's father's nakedness, not merely "seeing" his genitalia.

15. See also the comments in Kunin (1995, 173–175). Stanley Brandes's position is that anthropological evidence suggests that in many cultures, fathers make every effort to ensure that they do not reveal their genitals to their sons (1980, 99).

16. This is the first example of the genre of parental blessing and cursing. See all of Gen. 49 and the following as examples: "Then prepare for me savory food, such as I like, and bring it to me to eat, so that I may bless you before I die" (Gen. 27:4); "So he came near and kissed him; and he smelled the smell of his garments, and blessed him, and said, 'Ah, the smell of my son is like the smell of a field that the lord has blessed. May God give you of the dew of heaven, and of the fatness of the earth, and plenty of grain and wine. Let peoples serve you, and nations bow down to you. Be lord over your brothers, and may your mother's sons bow down to you. Cursed be everyone who curses you, and blessed be everyone who blesses you!'" (Gen. 27:29).

17. See, for example, the Wakefield pageant "The Deluge" in Gassner (1963, 57–71).

18. This play was adapted by Richard Rogers and Peter Stone and renamed *Two by Two*; it appeared on Broadway in 1970.

19. A *mishteh* (feast, banquet) is usually an occasion for drinking. See, for example, 1 Sam. 25:36; Isa. 5:12; Esther 2:18, 5:14, 8:17, 9:19.

20. Bronner offers three possible explanations: (1) the rabbis' silence may reflect deep revulsion on their part, a sentiment that comes to full expression only centuries later in the writings of the medieval commentators; (2) the rabbis, like modern commentators, saw homosexuality as the greater evil and therefore saw no point in castigating Lot in his no-win choice; (3) the Talmud does describe in great detail the depraved social, religious, and moral practices that prevailed in Sodom, and it is in the context of these descriptions that the rabbis hint at Lot's degeneracy (1994, 115).

21. See Rashkow (2000) for an elaboration of this theory.

22. See also Mieke Bal's analysis of Freud's essay in connection with the story of the sacrifice of Jephthah's daughter in Judg. 11 (Bal, 1988, 72–73).

23. Vawter argues that "this story, tenuously connected with the preceding narrative, obviously had little to do with the Sodom and Gomorrah saga and owes its preservation to other concerns" (1977, 242).

24. See, for example, Medlicott (1967) and Jones (1938).

25. Putti is the Italian word for the children who appear in paintings as allegorical creatures or little wingless angels.

26. Although no interpretation of the names of Judah's son is given in the text, a midrash and Targum Jonathan connect it with the Hebrew *'ariri*—"childless." Given that 'Er is "displeasing to YHWH" (Gen. 38:7), his name may be a word play on the Hebrew *ra'*—"evil."

27. The basic root meaning of the Hebrew is uncertain, but it is believed to be "to procreate" (Sarna, 1989, 266). In Deut. 25:7, the brother of the deceased husband is called the *yavam*—"progenitor."

28. Gen. Rabbah 55:5–6 understands this verse as saying that Onan practiced a primitive form of birth control through coitus interruptus. Another tradition (Yevamoth 34b) interprets the act as "unnatural intercourse."

29. See Rashkow (1993) for an elaboration.

30. Juliet Mitchell points out that psychoanalysis can hardly avoid being phallocentric in a society organized along patriarchal lines: "If psychoanalysis is phallocentric, it is because the human social order that it perceives refracted through the individual human subject is patrocentric" (1975, xv).

References

Alexander, F. (1948). *Fundamentals of Psychoanalysis*. New York: Norton.

Bailey, D. S. (1955). *Homosexuality and the Western Christian Tradition*. Hamden: Archon.

Bal, M. (1988). *Death and Dissymmetry: The Politics of Coherence in the Book of Judges*. Chicago: University of Chicago Press.

Bassett, F. (1971). Noah's Nakedness and the Curse of Canaan. A Case of Incest? *Vestus Testamentum, 21*, 236–274.

Beauvoir, S. de. (1961). *The Second Sex*, H. Parshley, trans. New York: Bantam Books.

Brandes, Stanley. (1980). *Metaphors of Masculinity: Sex and Status in Andalusian Folklore*. Philadelphia: University of Pennsylvania Press.

Brenkman, J. (1993). *Straight Male Modern: A Cultural Critique of Psychoanalysis*. New York: Routledge.

Brenner, A. (1997). *The Intercourse of Knowledge: On Gendering Desire and "Sexuality" in the Hebrew Bible*. Leiden: Brill.

Bronner, L. L. (1994). *From Eve to Esther: Rabbinic Reconstructions of Biblical Women*. Louisville: Westminster/John Knox Press.

Broome, E. C. (1946). Ezekiel's Abnormal Personality. *Journal of Biblical Literature, 65,* 277–292.

Carmichael, C. M. (1997). *Law, Legend, and Incest in the Bible: Leviticus 18–20.* Ithaca: Cornell University Press.

Cohen, D. (1987). Law, Society, and Homosexuality in Classical Athens. *Past and Present, 117,* 6–21.

Cohen, N. J. (1998). *Voices from Genesis: Guiding Us through the Stages of Life.* Woodstock: Jewish Lights Publishing.

Cole, W. (1959). *Sex and Love in the Bible.* New York: Association Press.

Conrad, J. (1912). *A Personal Record.* New York: Harper & Brothers.

Daub, D. (1986). Old Testament Prohibitions of Homosexuality. *Zeitschrift der Savigny-Stiftung für Rechtsgeschichte, 103.*

Dollimore, J. (1991). *Sexual Dissidence: Augustine to Wilde, Freud to Foucault.* New York: Oxford University Press.

Dover, K. J. (1989). *Greek Homosexuality.* Cambridge: Harvard University Press.

Edinger, E. (2000). *Ego and Self: The Old Testament Prophets from Isaiah to Malachi.* Toronto: Inner City Books.

Felman, S. (1980). *Literature and Psychoanalysis: The Question of Reading: Otherwise.* Baltimore: Johns Hopkins University Press.

Fletcher, J. (1989). Freud and His Uses: Psychoanalysis and Gay Theory, *Coming on Strong: Gay Politics and Culture,* S. Shepherd & Mark Wallis, eds. London: Unwin Hyman.

Fodor, A. (1954). The Fall of Man in the Book of Genesis. *American Imago, 11,* 203–231.

Freud, S. (1897). Abstracts of the Scientific Writings of Dr. Sigmund Freud, *The Standard Works of Sigmund Freud,* J. Strachey, ed. & trans., vol. 3. London: Hogarth Press and Institute of Psycho-analysis, 1953, 223–258.

Freud, S. (1905). Three Essays on the Theory of Sexuality, *The Standard Works of Sigmund Freud,* J. Strachey, ed. & trans., vol. 7. London: Hogarth Press and Institute of Psycho-analysis, 1953, 135–243.

Freud, S. (1909). On Infantile Sexual Theories, *The Standard Works of Sigmund Freud,* J. Strachey, ed. & trans., vol. 2. London: Hogarth Press and Institute of Psycho-analysis, 1953.

Freud, S. (1913). Totem and Taboo, *The Standard Works of Sigmund Freud,* J. Strachey, ed. & trans., vol. 13. London: Hogarth Press and Institute of Psycho-analysis, 1953.

Freud, S. (1916–1917). Introductory Lectures on Psycho-Analysis, *The Standard Works of Sigmund Freud,* J. Strachey, ed. & trans., vol. 15. London: Hogarth Press and Institute of Psycho-analysis, 1953, 15–239.

Freud, S. (1923). The Ego and the Id, *The Standard Works of Sigmund Freud,* J. Strachey, ed. & trans., vol. 19. London: Hogarth Press and Institute of Psycho-analysis, 1953, 12–66.

Freud, S. (1925). Some Psychical Consequences of the Anatomical Distinction between the Sexes, *The Standard Works of Sigmund Freud*, J. Strachey, ed. & trans., vol. 19. London: Hogarth Press and Institute of Psycho-analysis, 1953, 241–260.

Freud, S. (1928). Dostoevsky and Parricide, *The Standard Works of Sigmund Freud*, J. Strachey, ed. & trans., vol. 21. London: Hogarth Press and Institute of Psycho-analysis, 1953, 177–196.

Freud, S. (1931). Female Sexuality, *The Standard Works of Sigmund Freud*, J. Strachey, ed. & trans., vol. 21. London: Hogarth Press and Institute of Psycho-analysis, 1953, 223–245.

Gallop, J. (1989). The Father's Seduction, *Daughters and Fathers*, L. E. Boose & B. S. Flowers, eds. Baltimore: Johns Hopkins University Press, 97–110.

Gassner, J., ed. (1963). *Medieval and Tudor Drama*. New York: Bantam.

Gunn, D. (1980). *The Fate of King Saul*. Sheffield, UK: Journal for the Study of the Old Testament Press.

Halperin, D. J. (1993). *Seeking Ezekiel: Text and Psychology*. University Park: Pennsylvania State University Press.

Hamilton, V. (1990). *The Book of Genesis: Chapters 1–17*. Grand Rapids: Eerdmans.

Herman, J. L., & Hirschman, L. (1981). *Father–Daughter Incest*. Cambridge: Harvard University Press.

Horney, K. (1950). *Neurosis and Human Growth*. New York: Norton.

Irigaray, L. (1985). *This Sex Which Is Not One*, C. Porter & C. Burke, trans. Ithaca: Cornell University Press. (Original work published 1977)

Jones, E. (1938). *Papers on Psychoanalysis*. Baltimore: William Wood.

Kille, D. A. (2001). *Psychological Biblical Criticism*. Minneapolis: Fortress.

Kluger, Y., & Kluger-Nash, N. (1999). *A Psychological Interpretation of Ruth*. Einseideln, Switzerland: Daimon.

Knight, G. (1981). *Theology in Pictures: A Commentary on Genesis, Chapters One to Eleven*. Edinburgh: Handsel Press.

Kunin, S. (1995). *The Logic of Incest; A Structuralist Analysis of Hebrew Mythology*. Sheffield, UK: Sheffield Academic Press.

LaPlanche, J., & Pontalis, J. B. (1983). *The Language of Psychoanalysis*, D. Nicholson-Smith, trans. London: Hogarth.

Leibowitz, N. (1981). *Studies in Bereshit (Genesis): In the Context of Ancient and Modern Jewish Bible Commentary*. Jerusalem: Magnes.

Lerner, G. (1986). *The Creation of Patriarchy*. New York: Oxford University Press.

Levine, B. (1989). *Leviticus*. Jewish Publication Society Torah Commentary. Philadelphia: Jewish Publication Society.

Maimonides, M. (1904). *The Guide for the Perplexed*, M. Friedlander, trans. New York: Dutton.

Medlicott, R. (1967). Lot and His Daughters. *Australian New Zealand Journal of Psychiatry*, *1*, 134–139.

Mitchell, J. (1975). *Psychoanalysis and Feminism*. New York: Random House.

Negbi, O. (1976). *Canaanite Gods in Metal*. Tel Aviv: Institute for Archaeology.

Niditch, S. (1982). The "Sodomite" Theme in Judges 19–20: Family, Community, and Social Disintegration. *Catholic Bible Quarterly, 44*, 365–378.

Parker, K. I. (1999). Mirror, Mirror on the Wall, Must We Leave Eden, Once and for All? A Lacanian Pleasure Trip though the Garden. *Journal for the Study of the Old Testament, 83*, 19–29.

Philo. (1971). Questions and Answers on Genesis: Translated from the Ancient Armenian Version of the Original Greek, *Philo in Ten Volumes*, R. Marcus, trans, suppl. 1. Cambridge: Harvard University Press.

Piers, G., & Singer, M. (1953). *Shame and Guilt*. New York: Norton.

Piskorowski, A. (1992). In Search of Her Father: A Lacanian Approach to Genesis 2–3, *A Walk in the Garden: Biblical, Iconographical and Literary Images of Eden*, Deborah P. S. Morris, ed. Sheffield, UK: Journal for the Study of the Old Testament Press, 310–318.

Pitt-Rivers, J. (1977). *The Fate of Shechem*. Cambridge: Cambridge University Press.

Polka, B. (2001). *Depth Psychological Interpretation and the Bible: An Ontological Essay on Freud*. Montreal: McGill–Queen's University Press.

Pritchard, J. B., ed. (1958). *Ancient Near Eastern Texts*. Princeton: Princeton University Press.

Rank, O. (1912). *The Incest Theme in Literature and Legend: Fundamentals of a Psychology of Literary Creation*, G. Richter, trans. Baltimore: Johns Hopkins University Press, 1992.

Rashkow, I. N. (1993). *The Phallacy of Genesis: A Feminist-Psychoanalytic Approach*. Louisville: Westminster/John Knox Press.

Rashkow, I. N. (2000). *Taboo or Not Taboo: The Hebrew Bible and Human Sexuality*. Minneapolis: Fortress.

Robertson, J. (1900). *Christianity and Mythology*. London: Watts Publishers.

Rollins, W. G. (1999). *Soul and Psyche: The Bible in Psychological Perspective*. Minneapolis: Augsburg Fortress.

Sarna, N. (1989). *The Jewish Publication Society Torah Commentary: Genesis*. Philadelphia: The Jewish Publication Society.

Skinner, J. (1930). *A Critical and Exegetical Commentary on Genesis*. Edinburgh: T. and T. Clark.

Smith, J. H. (1986). Primitive Guilt, *Pragmatism's Freud: The Moral Disposition of Psychoanalysis*, J. Smith & W. Kerrigan, eds. Baltimore: Johns Hopkins University Press, 52–78.

Speiser, E. A. (1964). *Genesis: Introduction, Translation, and Notes*. Garden City: Doubleday.

Vawter, B. (1977). *On Genesis: A New Reading*. Garden City: Doubleday.

Wenham, G. J. (1979). *The Book of Leviticus*. Grand Rapids: Eerdmans.

CHAPTER 4

JUNG, ANALYTICAL PSYCHOLOGY, AND THE BIBLE

Wayne G. Rollins

> We must read our Bible or we shall not understand psychology. Our psychology, whole lives, our language and imagery are built upon the Bible.
>
> —C. G. Jung, 1976

It is a well-kept secret that the Bible played an extraordinary role in the personal life as well as professional work of Swiss analytical psychologist Carl Gustav Jung. No document is cited by Jung more often, and no cast of characters from any tradition is summoned to the stage of Jung's discourse with greater regularity than are the Adams and Abrahams, Melchizedeks and Moseses, and Peters and Pauls of Judeo-Christian Scriptures. To understand Jung's contribution to biblical interpretation, we must begin with the story of the Bible in Jung's life and work, as prelude to the significant contribution of Jungian thought to biblical understanding.

The Bible in Jung's Life and Work

Although the Bible is acknowledged as a factor in Jung's background, it is seldom recognized as a defining reality in the foreground of Jung's life and thought, constituting a major problem and project that Jung addresses throughout his career. Raised in a Swiss Reformed Protestant parsonage and engaged as a youth in active dialogue with six clergy on his mother's side and two clergy uncles on his father's, Jung was initiated into a lifelong relationship and dialogue with the

Bible. He writes in a 1957 letter, "you can rest assured that having studied the Gospels for a life-time (I am nearly 83!) I am pretty well acquainted with the foundations of our Christianity" (1975, 346). But it was precisely this nineteenth-century biblical context in tension with Jung's emerging thought and experience that framed the problem and provided the point of departure for the lifelong project that the Bible would constitute for him at both the conscious and unconscious levels, as well as providing guidelines for a biblical-psychological hermeneutical agenda today.

The Bible as Problem and Project for Jung

The problem the Bible presents for Jung can be seen in a series of four feeling-toned experiences and associations in which it becomes evident that the problem of the Bible in Western culture and its proper understanding and interpretation will become a major item in Jung's personal and professional agenda and will generate an autonomous complex that manifests itself at both conscious and unconscious levels in his life and work.

The first of these feeling-toned associations is the biblicism of the Reformed Protestant piety and theology that Jung recalls vividly from his youth. The theological language of Reformed Protestantism seemed unrelated to experience, and as a child he found it "stale and hollow, like a tale told by someone who knows it only by hearsay and cannot quite believe it in himself" (1963, 43). "So long as religion is only faith and outward form, and the religious function is not experienced in our own souls," Jung writes, "nothing of any importance has happened. It has yet to be understood that the *mysterium tremendum* is not only an actuality but is first and foremost rooted in the human psyche" (1953–1978, 12:13). Jung found too often that "the Christian puts his Church and his Bible between himself and his unconscious" (1971, 102), on the one hand rehearsing dogmatic formulae without thinking, and on the other, suppressing awareness of the "God within," of which Jung had read in Paul, John, and the mystics. Such types of religion seemed to Jung to be "more interested in protecting their institutions than in understanding the mystery that symbols present," having "stripped all things of their mystery and numinosity" (1971, 94). Jung observes, furthermore, that "such a religion . . . is incapable of giving help and having any other moral effect" (1953–1978, 11:52). Jung came to the conclusion, "Why, that is not religion at all" (1963, 55).

A second feeling-toned association that informs Jung's biblical "complex" is his assessment of the historical-biblical critical scholarship that proceeds from what Jung calls "the garish conceits of enlightenment" (1953–1978, 8:528). Jung found this type of "rationalistic historicism" guilty of excising the numinous aspect from the Bible, severing it from "the living religious process" (1953–1978, 11:748–751) and defusing its powerful symbols and stories through "demythologization" (1975, 206). In his Terry lectures at Yale Jung wrote: "Nor has scientific criticism . . . been very helpful in enhancing belief in the divine character of the holy scriptures. It is also a fact that under the influence of a so-called scientific enlightenment great masses of educated people have either left the church or have become profoundly indifferent to it. If they were all dull rationalists or neurotic intellectuals, the loss would not be regrettable. But many of them are religious people" (1953–1978, 11:34).

This is not to say that Jung was ignorant of or opposed to biblical scholarship; quite the contrary, as demonstrated in a letter to American writer Upton Sinclair, who had written asking Jung's opinion on his new novel, *A Personal Jesus*. Jung's response demonstrates his familiarity with biblical Greek, ancient Near Eastern literature, and the recent history of biblical scholarship. Recalling the "Life of Jesus research" of Ernest Renan, David Strauss, and Albert Schweitzer (1948), Jung criticizes Sinclair for excluding certain portions of the text as "later interpolations" in order to create a portrait of Jesus "convincing to a modern American mind." "You give an excellent picture of a possible religious teacher," he writes Sinclair, "but you give us no understanding of what the New Testament tries to tell, namely the life, fate, and effect of a God-Man." Jung concludes with the injunction, "sure enough, we must believe in Reason. But it should not prevent us from recognizing a mystery when we meet one. It seems to me that no rational biography could explain one of the most 'irrational' effects ever observed in the history of man. I believe that this problem can only be approached through history and comparative psychology of symbols" (1975, 88, 89, 91). Jung states that his critical approach to the Bible is more akin to that of Wilhelm de Wette (1780–1849), founder of the historical-critical approach to the Pentateuch and friend of Jung's grandfather, whose hermeneutical method was to "mythize" or extract the "symbolic value of marvelous" Bible stories (1975, 115–116).

A third feeling-laden association, directly related to the previous two, is the tragedy of Jung's pastor father, Johann Paul Achilles Jung, who was caught between the desire to remain loyal to the unquestioning "faith" of the biblical piety to which he had been ordained and, one suspects, the "rationalistic historicism" of Enlightenment biblical scholarship that fed the "doubt" he so much feared (1963, 73). "It was the tragedy of my youth," Jung writes, "to see my father cracking up before my eyes on the problem of his faith and dying an early death" (1975, 257). He died when Carl was twenty-one.

Jung had been told by his father at an early age, "You always want to think. One ought not to think, but believe" (1963, 43). Years later Jung wrote that "people who merely believe and don't think always forget that they continually expose themselves to their own worst enemy: doubt. Wherever belief reigns, doubt lurks in the background" (1953–1978, 12:170). Jung saw this belief–doubt scenario play itself out in the years preceding the death of his father, who had become increasingly lonely, irritable, and hypochondriac. "Once I heard him praying," Jung reports. "He struggled desperately to keep his faith. I was shaken and outraged at once, because I saw how hopelessly he was entrapped by the Church and its theological thinking. They had blocked all avenues by which he might have reached God directly, and then faithlessly abandoned him" (1963, 93).

The tragedy was heightened by the fact that Jung's father had once had an active intellectual life. He "had studied Oriental languages in Göttingen and done his dissertation on the Arabic version of the Song of Songs" (1963, 91). As a minister he had been "connected with the cantonal insane asylum" and was "very much interested in psychiatry," a fact that ironically had inclined the younger Jung at first in the opposite direction (1989, 7). Shortly before his death the pastor had begun reading Bernheim's book on suggestion in Sigmund Freud's translation. But none of this had succeeded in enabling the father to rise above the "sentimental idealism" of the "country parson, smoking a long student's pipe, . . . reading novels or an occasional travel book" (1963, 91, 94).

Not only had Jung's father made the *sacrificium intellectus* in his attitude toward the Bible and religion, but he had also failed to discover what the prophets, Paul, and the young Jung had come to know, namely, that the promptings of the "inner man" or the "God within" are to be accorded as much authority as the voice of traditional religion (1953–1978, 10:10–12). In Jung's words, his father "had taken the Bible's commandments as his guide; he believed in God as the Bible prescribed and as his forefathers had taught him. But he did not know the immediate living God who stands, omnipotent and free, above His Bible and His Church, who calls upon man to partake of His freedom, and can force him to renounce his own views and convictions in order to fulfill without reserve the command of God" (1963, 40).

Jung tells us, surprisingly, that his father's tragic end did not forestall his interest in religion but provided the "objective outer event that opened my eyes to the importance of religion," despite all the "negative conclusions" about religion that might have seemed warranted (1975, 257). Jung saw his father's tragedy as a mantle of unfinished business he was destined to assume. He writes, "I feel very strongly that I am under the influence of things or questions which were left incomplete and unanswered by my parents and grandparents and more distant ancestors. . . . It has always seemed to me that I had to answer questions which fate had posed to my forefathers, and which had not yet been answered, or as if I had to complete, or perhaps continue, things which previous ages had left unfinished" (1963, 233). His father's death marked the beginning of a project for Jung that included vindicating his father's life, his father's religion, and his father's commitment to the Bible, albeit from a "psychological" perspective that his father at best was only beginning to understand.

A final feeling-toned association Jung has with the Bible has to do with his personal acknowledgment of the significance of biblical archetypal images for his own life, as well as for Western culture in general. One example of the former, from among many, is his recounting how the image of Paul came to his rescue at the time of his father's death, when by all accounts he should have thrown in the towel on religion, but didn't, and in fact went on to develop his psychology:

> My education offered me nothing but arguments against religion on the one hand, and on the other the charisma of faith was denied me. I was thrown back on experience alone. Always Paul's experience on the road to Damascus hovered before me, and I asked myself how his fate would have fallen out but for his visions. Yet this experience came upon him while he was blindly pursuing his own way. As a young man I drew the conclusion that you must obviously fulfill your destiny in order to get to the point where a *donum gratiae* might happen along. But I was far from certain, and always kept the possibility in mind that on this road I might end up in a black hole. I have remained true to this attitude all my life. From this you can easily see the origin of my psychology: only by going my own way, integrating my capacities headlong (like Paul), and thus creating a foundation for myself, could something be vouchsafed to me or built upon it, no matter where it came from, and of which I could be reasonably sure that it was not merely one of my own neglected capacities. (1975, 257–258)

An example of the latter, that is, Jung's sense of the cultural impact of the Bible, is voiced in the text of Jung's *Visions Seminar* (1930–1934): "We must read the Bible or we shall not understand psychology. Our psychology, whole lives, our language and imagery are built upon the Bible" (1976, 1:156). On the basis of this dictum and the many feeling-toned associations Jung has with the Bible and the problems of its meaning and interpretation, it comes as no surprise that the Bible constitutes a project of major significance in Jung's life and work, at both the conscious and unconscious levels.

The Bible as Conscious Project in Jung's Life and Work

Although the ubiquity of the Bible in Jung's life and work is a matter of public record, it is seldom acknowledged by Jungian commentators or biographers. For example, Vincent Brome's *Jung: Man and Myth* (1981) includes an appendix of Jung's sources in which Brome cites philosophers, psychologists, novelists, poets, and history of religions texts—from Plato to Freud, Rider Haggard, Goethe, and the Tibetan Book of the Dead. Not once does Brome mention the Bible, the single text that is cited more often than any other document in the Jungian corpus. To set the record straight, I examine four moments in Jung's curriculum vitae that make his conscious and comprehensive use of the Bible manifestly evident.

The first example comes from Jung's medical student days, in January 1899. Jung was twenty-four years old and was taking his turn as lecturer for the "Basel section of the color-wearing Zofingia" society, which he had joined four years earlier and to which his father had belonged in his student days. The lecture title was an unlikely one for a medical student: "Thoughts on the Interpretation of Christianity, with Reference to the Theory of Albrecht Ritschl" (Wehr, 1988, 58). Ritschl (1822–1889) was a systematic theologian to whose thought Jung had recently been introduced (by his father's former vicar) as one of the "new aspects of Protestant theology . . . much in fashion in those days." Jung found the "historicism" of Ritschl's theology "irritating" (1963, 97), and in his lecture flew into Ritschl's antimystical interpretation of Christian origins. The remarkable feature of the lecture from our standpoint is the list of fifty-five numbered biblical passages (for example, Matt. 13:35, "I will open my mouth in parables; I will utter things which have been kept secret from the foundation of the world"; or Luke 12:49, "I am come to send fire on the earth") that Jung had mustered for the disquisition, demonstrating a practice that would mark Jung's career of enlisting biblical wisdom to combat mindless pietism and rationalistic positivism.

A second example of the nuclear role of the Bible in Jung's life is his *Answer to Job* (written in 1951), the single volume he addresses explicitly to a biblical theme (one that qualifies as an unconscious project as well as a conscious one in Jung's life and work). According to Jungian analyst Nathan Schwartz-Salant, *Answer to Job* was the only work of his own that Jung found "totally satisfying" (1987, 64). Jung wrote to Henry Corbin: "the Book 'came to me' . . . as if accompanied by the great music of a Bach or Handel" (1975, 116). In a letter to Aniela Jaffé in May 1951, he states: "In this way I have landed the great whale; I mean 'Answer to Job.' I can't say I have fully digested this *tour de force* of the unconscious." Later in July he writes, "if there is anything like the spirit seizing one by the scruff of the neck, it was the way this book came into being" (1975, 17–18, 20). In the "Lectori Benevelo" of the essay he adverts to the level of feeling and the depth of emotion that the subject matter touches in him:

> Since I shall be dealing with numinous factors, my feeling is challenged quite as much as my intellect. I cannot, therefore, write in a coolly objective manner, but must allow my emotional subjectivity to speak if I want to describe what I feel when I read certain books of the Bible, or when I remember the impressions I have received from the doctrines of our faith. . . . What I am expressing is first of all my own personal view, but I know that I also speak in the name of many who have had similar experiences. (1953–1978, 11:559)

Answer to Job is the product of a long-term agenda for Jung, addressing matters, he says, that "I have been occupied with . . . for years" (1953–1978, 11:357). He had hesitated for years to undertake the book, knowing its publication would cause fierce controversy. It occasioned a rift with longtime friend and theologian Victor White, and "even Emma Jung had misgivings." Jung proceeded, however, because of his compulsion "to write down from the heart everything that had formed an indelible part of his life for decades" (Wehr, 1988, 382, 392). *Answer to Job* is a reprise of the great themes and problems with which Jung had wrestled from the beginning. It speaks of Job's expecting "help from God against God"; it also reveals Jung expecting help from the Bible (and psychology) against the Bible as misunderstood by both biblicistic piety and rationalistic biblical criticism Jung had so profoundly opposed.

At a more personal level, *Answer to Job* was Jung's antidotal answer to the tragic route his father's life had assumed. Jung intimates this in his autobiography, speaking of his father: "He had to quarrel with somebody, so he did it with his family and himself. Why didn't he do it with God, the dark author of all created things, who alone was

responsible for the sufferings of the world? God would assuredly have
sent him by way of an answer one of those magical, infinitely profound
dreams which He had sent to me even without being asked, and which
had sealed my fate" (1963, 92).

A third genre of evidence for the role the Bible plays as conscious
project in Jung's life and work is the testimony of the twenty volumes
of the *Collected Works*, whose *General Index* lists twenty columns'
worth of citations under the entry "Bible," exceeding the number of
columns devoted to any other single text. The listing references all
but thirteen of the sixty-six books of the Old and New Testaments of
the Christian canon, as well as Old Testament apocryphal and pseud-
epigraphic writings (Life of Adam and Eve, Syrian Apocalypse of
Baruch, Ecclesiasticus, Book of Enoch, 2 Esdras, Tobit, and Wisdom
of Solomon) and New Testament apocryphal works (Book of Apostle
Bartholomew, Gospel of the Egyptians, *Epistolae Apostolorum*, Ascension of Isaiah, Acts of John, Acts of Peter, Gospel of Peter, Gospel of
Philip, Apocalypse of Zephaniah, and Acts of Thomas), along with references to the critical volumes by R. H. Charles on the apocrypha and
pseudepigrapha of the Old Testament and the works on the New Testament apocrypha by Edgar Hennecke and by M. R. James.

Beyond the enclave of twenty columns indexing the Bible is a vast
network of separate headings for biblical names, terms, stories,
themes, and phrases, along with references to theologians and biblical
interpreters. Proceeding through the *General Index* from *A* to *Z* one
finds 185 biblical names, many cited more than a dozen times. For
example, the entries under the letter *A* include the personal names
Aaron, Abel, Abraham, Adah (wife of Esau), Adoni-Bezek (a Canaanite
king), Ahasuerus, Ahijah, Andrew, Azazel (the scapegoat), and Augus-
tus. In addition to the personal names are biblical topics and themes,
for example, Abyss, Amorites, Antichrist, Annunciation, Antiochus,
Apostle, Ark of the Covenant, Areopagus, Ascension, along with terms
in Greek script, *anthropos* (man) and *agnoia* (ignorance), the Latin
phrase *agnata fides* (consanguine faith), and the Hebrew *adamah* (earth),
aleph, and *tau* (*A* and *Z*). It also includes ancient writers and biblical
commentators (Abelard, Albertus Magnus, Ambrose, Anselm, and
Augustine). At the other end of the alphabet, the letter *Z* yields an
appreciably shorter list, including Zecharias, Mt. Zion, Zipporah (wife
of Moses), and the related Zohar. Running through the alphabet
between *A* and *Z* is a panoply of biblical entities, including Balaam, the
Canaanites, Dagon the God of the Philistines, El Elyon (God most
High), the Flood, Gamaliel, Hagar, Immanuel, Jezebel, the Kingdom

of God, Lilith, Melchisedek, Nicodemus, the "only-begotten," the Paraclete, Queen of Sheba, Rahab, the Shulamite Woman, Terah (father of Abraham), the "unjust steward," the *vox dei*, the whirlwind, and Yehoshua.

In addition to this glossary of biblical names is a compendium of 230 biblical terms, phrases, and themes, for example, the "inner man," central to Jung's anthropology; the "mote in your brother's eye," which Jung adduces as an illustration of projection; and the Christological question "Why callest Thou me good?" which Jung often summons to demonstrate the humanity of Jesus in the Gospels. Repeatedly Jung finds that the Bible supplies him with archetypal images that inform his situation: the pearl of great price, the house built on sand, the grain of mustard seed, the journey of Adam out of the garden, and the buried treasure in the field.

A letter of Jung's from March 13, 1958, aptly demonstrates his perennially artful interpolation of biblical images (indicated by italics) that articulate ideas central to his self-understanding:

> The primordial experience is not concerned with the historical bases of Christianity but consists in an immediate experience of God (as was had by *Moses, Job, Hosea, Ezekiel among others*) which "con-vinces" because it is "overpowering." But this is something you can't easily talk about. One can only say that somehow one has to reach the rim of the world or get to the end of one's tether in order to partake of the terror or grace of such an experience at all. Its nature is such that it is really understandable why the Church is actually a place of refuge or protection for those who cannot endure the fire of the divine presence. *A logion says: "He that is near me is near the fire. He that is far from me is far from the kingdom."* I think I understand ecclesiastical Christianity but the theologians do not understand me. Their *raison d'étre* consists in the very fact of belonging to a Church, and mine in coming to terms with that indefinable being we call "God." Probably no compromise is possible except that of "coexistence," each allowing the other his say. At any rate, again and again the allegory is repeated of the *strait and steep path trodden by the few and the broad path trodden by the many.* (1975, 424)

A fourth and final demonstration of the Bible as conscious project for Jung is the vertical marker in the family graveyard plot at Küsnacht that contains the family crest and, on the side, two Latin inscriptions. The first is "Vocatus atque non vocatus, Deus aderit" (Summoned or not summoned God, will be present), the oracular Delphic utterance Jung found in Erasmus that he also had inscribed over the entranceway at Küsnacht for his patients to see. The second is from 1 Corinthians 15:47, "Primus homo terrenus de terra, secundus homo coelestis de coelo" (The first man is of the earth, a man of dust: the second is of heaven). The Bible is part of Jung's conscious project from beginning to end.

The Bible as Unconscious Project in Jung's Life and Work

One would expect, from what I've just described, that the Bible would seep into Jung's dream life, as it did on a number of occasions. The first occurred, in December 1913, at the onset of the four-year period during which Jung made his descent into the unconscious using himself as a case study to document images that appear spontaneously in the psyche. He recounts a dream in which two, and possibly three, biblical figures appear—an old man with a white beard who identified himself as Elijah and a young, beautiful, blind girl named Salome, in company of a black serpent that, Jung reports, "displayed an unmistakable fondness for me. I stuck close to Elijah because he seemed to be the most reasonable of the three, and to have a clear intelligence. Of Salome I was distinctly suspicious. Elijah and I had a long conversation which, however, I did not understand." Jung comments, "naturally I tried to find a plausible explanation for the appearance of Biblical figures in my fantasy by reminding myself that my father had been a clergyman. But that really explained nothing at all" (1963, 181–182; 1989, 63–64). Jung would later identify the black serpent as symbolizing the "introverting libido," Salome, the anima, and Elijah, the Mahatma, the Wise old Man (1989, 88–90, 92–99). Jung cited the dream as an example of the spontaneous manifestation of mythic themes in biblical guise, though he made no further speculation on why his unconscious chose biblical imagery to express the archetype rather than some other symbolic vocabulary.

Jung reports a second, and for our purposes, more significant dream in which the Bible and Jung's father are paired in key roles related to Jung's preoccupation with the issues addressed in *Answer to Job* (1963, 216–217). Jung writes, "the problem of Job in all of its ramifications had likewise been foreshadowed in a dream. It started with my paying a visit to my long-deceased father," who in the dream is not only the guardian of the sarcophagi of famous people at a large eighteenth-century home but also a "distinguished scholar in his own right." In the dream Jung meets his father in the study, where "oddly enough, Dr. Y—who was about my age—and his son, both psychiatrists, were also present." To illustrate a point in the conversation, Jung's father "fetched a big Bible down from a shelf . . . bound in shiny fishskin," opened it to the Pentateuch, "and began interpreting a certain passage." Jung recounts that he did this so swiftly and so learnedly that I could not follow him. I noted only that what he said betrayed a vast amount of variegated knowledge. . . . I saw that Dr. Y. understood nothing at all, and his son began to laugh. They thought that my father was going off the deep end and what he said was simply senile prattle. But it was quite clear to me . . . that there was nothing silly about what he was saying. On the contrary, his argument was so intelligent and so learned that we in our stupidity simply could not follow it. It dealt with something extremely important which fascinated him . . . his mind was flooded with profound ideas. I was annoyed and thought it was a pity that he had to talk in the presence of three such idiots as we. (1963, 216–217)

Jung's comment on the dream identifies the two psychiatrists, Dr. Y. and his son, as representations of the "limited medical point of view" that had in fact infected Jung's own thinking. The rest of the scene, for Jung, pointed to the unconscious task he was to undertake in the writing of Job, which he had left to his " 'father,' that is, to the unconscious." Jung comments that in the dream, his father "was obviously engrossed in the Bible (*Answer to Job*) and eager to communicate his insights. The fishskin marks the Bible as an unconscious content, for fishes are mute and unconscious. My poor father does not succeed in communicating either." In connection with a later scene in the dream, Jung adds, "something in me was defiant and determined not to be a dumb fish: and . . . if there were not something of the sort in free men, no Book of Job would have been written several hundred years before the birth of Christ" (1963, 219–220).

A second dream Jung reports as prelude to *Answer to Job* begins with Jung in his own house discovering a "large wing which I had never visited. . . . When I opened it, I found myself in a room set up as a laboratory. . . . This was my father's workroom. However, he was not there. On shelves along the walls stood hundreds of bottles containing every imaginable sort of fish. I was astonished: so now my father was going in for ichthyology!" (1963, 213). Jung interprets the fish (*ichthys*) as a clear reference to his preoccupation with Christ and finds it "remarkable" that the study of fish was attributed to his father. Jung's dream saw his father as a "caretaker of Christian souls" (as was his mother also, in a second part of the dream). For Jung the dream signified the contiguity of his vocational task with that of his parents. He writes, "both my parents appeared burdened with the problem of the 'cure of souls,' which in fact was really my task. Something had remained unfinished and was still with my parents; that is to say, it was still later in the unconscious and hence reserved for the future" (1963, 214). Jung's sense that he was taking over his father's unfinished business is also suggested in two dreams Jung had six weeks after his

father's death, in which his father returns and Jung is concerned
that he might "be annoyed with me for having moved into his room"
(1963, 96).

Jung discloses that "all problems that concerned me personally or
scientifically" were "accompanied or heralded by dreams" (1963, 213).
In response to the two dreams, Jung undertakes the daunting but
compelling task of *Answer to Job*, bringing together his lifelong wrestling with religion and the Bible in the service of the "many questions
from the public and from patients . . . about the religious problems of
modern man" (1963, 216), which for Jung included the question of biblical hermeneutics. In the writing, Jung hoped to point the way to a
solution of the problems on which his father had tragically foundered.
Jung writes, "he wanted to rest content with faith, but faith broke
faith with him. Such is frequently the reward for the *sacrificium intellectus. . . .* Blind acceptance never leads to a solution; at best it leads
only to a standstill and is paid for heavily in the next generation" (1963,
215). It was Jung's commission, from the voice of his unconscious, to
offset the debt of his father's irresolution, by reclaiming the meaning
his father had failed to detect in Scripture as well as in the recesses of
his own psyche, toward the final goal of the "cure of souls."

A Jungian Agenda for Reading the Bible
through a Psychological Lens

Jung's long-term agenda for the Bible is subsumed under his agenda
for the Christian tradition in general. As Murray Stein has so skillfully
argued in *Jung's Treatment of Christianity: The Psychotherapy of a Religious Tradition,* Jung's approach to Christianity is not primarily that of
the "empirical scientist" who wishes to lay bare the psychological
anatomy of religion, nor that of the "hermeneutical revivalist" who
wishes to reclaim the lost meaning of Christian symbolism, nor of the
"doctor of souls" who seeks to heal those wounded by religion, nor
of the "post-Christian modern man" who sifts through the detritus of
Christianity to repudiate the bad and assimilate the good. Jung's
approach is that of psychotherapist, with the "strong urge to heal
Christianity" (Stein, 1985, 17). Or as James Dittes frames it, Jung's
objective is that of "a prophet or reformer wanting to rescue the best
of his tradition from the worst of his tradition," calling for it "to grow
beyond a one-sidedness in which it is stuck . . . and beyond paralyzing
literalisms, rationalisms, and perfectionisms that dangerously remove
religion from its origins and mission in experience." In the end "he

wants Christianity, as he must have wanted his father and mother, to become transformed, liberated, renewing its vitality in restored connection with the roots from which it arose" (Dittes, 1990, 33–34).

What hermeneutical program does Jung advance to achieve this objective with the Bible? As Peter Homans observes in his essay "Psychology and Hermeneutics: Jung's Contribution," Jung does not provide a full-blown hermeneutical system, nor does he delineate "the full range of problems involved in a theory of interpretation of religious forms" (1969, 349). But the Jungian corpus leaves two resources for attempting the construction of a Jungian hermeneutical model. The first is a scattering of essays in which Jung addresses the problem of the hermeneutics of literature and art directly, for example, *Answer to Job* (1953–1978, vol. 11), "Commentary on 'The Secret of the Golden Flower'" (vol. 13), "On the Relation of Analytical Psychology to Poetry" (vol. 15), and above all, "Psychology and Literature" (vol. 15). The second is the myriad of interpretive comments Jung makes on biblical texts throughout the Jungian corpus. From these two sources, one can extract a number of hermeneutical *presuppositions*, an *agenda* of hermeneutical objectives, and a hermeneutical *method* for a psychological approach to the Bible.

Presuppositions

The first and fundamental presupposition for a Jungian hermeneutic is that religion and religious texts are "not only a sociological and historical phenomenon" but also a function of the "psychological structure of human personality" (1953–1978, 11:1). As Jung notes in the introduction to his essay "Psychology and Literature," although poetry "constitutes the proper province of literary science and of aesthetics . . . it is also a psychic phenomenon, and as such it probably must be taken into account by the psychologist." For Jung, "the human psyche is the womb of all the arts and sciences" (1953–1978, 15:132–133), which means that all human expression, including religion, art, and literature, has been processed through the human psyche and can be shown to bear evidence of the psychic habits, processes, dispositions, truths, and visions that gave birth to them. His goal therefore is to "discover psychological facts and processes that before were veiled in symbols and beyond . . . comprehension" (1953–1978, 13:373).

Jung is eager to distance his "psychological approach" from the "psychologizing" approach he identifies with Freud, an approach that tends to use psychological analysis to reduce a psychic artifact (for example, a poem, work of art, piece of literature, an image of God, or a dogma) either to an illusion or to a symptom of neurosis. The result of this approach in the popular mind, Jung claims, has been that "every attempt at adequate psychological understanding is immediately suspected of psychologism" (1953–1978, 11:749 n. 2). Jung argues that this need not be the case if psychological inquiry focuses on the content of symbolic expression rather than on the psychological state of the author:

> The personal life of the artist is at most a help or a hindrance, but is never essential to his creative task, . . . his personal career may be interesting and inevitable, but it does not explain his art. . . . The essence of a work of art is not to be found in the personal idiosyncrasies that creep into it . . . but in its rising above the personal and speaking from the mind and heart of the artists to the mind and heart of mankind. (1953–1978, 15:97–98, 156, 162)

A second psychological presupposition of an analytical-psychological approach, implicit in the first, is the recognition of the unconscious as a factor ineluctably at work in all human expression, including religious texts. Jung identifies three aspects of the unconscious at work in religious texts worthy of reflection as part of a psychological hermeneutic.

The first consists of the remnants of the pre-Christian or pre-Israelite consciousness that reside unconsciously in Christian and Hebrew sacred texts. Speaking of Christianity specifically, Jung writes, "everything has its history, everything has 'grown,' and Christianity, which is supposed to have appeared suddenly as a unique revelation from heaven, undoubtedly also has its history. . . . It is exactly as if we had built a cathedral over a pagan temple and no longer knew that it is still there underneath." Jung adds that the presence of pre-Christian factors in Christian texts, unconscious as they are, continue to have their effect, and that because contemporary Western culture has the unconscious stamp of Judeo-Christianity upon it, so "we are also stamped by what existed before Christianity" (1978, 342).

A second unconscious factor at work in religious texts worthy of psycho-hermeneutical attention is the personal unconscious of the author of the text. Jung, to be sure, is wary of focusing on the author or artist more than the final text, as noted previously, and insists that although "the personal psychology of the artist may explain many aspects of his work," it does not explain "the work itself" (1953–1978, 15:134). Be that as it may, a psychological approach from a Jungian perspective assumes two primary factors in the personal unconscious of the author at work in the text: (1) the psychological-type orientation of the writer (sensing, thinking, feeling, intuiting), which will manifest itself in the treatment and choice of materials in the text; and (2) the psychological history of the author, his complexes, projections, sublimations, urges, passions, and so forth, that will be at work in the warp and woof of the text as a psycho-hermeneutical factor, difficult to identify with any degree of accuracy to be sure, but nonetheless present.

A third unconscious factor at work in religious texts, and of consummate interest to Jung, is the collective unconscious, or as Jung also alludes to it, the objective unconscious, which Jung describes as "a sphere of unconscious mythology whose primordial images are the common heritage of mankind." Although the objective unconscious "will forever elude our attempts at understanding" (1953–1978, 15:125, 135), its traces can be detected in many genres of scriptural expression (for example, symbols, archetypal images, dream narratives, stories, myths, epic narratives, apocalypses, and stories of heroic figures). The contemplation and amplification of such images constitute a major part of a psycho-hermeneutical agenda, examining their function and effect in the biblical text and in Bible-reading communities, comparing their form and content with commensurate images in other cultural traditions, and inquiring into their meaning for the human condition.

Agenda

With this set of presuppositions implicit in a psycho-hermeneutical approach to the Bible, let us proceed to an eight-point agenda that would seem to be inferred in the Jungian corpus for the application of an analytical-psychological approach to the text.

The first point is that symbols, archetypal images, and myths provide the primary point of inquiry for a Jungian psycho-hermeneutic, because, as noted earlier, they seem to constitute the primary point of access to the great themes indigenous to the collective unconscious. A keystone of Jung's psychology is that the unconscious spontaneously produces images of direction and integration for the individual and culture, and that classical religions traffic in such images, which in the end have to do not just with history "back then" or "out there" but with the "now" and the "within." In a letter to Dorothee Hoch on July 3, 1952, Jung wrote: "Educated people . . . would be much more readily convinced of the meaning of the gospel if it were shown them the myth was always there to a greater or lesser degree, and moreover is actually present in archetypal form in every individual. Then people would understand where, in spite of its having been artificially screened off by the theologians, the gospel really touches them and what it is talking about" (1975, 75).

The purpose of symbols, archetypal images, and myths within the

economy of the psyche from Jung's perspective is to correct the
"course" of the psyche when it has become "one-sided or adopts false
attitudes." This occurs as a corrective not only to an individual psyche
but to the psychic attitude of an entire culture or age when it becomes
sidetracked or when it forgets its raison d'étre. The medium of psychic
expression in the case of the individual is often the dream, but in the
case of an entire culture it may be a "dream" mediated through great
literature, music, or art. "Herein lies the social significance of art,"
Jung writes. "It is constantly at work educating the spirit of the age,
conjuring up the forms in which the age is most lacking. The unsatis-
fied yearning of the artist reaches back to the primordial image in the
unconscious which is best fitted to compensate the inadequacy and
one-sidedness of the present." More often than not, the artist of which
Jung speaks bears social resemblance to the Old Testament prophets,
by virtue of their lack of adaptation to the culture around them, which
provides them with the eyes to see "the psychic elements that are waiting to play their part in the life of the collective." In this instance, Jung
writes, "the lack of adaptation turns out to his advantage" and to that
of the collective psyche (1953–1978, 15:131, 160).

How is one to approach these spontaneous and compensatory
images mediated through symbol, archetypal image, and myth?
Here the profound difference between Freud's hermeneutic and Jung's
becomes clear. Jung writes,

> For Freud . . . symbols . . . are not truly symbols but *signs* or *symptoms*
> of the subliminal [repressive] processes. The true symbol differs essen-
> tially from this, and should be understood as an expression of an intui-
> tive idea that cannot yet be formulated in any other or better way. When
> Plato, for instance, puts the whole problem of the theory of knowledge
> in his parable of the cave, or when Christ expresses the idea of the King-
> dom of Heaven in parables, these are genuine and true symbols, that is,
> attempts to express something for which no verbal concept yet exists. If
> we were to interpret Plato's metaphor in Freudian terms we would nat-
> urally arrive at the uterus and would have proved that even a mind like
> Plato's was still stuck on a primitive level of infantile sexuality. But we
> would have completely overlooked what Plato actually created . . . ;
> we would have missed the essential point. (1953–1978, 15:105)

A Jungian hermeneutical approach to symbols, archetypal images,
and myths therefore challenges the reader not only to understand
the manifest content of the story, fable, parable, or image in its own
linguistic and cultural setting but to contemplate the image toward
the end of finding "our way back to the deepest springs of life" that the

artist, poet, or storyteller has crystallized with his or her imaginal rendering (1953–1978, 15:130). This will not be a matter of a simple, univocal translation but an exercise in entertaining the paradoxical amplitude of the image in which "fullness of life" and the "incomprehensible" are expressed in forms that eschew the one-sidedness of "non-ambiguity and non-contradiction" (1953–1978, 12:18).

Dreams constitute a second focus for a Jungian psycho-hermeneutic of the Bible. Although Sigmund Freud provided the "royal road" to modern dream interpretation, Carl Jung developed the oneiro-critical theory that provided access to biblical dreams and dream interpretation from a perspective congenial to a biblical view of dreams. Freud's psychopathological approach, which regarded the dream as an intentionally disguised expression of repressed instinctual urges that should be dredged into consciousness, focused not on the dream itself but on its latent content. Freud used a method of free association to tease out that content for conscious recognition, in effect regarding the dream as a mask for a darker, repressed reality. Jung's theory, on the other hand, saw the dream in biblically compatible terms as part of the self-regulating system of the psyche, which provided images compensatory to and therapeutic for consciousness (Job 33: 15–17). As a result, the role, meaning, and significance of biblical dreams have become subjects for critical examination from a biblical-critical and Jungian perspective, with pioneer work done by Morton Kelsey in his invaluable history of dream interpretation, *Dreams: The Dark Speech of the Spirit* (1968), and by John Sanford in *Dreams: God's Forgotten Language* (1968).

A Jungian analytical-psychological approach can make a number of contributions to the study of biblical dreams, athough at the outset it should be noted that Jungian dream theory would preclude the possibility of interpreting a biblical dream from the standpoint of a biblical dreamer, given the unavailability of the dreamer for comment. Beyond this obvious caveat, a Jungian approach can contribute to the work of biblical exegesis in at least four ways. First, it can offer a classification of a given biblical dream from the standpoint of a Jungian typology of dreams (for example, initial dreams, "big dreams," recurrent dreams), locating the biblical dream in the broader context of human dreaming in general. Second, it can contribute to a history of dream interpretation, comparing the oneiro-interpretive approach of the Bible with that of Greco-Roman culture, Rabbinic Judaism, and later Christian writers, for example, Clement, John Chrysostom, and Augustine. Third, it can provide insight into the oneiro-interpretive approach of the biblical writers in their reporting of dreams, and of the dream interpretations proffered by figures within the biblical narrative, for example, Peter's recurrent "universalistic" dream and its interpretation in Acts 10: 9–16. Fourth, it can provide insight into the archetypal dimensions of certain dream images in the Bible.

Biblical personalities constitute a third subject on which a psycho-hermeneutic approach can cast light. As has been demonstrated in John Sanford's studies of the biblical portraits of Jacob, Joseph, Moses, Adam and Eve, and Saul, "the tragic hero" (1974, 1985), and in Edward Edinger's studies on Abraham, Jacob, Moses, Joshua, Gideon, Samson, Ruth, Saul, David, Solomon, and Old Testament prophets and kings (1986), in Walter Wink's essay on Jacob's wrestling with God (1978), or in André and Pierre-Emmanuel LaCocque's study of Jonah (1990), a psycho-hermeneutic approach to biblical personalities offers two, and possibly three, new lines of inquiry and exegesis to the study of the text. The first is simply character analysis from a psychological per-spective, analyzing the psychic habits, strategies, defenses, and so forth implicit in the textual portrait of a biblical figure, commenting, albeit tentatively, on the conscious as well as unconscious factors and inten-tions that appear to be operative within the psychodynamics of the nar-rative. Such analysis adds a psychological dimension to the rich inter-pretive work being done by the new literary and narrative criticism.

A second line of inquiry focuses on the biblical portraits of per-sonalities as models of individuation, consciously or unconsciously intended by the biblical author. Jung enjoins us "to examine carefully the psychological aspects of the individuation process in the light of Christian tradition, which can describe it for us with an exactness and impressiveness far surpassing our feeble attempts" (1953–1978, 9:2, 79), and he explicitly identifies such models of individuation in the fig-ures of Adam, Abraham, Paul, and preeminently Christ as the exem-plification of the archetype of the Self.

A third possible contribution of a psychological approach to biblical personalities is psychoanalytical. Although Jung in his time objected strongly to the Freudian focus on the psychopathology of biblical authors, it cannot be gainsaid that psychoanalytic observations on bib-lical portraits of personalities can be of value to the biblical inter-preter. Although a psychoanalysis of biblical figures in the strictest sense is ruled out given the absence of the analysand, and although the egregious defects of "bad psychoanalysis" have been indexed by Albert Schweitzer (as noted above), a number of recent studies have sug-gested that psychoanalytic observations in the hands of seasoned analysts can provide persuasively meaningful and compelling insight into the psychodynamic factors at work in author and text, for example, the work of David Halperin (1993) on Ezekiel, fulfilling as it were an observation by Bernhard Anderson in his classic *Understanding the Old Testament*, that "Ezekiel *himself* was an unusual person whose psychic peculiarities make a fascinating psychological study" (1986, 429).

Biblical religious phenomena constitute a fourth area of inquiry in which an analytical-psychological inquiry can enhance biblical understanding. Although Jung himself did not explore in detail the range of religious phenomena to be found in the Bible, he did manage to make passing reference to many of them, providing an occasional suggestion of their importance from a psychological perspective and in effect outlining an agenda for future work. In his essay "Freud and Jung: Contrasts," Jung offers the hint of a psychological interpretation of rites of initiation without mentioning baptism in particular, yet clearly alluding to the biblical phenomenon of baptism in the spirit: "For thousands of years rites of initiation have been teaching rebirth from the spirit; yet, strangely enough, man forgets again and again the meaning of divine procreation" (1953–1978, 4:783). Here, as at numerous points throughout the Jungian corpus, Jung points the way to a psychological hermeneutic of ritual practice (such as foot washing, Eucharist, burnt offering, purification rites), of mystical experience (for example, visions, dreams, prophecy, photisms, auditions, inspiration, revelation, the inner light, and *enthousiasmos*), of religious states ("twice-born religion," *metanoia*, *kenosis*, martyrdom, and the experience of sin, guilt, forgiveness, grace, and sanctification), religious practices (prayer, glossolalia), and religious experiences (miracles, transfiguration, resurrection).

The pathogenic and therapeutic elements in the Bible constitute a fifth dimension of special interest to Jung that can be illumined by a psychological hermeneutic. John Dourley, in his book *The Illness That We Are: A Jungian Critique of Christianity* (1984), identifies five pathogenic deficiencies in Christianity that, for our purposes, are equally characteristic of the Bible or of its traditional interpretation. In *Answer to Job*, Jung identifies and addresses some of these elements, but it is the task of a psychologically oriented hermeneutic to amplify the work already done by feminist and ideological critics in identifying the dark biases that enjoy advocacy in certain biblical texts. Dourley provides a starting point for such an undertaking with the pathogenic elements he identifies: (1) the "sacrosanct unintelligibility of religious language"; (2) the "systematic blindness to God within"; (3) the systematic exclusion of four realities from the God-concept: matter, the feminine, the "dark side," and the sexual-instinctual; and (4) the creation of a "militant monotheistic faith that kills."

The therapeutic dimension of the text is not one ordinarily explicated by biblical hermeneutics but is indigenous to a Jungian understanding of the text and would constitute a special telos of a psycho-hermeneutical approach. For Jung the goal of religion in all of its manifestations, including Scripture, is the *cura animarum*, the care and cure of souls. In his essay "The State of Psychotherapy Today," Jung writes that "religions are psychotherapeutic systems in the truest sense of the word. . . . They express the whole range of the psychic problem in mighty images; they are the avowal and recognition of the soul, and at the same time the revelation of the soul's nature" (1953–1978, 10:367), and as I noted earlier, they provide models of individuation. In approaching the therapeutic elements and potential effects of the Bible, a psychological hermeneutic can learn from the work of pastoral counselors Donald Capps (1981), Wayne Oates (1953), and Carroll A. Wise (1956).

Biblical ethics is a sixth area of inquiry to which a psychological hermeneutic can contribute. Although a definitive work has yet to be written on the "ethics of consciousness" advocated by Jung, it is clear he finds analogues for such an ethic in the life of Paul, as he indicates in his introduction to Erich Neumann's *Depth Psychology and a New Ethic* (1969), as well as in a variant logion of Jesus from the fifth-century Codex Bezae at Luke 6:4: "Man, if indeed thou knowest what thou doest, thou art blessed; but if thou knowest not, thou art cursed, and a transgressor of the law." Jung comments that "here the moral criterion is *consciousness*, and not law or convention" (1953–1978, 11:696 n. 6). The spectrum of ethical postures in the Bible—from the deontological ethics of the law codes, to the love ethic of the Johannine Christ, to the ethics of the spirit in Paul—would benefit from a psychological approach that examines the psychic habits and predilections as well as the archetypal urgings that are coming to expression in the various ethical modalities in the Bible.

The biblical reader and interpreter would also fall within the spectrum of inquiry for a psycho-hermeneutical approach to the text—a seventh area. Although Jung does not take up the concerns of current reader-response criticism, which focuses on the contribution of the reader to the construction (even the creation) of the text, Jung does acknowledge the fact of readers shaping texts. In his more cynical moments, he admits that "as we know, anything can be authorized out of the Bible" (1953–1978, 9:2, 276), but more constructively he develops the theory of psychological types to account for the diverse renderings that a common set of data enjoys from different interpreters, a fact also explored by Cedric Johnson in *The Psychology of Biblical Interpretation* (1983). The special task of a psychological hermeneutic would be to examine the conscious and unconscious objectives and motives at work in the psyche of the reader, commenting both on the effect of the text on the reader and the reciprocal metamorphosing effect of the reader on the text.

Biblical psychology as defined in eighteenth- and nineteenth-century works, such as Franz Delitzsch's *A System of Biblical Psychology* (1867), is the discipline devoted to articulating the biblical view(s) of the origin, nature, and destiny of the psyche/soul. A contemporary psychological hermeneutic would certainly include this objective in its agenda not only as a matter of record but as a possible source of insight for contemporary self-understanding. Jung spends no time at all reconstructing the biblical model of the psyche, because he is so caught up in the Herculean task of constructing his own. It is clear, however, that his own model bears what appears to be telling resemblance to that of the Bible. Jung appears in many respects to be a "biblical Mensch," as evidenced in the biblical character of his *Weltbild*, with its concern for the soul, its sense of destiny or call, its openness to the wisdom of dreams, revelations, and visions, its appreciation of the interplay between good and evil, its appreciation of the sequence of sin and grace in human experience, and its sense of the numinous. A psychohermeneutic might take notice of this comparison: first, identifying and clarifying the biblical model of the psyche; second, inquiring into the extent that this model might still be operative in Jung's thought in specific, and in Western culture in general; and third, raising the question whether the biblical model of the psyche provides a translatable corrective or paradigm for modern and postmodern models.

Method

In his book *The Bible and the Psyche: Individuation Symbolism in the Old Testament*, Jungian analyst Edward Edinger writes, "the events of the Bible, although presented as history, psychologically understood are archetypal images, that is, pleromatic events that repeatedly erupt into spatio-temporal manifestation and require an individual ego to live them out. As we read these stories with an openness to their unconscious reverberations we recognize them to be relevant to our own most private experience" (1986, 13). This statement summarizes Jung's pri-

mary hermeneutical goal, to bring the "metaphysical" "within the range
of experience" (1953–1978, 13:74) and to take the "thought-forms that
have become historically fixed" and "try to melt them down again and
pour them into moulds of immediate experience" (1953–1978, 11:148).
Although a psycho-hermeneutical approach to the Bible from a Jungian
perspective will use the findings of historical-literary critical research
and focus on the specific hermeneutical tasks enumerated in the preceding section, its ultimate goal is to relate the text to the life experience of
the reader and the reading community, diverting the reader from the
tendency, for example, to talk of "Christ's cross" "out there," rather than
"discover our own cross" within (1975, 76–77). "In religious matters,"
Jung writes, "it is a well-known fact that we cannot understand a thing
until we have experienced it inwardly" (1953–1978, 12:15).

The two methods Jung developed for this "final" hermeneutical step
of relating the text to lived experience are the processes of amplification and active imagination. Although originally designed for the
interpretation of dream material in the clinical context, they are
equally applicable in the "investigation of psychologems, mytholo-
gems, and psychic structures of all kinds" (1971, 86), rooted in the
assumption that "the eternal truths cannot be transmitted 'mechani-
cally,' in every epoch they must be born anew from the human psyche"
(1953–1978, 10:443).

The hermeneutical method of amplification aims at eliciting the
associations the text has evoked within the reader, and it proceeds at
both the subjective (personal) and objective (collective) levels, search-
ing for both the personal meaning the text may have catalyzed in the
reader as well as the larger transpersonal "collective" meanings it may
have inspired. Although at the personal level a psycho-hermeneutical
approach can do little more than alert the individual reader to the
potential personal meanings in the text, it can at the collective level be
of assistance in three ways. First, it can locate the collective imagery
of the Bible within the powerful glossary of archetypal images that
recur in the art, literature, and religion of the world, where they can
be seen to provide guidance and direction for individuals and whole
cultures, as they do in the Bible. Second, it can seek on the basis of its
research in comparative mythology and folklore to proffer an interpretation of biblical imagery, resting on Jung's psychological observation that the interpretation of art cannot rest on the artist but remains
a task for the future: "Being essentially the instrument of his work,
[the artist] is subordinate to it, and we have no right to expect him to
interpret it for us. He has done his utmost by giving it form and must

leave the interpretation to others and to the future." Third, a psychological hermeneutic can seek to draw out untapped meanings, resident in the text, that remain to be identified and articulated, especially in openly symbolic texts such as Goethe's *Faust*, in which meaning can exceed the conscious intent and awareness of the author. Thus the responsibility of the interpreter, humanly and professionally, is to occasion the birth of those meanings not yet consciously noted and articulated, for the good of the author, the good of the reader, and the good of the broader humanity for whom, according to Jung, the image has emerged and "been revealed" from the depths of the objective unconscious in the first place (1953–1978, 15:73–119, 161).

The hermeneutical method of active imagination takes the interpretive process one step further by "translating" the amplified message into new forms. The forms can range from painting, dancing, storytelling, and working with clay, to stained glass, liturgy, musical cantatas, mystery plays, and religious pageants, or even new translations or versions of the text. Its purpose is, in Jung's classical formulation, to enable the reader to "dream the myth onwards and give it a modern dress" (Philipson, 1963, 62). Walter Wink elaborates on this approach in his *Transforming Bible Study: A Leader's Guide* (1989), integrating a Jungian hermeneutic method with classical biblical scholarship.

The presupposition of the method is that because "a living symbol expresses something that is not fully conscious, or able yet to become fully conscious" (Dallett, 1982, 174), the imagination, catalyzed by a text, is enlisted to search for the unconscious content the symbol may have evoked in the self. To do this, conscious thinking is not enough. What is required is a method involving fantasy (regarded by Peter Homans [1969, 345] as the primary psychological activity in Jung's psychological hermeneutic) and reduced ego functioning, so that the wisdom of the unconscious can come into play. As Jung observes, "often the hands know how to solve a riddle with which the intellect has wrestled in vain" (1953–1978, 8:180). From a psychological standpoint, something is "gained in translation" rather than lost, because each of the techniques employed represents a curiously discrete angle of vision that can perceive and draw things out of the text that other faculties and modes of expression fail to catch. The potter, the dancer, the storyteller, the musician, playwright, and preacher all come to the text with sui generis aptitudes and appetites that render specific dimensions of the text susceptible to their vision and interpretation. As a result of this active imaginal dialectic with the text, which Janet Dallett likens to the unremitting dialogue of Tevya with God in

Fiddler on the Roof (1982, 176), new dimensions of the text are uncon-
cealed and new depths of the text are realized in concrete form. In
many instances, as in the case of religious art, literature, liturgy, music,
or drama, it becomes the *primary* mediator of the meaning of the text,
even more than the text itself—"modern dress" in which the *mythos*
is clothed.

The goal of a psycho-hermeneutical approach is to integrate these
methods with the panoply of critical methods extant in the field, but at
the same time seek to bend the hermeneutical effort as a whole into the
service of the ultimate goal it serves from a Jungian perspective,
namely, to "create more and more consciousness." "As far as we can
discern," Jung writes, "the sole purpose of human existence is to kindle
a light in the darkness of mere being" (1963, 326).

Note

This essay, with some modifications, was published originally under the
title "Psychology, Hermeneutics, and the Bible," in *Jung and the Interpretation
of the Bible*, David L. Miller, ed. (New York: Continuum Publishing Company, 1995), 9–30, and is reprinted with permission.

References

Anderson, B. (1986). *Understanding the Old Testament* (4th ed.). Englewood
    Cliffs: Prentice Hall.
Brome, V. (1981). *Jung: Man and Myth*. New York: Atheneum.
Capps, D. (1981). *Biblical Approaches to Pastoral Counseling*. Philadelphia:
    Westminster.
Dallett, J. (1982). Active Imagination in Practice, *Jungian Analysis*, Murray
    Stein, ed. Boston: New Science Library, 173–191.
Delitzsch, F. (1867). *A System of Biblical Psychology*, A. E. Wallis, trans. Grand
    Rapids: Baker Book House, 1966.
Dittes, J. E. (1990). Analytical (Jungian) Psychology and Religion, *Dictionary
    of Care and Counseling*, Rodney J. Hunter, ed. Nashville: Abingdon.
Dourley, J. P. (1984). *The Illness That We Are: A Jungian Critique of Christian-
    ity*. Toronto: Inner City Books.
Edinger, E. F. (1986). *The Bible and the Psyche: Individuation Symbolism in the
    Old Testament*. Toronto: Inner City Books.
Halperin, D. J. (1993). *Seeking Ezekiel, Text and Psychology*. University Park:
    Pennsylvania State University Press.
Homans, P. (1969). Psychology and Hermeneutics: Jung's Contribution.
    Zygon, 4(4), 333–372.

Johnson, C. B. (1983). *The Psychology of Biblical Interpretation*. Grand Rapids: Zondervan.

Jung, C. G. (1953–1978). *The Collected Works of C. G. Jung*, R. F. C. Hull, trans. (Vols. 1–20). Princeton: Princeton University Press.

Jung, C. G. (1963). *Memories, Dreams, Reflections*, Aniela Jaffé, ed.; R. Winston & C. Winston, trans. New York: Pantheon.

Jung, C. G. (1971). Approaching the Unconscious, *Man and His Symbols*. New York: Doubleday.

Jung, C. G. (1975). *C. G. Jung Letters, 1951–1961*, G. Adler & A. Jaffé, eds.; R. F. C. Hull, trans. (Vol. 2). Princeton: Princeton University Press.

Jung, C. G. (1976). *The Visions Seminars* (2 vols.). Zurich: Spring Publications.

Jung, C. G. (1978). *Psychological Reflections*, Jolande Jacobi & R. F. C. Hull, eds. Bollingen Series 31. Princeton: Princeton University Press.

Jung, C. G. (1983). *The Zofingia Lectures*, William McGuire, ed. Princeton, NJ: Princeton University Press.

Jung, C. G. (1989). *Analytical Psychology: Notes of the Seminar Given in 1925 by C. G. Jung*, William McGuire, ed. Bollingen Series 99. Princeton: Princeton University Press.

Kelsey, M. (1968). *Dreams: The Dark Speech of the Spirit*. New York: Doubleday.

Kümmel, W. G. (1972). *The New Testament: The History of the Investigation of Its Problems*, S. MacLean Gilmour & Howard Clark Kee, trans. Nashville: Abingdon.

LaCocque, A., & LaCocque, P-E. (1990). *Jonah: A Psycho-Religious Approach to the Prophet* (Studies on Personalities of the Old Testament). Columbia: University of South Carolina Press.

Neumann, E. (1969). *Depth Psychology and a New Ethic*, Eugene Rolfe, trans. New York: Harper Torchbooks.

Oates, W. E. (1953). *The Bible in Pastoral Care*. Philadelphia: Westminster.

Philipson, M. (1963). *Outline of a Jungian Aesthetics*. Evanston: Northwestern University Press.

Philp, H. L. (1956). *Freud and Religious Belief*. New York: Pitman Publishing.

Pontifical Biblical Commission. (1994). The Interpretation of the Bible in the Church. *Catholic International*, 5(3), 109–147.

Robinson, H. W. (1946). The Psychology of Inspiration, *Inspiration and Revelation in the Old Testament*. Oxford: Clarendon Press.

Rollins, W. G. (1983). *Jung and the Bible*. Atlanta: John Knox Press.

Rollins, W. G. (1999). *Soul and Psyche: The Bible in Psychological Perspective*. Minneapolis: Fortress.

Sanday, W. (1911). *Personality in Christ and in Ourselves*. Oxford: Clarendon Press.

Sanford, J. (1968). *Dreams: God's Forgotten Language*. Philadelphia: Lippincott.

Sanford, J. (1974). *The Man Who Wrestled with God*. King of Prussia: Religious Publishing.

Sanford, J. (1985). *King Saul, The Tragic Hero*. New York: Paulist.

Scharfenberg, J. (1988). *Sigmund Freud and His Critique of Religion*. Philadelphia: Fortress.

Schwartz-Salant, N. (1987). Patriarchy in Transformation: Judaic, Christian, and Clinical Perspectives, *Jung's Challenge to Contemporary Religion*, Murray Stein & Robert L. Moore, eds. Wilmette: Chiron Publications, 41–71.

Schweitzer, A. (1948). *The Psychiatric Study of Jesus: Exposition and Criticism*, Charles R. Joy, trans. Boston: Beacon Press. First published in German in 1913.

Scroggs, R. (1982, Mar. 24). Psychology as a Tool to Interpret the Text. *Christian Century*, 335–338.

Stein, M. (1985). *Jung's Treatment of Christianity: The Psychotherapy of a Religious Tradition*. Wilmette: Chiron Publications.

Taylor, V. (1959). *The Person of Christ in New Testament Teaching*. London: Macmillan.

Theissen, G. (1987). *Psychological Aspects of Pauline Theology*, John P. Galvin, trans. Minneapolis: Fortress.

Wehr, G. (1988). *Jung: A Biography*, David M. Weeks, trans. Boston: Shambhala Publications.

Wink, W. (1973). *The Bible in Human Transformation: Towards a New Paradigm for Biblical Study*. Philadelphia: Fortress.

Wink, W. (1978). On Wrestling with God: Using Psychological Insights in Biblical Study. *Religion in Life*, 47, 136–147.

Wink, W. (1989). *Transforming Bible Study: A Leader's Guide*. Nashville: Abingdon.

Wise, C. A. (1956). *Psychiatry and the Bible*. New York: Harper & Bros.

Wuellner, W. (1987). Where Is Rhetorical Criticism Taking Us? *Catholic Biblical Quarterly*, 49, 448–463.

CHAPTER 5

THEISSEN'S INTEGRATION OF PSYCHOLOGY AND NEW TESTAMENT STUDIES: LEARNING THEORY, PSYCHODYNAMICS, AND COGNITIVE PSYCHOLOGY

Dieter Mitternacht

In 1983 Gerd Theissen embarked on a scholarly journey that had in fact been shunned almost completely by New Testament scholars in Germany for decades. Outside of Germany a number of efforts had been made to re-introduce psychology to New Testament studies, but scholars in Germany were scarcely affected.[1] When Theissen's *Psychological Aspects of Pauline Theology* (1983) was first published, some hoped it might be a turning point in the history of research (Leiner, 1995, 73), and some welcomed the study with enthusiasm.[2] In general skepticism prevailed, however, and except for students of Theissen's there have been only a few publications on psychological aspects by New Testament scholars in Germany during the two decades since. Theissen knew, of course, that establishing psychological exegesis would be an uphill struggle.[3] Perhaps he found the aggravation greater than expected, considering how little he has continued to pursue the path he himself staked out.

To be sure, Theissen remains fully committed to the historical-critical paradigm, and he offers only limited reflections on pathogenic or therapeutic aspects. Yet his commitment to using experience and understanding of human life and religion in his work with historical-critical findings and insights into early Christianity constitutes, in my view, his most important achievement. In its own right, *Psychological Aspects of Pauline Theology* is a therapeutic contribution to New Testament studies.

The Historical Backdrop

Psychological interpretations of biblical texts have a history that stretches from antiquity to modern times.[4] As part of the historical-critical enterprise that began with the Enlightenment, historical and psychological approaches to biblical texts treated biblical history as any other history and "biblical persons" as any other human beings. The endeavour blossomed and reached its peak at the beginning of the twentieth century in works of scholars such as Bousset, Deissmann, and Pfister.

At this time, especially in Germany, those in the field saw a growing denigration of the use of psychology in New Testament exegesis, instigated in part by two influential scholars, Karl Barth and Rudolph Bultmann (Niederwimmer, 1970, esp. 262f.). They articulated two major objections. First, there was the charge of reductionism, that is, that the psychological approach either blocks out the transcendent (God and revelation) to which the texts testify (Barth), or it immunizes against participation in what the texts really want to communicate (Bultmann). Second, there was the allegation that psychology assumed the function of a worldview that subsumed actual life in history under an all-encompassing psychological reading of world and man.

The latter criticism was considered especially harmful from an existentialist perspective, where the main concern of the New Testament is considered to be the individual and intimate encounter with history, because "in every word he [the individual] says about history he is saying something about himself" (Bultmann, 1958, 3). In Bultmann's view, psychological exegesis "quantitatively collects many new facts *out of* history, but learns nothing genuinely new *about* history and man." Bultmann asserts also that "so far as purely psychological facts of the past are the object of investigation, such a method is (for the psychological expert) quite correct. There remains, however, the question whether such a method reveals the essentials of history, really brings us face to face with history" (1958, 6).[5]

A Hermeneutical Approach

Aware of this milieu and determined to reinstate psychology among the historical tools of New Testament exegesis, Gerd Theissen conceived his careful approach to psychology and New Testament studies, determined to overcome the weaknesses of earlier attempts. What could be gained from psychological insights concerning the New Testament and early Christianity should not be easily wasted again, either by unwarranted psychological speculation or by interpretations that fall into the trap of a historical generalization.

Theissen's goal was a hermeneutical integration of three psychological models: learning theory, psychodynamics (Freud/Jung), and cognitive psychology. His basic premise was that every psychological model constitutes a historically conditioned self-interpretation. There is no absolute or exclusive representation of reality. Learning-theoretical models breathe Anglo-Saxon optimism, with its expectation of a successful command over the circumstances of life. Psychoanalytical models that view humans as limited by their collective or individual past reflect something of early twentieth-century European catastrophes. The interest in cognitive psychology corresponds to a renaissance of Enlightenment ideas, which in turn may be an effect of the economic and political stability between the 1950s and 1980s.

Notwithstanding these contingencies, Theissen asserts that modern psychological theories are suitable for the interpretation of ancient texts because of the interplay between the history of traditions and human psychology. Affinities are not so much proof of the idea of a universal human nature as of the fact that the cultural environment of Greco-Roman antiquity is the historical seedbed of modern psychological perceptions and that historical traditions provide a framework of possible models of human experience and behavior. This foundation becomes all the more obvious as one realizes that already in antiquity there existed psychological theories with affinities to our modern models. Critias' fragment (possibly from Euripides), for instance, seems to resound learning-theoretical ideas (Diels, 1912). In Plato we find an awareness of imitative learning (Laws, 887 d/e). Knowledge of the unconscious is found in Augustine's writings, in both the inward longing for God (Conf. 1:1) and the struggle with pre-Christian dreams (Conf. 10:30). Cognitive theories are prefigured in Epictetus, who states that not the things as such but our opinions of them govern our behavior and experiences regarding them (Theissen, 1983, 51–54).[6]

Using Psychological Models for Historical Research

The objective of Theissen's psychological exegesis is to describe and explain human behavior and experience in early Christianity. To that end he asserts five premises that justify a hermeneutical adaptation of the three psychological models: (1) Human experience and behavior are transmitted as interpretations of one's self-understanding, which in turn can be interpreted. (2) Human experience and behavior are historically conditioned, which means that their interpretation is based on interchanges between situation and tradition. (3) Human experience and behavior are objectified in texts as expressions and performances (prayer, intercession, thinking, interpretations, and evaluations). (4) The interpretation of human experience and behavior presupposes a pre-understanding of unity that is affirmed, a priori, by personal experience. Understanding, therefore, operates in a hermeneutical circle between part and whole. (5) Human experience and behavior are defined by content, as seen, for example in the fact that the *psychology of religion* is to be differentiated from *general psychology* in terms of its content (Theissen, 1983, 11–13).

Learning Theory

According to learning theory, religious experience and behavior are acquired socially, by way of *associative learning* (external and internal stimuli), *operative learning* (material, social, and symbolic reinforcers), and *imitative learning* (real and symbolic models). Although learning theory is akin to behaviorism (Watson, Skinner) in that it operates with stimuli, reinforcers, and models, it is also contrary to behaviorism in that it includes internal and symbolic stimuli, reinforcers, and models. According to Theissen, internal and symbolic stimuli, reinforcers, and models are indispensable to religious psychology, especially in biblical religion. Internal stimuli explain how an emancipation of religious experience and behavior from external stimuli (i.e., the image prohibition in the Hebrew Bible or the internalization of purity regulations by Jesus) can occur. In biblical religion we also find symbolic reinforcers such as the parousia, that is, a means of operative learning located completely in the future. And there is the symbolic model of Christ, reenacted by the real model Paul (2 Cor. 4:10). Inasmuch as real stimuli, reinforcers, and models can be internalized by the use of cognitive modification, they can also surface in a text and become available for a learning-theoretical analysis (Theissen, 1983, 16–20).

Psychodynamics

The recognition of an inner world of man, with depth dimensions that are hidden to the conscious mind, has resulted in theories about subliminal and repressing transformation processes of the unconscious. Changes in experience and behavior occur as the borderline between the conscious and the unconscious is narrowed. For Freud the unconscious contains dysfunctional traumata and fixations from early childhood experiences. It is like a swamp that needs to be dried up in order to reduce unconscious tension and attain constructive conscious behavior. The Jungian paradigm assumes a collective unconscious, with genetically inherited patterns of behavior and experience (archetypes) that express themselves in motifs, pictures, and symbols. These patterns constitute constructive resources; the unconscious is perceived as a life-giving well, which if discovered enables a person to reconnect and thus cope with the external world.

Freudian and Jungian perspectives would seem to be in opposition with one other. Theissen agues, however, that if one accepts their hermeneutical character, they can be united—that is, if one accepts, on the one hand, that archetypes are affected by historical processes, shaped, modified, and prone to hermeneutical interchange, and on the other that early childhood impressions do not suffice to explain religious experience and behavior (as Freud himself recognized) (Theissen, 1983, 29). Conflict symbolism (Freud) and goal-oriented symbolism (Jung) are thus seen to complement each other (Theissen, 1983, 20–32).

The concept of the Self, the uniquely human aspect of the psyche in which consciousness is able to distinguish itself from the unconscious, may serve as an illustration. For Jung, the Self (for which, in Jungian psychology, Christ is a symbol) is an archetype that instigates the aspiration for wholeness and self-realization, the longing for oneness, and the integration of conscious and unconscious. Thus the Self represents the subjugation of basic human conflicts, such as rebellious autonomy versus dependence, male versus female, power versus powerlessness, the ideal self versus the shadow/inferior self. If viewed as something that has come about historically, the symbol can represent a variety of psychic factors (Theissen, 1983, 34).

According to Theissen, Jung's identification of Christ as a symbol of the Self provides the best explanation so far for a crucial historical problem within early Christianity, namely, how the perception of the historical Jesus could be transformed into that of the preexistent divine Christ within such an astonishingly short time (Theissen, 1983, 25). The concept makes plausible how an image of Self-realization could generate an experience of a preexistent being and how impulses from the unconscious could reinforce a learning-theoretical process.

Freud's attribution of religious experience and behavior to parental impression and his definition of symbols as symptoms of repression require hermeneutical modification as proposed by Ricoeur (1969, 1974), Scharfenberg (1968, 1980), and others. Theissen affirms

Scharfenberg's assertion regarding symbols: "It is not repression which occasions the necessity of symbolization, but refraining from using symbols which causes repression" (1987, 23). Symbols as a language of the unconscious are not only subjected to interpretation but are themselves interpretations. They do not simply emerge from the innermost dynamics of the psyche but are cognitive structures that embrace cultural elements and then again influence psychological processes. In other words, religious symbols are capable of both revealing deeply rooted conflicts within an atmosphere of hope and presupposing already overcome conflicts that have taken shape as archetypical structures.

Cognitive Psychology

Cognitive psychology differs from the other models in that it focuses on the human cognitive activity of structuring and interpreting one's world. In order to avoid chaos, man structures his world topically (close–far, approachable–inapproachable) and dynamically (decreasing and increasing tension, reducing and inducing cognitive dissonance). Man is also conscious of the fact that he will never fathom the depths of reality, and that is where religion comes in. In the New Testament we can observe how depth dimensions are introduced into present time. The creation myth and final judgment in the remoteness of time are materialized in the present through the second Adam. Again, through norms that define the status quo and regulatory functions such as forgiveness of sins, penitence, and expiation rites, religion helps us structure a dynamic balance in life. The task of religion consists of providing hope and meaning even for the most extreme situations (such as terminal illness) (Theissen, 1983, 38–43).

How then do human beings go about structuring their "interpreted world"? Theissen considers four techniques of interpretation as the most relevant for the analysis of religious texts (akin to the psychodynamic defense mechanisms of projection, sublimation, rationalization, and identification): causal attribution, anticipation (decision making about future conduct), self-esteem, and role adoption.

As we attribute causes to experiences and behaviors that we observe, we seek to determine our own behavioral options and conditions. Attributions of cause are not predetermined but depend on our perceptions of reality. These perceptions change; in fact, they can be altered by religion to such a degree that one causal attribution is replaced by quite a different one. That is why, for instance, Paul can state in Romans 7:17: "It is not me who does it, but sin that dwells in me"; or in Galatians 2:20: "I live, yet not I, but Christ lives in me."

In pluralistic societies (and the Roman-Hellenistic society may well have been the first pluralistic society in the world), different normative systems exist side by side. A person may find herself challenged by her convictions and anticipations to question whether she should comply with the normative system to which she usually adheres. In anticipation of the ramifications, she may decide to include the normative system among the pros and cons of her decision. This is what Theissen (leaning on Thomae) calls a change from regular normative decision making to existential decision making. Again Theissen argues that the relevance for New Testament studies can be illustrated by Paul, who inaugurates a paradigmatic transition from normative to existential decision making.

Self-esteem increases if failure can be attributed to external instead of internal causes (which exemplifies the interdependence with causal attribution and anticipation). Self-esteem is always determined through comparison with others, be it real people or ideal role models of a certain culture. Religions can provide means to overcome lack of self-esteem, for instance, by negating the self as an illusion (Buddhism) or by attributing absolute value to every human being (for example, the equal wages to the laborers in the vineyard [Matt. 20:1–16] or the justification by grace that excludes any boasting of one's achievements).

Ultimately, religion's gift of a holistic, complete self-understanding and self-esteem, such as "child of God" or "nomad in search for the promised land," can be realized through role adoption. Sundén (1959) has demonstrated that as one assumes a certain role, one's perception of oneself and the world is restructured. Theissen asserts that Sundén's role theory overcomes the false antithesis of tradition and experience. Religious traditions define the spectrum of possible religious experiences by offering religious roles. Again, Paul provides ample information about himself to illustrate role adoption. In relation to his tradition, he defines himself in terms of Adam and Moses in the negative, Abraham and Christ in the positive (Theissen, 1983, 44–49).

Evolutionary Stratification and Transcendence

Theissen's hermeneutical program culminates in an evolutionary integration of the three psychological models. The models, he suggests, correspond to different stages of human development. Psychoanalysis traces archaic aspects of human behavior and experience and perceives religion in terms of an interaction with genetic, unconscious archaisms. The learning-theoretical model investigates higher levels of interactions between individual and society. Here religion appears as the consequence of social learning. The highest and most recent form of psychological evolution corresponds to the cognitive integration of life circumstances into an interpreted world by means of an interaction with archaisms and societal influences. Religion functions as the regulatory system in this process, aspiring to a balance between the different layers of man's psyche (Theissen, 1983, 59–61).

Thus, man's perception is constantly involved in a process of adapting to the reality that surrounds him, storing archaic structures inside himself next to new and possibly competing structures. However, any structure of adaptation to reality is but one example of a variety of possible perceptions. Because of man's awareness of the discrepancy between his ability to perceive and the world "in itself," there will always be a need for a concept of the inaccessible, the unconscious. This is the *conditio humana*.

In his evolutionary development man moves with ever-changing structures of adaptation toward a reality that is as yet undefined, a premonition of the "wholly other."[7] The unconscious reiterates previous evolutionary phases that find themselves in an ongoing struggle with new perceptions of reality. Through a process of mutation and selection, these structures are continually refined as they interact with outside "objective" powers of reality. Similarly, we find a conscious (learning-theoretical) selection in the act of conversion, in identity crises, in rejections of philosophies of life. Behind this pressure of selection, this restriction of man's own will, there is an *ultimate reality*, the "creator" of the conditions of our lives. Everything inside man partakes in the experiment of adaptation. And so the scholar arrives at the "unscientific" question: "Is it unjustified to call this reality 'God'?" (Theissen, 1983, 65).[8]

Identifying Psychic Processes in Texts

Besides more or less straightforward *descriptive* and *comparative* ways of identifying psychological processes in texts, Theissen proposes that even *analytical* insights can be gained from texts. Presupposing that religious symbols make unconscious elements accessible to consciousness, we find six kinds of expressions with a semantic stratification of *conscious-near* and *conscious-far* layers that reveal unconscious dynamics: metaphors, exegeses, homologies, motif displacements, contradictions, and exaggerations.[9] Two examples suffice to illustrate the procedure. *Metaphors* combine unconscious image-provision with conscious image-reception. For instance, when God is addressed as father, the conscious intention is to make a statement about God. Yet whenever the metaphor is invoked, it also arouses associations from childhood. These associations can be ascertained in the connotations of the whole word field. *Exegeses* are texts that interpret other texts. A comparison of the two always reveals something unconscious about the interpreter, who intends simply to reproduce the meaning of the text. Thus, when Paul presents his interpretation of the veil of Moses in 2 Corinthians 3:6–18, he imports his ambivalence toward Moses into the Old Testament text, distancing himself from Moses on the one hand and making him a model for conversion on the other (Theissen, 1983, 55–58).

Finally, Theissen warns against interpreting psychological phenomena in isolation. They are always parts of wholes, that is, of complete texts, authors' complete works, or a whole group's literary assets. The decisive criterion of a hermeneutically oriented psychological exegesis is not the coherence of theories (theories may even have to be adjusted) but the compatibility of a single insight with the text as a whole. But the criterion of "compatibility of the singular with the whole" must not be misunderstood as something like a private, eclectic impression; rather, it is the disciplined commitment to the sources.

With this impressive battery of hermeneutical reflections, Theissen proceeds to apply his perspectives to five sets of Pauline texts. The titles of the sets epitomize his findings. First set: "The Secrets of the Heart: The Disclosure of Unconscious Motives through Pauline Theology" (1 Cor. 4:1–5; Rom. 2:16; 1 Cor. 14:20–25). Second set: "The Veil of Moses and the Unconscious Aspects of Law" (2 Cor. 3:4–4:6). Theissen interprets the unveiling as the process of stripping the normative system of its holiness and revealing its aggressive power. Third set: "Law and Sin: Raising the Conflict to Consciousness According to Romans 7:7–23" (Rom. 7, 8). The unconscious rebellion of the *sarx* against the law is made conscious. It was hidden before, because the *sarx* employed the most holy norms of life and fooled and threatened man with them. Fourth set: "Glossolalia—Language of the Unconscious?" (1 Cor. 12–14). Fifth set: "Wisdom for the Perfect as Higher Consciousness" (1 Cor. 2:6–16).

Theissen's exegetical procedure is consistently threefold and fully in accord with his hermeneutical program. Every text is interpreted according to synchronic text analyses, diachronic tradition analyses, and a threefold psychological analysis, along the models discussed earlier. One of the applications looks at Romans 7:7–23, as follows.

The termination of decades-long attempts to interpret Romans 7 psychologically, among German exegetes at least,[10] is clearly linked to W. G. Kümmel's *Röm 7 und die Bekehrung des Paulus* from 1929 (reprinted as Kümmel, 1974). Kümmel's three major arguments against psychological interpretations were as follows: (1) the "I" of the chapter is rhetorical-fictitious; (2) Romans 7:9 can only be nonbiographical; and (3) the contradiction between (the autobiographical) Philippians 3:6 and Romans 7:7 confirms arguments (1) and (2). Kümmel's conclusion: Romans 7 is neither personal-biographical nor typical but theoretical.

In Theissen's judgment, Kümmel's exegetical analysis of the background material regarding the use of "I" is not convincing. His own analysis of the material leads him to the conclusion that the "I" of Romans 7 combines personal (autobiographical) and typical qualities, analogous to the "I" in the psalms of the Old Testament or the psalms of Qumran, and in line with role adoption theories. In fact, he states emphatically with respect to Romans 7 and 8: "If any Pauline texts can be interpreted psychologically, it is these chapters" (Theissen, 1987, 222).

Text and Tradition Analyses

Theissen follows a standard interpretation of the context of chapters 6 and 7. The chapters show Paul's concern for rebutting the accusation of anomism (Rom. 6:1, 6:15, and 7:7 resound the explicit accusation of 3:8). The images of funeral (6.1–14), power exchange (6:15–23), and marriage (7:1–6) parallel the conditions before and after conversion as a break with the past and the transposition of authorities. Theissen does not consider Romans 7:7ff. to be a diversion from but rather a natural continuation of the argument against antinomism, placing *anomia* (lawlessness) semantically together with *nomos* (law) and against *charis* (grace) and *dikaiosune* (righteousness). On the question of the transition from chapter 7 to chapter 8, he sides with Kümmel and Althaus against Cranfield and Dunn and opts for a shift from the old to the new life.[11]

In Romans 7:7–23 Theissen sees Paul constructing his apology for the law by correcting a dualistic antagonistic model (law versus sin and a *sarx*-dominated ego) with a threefold model, where law, sin, and the human ego interrelate closely. To achieve this, Paul divides the function of the law in two: a bright law of God that serves the mind, and a dark, intractable law of the members. Between the two is the human ego. The initially clear opposition is replaced by a complicated model of interactions, with the effect that the *nomos* (law), despite its incongruity with *epithumia* (desire), kindles covetousness.

In light of the threefold pattern, the anthropological-theological conceptions of Paul parallel modern psychoanalytical models of the psyche. Further, the parallelism is historically determined: Paul's argument is based not on the law's nature but on its function at a particular point in time. Likewise, man's predicament is rooted not only in man's nature but in his culture. In other words, Paul's perception of the conflict is determined by cognitive restructuring (Theissen, 1983, 193).

Learning Theoretical Aspects: The Law as a Stimulus of Sin

"Apart from the law sin is dead" (Rom. 7:8). With this assertion Paul in fact contradicts psychoanalytical impulse theory. The power of sin is not autochthonous, that is, an original inhabitant of the flesh, nor a hypostasis that replaces the ego, but a socioculturally embraced norm; the concept of sin presupposes a norm. In Theissen's view, it may well have been Paul's great achievement to discover that there is no innate evil power and that the conflict is not between nature (*sarx*) (flesh) and norm but between different aspects of the same historically conditioned normative system: *nomos* (law) as *pneuma* (spirit) and *nomos* (law) as *gramma* (letter).[12] Recognizing the dichotomy, Paul finds himself exposed to contradictory stimuli, reinforcers, and models. The holy and good law promises life but also constantly poses the death threat, thus psychologically constituting an *Angstauslöser* (anxiety-triggering entity) for Paul (Theissen, 1983, 227).

Christ becomes Paul's learning model to overcome the angst, not by denying the threat but—as in implosion therapy—by overdoing it for one last time. The crucified Christ embraces the wrath of God once and for all. In the Christ event, fear of the threatening law evaporates by means of the symbolic participation in his crucifixion (Gal. 2:19). Man participates in the condemnation of Christ, and thus his own fear of condemnation is overcome. As a result, Paul can now speak of the demands of God without fear. Not norms but the loving fellowship with transgressors of norms (Gal. 6:1) has become the imperative. This new relationship to normative systems is, in Theissen's view, one of the most valuable contents of the New Testament (1983, 228–230).

Psychodynamic Aspects: The Unconscious Conflict with the Law

If, as Theissen argues, both Romans 7:7ff. and Philippians 3:6 are authentic references to the pre-Christian Paul, we seem to be faced with a logical contradiction. In the Romans passage Paul depicts the "I" as a wretched man, one suffering under the law. In the letter to the Philippians he looks back on his former life as a Pharisee with the words "as to righteousness under the law blameless." What appears to be a logical contradiction may dissolve in the recognition that the Philippians passage reflects the consciousness of the pre-Christian Paul, whereas the description in Romans refers to an unconscious conflict of which Paul the Pharisee wasn't consciously aware.

Philippians 3:6 is confirmed by Galatians 1:13–14. When Paul looks back on his life as a Pharisee, he emphasizes the zeal with which he identified and fought the enemies of his own group. The picture of a person marked by over-identification and aggression emerges. The impression is further strengthened by Paul's general criticism of Jewish over-identification with the law in Romans 2:17–23. Again, at first sight there seems to be a contradiction. Although Philippians 3.6 contains an emphatic assertion of righteousness under the law, in Romans 2.21ff. the one who has his pride in the law is accused in no uncertain terms of breaking the law; the passage as a whole amounts, in fact, to an unjustified caricature (Theissen, 1983, 241). However, the two passages coincide if one recognizes that Paul the Pharisee shares the outlook on life under the law of the Jews of Romans 2:17ff.; both boast in the law and lack awareness of breach of law (Theissen, 1983, 242). Recognition of the inability to comply with the requirements of the law has been repressed in the pride of over-identification. Romans 7:7ff. differs from Philippians 3:6 and Romans 2:17–20 in that now the same life period is portrayed in light of the knowledge of Christ. Theissen writes, "the thesis defended here, therefore, is that Phil. 3:4–6 reflects the consciousness of the pre-Christian Paul, while Rom. 7 depicts a conflict that was unconscious at the time, one of which Paul became conscious only later" (1987, 233).

Cognitive Aspects: Role Adoption and Conflict Structuring

Role theory in religion psychology has shown that as people identify with traditional roles, their cognition of themselves is restructured. The role adopted and personal experience can never agree completely.

Yet tensions that arise from this disjunction are not perceived to be a problem but to provide new opportunities for self-perception.

These insights seem applicable to Paul's use of the Adam figure in Romans 7. To interpret his conflict with the law, Paul lets his "I" in Romans 7:7 adopt the role of Adam. Thus, even though Adam never becomes the subject of 7:7–13, he still functions as the model for Paul's interpretation of conflict with the law. Paul could have never said of himself, "I was once alive apart from the law" (7:9). And of Adam it could not have been said that he had broken the Decalogue from Sinai. Through the process of role adoption, seemingly contradictory conditions appear plausible.

In support of this contention of irrational reinterpretation activity, Theissen lists three other cases in Paul's letters that seem to indicate role adoption. The first case is Galatians 1:15, where Paul, contrary to his autobiography, identifies himself with the servant of God, who claims with Isaiah 49:1: "The Lord called me from the womb." Similarly in Philippians 3:12ff. he adopts the role of an athlete (cf. 1 Cor. 9:24–27), asserting that, like a dedicated competitor, he would not look back and was in fact "forgetting what lies behind," although of course he never forgot his Jewish heritage and never abandoned his roots. Third, in 1 Corinthians 9:9–23, Paul assumes the role of Christ in a way that does not only cause tension with his autobiographical reality but leads into obvious contradiction. Like Christ (Phil. 2:7), he became a slave. Like Christ, he put himself under the law (Gal. 4:4), and so forth. Again the role adoption creates tension with autobiographical facts. How could Paul have been able to become a Jew for the Jews—he who was circumcised on the eighth day, a Hebrew of Hebrews (Phil. 3:5; cf. 1 Cor. 11:22)? That which he was by birth he could not become (Theissen, 1983, 254–256).

Having thus established the probability of autobiographically fragile and even contradictory identifications through role adoptions, Theissen asserts that there is no good reason not to accept that the same could occur in Romans 7. The subject of the "I" includes Paul, but the model of the "I" is Adam—yet Adam also is reinterpreted in light of Paul's own conflict with the law.

Conclusion

Theissen's hermeneutical psychology of biblical religion constitutes an impressive demonstration of how to gain a multitude of psychological insights into biblical texts within their historical setting. The

hermeneutical adaptation and mixing together of Freudian and Jungian perspectives and the evolutionary integration of different psychological models into a dynamic and comprehensive whole seem both
fascinating and plausible. Because my field is New Testament studies
and not psychology, I leave it to others to decide whether the hermeneutical intermingling of what, from traditional vantage points, seem
to be contradictory models is theoretically permissible. Whether one
can in fact identify Pauline expressions such as "the hidden parts of
man" or "the veil" to represent what the psychological analyst calls the
unconscious will continues to be a matter of dispute among scholars.
I am convinced, however, that Theissen's assertion that there is no
direct knowledge of psychic processes and that every model is historically conditioned and thus hermeneutically dynamic is valid. If we
accept this presupposition, it would seem that the relationship between
then and now, tradition and experience, history and nature becomes
less a matter of terminology and more one of phenomenology.

At times the temptation of finding "one too many" historical analo-
gies seems to haunt Theissen, as in the case of scapegoat symbolism.[13]
The act of projecting on a scapegoat is an unconscious activity that
psychological analysis aims at dispersing. Successful analysis implies
getting rid of the projection. Paul, however, must have taken the
image of the scapegoat as a sacrificial representation of Christ. Trying
to get rid of the projection would therefore for Paul have meant to
cease aspiring to the atonement of Christ. Similarly the identification
of Christ as a symbol not only of the Self but also of "the super-ego and
the id . . . , the ideal ego and its shadow" (Theissen, 1987, 114) seems
to strain the imagery beyond reasonable limits (Theissen, 1983, 81).[14]

Theissen's psychological exegesis generally presupposes descriptive textual analysis. The text expresses what the author wishes to
convey, and for Theissen that is all there is to look for at the textual
level. This presupposition is apparent from his consistent threefold
procedure: text analysis, tradition analysis, and then psychological
analysis (even though he may assert that tradition analysis can really
be a part of the cognitive psychological analysis) (Theissen, 1983, 204).
Somewhat troubling is the fact that descriptive textual analyses are
influenced by the perspectives and presuppositions of the one doing the
analysis, wherefore psychological insights drawn may be considered
invalid had a different textual analysis been done. Thus, for instance,
Paul's identification with the servant of Isaiah 49:1 in Galatians 1:15,
where he claims that "the Lord called me from the womb," is taken
by Theissen to exemplify how role adoption can create tension with

autobiographical reality. This assertion, however, is based on Theissen's reading of the text that Paul in fact could not conceive of his calling as being from his mother's womb. Other exegetes have suggested otherwise. Also, the assertion that the addressees of Romans 2:17ff. were Jews has recently been challenged in a dissertation from Lund University. According to this textual analysis, the interlocutor of Galatians 2:17–29 is not a Jew but a Gentile Christ-believer who contemplates circumcision and "wants to call himself a Jew" (Thorsteinsson, 2003, 196–211). Should this "descriptive" text analysis prevail (which only time can tell), the passage will not yield the psychological insights Theissen has drawn from it.

Theissen does not engage in text-pragmatic analyses, communication psychology, analyses of rhetorical strategy, and the like. He does not really seem concerned with the historical and psychological contingencies of each letter's individual communication situation. What concerns him is the lasting impact of the theological content of what is being articulated. And in this concern he is unveiling with great skill the luminous psychological beauty of Pauline theology.

Notes

1. To the evidence of change in the late 1960s and early 1970s gathered in Rollins (1999) one should add Niederwimmer (1968 and 1970, 257–272). Because the purpose of this introduction is to sketch the climate surrounding Theissen's work, my focus in this chapter refers primarily to the situation in Germany.

2. The English edition was published in 1987, and a Japanese edition in 1991. Rebell (1986) appeared soon after the first edition of Thiessen. See, for instance, Luz (1985, 186–189, 187): "Ich gestehe, daß mich in den letzten Jahren selten ein Buch so fasziniert hat wie dieses" (I have to say that in the last ten years rarely has a book fascinated me as much as this).

3. Leiner (1995, 74). Theissen's colleague in Heidelberg, Klaus Berger (1991, 18), acknowledged especially the value of Theissen's exhaustive introductory treatment of the different psychological models: "eine vorzügliche Einleitung" (an excellent introduction). He did, however, remain skeptical of the work, charging it with covering up the historical truth rather than enlightening it (1991, 19). In Berger's view, the social-psychological aspects of Theissen's work were the most promising. My own dissertation (Mitternacht, 1999) was inspired in part by Theissen's work, even though the communication-psychological approach I apply has little affinity with the approaches developed by Theissen.

4. Convenient overviews of the history of psychological interpretation can be found in Leiner (1995, 41–76) and Rollins (1999, 1–87). For a description

of the different methodological dimensions of psychological interpretation, see Kille (2001, 5–37).

5. The use of Heidegger's philosophical anthropology by Bultmann was of course no less a generalization than the one he opposes (see Berger, 1991, 19).

6. Cf. Siebeck (1880–1884), which demonstrates the psychological awareness of ancient writers.

7. At this point Theissen's ideas touch Ricoeur's perception of religious symbols as both archaeological and teleological (cf. Ricoeur, 1969, 470ff.). Whereas psychoanalysis sheds light on the archaeological, Hegelian theories are used to explain the teleological. Theissen differs from Ricoeur in that he replaces the Hegelian philosophy with evolutionism (Theissen, 1983, 63 n. 61).

8. Theissen has further elaborated on the role of religion in the evolutionary "experiment" man (1984).

9. Cf. Berger's identification of three levels of perception (Berger, 1991, 123).

10. Cf. Packer (1964, 621–626), which is convinced Paul is describing his own experience. See also Buber (1950, 150), which considers Rom. 7 to be "processed memory" ("verarbeitete Erinnerung").

11. Kümmel (1974, 104–110); Althaus (1951, 27–30); Theissen (1983, 185–186); Cranfield (1975, 344–347, 355ff.); Dunn (1975, 257–273).

12. The idea that there is no covetousness without a law that says "You shall not covet" is not original to Paul. Similar insights can be found in the works of Euripides, Ovid, and also Judaism (Theissen, 1983, 225).

13. Pointed out correctly in Neidhart (1985, 79–81, 81).

14. Similarly Rollins (1990, 154–156).

References

Althaus, P. (1951). *Paulus und Luther über den Menschen. Ein Vergleich.* Gütersloh: Bertelsmann.

Berger, K. (1991). *Historische Psychologie des Neuen Testaments.* Stuttgart: Verlag Katholisches Bibelwerk GmbH.

Buber, M. (1950). *Zwei Glaubensweisen.* Zürich: Gütersloher Verlagshaus.

Bultmann, R. (1958). *Jesus and the Word.* New York: Charles Scribner's Sons.

Cranfield, C. E. B. (1975). *Romans.* ICC. Edinburgh: T&T Clark.

Diels, H. (1912). *Die Fragmente der Vorsokratiker II.* Berlin.

Dunn, J. D. G. (1975). Romans 7:14–25 in the Theology of Paul. *Theologische Literaturzeitung, 31,* 257–273.

Kille, D. A. (2001). *Psychological Biblical Criticism.* Minneapolis: Fortress.

Kümmel, W. (1974). Röm 7 und die Bekehrung des Paulus. *Theologische Beiträge 53.* München: Kaiser Verlag.

Leiner, M. (1995). *Psychologie und Exegese: Grundfragen einer textpsychologischen Exegese des Neuen Testaments.* Gütersloh: Kaiser/Gütersloher Verlagshaus.

Luz, U. (1985). Review of Theissen, Gerd, *Psychologische Aspekte paulinischer Theologie*. *Theologische Literaturzeitung, 110,* 186–189.

Mitternacht, D. (1999). *Forum für Sprachlose. Eine kommunikationspsychologische und epistolär-rhetorische Untersuchung des Galaterbriefs.* Stockholm: Almqvist & Wiksell.

Neidhart, W. (1985). Review of Theissen, G., *Psychologische Aspekte paulinischer Theologie*. *Theologische Zeitschrift, 41,* 79–81.

Niederwimmer, K. (1968). *Jesus.* Göttingen: Vandenhoeck & Ruprecht.

Niederwimmer, K. (1970). Tiefenpsychologie und Exegese. *Wege zum Menschen, 22,* 257–272.

Packer, J. I. (1964). The Wretched Man in Romans 7. *Studia Evangelica, 2,* 621–626.

Rebell, W. (1986). *Gehorsam und Unabhängigkeit. Eine sozialpsychologische Studie zu Paulus.* München: Chr. Kaiser Verlag.

Ricoeur, P. (1969). *Die Interpretation. Ein Versuch über Freud.* Frankfurt: Suhrkamp Verlag.

Ricoeur, P. (1974). *Hermeneutik und Psychoanalyse.* München: Koesel Verlag.

Rollins, W. G. (1990). Review of Theissen, G., *Psychological Aspects of Pauline Theology. Journal of Biblical Literature, 109,* 154–56.

Rollins, W. G. (1999). *Soul and Psyche: The Bible in Psychological Perspective.* Minneapolis: Fortress.

Scharfenberg, J. (1968). *Sigmund Freud und seine Religionskritik als Herausforderung für den christlichen Glauben.* Göttingen: Vandenhoeck & Ruprecht.

Scharfenberg, J. (1980). *Mit Symbolen leben.* Olten: Vandenhoeck & Ruprecht.

Siebeck, H. (1880–1884). *Geschichte der Psychologie,* 2 vols. Gotha.

Sundén, H. (1959). *Religionen och rollerna. Ett psykologiskt studium av fromheten.* Stockholm: Diakonistyrelsen.

Theissen, G. (1983). *Psychologische Aspekte paulinischer Theologie.* Göttingen: Vandenhoeck & Ruprecht.

Theissen, G. (1984). *Biblischer Glaube in evolutionärer Sicht.* München: Chr. Kaiser Verlag.

Theissen, G. (1987). *Psychological Aspects of Pauline Theology,* John P. Galvin, trans. Philadelphia: Fortress.

Thorsteinsson, R. (2003). *Paul's Interlocutor in Romans 2: Function and Identity in the Context of Ancient Epistolography.* Stockholm: Almqvist & Wiksell.

CHAPTER 6

Developmental Psychology in Biblical Studies

Lyn M. Bechtel

Developmental Theory

Human development is an unfolding process of psychological and physical growth during the course of a lifetime. It is divided into chronological stages of transformation, which are more or less stable and patterned, so that an enduring system can generally be observed (see Erikson, 1963, 1968, 1979a, 1979b; Baldwin, 1966; Cole & Cole, 1989). Between each pair of stages is a period of transition or flux, when one stage has disintegrated and the new stage is not firmly in place (see Lifton, 1976). During the twentieth century, developmental theories became numerous, yet adherents to all the major theoretical approaches refer to the same five stages—infancy, early childhood, middle childhood, adolescence, and adulthood. During these stages, the brain has the capacity for increasingly complex thinking, but only because there is a slow building up of cognitive and social learning, acquired as children gradually piece together a deeper understanding of the world and their place in it. This accretion forms the foundation of adult maturation. The importance of infancy and childhood in shaping later behavior cannot be overemphasized.

In general, psychoanalytic theory must be used with great care in biblical studies, because it is based on the behavioral tendencies of modern Western individual-oriented people whose assumptions and circumstances are very different from those that belonged to members

of ancient Middle Eastern societies. However, because developmental
theory is based on careful observation of the genetic program locked
into the cells of each human as well as of forces in the external environment, it has a universal quality that makes it particularly appropriate for use in biblical interpretation. It can allow the text to speak in
ways that have largely gone unobserved in past interpretation.

Infancy

From birth infants are biologically ready to experience the fundamental human sensory capacities (visual, auditory, olfactory, gustatory, and tactile), but they are dependent on the environment to provide their basic necessities, particularly nutritional needs, and the
optimal conditions for development and growth. Thus, Erikson (1968)
identifies infancy as the period of trust or mistrust of others.

Early Childhood

The onset of walking and increased mobility occurs in early childhood. It is a time of exploration and development of a sense of autonomy (Erikson, 1968). During this period children are permitted to
make simple choices, so initial socialization focuses on a combination
of acceptable behavior and restrictions on behavior that is undesirable
at this stage of life. Much significant learning occurs at this time, with
the beginning of vocalization, language comprehension, speech development, and learning to interact and relate in order to eventually
acquire a social identity. Language is one of the chief agents of cognitive development and reasoning (Erikson, 1979a).

Middle Childhood

Middle childhood propels children into new activities and contexts
in which they learn to be competent and effective at activities valued
by adults. There is declining egocentrism, an expansion of the social
environment and perspective, and integration into new peer groups
along with developing friendships and more awareness of sexual difference. With increased capacity for perspective taking, observation,
and reasoning, a child during this period develops an important cognitive knowledge base (Erikson, 1979a).

Adolescence

According to Jung (1968), any confining pattern of existence or
state of mind that is too immature, fixed, or final discloses a need for

psychological transformation. Once there is an awareness of this need, submission to the process of change and symbolic death of the old way of thinking are essential, and a new, changed way of thinking can then begin. Because adolescence is a period of heightened instability and emotional conflict, brought on by biological maturation and fundamental changes in the cognitive process, it is a time for important psychological transformation. Puberty transforms the child from a state of physical immaturity to one in which there is biological maturity and the capacity for sexual reproduction. These physical changes create profound adjustment demands as young people come to terms with sexual maturity and the need to adapt to adult roles (see Dragastin & Elder, 1973).

Adolescence is also is a period of integration (Erikson, 1968). If a healthy adult personality is to result, the adolescent's fundamental task is the process of identity formation, which requires the integration of learning from the experiences of the previous three stages. For the first time, newly acquired cognitive skills and social experiences make it possible for young people to sort through and synthesize their childhood identifications in order to construct a more mature thinking pattern with increasingly complex reasoning, a multifaceted perception of right and wrong, and the ability to examine the basis for moral principles (see Cole & Cole, 1989, 584). This process contributes to an integrated adult sense of identity, as an individual who is part of a social group and interdependent (Erikson, 1979b). However, two of the cognitive characteristics of adolescents are idealism and dualistic thinking (see Flavell, 1982, 1985).

If any of the previous stages have been skipped, adolescents may remain in an immature thinking pattern and may suffer from identity confusion. They can become confused about who they are and what they want to do in life. Those who suffer from identity confusion often take out their frustrations on others through antisocial or criminal behavior (see Cole & Cole, 1989, 585).

The transition between adolescence and adulthood is well marked with profound changes. In many societies it coincides with marriage, the adoption of adult roles, and work, which is a vital factor in making the transition into adult responsibility and status (see Smelser & Erikson, 1980).

Adulthood

Not until the twentieth century did the period of adulthood begin to command the attention that previously had been devoted to infancy, childhood, and adolescence. In early adulthood, people find an intimate life companion or they risk loneliness and isolation. In middle age, they must be productive in their work and willing to raise the next generation or they risk stagnation and regression into self-centeredness. In old age, they try to make sense of their prior experiences and to assure themselves that their lives have been meaningful or they despair over their unaccomplished goals and ill-spent lives. Although a mature understanding of life is an ongoing process, it is grounded in the slow accumulation of the cognitive and social learning acquired in infancy, childhood, and adolescence (see Neugarten, 1968; Erikson, 1978; Hareven, 1982; Erikson, Erikson, & Kivnick, 1986).

Developmental Theory and Genesis 2-4

Most interpretations of the Genesis 2:4b–3.24 myth are variations on the "sin and fall" of humanity, in which the human is assumed to be created as a fully grown adult. In that respect and many others, the interpretation does not fit reality. "Sin and fall," however, may not be the most convincing and certainly not the only interpretation. The developmental character of Genesis 1 should point to the interpretation of Genesis 2–4. If Genesis 2–4 is interpreted as a portrayal of the stages of human maturation, the story reveals a very sophisticated and multifaceted understanding of life. Humans go from being immature, infertile, dependent infants (2:7–9) and children (2:16–23), to increasingly independent adolescents (3:1–19), and finally to maturing, fertile, interdependent adults (4:1–16).[1] The characters should grow out of their immature understanding of life in the childhood world of the garden and into a mature discernment and acceptance of life in the adult world. Genesis 4:1–16 deals with one of the pitfalls of adult maturation—overcoming self-centeredness and threatened egotistic reactions. The four developmental stages are differentiated by three literary transitions that separate infancy from childhood (2:10–15), childhood from adolescence (2:24–25), and adolescence from adulthood (3:20–24). These literary transitions foreshadow the essential characteristics of adulthood. The three transitions and four developmental stages make human maturation resemble a seven-day week in which days are differentiated yet one day flows seamlessly into the next. A brief introduction (2:4b–6) lays out the time before birth of humans, and we see the change from infertility to fertility that exemplifies the natural world and foreshadows the human process in adolescence.[2] In what follows, I give a brief description of the creation myth interpreted, by drawing on developmental theory and general psychological insights.

Infancy

In the story of human development, the human begins as an infant. An important clue indicating that the biblical characters are infants and children is found in Genesis 2:25, when, according to the text, "the two of them are naked and not ashamed of themselves."[3] Infancy and childhood are the only time people are publicly naked and not ashamed because they have not developed enough self-consciousness to stimulate shame.[4]

The infant is called an *'adam* because of the wordplay between *'adam* (human) and *'adama* (ground). Because the word *'adama* contains the word *'adam,* the wordplay symbolically describes the foundational unity, relatedness, and dependence between humanity and the ground/ earth.[5] In birth, humanity (*'adam*) is separated from the ground (*'adama*), while always retaining unity with it. As an adult, the human's primary role (*'adam*) is to cultivate the ground (*'adama*) in order to produce food to sustain life, so congruence is essential. In death, the human (*'adam*) returns to unity with the ground (*'adama*).

After forming the human, the parent God plants a garden, a distinct controlled place within the world.[6] The garden is "toward the east," symbolic of the beginning of the day or the beginning of individual life.[7] It is in *'eden* (pleasant), suggesting an enjoyable, pleasing location more than an actual geographic location. The garden has nothing but trees, which are described as a "delight to see" and "good to eat," stimulating the visual and gustatory capacities and filling the nutritional needs of the infant. Thus, the garden is symbolic of a distinct, cultivated *childhood world,* an environment of trust, enjoyment, and learning that provides optimal conditions for growth. In the ancient Near East, trees symbolize growth, maturation, and the continuation of life generation after generation through sexual reproduction. They acquire this symbolism because of (1) their slow imperceptible growth, much like human growth, (2) their phallic-shaped trunks as symbols of male sexuality, (3) their production of "seeds/fruit" as symbols of female sexuality, and (4) their seasonal shedding of leaves, which makes them appear to die and begin life anew over and over. The trees in the garden indicate that growth and maturation are the goals of humanity that lead to the procreative capacity of "being fruitful and multiplying" (Gen. 1). Because the central functioning of God in Genesis 1 is advocating the continuing existence of life, sexual functioning allows humanity to function in the "image of God." However, at this point the infant is symbolically fed, cared for, and protected by his environment in a secure childhood world, which allows him to develop a sense of trust.

There are two *specific* trees in the childhood world: the tree of life and the tree of knowing good and bad. The meaning of the tree of life is found in the Babylonian myth of Gilgamesh, in which the tree represents a constant return to infancy and childhood, with its immature understanding of life each time a person approaches adulthood. The myth allows adults, like children, to have the illusion of perpetual life. Consequently, the tree of life can also be called *the tree of immature understanding of life.* In infancy and childhood, there is no prohibition concerning this tree. Eating of the tree then would simply place the child where he is—in an immature understanding of life.

The meaning of the tree of knowing good and bad centers on the verb *to know*, which connotes a broad intellectual, experiential, and sexual understanding of life, along with the complex reasoning and multifarious perception of right and wrong that broad understanding requires. In the Old Testament, this tree is essential for adults. However, because adult knowledge cannot be imposed, the tree of adult knowledge requires the slow buildup of life experiences throughout childhood and is therefore prohibited to children. Once adolescent psychological and physical maturity begins, then the tree of life with its immature discernment of life is prohibited.

Transition

The river section (Gen. 2:10–15) functions as the transition between infancy and childhood. It foreshadows the process of unity and separation that characterizes adult life and marriage. The river represents life as continually gushing forth from the childhood world of the garden and multiplying into four rivers that encircle the four corners of the world to make it "fruitful."[8]

Childhood

The development during childhood is essential because without the insight from each experience, the child will not have the foundation for the capacity to discern good and bad. With the onset of walking and mobility, the child experiences initial socialization into the behavior that is acceptable and unacceptable at this stage in life. The child is now permitted to make simple *choices.* God says, "From the trees in the garden you may certainly eat" (Gen. 2:16). Eating of the trees is indicative of maturation and is necessary to sustain life in the face of death. It is the first step in understanding death and developing a mature understanding of life. Although God has filled the garden with the potential for maturation and for eventually acquiring adult knowledge, *in childhood* the tree of knowing good and bad (that is, adult discernment) is prohibited because attaining this tree before the child is ready could retard his growth by skipping over essential experiences that form the foundation for a broad intellectual, experiential, and sexual understanding of life. The limitation is *protective* because all children are curious and anxious to grow up and be like their parents. In childhood, all things are possible, *except growing up too fast.* As Rowan Williams, archbishop of Canterbury, points out, the childhood world cannot be stifled or shortchanged. A society that does not protect the childhood world will produce childish and dangerous adults (Williams, 2002, 2–4).[9]

As children grow and learn from their experience, however, their possibilities and limitations change. Then God says that if you eat from the tree of knowing, "you will certainly die." The audience assumes that the child will instantly die, but he does not. The audience misunderstands God, which seems to be a human tendency. Although the wise snake tries to correct this misunderstanding of instant death, God's statement remains *ambiguous.* It could imply that as a result of eating from this tree, the child enters adulthood and develops an awareness of the function and inevitability of death. Or it could indicate that upon eating from this tree the human goes through a rite of passage into adulthood. A rite of passage entails the symbolic death of an old, immature perception of life in order to begin a more mature, more intricate level of understanding. That the child lacks the capacity for critical thinking is reflected in his never asking what "you will certainly die" means. He simply unquestioningly obeys.

One of the bothersome aspects of the limitation is that it is never rescinded. The answer lies in the prohibition given by most parents to their young children that they not cross the street alone. Because maturity cannot be imposed, there is no static formula to determine when children are mature enough to cross alone. When they are ready, parents normally remain in the background and watch as their children test their newly acquired autonomy and capacity for discernment. Because few parents ever rescind the prohibition, disobedience affords the definitive break with the past that allows a new capacity to be used.

God declares that being alone is *not good.* Humans need a sense of relationship to the ground, other beings, and one another. Thus, God forms the animals from the ground as "helping companions."[10] Because animals do not bring ego concerns into the relationship and accept people just as they are, they are excellent companions for children learning to relate. In addition, when the child becomes an adult, animals remain helping companions, "co-producing" food to "sustain life."

The creation of the animals adds three new capacities: (1) the acquisition of language skills with which to conceptualize, name, and categorize reality; (2) the beginning of identity formation through differentiation of the self from others; and (3) the relational skills with which to foster social identity. In Genesis 1, God conceptualizes and names, which is what the child now does; he is beginning to function in the image of God. As the child categorizes the animals, he becomes aware of the life-preserving domesticated beasts and the life-threatening wild animals, which leads to a "re-sorting" of the animals according to their helpfulness. Because language is one of the chief agents of cognitive development and reasoning, these experiences initiate the capacity for discernment necessary for the tree of knowing.

In the Genesis story, there is no division of childhood into early and middle, unless there is a conceptual division between the creation of the animals and the creation of the woman. Now the child has a deeper existential need—a helping companion to "co-produce" life. Having learned to relate to the animals, the child is ready for gender differentiation, so he can learn to interact with the opposite sex and acquire a social identity. Consequently, God "builds" the woman by putting the man into a deep sleep or symbolic death—demonstrating that new life springs from death.[11] This symbolic death prefigures the symbolic death of the adolescent's rite of passage.

The imagery of God "building" the woman from a rib is fascinating. The Hebrew word for *rib* has an architectural dimension, like Sumerian "rib vaulting" that supports and protects the entire structure, implying symbolically that the woman is built from strength. In addition, in Genesis 6:1–4 women "build" houses, that is, households or dynasties. Thus, when the woman is named, she is called Eve/Life, the Mother of all Life, because she "builds" life. God builds the builder.

Because the child has benefited from his conceptualization experience, he speaks for the first time, declaring that the woman is bone of his bone and flesh of his flesh.[12] In the second wordplay, woman/man (*'iššâ/ 'iš*), the child demonstrates his ability to discern *unity and separation,* which is foreshadowed in Genesis 2:10–15 and 24–25. He comprehends that a man is "flesh and bone," "formed" from the flesh-like clay of the ground, and a woman is "flesh and bone," "built" from a rib/bone.

The woman/man wordplay is peculiar, however. In the *'adam/ 'adama* wordplay, the word *'adam* can be taken out of the word *'adama*, demonstrating that the human is born from the ground yet always retains unity with it. But here the word *woman* (*'iššá*) cannot be taken out of the word *man* (*'iš*); linguistically the wordplay does not work. Although it demonstrates the differentiated unity between men and women, it does not represent the natural process of men being born from women. However, because the children still *lack* full understanding of life and the sexual maturity to produce life, the noticeable incongruity in the wordplay points to the need for a change, namely, physical and intellectual maturation. When the man and woman are sexually mature, the wordplay is set right in Genesis 4:1, where a man (*'iš*) is born from a woman (*'iššá*).

Transition

The text of Genesis 2:24–25 functions as the transition between childhood and adolescent, and it foreshadows what is to come in adult life: marriage and producing children. Marriage, at the threshold of adulthood, is a rite of passage into adult society. Marriage bonding is described in terms of separation and unity: "A man separates from his father and mother and unites/bonds with his woman and they become one flesh." This psychological separation from his father and mother is demonstrated when God sends the man forth from the childhood world of the garden into the adult world (Gen. 3:22–24), and he "knows" his woman/wife (Gen. 4:1). Separation from parents is essential in forming the new bonding to his woman/wife, so that they become "one flesh." The phrase "one flesh" symbolizes (1) the psychological unity between a man and a woman and (2) the physical unity that can produce a child, who will separate from father and mother, unite with a spouse, and produce a child, and on and on. Marriage requires a secure sense of separate identity because it involves simultaneous unity.

To emphasize that all these experiences are in the future, the text stresses that the man and the woman are naked and not ashamed of themselves. Their lack of shame and self-consciousness places them in childhood, but they are approaching the threshold of adolescence, in which sexual maturity stimulates self-consciousness.

Adolescence

Adolescence is not "rebellion" or "sin" but natural and critical growth in which there is questioning, a quest for freedom, and new identity formation (Erikson, 1963, 1968). Maturation into adolescence occurs with the accumulation of experiences, and so children are ready to engage life on a more multifarious level. Now *disobedience is appropriate and necessary* because obedience would stifle psychological maturation and critical thinking.

Previously, the experiences that have stimulated growth have been instigated by God the parent. In contrast, it is *life*, symbolized by the snake, that initiates adolescent maturation. Consequently, understanding snake symbolism in the ancient world is central to this section of Genesis. The snake is a symbol of wisdom, a mediating figure that represents an *understanding of the complexity of life*, including its simultaneous inherent life-threatening and life-preserving dimensions. On a practical level, snakes are wild animals that in the cultivated areas are life preserving and protecting in that they rid farms of rodents that consume stored grain. Yet some snakes are poisonous and potentially life threatening. However, if people "know" what kind of snake it is, they will know if it is life threatening or life preserving. Knowledge is critical to experience with the snake. On a symbolic level, snakes represent the continuous life process, symbolizing male sexuality with their phallic shape and female sexuality with their ability to shed their skin and appear to continually begin life anew. As a symbol of wisdom, the snake comprehends the tree of knowing good and bad, which stimulates a mature complex understanding of life. Consequently, the snake is described as more intuitively wise than the other wild animals. As a mediating figure from the adult world, the snake is instrumental in the rite of passage between adolescence and adulthood. What the snake initiates is a transformation in the man and woman's perceptions of life by encouraging the capacity to *see reality*, that is, to see life *as it really is*—with their eyes opened.

It is the woman who interacts with the snake. Observation reveals that females begin their physical and cognitive maturation earlier than males. Thus, with its intuitive understanding of life, the snake asks the woman rhetorical questions that test her readiness for the tree of adult knowing. The snake's pedagogy is excellent; the questions force her to sort through her information and carefully formulate her knowledge. God's statement about the tree, from which she is not to eat, is clear. She knows she will die if she eats from the *tree in the middle of the garden*, but she does not know the tree's name. Unfortunately, the tree of life is in the middle of the garden, and the location of the tree of knowing is ambiguous. The woman has partial understanding. The snake corrects the misconception about dying instantly, although it does not interpret the meaning of death. The woman's understanding of death has to come with experience, not instruction.

Then the snake identifies what the tree of knowing accomplishes: the potential opening of the eyes, so that a more mature understanding can begin (for example, Gen. 21:19). Because humans are created in the image of God, once their eyes are opened, they will "be like God," knowing the complexity of good and bad. However, typical of an adolescent, the woman views the tree idealistically and dualistically. She focuses on the good but ignores the simultaneous bad. Dualistic thinking is a pitfall of adolescence.

The genius of this story lies in the fact that in ancient Israel, the capacity to know good and bad is essential for adults. In Deuteronomic theology, it is assumed that with this capacity people can choose "good" (i.e., Deuteronomic theology) and then be absolutely obedient to its law. On the other hand, people who choose "bad" (i.e., another theology) are disobedient and are punished. Unfortunately, assuming that punishment eliminates disobedience is a misperception. Punishment may suppress disobedience, but most often it creates more disobedience. In this story, however, before the capacity to know and choose good and bad with its mature understanding of life can be acquired, there must be disobedience. In adolescence, disobedience creates the disjuncture and conflict that are necessary for change. In fact, in adulthood, God definitively blocks the way to the tree of life with its immature perception of life; for adults, immature knowledge of life should *not* be an option. Genesis 4 describes what happens when an immature view of life determines adult choices. In addition, although there is disobedience, there will be no punishment.

Eating the fruit of the tree of knowing becomes a rite of passage in which old, immature perceptions of life, as symbolized by the humans, die in order for a new, more mature understanding to be reached. This may be the symbolic death to which God refers in Genesis 2:17. It should be noted that the woman questions and thinks, yet there is no record of the man deliberating or wrestling with the issues. He blindly obeys the woman without evidence of thought.

Now their eyes are opened, and they have a new capacity to know. Contrary to their adolescent expectations, they are now self-conscious and aware of their nakedness. Nakedness generates the kind of exposure that produces feelings of psychological vulnerability, defenselessness, fear of inadequacy, and shame (see Bechtel, 1991). For adolescents, this exposure is particularly threatening because their ego identity is not well formed. Consequently, they are afraid of their

vulnerability and hide their shame and nakedness by covering themselves with leaves, which in modern society are similar to jeans and a
tee shirt.[13]

Like the snake, God asks rhetorical questions that stress discernment and responsibility and are intended to make the humans think
deeply. However, God does not mention judgment or disobedience.
The man is self-defensive and places the blame on God, who has given
him the woman, and on the woman. In doing so, he virtually admits
that he has not deliberated but instead blindly obeyed the woman.
Because assuming responsibility for one's actions represents maturity
at its most accomplished level, its absence signals that the man has
not reached a mature stage of development. The woman is also self-
defensive and blames the snake/life, indicating that she has been
enticed away from her childlike perception of life, which is relatively accurate.

Because adolescence is a time of identity formation and profound
adjustment demands as young people come to terms with sexual maturity and adult roles, God explains the essential potentials and limitations of adult female and male life. Awareness of the fundamental
dynamics of adult life should generate a transformation of perceptions
of young people, but *not* a change in the conditions of life—this is not
punishment. Adult work is a vital factor in making the transition to
adult status.[14] The work of the woman contains multifaceted potentials and limitations, which are interconnected with the potentials and
limitations of the man, just as the multifaceted potentials and limitations of the man are interconnected with the potentials and limitations
of the ground. The woman's most essential capabilities are her sexual
desire for her husband and her power of conception, pregnancy, and
childbearing. This potential is critical to her identity, giving her an
awareness that she is part of the whole life process and making her feel
at home on the earth. In addition, her potential is part of God's bene-
diction to be fruitful and multiply; it allows her to function in the
image of God. Yet her life-producing role is not merely restricted to
production of her own children. As the mother of *all* life, she should be
an advocate for all life. Of course the incredible power of conception
and pregnancy is also risky, in light of the possibility of death in childbirth for women and infants.[15] Although she has the potential to produce life, she can also produce death; her potential resides in the tension between life and death.

The woman has dual limitation. First, she is limited by the increased
labor or physical effort that producing and sustaining a large house-

hold requires. Second, because of the huge amount of physical effort that children require, the man needs to control the woman's sexual desire in order to limit the number of children the woman produces. This is not generalized male domination of women but practical limitation. Producing a large number of children gives a woman a great deal of status and ego elevation, so the man should limit the number of children she produces to the number that the man can sustain by his food-producing effort. Yet her sexual desire cannot be completely controlled; children are necessary to sustain the two in their old age.[16] Potential cannot be unlimited, and limitation cannot destroy freedom and potential.

As with the woman, God explains to the man the essential potentials and limitations of adult male life. Because the man's ability and his adult work show his potential to produce life-sustaining food through cultivation of the ground, he must realize that the ground has both the potential of producing edible cultivated vegetation and the limitation of producing inedible wild vegetation (thorns and thistles). This limitation and potential of the ground/earth should not come as a surprise, because wild and cultivated vegetation is mentioned at the beginning of the story (Gen. 2:5). It too is not punishment but the reality of life. The man's relationship to the ground is critical to his identity, giving him an awareness of being part of the whole life process and making him feel at home on the earth. Again, his adult life-sustaining role is not limited to food production for himself. It has a broader scope: he is the sustainer of *all* life.

The man also has dual limitation. First, he is limited by the tremendous labor or physical effort required for food production, in light of the wild vegetation that the ground produces.[17] The larger his household, the greater his effort. Second, his productivity is controlled by the ground. Stockpiling a large amount of food gives a man a great deal of status and ego elevation. Although the ground continues to sustain life, according to Genesis 4:12 the ground does not continually increase its power exponentially to fill the man's excessive needs. The man's ego needs are controlled by the ground in the same way that the woman's ego needs are controlled by the man. Consequently, the man's control of the woman should pattern the ground's control of the man. In both cases, control comes from something with which they have unity and are intimately related.

Finally, when he dies, the 'adam returns to his unity with the 'adama (ground). He has retained his unity with the ground throughout life, despite his apparent separation from it at birth. Death is a return to the womb, the matrix of life; it is a return to unity with the source of continuing new life.[18] In addition, after death one eventually turns to fine dust, appearing to return humanity to the dust/clay of the ground. These concepts are central to people's acceptance of the life/death process; they give death a positive value.

Transition

In Genesis 3:20–24 it is reported that the woman is given her adult name, Eve (Life). Naming her indicates a change: she is now sexually mature and ready to separate from the childhood world and fulfill her life-producing potential. In the ancient world her name is an honorific title, pointing to her greatest natural power, which is associated with God. If, according to the traditional interpretation, the woman is responsible for bringing evil and death into the world, why is she given an honorific name that is linked with God's functioning?

In the same way that parents prepare their children to leave home and live on their own, the parent God prepares the young human to leave the childhood world of the garden and enter the adult world. As a sign of adult maturation and socialization, God clothes the young human a second time with garments of animal skins,[19] which is the ancient equivalent of a two-piece suit, and which demonstrates that the animals are still his helping companions.

Now God says the human has become "like one of us," which is a reference to Genesis 1:26–27, where humanity is created in the image of God. The young human has the capacity to conceptualize, differentiate, and name, as God does in Genesis 1. He has acquired the capacity for complex reasoning, a multifaceted perception of right and wrong, and the ability to examine the basis for the moral principles of the changing dimensions of good and bad. As God creates and sustains life, so the human is ready to produce and sustain life as a sexually mature adult, either by sexual reproduction or cultivation of the ground/earth. In that respect, the human is *like* God.

Then like any parent, God sends him forth as an adult from the childhood world. In the ancient world this separation coincides with marriage (foreshadowed in Gen. 2:24, where a man separates from father and mother and unites with his woman) and the beginning of adult work. It is emphasized that God drives him out, which accentuates the definitive break necessary for this radical change. It may also reflect human reluctance to leave the security of the childhood world.

Now God definitively blocks the way to the tree of life. For adults, eating of the tree of life means constantly returning to childhood and embracing immature thinking. It is a retreat from the complexity, change, and interrelatedness of life as well as a denial of death as an essential aspect of life. Consequently, a guarding cherubim and revolving flaming sword prevent adults from eating of the tree of life and its childlike thinking. For adults, God's prevention of recoiling into immaturity is considerably more decisive than God's statement to the young child about not eating from the tree of knowing. An immature view of life is good, even essential, for children, but bad and unacceptable for adults.

Adulthood

Genesis 4 describes what happens when immature thinking determines adult choices. In Genesis 2:17, the prohibition *in childhood* against the tree of knowing good and bad (the tree of mature thinking) is there so that children do not grow up too fast and skip the slow accumulation of the learning that forms the foundation of mature adult thinking. In Genesis 4:1, Cain appears to go from infancy to adulthood with no mention of his childhood or adolescence. Cain retains an immature understanding of life with its consequent self-centeredness and threatened egotistic responses. His immature thinking in adulthood may symbolize the result of a violation of the Genesis 2:17 prohibition in childhood.

Cain is the firstborn and displays many of the psychological tendencies of firstborn children. They begin life by receiving all the family's attention, which can make them feel entitled to the kind of honor, respect, and privilege that maintains their superiority (Katz, 1991, 501–512). In Israelite society, firstborn sons inherit family power, authority, a double portion of the property, and responsibility for the family's welfare and continuation (for example, Gen. 25:25). Cain receives preferential treatment from Eve in that she makes a statement about Cain's birth, but not about Abel's.

Yet the elevated status of the firstborn is rarely secure; other sons can buy or steal the birthright through cunning behavior. Moreover, one of the greatest blows to the psyche of the firstborn is having a younger sibling appear to be treated better. As a result, the firstborn often seeks special attention and can become abnormally self-centered. Any real or imagined threat to firstborns' sense of superiority makes them hypersensitive to slighting remarks, gestures, or situations and causes them to be anxious, self-defensive, and intensely angry (Leman, 1984, 1989). It can lead to threatened egotistic responses such as violence and ultimately murder.

After the brothers make an offering appropriate to each of their occupations, God is perceived as "looking at" one brother and his offering and not at the other. Abel has offered the *firstborn* of his flock, which would *not* be preferable to God, but because of his hypersensitivity, Cain could misinterpret reality and assume that Abel has become the center of God's attention. Cain's face falls and he becomes intensely angry, expressing the kind of unseen, intense anger that fills the world with violence and leads to retaliation and revenge. When people concentrate on themselves and are self-centered, it can be expressed symbolically by having the "face fall." This downward-inward focus creates a wall of separation that prevents awareness of brotherhood and relationship with God. Both Cain's intense anger and his face falling point to a threatened egotistic reaction.

God asks Cain rhetorical questions that have the potential to transform Cain's thinking. Although self-focus can never be completely lost, God states that "doing good" is lifting the face upward out of self-centeredness. When the face is lifted up, people can see beyond their limited self-interests, and reality can be discerned with more clarity, without being colored by excessive ego needs. "Not doing good" is having the face down and being self-centered, preoccupied with self-interests and self-superiority, so that the world becomes threatening to the fragile ego. God draws on the image of a crouching wild animal, ready to spring up in attack with ego-centered desires. In regard to sin, God shifts the emphasis from an external act to internal motivation by implying that threatened egotistic responses lie at the heart of sin.

Cain ignores God's offer to transform his attitude, retains his threatened egotism, springs up like a defensive wild animal, and kills his brother. Again God asks a rhetorical question, ignoring the issue of murder and focusing on the heart of the matter—Cain's responsibility for severing his brotherhood with Abel.

However, when asked where his brother is, Cain disavows his brotherhood by stating, "I do not know." Ironically, his not knowing is a denial of his firstborn responsibility for the welfare and continuation of the family. Because of his threatened egotism, Cain is now rejecting the responsibility of the firstborn in that he has killed a member of his family.

Then, instead of accusing or judging Cain, God tries to make Cain accept accountability for the consequences of his choice by subtly linking what Cain has done to issues of superiority and inferiority. God implies that in defending his superiority, Cain has put Abel down into the lowest, most inferior position—that is, into the ground. In addition, part of what need to be transformed are Cain's ideas about the dynamics of life. Potential has to be balanced with limitation. God gives the example of the ground, which continues to sustain life but cannot exponentially increase its power to grow more and more food to fill Cain's excessive need, as a farmer, to stockpile. Likewise, Cain should realize that he cannot exponentially increase his status and power to fill his extreme need for superiority.

Most exegetes associate this story with Deuteronomic ideas of trial, punishment, and divine justice. In the dialogue with Cain, however, God never accuses or mentions imposing anything on Cain as punishment. It is Cain who has made the choice; he has preferred to exist and act with his face down in self-centeredness. God simply points out the normal consequences of Cain's choices, consequences that Cain has imposed on himself. Unfortunately, because of his self-centeredness, Cain presumes his circumstances are inflicted on him as punishment and that God is to blame. He is playing the blame game, so he does not have to be accountable himself.

Having killed to defend his threatened ego, Cain now fears the same ego response from others in the form of revenge. God describes the sevenfold revenge of the human community as "springing up," demonstrating the interconnectedness between "springing up" to murder and "springing up" in revenge. Both are motivated by ego defensiveness, and both are linked to the imagery of a crouching wild animal about to spring up in attack.

Contrary to expectations, God sustains the murderer's life through a sign that protects him from being struck or killed. The sign can simply be the fact that the murderer lives and that God does not kill him as punishment for his crime. It may be God's attempt to stop the cycle of violence, which threatened egotistic reactions perpetuate.

Although scholars imagine that Cain is banished from the human community and lives as a nomad on the fringes of the life-giving world, Cain settles down, marries, has children, and becomes a city builder (Gen. 4:17). Even though he leads a seemingly normal life, his existence is described as "shameful-shaking and sorrowful-straying,"[20] a phrase that depicts Cain's psychological state of existence, not his physical one. Cain's sensitivity to ego diminishment leaves him self-defensive, shaky, and fearful, because aspects of life appear threatening to his need for superiority. He has also strayed from his natural brotherhood with Abel and from relationship with the ground and God, so he laments that he is not psychologically at home on the earth. Because he is incapable of lifting his face and identifying with some-

thing greater than himself, his identity is insecure. All of this is shameful because it reflects a weakness and inadequacy at the core of his
being. Because Cain's psychological attitude is a place where many
people settle, Cain's city is called "the Land of Sorrowful Straying."
Many people with immature thinking caused by threatened egotistic
attitudes settle there.

This essay is simply one example in biblical interpretation of the use
of developmental theory and general psychological insights and
the way these tools can open the eyes of interpreters to elements of the
text that previously have been overlooked.

Notes

1. For a fuller exegesis of Gen. 2–3 as a maturation myth, see Bechtel
(1993, 1995).

2. Lévi-Strauss (1963) stresses that humans need consonance between
their perceptions of social and cosmic levels of experience.

3. For the importance of shame in ancient Israel, see Bechtel (1991, 47–76).

4. In Egyptian artistic convention, a child pharaoh was portrayed as a
naked fully grown man, and an adult pharaoh as a *clothed* fully grown man.
Nakedness indicates infancy/childhood and clothing adulthood.

5. In Gen. 4.1, Cain at birth is called an *'îš* (man), a word specifically used
for *adult* males. *'Îš* is used to set right the wordplay, begun in Gen. 2.23, by
having the man (*'îš*) born from the woman (*'iššâ*).

6. The traditional understanding of the garden has been that of a "paradise," which comes from the Septuagint translation of Hebrew *gan*. The Greek
word *paradeisos* indicates an enclosed park and place of sensual pleasure.

7. In Egyptian theology, the path of the sun across the sky symbolizes
the continuing process of life, day after day, generation after generation. The
god Re is born in the east at sunrise and dies in the west at sunset, and this
episode happens day after day, as in generation after generation.

8. Egyptian theology uses the Nile for the same kind of symbolism.

9. We are, or should be, shocked and sickened by pictures of thirteen-
year-olds conscripted into an army (as occurred in the Iran–Iraq War and
practiced in some of the rebel militias of Africa); by parentless, homeless,
criminalized children in the urban streets of Brazil or Guatemala, regularly
butchered by police and security forces; by child prostitution and sexual
abuse. There is a peculiar horror and pathos in children not allowed to be
children (Williams, 2002, 2).

10. In the Gilgamesh myth, before Enkidu begins to mature and can relate
to women, he runs with and relates to the wild animals.

11. In the Gilgamesh myth, sleep is portrayed as the "brother" of death—
different yet related.

12. Actually, the human's response should have been "Boy, is she built!"

13. Although guilt is often stressed by the traditional interpretation, guilt does not become the major means of social control in ancient Middle Eastern society until the late Hellenistic period, the time at which the traditional interpretation begins to develop. Guilt is considerably less important as a means of social control during the monarchical and Persian periods.

14. In the "sin and fall" interpretation, this section is considered a "curse and punishment." Conveniently, the interpretation ignores the potential given for both the woman and the man and focuses only on the limitation or punishment/curse. Many exegetes consider work or physical effort to be a curse/punishment, yet in Gen. 1, God works, and it is never considered a curse. Because humans are made in the image of God, part of that image is both work and ceasing work. Work/physical effort is essential to the health and well-being of the body, so it is both a potential as well as a limitation.

15. See Meyers (1983, 1988) for a fuller explanation of the socioeconomic conditions of the Israelite highlands.

16. The nature of control has been demonstrated in Gen. 1, where the control of lights over the day and night is determinative, mutual, and passive, allowing complete freedom of existence within the potential and limitation of reality. Control is never absolute.

17. However, although for the human, thorns and thistles are a limitation, for the animals and birds whose lives are sustained by this wild vegetation, they represent a potential.

18. In the ancient world, the dead are placed in caves, which is like being placed in the mouth/womb of the ground.

19. In the Gilgamesh myth, Enkidu is initially clothed with leaves and receives a second set of clothing as a sign of adult maturation.

20. The Hebrew phrase *na' wa nad* is difficult to translate. The equivalent English words all need to begin with the same letters yet still convey the sense of the Hebrew and capture the consequences of Cain's threatened egotism.

References

Baldwin, A. L. (1966). *Theories of Child Development and Behavior*, vol. 8. Hillsdale: Erlbaum.

Bechtel, L. (1991). Shame as a Sanction of Social Control in Biblical Israel: Judicial, Political, and Social Shaming. *Journal for the Study of the Old Testament, 49*, 47–76.

Bechtel, L. (1993). Rethinking the Interpretation of Genesis 2.4b–3.24, *The Feminist Companion to Genesis*, A. Brenner, ed. Sheffield, UK: JSOT Press, 77–117.

Bechtel, L. (1995). Genesis 2.4b–3.24: A Myth about Human Maturation. *Journal for the Study of the Old Testament, 67*, 3–26.

Cole, M., & Cole, S. (1989). *The Development of Children.* New York: Scientific American Books.

Dragastin, S., & Elder, G. H., Jr. (1973). *Adolescence in the Life Cycle.* New York: Wiley.

Erikson, E. H. (1963). *Childhood and Society.* New York: Norton.

Erikson, E. H. (1968). *Identity, Youth and Crisis.* New York: Norton.

Erikson, E. H. (1978). *Adulthood.* New York: Norton.

Erikson, E. H. (1979a). *Identity and the Life Cycle.* New York: Norton.

Erikson, E. H. (1979b). *Life Span Development and Behavior,* vol. 2. New York: Academic Press.

Erikson, E. H., Erikson, J. M., & Kivnick, H. Q. (1986). *Vital Involvement in Old Age.* New York: Norton.

Flavell, J. H. (1982). Structures, Stages, and Sequences in Cognitive Development, *The Concept of Development: Minnesota Symposium on Child Development,* W. A. Collins, ed., vol. 15. Hillsdale: Erlbaum.

Flavell, J. H. (1985). *Cognitive Development* (2nd ed.). Englewood Cliffs: Prentice Hall.

Hareven, T. K. (1982). *Aging and Life Course Transitions: An Interdisciplinary Perspective.* New York: Guilford.

Jung, C. (1968). *Man and His Symbols.* New York: Dell Publishing.

Katz, G. A. (1991). The First-Born Son, Rivalry, Entitlement, Loss, and Reparation: Illustrations from Biblical Legend and Freud's Biography. *International Review of Psycho-Analysis, 18,* 501–512.

Leman, K. (1984). *The Birth Order Book: Why You Are the Way You Are.* New York: Dell.

Leman, K. (1989). *Growing up Firstborn: The Pressure and Privilege of Being Number One.* New York: Delacorte.

Lévi-Strauss, C. (1963). *Structural Anthropology.* New York: Basic Books.

Lifton, R. J. (1976). *Boundaries.* New York: Basic Books.

Meyers, C. (1983). Procreation, Production, and Protection: Male–Female Balance in Early Israel. *Journal of the American Academy of Religion, 51,* 569–593.

Meyers, C. (1988). *Discovering Eve: Ancient Israelite Women in Context.* New York: Oxford University Press.

Neugarten, B. L. (1968). *Middle Age and Aging.* Chicago: University of Chicago Press.

Smelser, N., & Erikson, E. H., eds. (1980). *Themes of Love and Work in Adulthood.* Cambridge: Harvard University Press.

Williams, R. (2002). *Lost Icons.* London: Continuum.

CHAPTER 7

Winnicott's Squiggle Game and Biblical Interpretation

Ralph L. Underwood

Peter Gomes once said that the basic obstacle to biblical preaching is that we trust neither the text nor ourselves. Of course hermeneutics is not preaching, nor is hermeneutics solely preparation for preaching. Even so, in the context of self-understanding and intellectual inquiry, we might ask what sense of playful proportion and careful craftsmanship is called for to foster a meaningful dynamic of trust and distrust of text and self? And so I raise this question: what kind of work, and what kind of nonwork (pure attending), escort us to the place where we do trust both the text and ourselves in the midst of reasonable distrust? Object relations theory, I suggest, can contribute to our response to this question.

In this chapter I argue that object relations theory and its implications help to depict a vital dimension of the *process* of interpreting biblical texts. To claim this, however, is not to suggest that object relations provides a complete model of interpretation as a whole. One can say that an object relations perspective contributes to reflection on the interpretive process but need not reduce hermeneutics to psychological categories.

Before I address the implications of object relations theory for biblical hermeneutics, it is necessary to introduce briefly some key concepts and assumptions in object relations theory.

What Is Object Relations Theory?

So what is it? The psychoanalytic story of object relations begins, of course, with Sigmund Freud. He tried to describe how relations with primary others are introjected inside the person, in the psyche, where in due course they take up residence as stable mental images. In psychoanalysis the term *object* refers to persons or to mental representations of persons (Greenberg & Mitchell, 1983, 14). An assumption of all psychoanalytic theory is that the inner world of the infant is fragmentary, and that over time the fragments of body parts, emotional impressions, and the like are organized into wholes—objects within the psyche that represent other persons, in however distorted or realistic a fashion, and that include, in however distorted or realistic a fashion, a mental representation of one's own self. Such processes make outside realities available internally to be the object of the investment of emotional energy. Because of the conflicts between the id and the demands of outer reality as perceived and assimilated by the individual, these internal images of the psyche are largely unconscious. They have visual elements and thus are images; at the same time they have elements that represent the other senses, and they harbor emotional components. In Freud's economy of the psyche, instinctual energy represents biological processes and is characterized by an urge or drive to attach to some object. In a sense the realistic qualities of a person or personal object are not as significant as the drive for pleasure. By and large, objects are a means to an end (Freud, 1905, 135, 136; 1909; 1915, 122, 123).

The key drama for Freud that displays the conflicts of id and reality is found in the Oedipus complex. The psychoanalytic process of hermeneutics, that is, of interpreting dreams, the products of free association, and cultural objects, enables the ego to discern the hidden desires and objects of the psyche, and thus expose and analyze internal conflicts.

Since Freud, numerous movements within the psychoanalytic tradition have come to emphasize the significance of the social world on psychic organization as well as the influence of the world of interpersonal relations and dynamics on the formation of character. One of these movements is object relations theory. In object relations theory, objects are not merely means to the end of an instinctual drive. Rather, biological drive and psychological instinct are inherently wedded to interpersonal relations. The child is, as it were, instinctively social and seeks relationship with others. The Freudian self is instinctively motivated and seems isolated by comparison. The object relations self exists in and by its social relations, and its most abstract thoughts, visionary aspirations, and ingenious interpretations bear the traces of the interpersonal world.

Object relations theory focuses on how a sense of self in relation to others originates, and it assumes that interpersonal relations are important or primary in their own right. The scene for the new psychoanalytic myth is the mother–infant relationship. The first field of vision, then, is not the oedipal conflict but the dynamics of interaction between mother and child that eventuate hopefully in the child's development of an organized psyche with a stable sense of self and other in contact with external reality.

Transitional Space

Does this relocation of psychoanalytic attention have implications for biblical hermeneutics? Does it have something to say about trust and distrust of texts and ourselves? To address this we must move along to consider *transitional space.* The movement from an assumed infantile and narcissistic illusion of grandeur, in which the child is all and what the child wishes comes to pass, to the healthy organization of the world into self and other entails a transitional period during the first two years of life. During this time the primary caring person, usually the mother, provides an atmosphere, an environment, a space that holds and contains the infant's fragmentary experiences. Essential to this process is time when mother and infant are together and neither is making demands on the other. In addition the mother's responsive face mirrors the child's expressions and so paves the way for the child to discover his or her own appearance and eventually to develop a sense of self.

In this transitional period, before self and other are clearly formed and separated in the psyche of the infant, a particular quality of experiencing, labeled transitional space by Winnicott, and a peculiar discovery of beginning-to-be objects, called transitional objects, provide a pathway from illusion to encounter with external reality. Initially the mother is so over-adapted to the child that when the child is about to hallucinate an object—the breast, for example—the mother provides what is needed, and the child imagines that the wish created the object. In other words, this adaptation is so close that one can infer that initially the infant experiences a magical fusion of inner wish and outer reality. The paradox is that the infant cannot experience this illusion unless in fact the environment embodied in the mother makes it possible. As the child develops, the mother gradually becomes less symbiotically adapted to the child, who becomes disillusioned about the omnipotence of wishes. Without such frustration, an awareness of the mother's otherness, her being a separate person and reality, would not emerge. Through this time of transition, disillusionment, and creative interaction, the child comes to recognize the presence and reality of another, the reality of self, and relationships between self and other. This development entails recognition of an object as an entity in its own right that is not under the control of subjective desire. In short, object relations theory assumes that this first human relationship is crucial for the formation of a person who has the capacity to develop internal images of self and other out of which to engage in creative living (Winnicott, 1971a).

But more than this is at stake in this time of early development. In the transition the child adopts a special object, a blanket or teddy bear, to provide consolation and companionship. The transitional object symbolizes the other who may literally be absent but who is nonetheless present through the use of the symbol. We might say that the transitional object is the child's first cultural object; the child has developed capacity for symbolic creativity. Rizzuto has speculated about how a mental representation of God in relation to self is formed in the latter stages of this transitional period in childhood (1979). Much has been made of the way this early image of God draws on the image of the mother and one's relation with the mother.

The quality that is vital here, especially in Winnicott, is that transitional space is neither entirely inside nor outside the person. It is a limbo-like location in which everything is in transition and nothing is settled down into either an internal or an external place. In an object relations view, transitional phenomena are first discovered in the original formation of a sense of self in relation to others, but at the same time transitional phenomena characterize the creative process that goes on through life, including the creative dimension of adult lives. The play of the child's early relations becomes "the enjoyment of the cultural heritage" (Winnicott, 1971a, 108). Cultural activity is an extension and development of the same relational process encountered in early childhood. Object relations perspective entertains the idea of some continuity between the primitive and the mature, a continuity based on the notion of play. Playful openness connects the infantile and the mature, the deep and the high, the primordial and the sensible. These transitional phenomena produce, sustain, reform, and transform culture and religion. If there are no transitional phenomena, there is neither culture nor religion. Likewise, if there are no transitional phenomena, there is neither meaningful reality nor hermeneutics.

Thus object relations theory posits a continuity, insofar as process is concerned, between infantile experience and mature, adult creativity. If you will, the object relations myth of the child tells the story of processes that are creative as well as defensive in nature. In this myth the very illusion of the infantile creature is made possible by external relation in the form of the mother's overadaptation to the child. The process of disillusioning occurs in that special place that makes illusions possible and is playfully accompanied by the process of re-illusioning. The word *illusion* derives from Latin for "play." Along with Winnicott, Pruyser believes that culture and religion derive from the play of the imagination in the context of a reality that basically is social or relational in nature (Pruyser, 1974). As I read him, Winnicott emphasizes the continuity between the child's transitional phenomena and the adult world of religion and culture. Pruyser, on the other hand, acknowledges this continuity but stresses an element of discontinuity, recognizing tension between the primitive world of the infant and the mature forms of object relations possible in culture and religion (1991, 47–82). In object relations perspective, hermeneutics involves the capacity to play with texts and with the worlds they occupy. Playing is the mode of relating to tradition in order to be creative in contributing to the unforeseen and unforeseeable.

A child's first image of God may be parentally based, but a child's imagination is not limited to a parental template. Children's play and imagination produce a wide variety of fantasy playmates, not all of which are based on a parental image. The first transitional object and the quality of relations with mother, when a sense of self and other is formed, introduce the child to a vast world of imagination and to the world of making sense of all kinds of phenomena—that is, to the world of interpretation. Object relations is interested in the play of the mind not only with objects born in persons' earliest relationships but also with objects developed in history and transmitted culturally from one age to another.

This then is how I summarize object relations thinking and the transitional phenomena that bring into being the interpersonal world of self and other, and that constitute the playing field of human culture and religion. Certain implications for hermeneutics are evident. In object relational perspective, interpretation is a transitional process, the play of the imagination in a numinous, transcendent location neither inside nor outside of the person. At the same time, interpretation is a relational process, and any wedding of imagination with human relationship is a community event.

The Squiggle Game: Hermeneutical Model

For many of us it may seem quite a stretch to connect the imagination of the infant with creative reflections on cultural and religious objects. And the distance to biblical hermeneutics may seem farther still. So come one more step with me and consider another phenomenon—not the mental life of the infant but that of an older child interacting with an adult, a kind of halfway spot between the transitional world of the infant and the cultural world of adults.

In London today there is a foundation named the Squiggle Foundation, whose unusual name derives from a game that Don Winnicott played with the children he treated in his psychiatric practice. The squiggle game went something like this. Dr. Winnicott told the patient that he would draw a squiggle, a line or drawing that had no particular meaning, and the child was to draw and make something from this squiggle. Then the child could draw a squiggle, and Winnicott would make something of it. Typically, the psychiatrist would start by closing his eyes and drawing a line. Then the patient would respond by adding a line drawing onto the squiggle in order to give it some meaning. As the child and therapist played this game, reversing roles in turn, they would talk as much as the child wanted. One child, for example, before drawing his response to Winnicott's squiggle, asked about what he could or could not do, and the psychiatrist's response was "There are no rules." On another occasion, the child might begin to tell a story or a dream (Winnicott, 1971b). Accordingly, a dialogue accompanied the activity of drawing together. When by this means Winnicott began to know a child, he would say, "I do not have a diagnosis of the child, but a diagnosis of my relationship with the child."

To be sure, although this relationship-forming process is play, it has a critical dimension to it. Some problematic process has brought patient and doctor together. The youngster and the adult choose to respond to each other's moves in selective, discerning ways. Still, one can hope that once the game has been played, the psychiatrist can interpret the relationship with the child in a playful spirit.

The squiggle comes from the unconscious and has a primordial quality that reflects the impulse of the moment. The response to the squiggle intends to create a meaningful object, an object that evokes some recognition from both persons. This response is marked by intentionality and creativity. It gives expression to ego qualities.

For an object relations perspective on hermeneutics, I proffer the squiggle game as an analogy for the hermeneutical process. The squiggle game is like the process of developing a relationship with a text and of being in a position to interpret the relationship in a meaningful way. Similarly, hermeneutics emerges out of a process of relationship building such that our interpretations of texts are hunches or declarations about our relationship with these texts. An object relations approach frames hermeneutics as a dynamic relationship between text and readers. Hermeneutics is not simply a task of making a meaning from the text that suits the needs of the readers, nor simply a task of unlocking some a priori meaning ensconced in the text. Rather, hermeneutics is a process in which a unique relationship between text and readers evolves.

A squiggle is symbolic for me of anything in biblical texts that challenges meaningful interpretation, something that says, "What are you going to do with me?" Squiggles are fragments. Responses to squiggles are ways of making meaning that in some fashion include the squiggles. No interpretation produces meaning or truth as a complete whole. Rather, responses or interpretations are more or less creative, evoking a liveliness of relationship with a text.

For example, the following is a brief summary of a line of interpretation of some elements in Luke 8:26–39. This interpretation is possible because of contemporary sensitivities and issues. The demoniac falls at Jesus' feet and cries out. The word comes from Greek *anakrazō*, which had a connotation of to choke, and later to cry out. The image that comes to mind is that of an unnatural sound, not the person's own voice at all. Jesus had to subject demons to discourse because they had the power of speech; the person who had thrown himself at Jesus' feet did not. Then it becomes all the more significant at the end of the story that Jesus refuses to allow this person to go with him but bids him tell his story in detail (Greek, *diēgou* from *diēgeomai*). What is wondrous in this narrative is that the person now is able to declare God's praise in his own voice among his own people. The legion of demons, the chaotic fragmentation of this person's life, had to be exposed, yet they were not originally part of him. However long ago, they entered his life. The legion of demons was alien and robbed him of his own voice, and when the kingdom of God came near it was time for them to depart, whatever the cost. Note the swine rushing to the lake that scholars cannot locate.

Such an interpretation highlights certain particulars of the text because of their potential significance for readers today who are sensitive to the way that persons struggle with the chaotic, desire to find their own voice, and want to be heard. The interpretation is not objective in the sense of being the one understanding that makes sense for all time and places. On the other hand, it is not merely subjective in the sense of imposing self-serving agendas on the text regardless of its content or context. The interpretation reflects an emerging relationship between text and readers. The text lives for readers and speaks to them.

For another kind of example, one can consider the interpretations of scholars such as Phyllis Trible (1984). Clearly her work is the result of a literary method of analysis, but also it reflects the sensitivities of an age, the kind of questions being raised in a community, and the struggles and gifts of a particular person. One might say that Jacques Derrida (1978), a key figure in the contemporary deconstruction movement, has set forth an attention-getting squiggle for advocates of hermeneutics. The response of Francis Watson, to cite one example, produces interesting comments on glossolalia texts in the New Testament (1994, 89–106). Contemporary issues and discussions in communities of discourse create relations with texts that have new problematics and possibilities for understanding.

By providing interpersonal contexts, communities such as communities of faith and communities of scholarship establish systems of checks and balances between imagination and external reality, between creative openness and critical distance. In this sense, hermeneutics is a community as well as a personal undertaking.

Transitional space is the realm of the symbolic. To be in this space entails more than mere openness to other people. Hermeneutics entails a process of negotiating tensions and possibilities between personally primordial texts and culturally primordial texts. Texts open the way to the unspeakable, to what cuts across language and thought, to what can be voiced only in metaphors and stories, known only in silence. Psychologically, the stereotypical view is that interpreting in the sense of explaining is the paternal function, and holding is the maternal function. The two cannot be separated, however. The community locus of hermeneutics—the holding function—is as significant as are the proffered contents of explanation and understanding. Consequently, hermeneutics is a movement from orientation to disorientation to new orientation, as Brueggemann (1984) has suggested. When the aliveness of a creative orientation fades, a time of transition, disorientation, and fragmentation ironically comes to the rescue.

It is a squiggle game, a way in which trusting and distrusting dance together.

Consequently, hermeneutics is a process that interweaves written and oral processes. The oral is essential and in its fullness involves a bodily presence to one another—despite the Internet—so that we know not only the context of the interpretation but also how people are talking about texts, and how texts move and enliven people. The oral dimension opens up a way for a community of discourse to create a relation with the text and a way to be created by the text. Yet bodily absence and solitude are vital aspects of the interpretive process as well. Through their symbolic power, texts disclose the presence of what is absent.

Numerous similarities, then, between Winnicott's squiggle game and hermeneutical process can be noted. Like the squiggle game, hermeneutics is a process of interaction between the primordial and the constructive, between chaos and order, between the deeply emotional and the highly rational. Object relations acknowledges multiple, primitive selves and fragmentation of persons, yet playfully proclaims a paradox in human relations and in the human psyche such that this fragmentation is the essential partner to creativity, including the interpretation of texts. Like the squiggle game, hermeneutics is a process that embodies and forms a relationship between text and person or text and community. Like the squiggle game, hermeneutics takes place in a space in which there is no complete dominance of either objectivity or subjectivity. Like the squiggle game, hermeneutics involves both written and oral communication in the context of community.

Authority and Illusion

These similarities pertain to hermeneutics in general. What about biblical hermeneutics in particular? A dynamic we have not yet considered is a dynamic that is particularly significant for biblical hermeneutics. I call it the dynamic of authority and illusion. For communities of faith and also for cultures influenced by the Scriptures, the question of authority constantly reappears. Hermeneutics, especially biblical hermeneutics, explores the meaning of *canon*, a diverse library of special texts that form and transform persons and community. As canon, the Scriptures are held out as a basis for judgment, a standard. They provide authority for communities of faith as a check on boundless human desire. Questions concerning canon are questions about relationships with texts.

Psychologically, this status in communities of faith lends a certain aura to biblical texts. Just as the earliest objects of affection and hatred from a person's childhood have a privileged place for influencing personality and personal apprehension of the world, so too what is canonical among the enduring texts of human culture occupies a special place. From an experiential standpoint, Scripture is a transitional reality, transgressing internal and external boundaries of self and other.

At the same time, an object relations approach regards the relationship that communities of faith or communities of scholarship have with biblical texts to exist in the realm of illusion.

What is illusion? For Freud it was any claim to truth that could not be verified scientifically yet could not be disproved either. Freud held that religion belongs to the realm of illusion, and he believed that scientific knowledge was making religion and its illusions no longer necessary (1927). In contrast, an object relations perspective holds that all cultural creativity, including the creativity of psychoanalytic theorizing and powers of religious belief, operates in the transitional sphere of illusion and is essential to human creativity and maturity. For the child, illusion is the royal road of transition from inner fantasy to outer reality. Without illusion there could be no encounter with such reality (Winnicott, 1988, 34). Likewise, without illusion, external reality has no possibility for meaning. This beginning point of human discovery and making of meaning extends to the art of interpretation. The hermeneutics of suspicion, to use Ricoeur's phrase (1970), has become the hermeneutics of playful suspension. Winnicott's concept of illusion does not constitute a full theory of culture, religion, or hermeneutics. Rather, it is his own suggestive squiggle, waiting for players.

Of course, one should not forget that illusion as such may express defensive relations as well as creative relations between person and object, person and text, and one should not forget that the popular connotation of the term *illusion* is "erroneous belief." It should be no surprise, then, that however much object relations tries to turn Freudian orthodoxy on its ear, object relations is not a psychoanalytic leap of faith in the sense that it does not provide a psychological foundation for a particular belief system or a particular canon. The heritage of psychoanalytic suspicion lives on but no longer occupies center stage. The psychological orientation of object relations theory does not provide grounds for affirmation of faith, but it does suggest a rationale for a suspension of disbelief that occurs in the creative encounter between persons, communities, and scriptural texts. An object relations approach calls off the dogs of disbelief and invites the world to play.

The field of play is the place of equilibrium between psychological defense and cultural creativity, and for object relations perspective this also is the playing field for biblical hermeneutics. What does one do with the squiggle of inner impulse and defense, and with the squiggle of the nonsensical in biblical texts? An object relations approach suggests that we accept these as part of a relational field inherited from the past and available potentially for the creation of patterns of participation in contemporary communities. So-called illusion is the currency of human interaction seeking to discern ultimate significance.

So we find this irony: interpretations of biblical texts are illusions, yet these illusions have authority. To the extent that we are constituted by our fundamental relationships, to the extent that interpretations of biblical texts mediate fundamental issues of human life and belief, these interpretive illusions have power to speak, author who we are, form and transform us, and make authors of us. A quality of mutual agency has emerged.

Biblical scholars have opportunity today to sharpen awareness of the dynamics of the authoring potential of biblical texts for the communities of faith that gave birth to these texts, and to continue to interpret them and the authoring potential of these texts for others also. For this reason, biblical scholars ought to analyze texts and also proffer reflective syntheses that describe our relationships with texts.

The Bible is both canonical text and primordial object, which is why there is a perennial danger in this inevitable locus of the people's canon. Perhaps this is why we find the phrase "cultural icon" used in the 1995 program of the Society of Biblical Literature. There is potential for harm; there is potential for liberation. These words slay and resurrect. Dynamically the meaning of Scripture is not only what it says but also what happens to us as we study Scripture. The process of interpreting yields new perceptions of texts and new understandings of ourselves. Could it be that in studying these texts, scholars subject themselves to a discourse that is not totally within their control, however disciplined they try to be?

Conclusion

Object relations theory sets forth a contemporary myth that is a resource for understanding the *process* of biblical interpretation. This psychology emphasizes the relational nature and imaginative character of interpretation. Can we learn to trust biblical texts and ourselves in the midst of reasonable distrust? An object relations approach suggests that biblical interpretation is an ongoing process that forms and transforms dynamic relations with biblical texts. The critical methods of scholarship fascinate when they are brought into concert with the unpredictable power of imagination that moves in individuals and communities. Given that nature, object relations envisions a trust–distrust dynamic that energizes the way persons and communities read and understand cultural texts, including biblical texts. An object relations approach to biblical hermeneutics is interested in the images of texts, the objects they present and the objects they are, their poetry as well as their narrative. Such an approach is interested in the rhythm, the musical quality of play, among texts, readers, and communities. Prolonged attention to biblical texts in communities of faith and in communities of scholarship has potential to form and reform persons, communities, and cultures.

In all this, object relations as such maintains a playful distance in relation to biblical hermeneutics. It remains a psychology and does not become a theology, but in principle there is space for potentially creative dialogue among object relations, theology, and biblical hermeneutics. As I interpret it, an object relations perspective hopes that the critical tradition in biblical hermeneutics, the obedient elder sibling, will make peace with the unpredictable return of prodigal imagination, for both of them, you see, belong to the same household.

Note

This article is based on a lecture delivered as a session of the Psychology and Biblical Studies Group, the Society for Biblical Literature, Philadelphia, Pennsylvania, November 21, 1995. It was first published in 1997 in *Pastoral Psychology*, 45(3), 181–192. It appears here with permission of *Pastoral Psychology*.

References

Brueggemann, W. (1984). *The Message of the Psalms: A Theological Commentary.* Minneapolis: Augsburg Press.

Derrida, J. (1978). *Writing and Difference.* Chicago: University of Chicago Press.

Freud, S. (1905). *Three Essays on the Theory of Sexuality, The Standard Edition of the Complete Psychological Works of Sigmund Freud,* vol. 7. London: Hogarth Press, 1953, 125–245.

Freud, S. (1909). Analysis of a Phobia in a Five-Year-Old Boy, *The Standard Edition of the Complete Psychological Works of Sigmund Freud,* vol. 10. London: Hogarth Press, 1953, 1–149.

Freud, S. (1915). Instincts and Their Vicissitudes, *The Standard Edition of the Complete Psychological Works of Sigmund Freud*, vol. 14. London: Hogarth Press, 1953, 117–140.

Freud, S. (1927). The Future of an Illusion, *The Standard Edition of the Complete Psychological Works of Sigmund Freud*, vol. 21. London: Hogarth Press, 1953, 5–56.

Greenberg, J. R., & Mitchell, S. A. (1983). *Object Relations in Psychoanalytic Theory*. Cambridge: Harvard University Press.

Pruyser, P. W. (1974). *Between Belief and Unbelief.* New York: Harper & Row.

Pruyser, P. W. (1991). *Religion in Psychodynamic Perspective*. New York: Oxford University Press.

Ricoeur, P. (1970). *Freud and Philosophy: An Essay on Interpretation*. New Haven: Yale University Press.

Rizzuto, A. (1979). *The Birth of the Living God: A Psychoanalytic Study*. Chicago: University of Chicago Press.

Trible, P. (1984). *Texts of Terror: Literary-Feminist Readings of Biblical Narratives*. Minneapolis: Fortress.

Watson, F. (1994). *Text, Church and World: Biblical Interpretation in Theological Perspective*. Grand Rapids: William B. Eerdmans.

Winnicott, D. W. (1971a). *Playing and Reality*. London: Tavistock Publications.

Winnicott, D. W. (1971b). *Therapeutic Consultations in Child Psychiatry*. London: Hogarth Press.

Winnicott, D. W. (1988). *Human Nature*. London: Free Association Books.

CHAPTER 8

Gospel Narrative and Psychoanalytic Criticism: Peter Brooks, Norman Holland, and Jacques Lacan

Petri Merenlahti

As evidenced by the emergence of methodological movements such as narrative criticism, New Testament scholars have recently taken a great interest in the nature of the Gospels as narratives (see, for example, Rhoads, 1982, 1999; Moore, 1989, 1–68; Powell, 1990; Malbon, 1992). In literary criticism, on the other hand, scholars have drawn on psychoanalytic theories in order to find dynamic models pertinent to the dynamics of narrative texts. In this chapter, I ask whether psychoanalytic criticism might contribute to a dynamic approach to Gospel narratives. For this purpose, I assess three cases of psychoanalytic criticism: (1) the psychopoetics of Peter Brooks, (2) transactive criticism proposed by Norman Holland, and (3) structural psychoanalytic criticism inspired by the psychoanalysis of Jacques Lacan.[1] I hope to show that despite their limitations, psychoanalytic theories and their adaptations to criticism can be useful to biblical scholars who are interested in narrative studies.

From Formalism to Freud: The Psychopoetics of Peter Brooks

In his well-received book *Reading for the Plot: Design and Intention in Narrative*, Peter Brooks uses "two different models derived from Freud to talk about two different aspects of narrative" (1984, 320; cf. Rickard, 1994, 6). The first model is taken from Freud's *Beyond the Pleasure*

Principle (1920), which Brooks transforms into a paradigm for how narratives work.

Brooks starts with the notion that narrative is an act of *repetition*. To narrate is to reproduce a sequence of events that is supposed to have taken place "once upon a time" in the world of the story. Moreover, various narrative techniques are, essentially, techniques of repetition. Thus, when Freud says that neurotic behavior is *a compulsion to repeat* events or fantasies of the past, this allows Brooks to conclude that structurally, narrative and the neurosis are driven by a similar kind of force.

In *Beyond the Pleasure Principle*, Freud links this repetition compulsion to a more general, instinctual "urge inherent in organic life to restore an earlier state of things" (1991, 244).[2] Ultimately, this urge leads to a state in which the organism becomes inorganic once again, which means that, in Freud's words, "the aim of all life is death" (246). However, Freud also assumes that the organism's self-preserving instincts make it react to various external stimuli so that death will not take place too soon, or in "an improper manner." What results is— the course of life: detours and modifications that delay the end.

Similarly, says Brooks, every narrative is initially directed toward its own termination, that is, a state in which everything is said, the story is told, and the narrative has lost all of its "narratability."[3] Before this end can be reached, however, the narrative also has to resist the threat of ending too soon. As a consequence, it produces a series of repetitions that bind its narrative energy until the point where, in an ideal case, all narratability is consummated. What results is *plot*— lifelike detours and complications that delay the end.[4]

The second model Brooks takes up from Freud is that of psychoanalytic *transference*, which Brooks considers "consonant with the narrative situation and the text" (1984, 320). Like the analyst and the analysand, the reader and the text of a narrative interact to construct an integrated interpretation of whatever happened in the past, or at the time of the story. Notably, this interpretive construction never becomes either fully complete or objectively verifiable. Instead, narrative and transference involve—to quote Brooks—"an unspecifiable network of event, fiction, and interpretation" (278).

Finally, what unites Brooks's two applications of Freud is his idea of the narrative form as an expression of the typically human need to find meaning in temporal existence (cf. Rickard, 1994, 4–5). According to Brooks, the narrative form implies that we can learn the truth of our present situation by recovering the origins of that situation in the past. This belief is portrayed in the structure of every narrative. A narrative revives a particular chain of events, structures it, and supplies it with meanings in order to present a retrospective explanation of its own ending. As a result, its readers will see that what brought that ending into being was not an irrelevant series of accidents but a genuine story. Even though the readers may realize that this vision of intentionality and integrity is fiction, it remains reassuring fiction that gives a sense of meaning to life in its temporality.

What kind of contribution might Brooks's reading of Freud make to a reading of the Gospel narratives? First of all, his project is not without problems. Even though he says he wants to avoid "sterile formalism" (1994, 44), his basic starting point is nevertheless a genuine formalist one. For him, narrative is still an objective category of the mind, "one of the ways in which we speak, one of the large categories in which we think" (1984, 323). Indeed, he believes that "in the case of psychoanalysis, paradoxically we can go beyond formalism only by becoming more formalistic"; to find "that desired place where literature and life converge we need to become convinced that we make our art in our own image, that the very same basic drives that determine our psychic construction also determine aesthetic form" (1994, 26).

In Brooks's use, the word *we* has a marked ring of universalism. What he seems to be saying is that psychoanalysis after all presents an objective as well as a universal model of the workings of the human psyche. Accordingly, a psychoanalytic model of narrative would give us an objective description of how all narratives work.

Not many people would be willing to concede so much. In contemporary narrative theory, the dangers of false universalism are well known. Yet we should be able to apply Brooks's ideas in a more metaphoric sense, too. (In fact, several critics of Brooks would prefer just that: see Brooks, 1994, 36–44.) Observing the narrative form *as if* its functions paralleled (and who knows if they actually do) those of a psychic organism as conceived through psychoanalysis might then offer us inspiring insights into how Gospel narratives work. In any case, observing how one narrative of considerable cultural relevance interprets another should teach us something important about each.

The use of the narrative form enables the Gospels to make meaning and establish truth in a particular way. This truth is taken to reside in the primeval past, and in order to recover it, the Gospels present the *beginning* of the good news that Jesus' followers proclaim. Thus, the Gospel of Mark begins with "*the beginning* [italics added] of the good news of Jesus Christ, the Son of God" (Mark 1:1); the Gospel of

Matthew opens with an account of the *genealogy* of Jesus; the Gospel
of Luke refers to "those who *from the beginning* [italics added] were
eyewitnesses and servants of the word" as well as to his own personal
investigations "*from the very first* [italics added]" (Luke 1:2–3); finally,
the Gospel of John takes us to the beginning of all beginnings, the
time before the creation.

Furthermore, the redactional work done by the evangelists resem-
bles the situation of psychoanalytic transference. What the evangelists aimed at was integrating the diverse material they found in their
oral and written sources into an organized literary and ideological
whole that would suit the present faith and practices of their respective communities. This aim was somewhat similar to the aim of the
classical Freudian analyst: "Wo Es war soll Ich werden" (Where id
was, there ego shall be)—the irregular impulses stemming from the
past should be brought under the control of some overarching principle, so that a recognizable identity in the present might emerge. As a
result, each Gospel is reminiscent of an analysis session (or a series of
them). Like analysis, a Gospel narrative is perpetually incomplete and
full of tension. Diffuse primary experience and integrated secondary
interpretations combat ceaselessly within the artificial—indeed, fictive—boundaries of narrative.

Interpretation as a Function of Identity:
Reading with Norman Holland

In many respects, Norman Holland's ideas of psychoanalytic criticism
are in diametric opposition to those presented by Peter Brooks. Brooks
believes that "the bad name" psychoanalytic criticism "has largely
made for itself" has to do with the tendency to displace the object of
analysis from the text to some person, be that person the author, the
reader, or the fictive persons in the text (1987, 1–2). To serve its purpose, psychoanalytic criticism should be textual and rhetorical. Holland, for his part, maintains that "the literary critic comes to psychoanalysis because psychoanalysis promises to tell him something about
people. Psychoanalysis has nothing, absolutely nothing, to tell us
about literature *per se*. But psychoanalysis, particularly in its theories
of character, has a great deal to tell us about people engaged in literature, either writing it or reading it or being portrayed in it" (1982, 31).

On the other hand, Holland, just as Brooks, builds on the idea of correspondence between literary and psychic process. In brief, Holland's
version of this correspondence reads: "Unity is to text as identity is

to self" (1980, 121). In his terms, the decisive correspondence prevails between how people interact with other people and how people interact with texts. He believes that both types of transactions are governed by the participating person's personal style, that is, the unchanging personal identity that the child first establishes through its relation to its mother and later maintains through its entire adult life. Thus, the way a reader interprets a text corresponds to the reader's own characteristic identity theme so that, ultimately, "interpretation is a function of identity. . . . The overarching principle is: identity re-creates itself, or, to put it another way, style—in the sense of personal style—creates itself. That is, all of us, as we read, use the literary work to symbolize and finally to replicate ourselves. We work through the text our own characteristic patterns of desire and adaptation. We interact with the work, making it part of our own psychic economy and making ourselves part of the literary work—as we interpret it" (1980, 123–124).[5]

The meaning Holland gives to his key concepts *identity* and *interpretation* helps us to define his position. The notion of identity to which he refers originates from a distinct post-Freudian tradition, namely, ego-psychology.[6] Typically, ego-psychology focuses on the human self as an integrative force that maintains identity by adjusting the inner, instinctual drives of the id to external prohibitions, thus helping the individual adapt to human society. When seen in this framework, literature is a subtle means of socialization that helps the people engaged in it to manage their instinctual energies and, consequently, to maintain a unified self. The aesthetic pleasure literature gives results not so much from the fulfillment of the reader's private fantasy (as Freud thought) as from the managing of this fantasy and transforming it into some socially acceptable form.

In Holland's model, the inherent unity that the ego-psychology attributes to the self corresponds to another type of unity at which Holland thinks critics should arrive in literary interpretation. For him, the aim of interpretation is very much the same as it was in conventional formalist criticism: to discover the meaning of the work by showing how all its elements relate to one central theme. Consequently, even though he speaks emphatically of "the dynamics of literary response,"[7] the type of comparison he makes of text to self has been criticized for merely transforming a static, formalist notion of text fully intact into a static, essentialist notion of the self (thus, for example, Freund, 1987, 125).

Those who have criticized Holland have a point. There is no reason to believe that our texts were any more unified than we are (cf. Moore, 1994, 74–81). Yet to view interpretation as a function of identity might still be rewarding. Although our texts as well as our selves may well be liable to division and deconstruction, the conventions of unity of texts and of assurance of the self have a strong enough history of dominance to make a comparison between them interesting. Even as a similarity of two corresponding fictions, this just might turn out to be informative.

In any case, a particular, de facto ego-psychological view of interpretation as a function of identity seems to be an unspoken assumption in quite a few exegetical studies already. As such, it is a fine case of how deeply Freudian discourse has naturalized itself within our speech and modes of thinking (cf. Freund, 1987, 132).

Take the widely accepted idea of Deuteronomist theology, for example. This theology is suggested to have motivated the final redaction of the so-called Deuteronomic History Work in the Hebrew Bible.[8] The core idea expressed in Deuteronomist theology is that the destruction of Jerusalem in the year 587 B.C.E. was not a sign of the God of Israel's failure but was God's premeditated punishment of the infidelity of his chosen people.

In scholarship, Deuteronomist theology is generally considered an attempt to master an acute identity crisis. It enabled the Judeans to interpret a national catastrophe so that the national religion and, consequently, national identity need not be rejected. In other words, it helped the Judean collective self to defend its integrity in the face of external pressure.

On the New Testament side, questions concerning the way the human self deals with the threat of disintegration seem equally pertinent. For early Christianity, conflict with and departure from first-century Judaism constituted a case of identity crisis. While the first followers of Jesus held fast to their traditional Jewish identity, a gradually growing number of newcomers saw the Old Israel as being replaced by a New Israel, a new constitution of the Chosen People with an entirely new kind of covenant with God. What resulted were conflicts, traces of which can be detected in various New Testament writings. Paul's Letter to the Galatians, for example, is a direct witness of one such conflict.

As to the more specific issue of reading as a function of identity, the Gospel narratives present a suggestive case. After all, the Gospels are readings. Studies of their origins indicate that they were composed so as to interpret other texts and traditions that the evangelists used as their sources. During a process of redaction, each evangelist sought to subordinate earlier material to his own fresh narrative and ideological vision. In an ideal case, this vision would be a formal and conceptual unity that would match a particular idea of Christian identity, typical of the community in which the Gospel in question originated. Thus, the process of redaction might be seen as a process of textual socialization, that is, adaptation of texts, traditions, and their ideologies to external norms and expectations. These norms and expectations could have been ideological—the theological content of a true Christian Gospel should be such and such—or literary: a Gospel should (or should not) resemble this or that known literary genre or text type. In either case, the way the text of a Gospel, as a particular reading of early Christian tradition, reaches toward integrity matches the psychosocial efforts (be they epistemologically well grounded or not) of those people among whom the text originated.

The Necessity of Absence:
Jacques Lacan's Structural Psychoanalysis

The models of Brooks and Holland draw on the idea of a correspondence between literary and psychic process. In this respect, these two models are by no means unique. On the contrary, most psychoanalytic readings of literature since Freud have, at least implicitly, assumed a similar type of correspondence.[9] The most radical and by far the most influential version of this idea is presented by the tradition of *structural psychoanalytic criticism*. This tradition relates, most notably, to the reinterpretation of Freud proposed by Jacques Lacan.[10]

For Lacan, language and textuality play a crucial role in the creation of the unconscious, whereas the unconscious, in turn, resides very much in the structure of language. It is the very experience of language that causes the individual subject to split into the conscious and the unconscious.

At a prelinguistic stage, says Lacan, the child maintains an illusion of the absolute, enduring presence of the mother as a source of immediate satisfaction. Lacan calls this stage the realm of the Imaginary. When the child gains access to language, the illusion previously held breaks up. From the realm of the Imaginary the child enters the rule of the Symbolic. Expected to express her desire in articulate words, the child understands that desire is not met with satisfaction automatically. According to Lacan, this causes what Freud called *primal repression*: ideas attached to instincts are denied entrance into the conscious; as a result, the unconscious comes into being.

Lacan draws on Ferdinand de Saussure, the father of structural linguistics, who regarded the sign as a combination of two elements, a *signifier* and a *signified*. A signifier is a distinct word-sound; a signified, a concept the word-sound stands for. According to Saussure, the link between the two is entirely arbitrary; any word-sound can be linked with any concept. Once the link is made, however, Saussure took it to be firm and secure. In his terms, the signifier and the signified are as inseparable as the two sides of a sheet of paper.

In Lacan's view, on the other hand, the link between the signifier and the signified is not secure at all because the identification of the signified is, ultimately, a matter of human judgment. Thus, contrary to what Saussure said, any given signifier does not correspond to some one signified. Rather, signifiers signify other signifiers that signify other signifiers, and so on, ad infinitum. On the level of the conscious, then, language operates like an endless chain of words in which each word signals the absence of what it stands for. This absence keeps frustrating the unconscious wherein the desire for immediate satisfaction—that is, a symbiotic union of signifiers and signifieds—still lives in exile.

Thus—and this is worth noting—the Symbolic never succeeds in taking over completely; here Lacan's reading of Freud differs markedly from the notion of ego-psychology. Although ego-psychology postulates a unified identity that is taken to be the result of the ego's success in its "progressive conquest of the id" (Freud, 1923, 56), Lacan introduces a notion of a *divided subject* permanently split into two parts, an ego that recognizes the inevitable absence of satisfaction and an unconscious that keeps reaching out after its lost objects of desire. In Lacan's own terms, the Imaginary and the Symbolic compete ceaselessly for the control over the unattainable *Real*.

How to make use of Lacan's thoughts in the study of the Gospel narratives? Although Lacan's own readings of literature have inspired a great number of commentators, the main effect of his work has been felt not so much in critical praxis as in the field of literary theory.[11] Correspondingly, in Lacan's case the use of psychoanalysis as an intertext rather than a method comes most naturally. This is all the more so because in certain respects there seems to be a close family resemblance between Lacan's thought and that of the evangelists—in particular the idea of the *absence of meaning*.

A number of paradigmatic biblical passages emphasize the utmost importance of understanding correctly the true, hidden meaning of what one sees or hears. These passages include the Markan parable theory, the Johannine misunderstandings, and the encounter of Philip and the Ethiopian official in the Acts of the Apostles, to name but a few.

According to the Markan parable theory (Mark 4:10–12), Jesus' parables are riddles whose true sense can be attained only by interpretation. The key to this interpretation is given only to a group of insiders, that is, to the followers of Jesus.

The Johannine misunderstandings consist of one typical scene that is repeated over and over again in the Fourth Gospel. The key element of this scene, in all its variations, is the confusion of the literal and the spiritual sense: people think that Jesus is speaking of earthly things when in fact he is speaking of heavenly ones (John 3:12). What results is a comic, often grotesque effect, while the character who commits the misunderstanding is shown in an ironic light.

In the story of Acts 8:26–40, the Ethiopian court official learns that understanding the Scriptures is only possible by gaining access to the way insiders (that is, Christians) read. He decides to become an insider and asks Philip to baptize him.

Essentially, all these episodes reach beyond appearances and representations—that is, beyond the Imaginary and the Symbolic—to the realm of the secret Gospel truth: the Real. Because the Real resides beyond the letter, it is of necessity unspeakable. As a consequence, words are denied their literal sense and are taken as enigmas. Instead of using literal language, the Gospels are forced to apply figurative speech, parables, and metaphors. The trouble is, as shown in all the passages mentioned as examples, this mode of speech makes the message incomprehensible. Unless they are given the key to the correct interpretation, the Ethiopian cannot understand what he is reading, the disciples have to ask Jesus to explain his parables, and Jesus' audience in John is bound to perform one act of misunderstanding after another.

The correct interpretation, if given, however, will only take us all the way back to the realm of the Symbolic. The attempt to bypass the signifier and reach the signified only results in adding one more signifier to an infinite chain of signifiers. The signified, the Real, the object of desire, remains lost. Boldly, however, the Gospels continue their quest, even though their frustrated attempts to formulate their desire in terms of language repeatedly render their mission impossible. In this sense, the Gospels speak in the language of the unconscious. Words of absence are their native tongue.

Conclusions

Although I do not believe that psychoanalytic criticism can provide us with any objective models of how narratives work, I do believe that psychoanalysis can serve as a fruitful intertext for reading the Gospels—not the least because the psychoanalytic discourse is "deeply engaged in many of the same issues that pervade the biblical texts" (Bible and Culture Collective, 1995, 222).

On which particular type of psychoanalytic criticism one should rely depends on what one's interests are. If one wants to focus on the textual features of the complete narratives of the Gospels, Peter Brooks's textual and rhetorical approach can provide an intriguing starting point. In light of Brooks's ideas, the Gospels present themselves not so much as static, spatial end-products of telling as they do dynamic, temporal processes of meaning making.

Yet if one is more interested in the origin and composition of the Gospels, one might draw on ego-psychological criticism. From an ego-psychological viewpoint, the composition of the Gospels as narratives can be seen as a process structurally comparable to the ego's "progressive conquest of the id" in its maintenance of a coherent and intelligible identity.

Finally, if one is to investigate the essentially ambiguous, parabolic, and indeterminate nature of the language that the Gospels use, one might consider making use of Jacques Lacan's ideas concerning the frustrating but inevitable absence of meaning.

Notes

A previous version of this article is included as Chapter 9, "Poetics and Psychoanalysis: A Case for Instrumental Metaphors?" in Petri Merenlahti, *Poetics for the Gospels? Rethinking Narrative Criticism* (T&T Clark: London & New York, 2002). Reprinted with permission.

1. The three cases are interconnected in that Lacan was a source of inspiration for Brooks and a vehement critic of ego-psychological approaches represented by Holland.

2. The page numbers of my notes refer to the *Standard Edition's* text (18,7) as reprinted in Freud (1991).

3. Cf. Steiner (1989, 141): "in their terminal structure, narrations are rehearsals for death."

4. Cf. Kermode (1967, 18): "The story that proceeded very simply to its obviously predestined end would be nearer myth than novel or drama. Peri-

peteia, which has been called the equivalent, in narrative, of irony in rhetoric, is present in every story of the least structural sophistication."

5. To find empirical support for his thesis, Holland put up an experimental program whose results are described in Holland (1975): he recorded and analyzed interviews about students' responses to William Faulkner's "A Rose for Emily" and discovered that these responses conformed to the readers' personality profiles as shown in standard psychological tests. Holland has reiterated his thesis in a vast number of publications since the early 1980s.

6. Among the founders of ego-psychology are Ernst Kris, Heinz Hartmann, Rudolph Loewenstein, and Erik Erikson. In his early works, especially in Holland (1968), Holland builds on the basis of Freud's "Creative Writers and Day-Dreaming" (1908), but he is also strongly influenced by the theories of Kris. The notion of identity presupposed in Holland (1980) derives from Heinz Lichtenstein, whom Holland introduces as "the most precise of the modern theorists of identity" (1980, 120). For an assessment of ego-psychological contributions to literary criticism, see Wright (1984, 56–68).

7. This is the title of Holland (1968), the book that begins his project.

8. The theory of the Deuteronomi(sti)c History Work (Deut., Josh., Judg., 1–2 Sam., 1–2 Kings) and the ideology behind it originated with the publication of Noth (1943) (English translation, 1981).

9. Lionel Trilling (1964) was the first to make this connection explicit. After Freud, most psychoanalytic readings of literature had focused predominantly on the author's psychic processes. At the same time, however, they had also given attention to how these processes were *figured in the text*, thus anticipating an openly textual and rhetorical approach (see Wright, 1984, 36; Freund, 1987, 131).

10. For a concise introduction to Lacan's ideas, see, for example, Richardson (1983); Wright (1984, 107–132); from the point of view of biblical studies, Bible and Culture Collective (1995, 196–211); Schwall (1997). My own presentation here is based mainly on these secondary introductions, as well as on Lacan (1977), an English selection from Lacan (1966). Although books on Lacan written by other people abound, his doctoral dissertation was the only book he himself published until he was sixty-five. Then, in 1966, *Écrits*, a massive collection of papers, appeared. Instead of books, Lacan's major contribution was the oral teaching he gave in his famous seminar.

11. Lacan's famous "Seminar on 'The Purloined Letter'" (1972, originally published in Lacan, 1966) gives an idea of how Lacan approached a literary text.

References

Bible and Culture Collective. (1995). *The Postmodern Bible*. New Haven: Yale University Press.

Brooks, P. (1984). *Reading for the Plot: Design and Intention in Narrative*. Oxford: Clarendon Press.

Brooks, P. (1987). The Idea of Psychoanalytic Literary Criticism, *Discourse in Psychoanalysis and Literature*, Shlomith Rimmon-Kenan, ed. New York: Methuen, 1–18.

Brooks, P. (1994). *Psychoanalysis and Storytelling*. Oxford: Blackwell.

Freud, S. (1905–1906). Psychopathic Characters on the Stage, *The Standard Edition of the Complete Psychological Works*, vol. 7. London: Hogarth Press and Institute of Psychoanalysis, 1953, 303–310.

Freud, S. (1907). *Delusions and Dreams in Jensen's "Gadiva," The Standard Edition of the Complete Psychological Works*, vol. 9. London: Hogarth Press and Institute of Psychoanalysis, 1953, 1–97.

Freud, S. (1908). Creative Writers and Day-Dreaming, *The Standard Edition of the Complete Psychological Works*, vol. 9. London: Hogarth Press and Institute of Psychoanalysis, 1953, 141–154.

Freud, S. (1920). *Beyond the Pleasure Principle, The Standard Edition of the Complete Psychological Works*, vol. 18. London: Hogarth Press and Institute of Psychoanalysis, 1953, 1–64.

Freud, S. (1923). *The Ego and the Id, The Standard Edition of the Complete Psychological Works*, vol. 19. London: Hogarth Press and Institute of Psychoanalysis, 1953, 1–66.

Freud, S. (1991). *The Essentials of Psycho-Analysis*. Reprints from the *Standard Edition*. New York: Penguin Books.

Freund, E. (1987). *The Return of the Reader: Reader-Response Criticism*. New York: Methuen.

Holland, N. N. (1968). *The Dynamics of Literary Response*. New York: Oxford University Press.

Holland, N. N. (1975). *Five Readers Reading*. New Haven: Yale University Press.

Holland, N. N. (1980). Unity Identity Text Self, *Reader-Response Criticism: From Formalism to Post-Structuralism*, Jane P. Tompkins, ed. Baltimore: Johns Hopkins University Press, 118–133.

Holland, N. N. (1982). Why This Is Transference, or Am I Out of It. *Psychoanalysis and Contemporary Thought*, 5, 27–34.

Kermode, F. (1967). *The Sense of an Ending: Studies in the Theory of Fiction*. New York: Oxford University Press.

Lacan, J. (1966). *Écrits*. Paris: Seuil.

Lacan, J. (1972). Seminar on "The Purloined Letter." *Yale French Studies*, 40, 38–72.

Lacan, J. (1977). *Écrits: A Selection*. New York: Norton.

Malbon, E. S. (1992). Narrative Criticism: How Does the Story Mean? *Mark and Method: New Approaches in Biblical Studies*, J. C. Anderson and S. D. Moore, eds. Minneapolis: Augsburg Fortress, 23–49.

Moore, S. D. (1989). *Literary Criticism and the Gospels: The Theoretical Challenge*. New Haven: Yale University Press.

Moore, S. D. (1994). *Poststructuralism and the New Testament: Derrida and Foucault at the Foot of the Cross*. Minneapolis: Fortress.

Noth, M. (1943). *Überlieferungsgeschichtliche Studien*. Halle (Saale): Max Niemeyer Verlag.

Powell, M. A. (1990). *What Is Narrative Criticism?* Minneapolis: Fortress.

Rhoads, D. M. (1982). Narrative Criticism and the Gospel of Mark. *Journal of the American Academy of Religion*, *50*, 411–434.

Rhoads, D. M. (1999). Narrative Criticism: Practices and Prospects, *Characterization in the Gospels: Reconceiving Narrative Criticism*, D. Rhoads & K. Syreeni, eds. Sheffield, UK: Sheffield Academic Press, 264–285.

Richardson, W. J. (1983). Lacan and the Subject of Psychoanalysis, *Interpreting Lacan*, J. H. Smith & W. Kerrigan, eds. New Haven: Yale University Press, 51–74.

Rickard, J. S. (1994). Introduction, *Psychoanalysis and Storytelling*, by Peter Brooks. Oxford: Blackwell.

Schwall, H. (1997). Lacan and the Bible. *Literature and Theology*, *11*, 125–144.

Steiner, G. (1989). *Real Presences*. Chicago: University of Chicago Press.

Trilling, L. (1964). Freud and Literature, *The Liberal Imagination*. London: Heinemann, 34–57.

Wright, E. (1984). *Psychoanalytic Criticism: Theory in Practice*. New York: Methuen.

CHAPTER 9

POST-TRAUMATIC STRESS DISORDER AND VICARIOUS ATONEMENT IN THE SECOND ISAIAH

William Morrow

> The conflict between the will to deny horrible events and the will to proclaim them aloud is the central dialectic of psychological trauma.
>
> —Herman, 1997, 1

The words of the epigraph describe a dilemma faced by victims of chronic post-traumatic stress disorder (PTSD). They also apply to the community that first heard and preserved the famous poem about the "suffering servant" in Isaiah 52:13–53:12 (hereafter referred to as Isa. 53). By the rivers of Babylon (cf. Ps. 137), expatriate exiles from Zion bewailed the cruel fate of Jerusalem, destroyed by the Babylonians in 587 BCE, and their own forced displacement to Mesopotamia. Survivors of this catastrophe were addressed by an anonymous prophet known to scholarship as the Second Isaiah (Isa. 40–55). He (or is it she? see McEvenue, 1997) attempted to convince this discouraged community, suffering the stigma of a story of captivity and divine abandonment, that their God intended a bright future for them. Isaiah 53 portrays psychological dynamics implicated in the community's appropriation of the Second Isaiah's message of hope. Acceptance of their suffering as a vicarious sacrifice for coming generations resolved the conflict between angrily turning blame for the violence inward (self-hatred) or outward (toward God and Israel's religious heritage).

To substantiate these claims, I defend the idea that the contemporary diagnosis of PTSD is relevant for reading Isaiah 53, an ancient

biblical text. I demonstrate how Isaiah 53 models a process of rationalization that enabled the exiled community to overcome a psychological and theological impasse created by grief and anger, which stood
in the way of coming liberation. The portrayal of the community's suffering as a form of vicarious atonement gave a mythic dimension to
their plight, which facilitated reconnection with a disowned religious
identity: as God's servant Israel. This effort at reframing the community's self-concept is connected to other vicarious processes. On the
one hand, the community of exiles vicariously bore the shame of a previous generation that had endured the destruction of Jerusalem. On
the other hand, the prophet/poet who wrote Isaiah 53 not only
observed the PTSD symptoms of the exiles but also experienced them
as an enlightened witness. As a witness to undeserved suffering, the
writer of Isaiah 53 communicated an empathy with the people that
would have promoted trust in the prophet's message.

The Effects of Violence on Exiled Israel

Exposure to extreme stress such as rape and other crimes of violence, natural and human-caused disasters, torture, prolonged captivity, and war bring about predictable psychological changes in human
beings. The term *post-traumatic stress disorder* is used to diagnose psychological problems that attend victims of such severe trauma. PTSD
may be defined as a set of chronic symptoms and coping mechanisms
that cause clinically significant distress and impairment in social, occu-
pational, or other important areas of functioning (American Psychiatric Association, 1994, 424). Symptoms can affect groups as well as
individuals. Victim populations include war veterans, Holocaust survivors, and those who have suffered various forms of captivity, including hostages and political prisoners (Herman, 1997).

One has to be cautious about associating PTSD symptoms with an
experience of trauma. Although only about 25 percent of persons
exposed to a traumatic event will develop PTSD (Meichenbaum, 1994,
23), nevertheless some conditions lend themselves to its development.
These indicators have to do with the cognitive aspects of extreme
stress and the ways in which violations of the victim's prior system of
meaning contribute to the development of PTSD. They are important
for my study because they are suggestive for a diagnosis of PTSD in
the symbol of exiled and captive Israel.

Traumatic stress disrupts various cognitive schemas that human
beings use to communicate basic relational needs. Among these needs

is the desire for a coherent frame of reference or worldview (McCann & Pearlman, 1990, 62–66). Alternatively, one can speak of the capacity of trauma to shatter "the assumptive world," thereby altering basic assumptions about self and worldview (50–51). In other words, severe psychological trauma entails disruptions in victims' capacity to feel meaningful or to make meaning out of their lives. Shifts in the system of meaning include loss of faith, a sense of hopelessness, and despair (Meichenbaum, 1994, 49).

What warrant is there for applying a contemporary description of traumatized persons to an ancient text? The way people react to psychological trauma does not seem to be very dependent on cultural background (van der Veer, 1998, 76). For example, child abuse and neglect appear to have consistent effects across race, ethnicity, culture, and time period (Erkman, 1992, 384). The probability that there are similarities between the ways in which ancient and modern persons respond to trauma is underscored by the observation that predictable physiological as well as psychological changes are involved (Herman, 1997, 35–36). Because the human genetic pool does not appear to have changed substantially over the roughly 5,000 years of recorded history, there is reason to believe that human responses to extreme stress might have continuity as well.

In the Bible, significant social entities such as the people of Israel or Zion can be regarded as symbolic or "corporate" persons (Rogerson, 1992, 1,157). Zion/Jerusalem and Jacob/Israel are depicted as experiencing terrible violence as a result of conquest by the Neo-Babylonian Empire. Although it may appear problematic to apply the psychology of violence to a classical literary symbol, there are precedents. For example, the effects of war seem to be described in similar ways whether the source is Homer, Shakespeare, or contemporary reports on combat stress (Meichenbaum, 1994, 57; Shay, 1994). The myth of Oedipus has been subject to various studies that appeal to the psychoanalysis of victims of abuse and violence (Girard, 1986, 25–30; Shengold, 1989, 41–68).

The Babylonian Empire conquered the kingdom of Judah and its capital city of Jerusalem both in 597 and 587 B.C.E. The second time, there was considerable destruction: large numbers of persons lost their lives, Jerusalem was turned into a ruin, the temple was burned to the ground, the city walls were torn down, and the kingdom of Judah ceased to exist as a political entity (Miller & Hayes, 1986, 406–415). Deportations occurred in both 597 B.C.E. and 587 B.C.E., when significant portions of the population were uprooted in order to suppress the country's capacity to rebel. By any account, thousands of inhabitants of Judah and Jerusalem were transported to Mesopotamia (Miller & Hayes, 1986, 417–420).

Trauma can be defined as (violent) stress that is sudden, unexpected, or nonnormative, exceeds the individual's perceived ability to meet its demands, and disrupts various psychological needs (McCann & Pearlman, 1990, 10). The defeat, captivity, and exile of the inhabitants of Jerusalem qualifies as trauma under this definition. For many persons, these events exceeded their capacity to continue living within the perspective of faith in Israel's god, and their needs for self-esteem, independence, and a coherent worldview, among other psychological needs, were injured (see, for example, Lam. 5).

When the experience of violence conflicts with prior beliefs, the victim is often less able to reconcile the violating event and recovery is more difficult. For example, among rape victims, it is the woman who thought she was particularly invulnerable or safe who usually has more difficulty recovering than others (Meichenbaum, 1994, 73). In this connection, it is significant that rape imagery is common in descriptions of the devastation of Jerusalem (for example, Ezek. 16, 23; Lam. 1). Biblical records attest to an exaggerated sense of confidence held by the population of Jerusalem about the safety and inviolability of the city as a result of the presence of the temple (see Jer. 7). It would not be surprising if the faith community that had counted on divine protection was overwhelmed by the experience of profound violation.

The victims of both deportations were settled in regions south of Babylon. It appears that most were reduced to the status of peasants who farmed plots of land assigned them by the state (Lemche, 1988, 179–180). The Second Isaiah addressed the deported Jewish population resident in Babylonia during the years 547–539 B.C.E. (Dion, 1970, 18), when significant political events were taking place that would bring the conditions of exile to an end. Cyrus, a Persian ruler, was the leader of a coalition of forces threatening the domination of the Neo-Babylonian Empire that had held sway over much of the ancient Near East since 605 B.C.E. Babylon fell to Cyrus in 539 B.C.E., and this victory inaugurated the beginning of the Persian Empire. The next year, 538 B.C.E., effectively ended the exile when a decree by Cyrus authorized captive peoples in Babylonia to return to their homelands (Miller & Hayes, 1986, 438–443).

The substance of the Second Isaiah's prophecies is conveyed through various poetic genres (Schoors, 1973, 29; Gottwald, 1987, 493–494). Two classes of poetry promise deliverance: oracles of salvation and proclamations of salvation. There are also two argumentative genres meant to defend the validity of the prophet's message: trial speeches and disputations. Throughout this body of poetry, the prophet addressed a community that was full of hostility toward its God, its own religious identity, and the prophet's message.

Violence alters a basic sense of self and world. The Second Isaiah's prophecies were intended to help the exiled community reframe its sense of self and its worldview. The need to promote resiliency impels traumatized victims to find meaning by constructing new and coherent narratives that make sense of their sufferings and their shattered world.

According to Meichenbaum, trauma brings out the poet in victimized persons and in those who attempt to help them. Language, metaphor, ritual, religion, and psychotherapy all have an important role in fostering change through the construction of new narrative perspectives (1994, 544–548).

It would be difficult to find a better description of the efforts of the brilliant, religious poet responsible for the compositions transmitted in Isaiah 40–55. Important themes in the prophet's message addressed both the exiles' sense of self and their worldview. The following summary of the prophet's message is adapted from Gowan (1998, 148–159):

Worldview
- YWHW is about to bring the Babylonian Empire to an end.
- YHWH can do this because he is the only God, and has created everything there is.
- YHWH will lead Israel back to the homeland, and Jerusalem will be rebuilt in splendor.
- All this will come to pass so that YHWH shall be glorified in all the earth.

Self
- The time of punishment (exile), which Israel deserves because of its sins, is over. They are still God's elect, and YHWH has forgiven their sins.
- The nations will bow down to Israel, recognizing that they are the favorites of the only God.

Indications of PTSD symptoms can be discerned by reading between the lines of the prophet's appeals to the people. These include the stigma of a shameful identity and symptoms of learned helplessness. I have documented these syndromes elsewhere at length (Morrow, 2004) so I only summarize the results of that study here.

The prophet encountered a collective story of violence and rejection that left little hope for the future of the faith community. Traumatic suffering associated with the conquest of Judah and Jerusalem was transmitted vicariously to second-generation survivors through the continued rehearsal of this catastrophe in liturgies of lament. The exiles believed that God had ignored Israel (Isa. 40:27), forsaken Zion (Isa. 49:14), and divorced Jerusalem (Isa. 50:1). Consequently, the exiles were burdened with low esteem for the faith community to which they and the previous generation—the generation that had actually suffered the violence of the Babylonian conquest and deportation—belonged. The children of the survivors continued to carry their parents' shame as those judged and rejected by YHWH.

Loss of a sense of order and continuity in life has discernible effects on spirituality. Persons suffering from PTSD often cannot trust or hope. They do not feel connected to their inner selves, much less to anyone else or to God. The term *abandonment despair* has been used to describe this profound sense of spiritual alienation and emptiness (McBride & Armstrong, 1995, 6–8). The motif of abandonment despair is discernible in the lament fragments preserved in the Second Isaiah. This attitude of religious distress apparently intensified as the exile continued. It is prominent in the prophet's trial speeches against Israel in which Israel's charges against YHWH are answered (Isa. 42:18–25, 43:22–28, 50:1–3). The community indicted YHWH for breaking the covenant by delivering them into the hands of the enemy. There was doubt whether YWHW was able to keep his promises and a conviction that he had abandoned his people (Albertz, 1994, 413; Schoors, 1973, 239).

Diminished hopes for divine redemption led to the syndrome of learned helplessness among the faithful—a syndrome that results when people believe or expect that their responses will not influence future outcomes. Prolonged captivity is an indicator for such behavior (Herman, 1997, 121). The lack of a visible response by YHWH to the exiles' liturgies of lament left the faith community with the sense that Israel had no control over its destiny. Symptoms of learned helplessness among the exiles can be discerned both in their refusal to embrace the prophet's message of imminent salvation and in the prophet's polemics against idolatry (for example, Isa. 44:9–20). The second-generation captives were becoming resigned to permanent Babylonian hegemony, which included a growing fascination with the religion of their conquerors.

The Servant Songs and the Sufferings of Israel

Scholars typically identify four "servant songs" in the poetry of the Second Isaiah: Isaiah 42:1–4, 49:1–6, 50:4–9a, and 52:13–53:12 (Dion, 1970, 34; Whybray, 1987, 70). Studies on these enigmatic poems, especially Isaiah 53, are numerous (see, for example, Baltzer, 2001, 19; Kaufmann, 1970, 128–134; North, 1956). Two disputed issues especially concern this study. First, does the servant have a collective or an individual identity? Second, were the servant songs composed by the Second Isaiah or later?

It is a matter of intense and ongoing debate whether the servant of Isaiah 53 is an individual or a collective referent (see Clifford, 1992, 499–500; Gowan, 1998, 160–161). Nevertheless, there is strong support for the traditional Jewish interpretation that the servant refers, in the first place, to Israel (Dion, 1970, 35; Kaufmann, 1970, 148–149; North, 1964, 20–22). An indicator that the servant can be taken collectively may be derived from the use of the term in the Second Isaiah. Altogether there are twenty references to the servant in Isaiah 40–55; of those, it is agreed that the thirteen occurrences outside 42:1–4, 49:1–6, 50:4–9, and 52:13–53:12 refer to the community Israel as servant (Clifford, 1992, 499).

This argument does not necessarily rule out an individual identification of the servant. It is problematic to impose this choice on an ambiguous symbol, especially in light of biblical ideas about personality. A representative of the community can be identified with that collective persona as well as speak for it. The prophet who spoke to Israel could also speak as Israel. There are grounds for assuming, therefore, that Israel in the servant songs can represent both the people and the prophet (Robinson, 1980, 41–42). The relationship of the prophet's suffering to Israel's is explored later in the chapter.

The association of the servant with Israel suggests that the Second Isaiah wrote the servant songs, although this conclusion is not universally accepted (Clifford, 1992, 499). The question of authorship is most vexed in connection with Isaiah 53 (North, 1964, 20). Dion is of the opinion that although the first three poems are compositions of the Second Isaiah, Isaiah 53 was likely written by a disciple of the prophet (1970, 35–36). This is a delicate issue and reflects an opinion that the servant songs seem written slightly later than the other genres of the Second Isaiah's poetry (North, 1956, 188), with Isaiah 53 the latest of all (Dion, 1970, 36). Because the Second Isaiah probably operated among the exiled community in Babylon for most of a decade, it is possible that Isaiah 53 comes at the very end of that period. But even if Dion is correct to assign its composition to a disciple of the Second Isaiah, we still have a poem that meditates on the effect of the prophet's message on the community. The discussion that follows is not substantially affected by the assumption that Isaiah 53 was written by the Second Isaiah or an immediate disciple.

There are indications that servant Israel, as described in the four servant songs, was suffering PTSD symptoms. The servant experienced injury to his self-esteem commensurate with the loss of meaning that accompanies chronic difficulties in recovering from trauma. Isaiah 42:2 describes the servant as frail and submissive, unable to cry out or cause his voice to be heard in the marketplace. There is an expression of abandonment despair in Isaiah 49:4: "I thought, I have laboured in vain, I have spent my strength for empty breath." Finally, with respect to Isaiah 53:2–3, Kaufmann points out: "He is without form or comeliness, ill and in pain, and remote from the society of men . . . these are metaphors for contrition and heartbreak and permanent melancholy" (1970, 158).

Isaiah 53 is also noteworthy for images of dissociation. In trauma victims, dissociation is the mechanism whereby intense sensory and emotional experiences are disconnected from the social domain of language and memory (Herman, 1997, 239). Dissociative actions and conditions in Isaiah 53 include the following: what appeared was reduced to humanly understandable categories (52:14); the servant was despised and cut off from human contact (53:2–3); he was silent before his slaughterers (53:7); and he was cut off from the land of the living and taken away (53:8–9).

Another indicator of emotional distance is found in the way the poem describes the affect of the various parties mentioned. According to Clines, Hebrew poetry and prophecy typically are steeped in affective terminology. But affective terms are almost totally absent in Isaiah 53: "Yahweh does not say how he *feels* about the servant, of the servant himself not a single emotion is expressed, the 'we' say nothing about how they feel about 'him' except to deny the feeling they once had, while of the 'they' it can only be said that if astonishment is an affect, that emotion passes quickly enough" (1983, 44). This sustained lack of affect communicates distance between the servant and those who observe him.

But who are the observers? One class of observer is designated by first-person common plural references: *we* in Isaiah 53:1–6. The identity of this reference has been subject to much discussion (Clines, 1983, 29–31), but an important clue comes from considering the function of the "we" references in the act of reading. This use establishes common ground between the observers and the readers/listeners of the poem (63). I conclude, therefore, that one group of listeners who could identity with "we" in Isaiah 53 would be the audience to whom the poem was originally addressed: the exilic community.

The poem shows, therefore, the process of dissociation that observation of the servant's sufferings caused in the community that witnessed them. Barré notes that the servant's sufferings are primarily inflicted on him by YHWH for his own mysterious purpose. What the servant suffers at the hands of his fellow human beings, by comparison, consists almost exclusively of being arrested, taken from his homeland by judicial decree, and classified with sinners. In the ancient Near Eastern context of the poem, it would be logical for observers to shun the servant as one who was accursed by God (Barré, 2000, 24).

Isaiah 53 as a Therapeutic Response to Israel's PTSD

One must be cautious about generalizations in proposing that the trauma of the exile caused PTSD symptoms among the deported Jewish populace of Babylonia. The Murashû archive, written about a hundred years after the exile, in the fifth century B.C.E., indicates that the Jewish community that remained after the exile was able to integrate successfully into Babylonian society (Stolper, 1992, 928). My claim of traumatic injury is limited to the religious identity of the exiles. The servant songs agree with other passages in Isaiah 40–55 that indicate the exiles had difficulty appropriating the identity of Israel.

A description of the therapeutic dynamics of Isaiah 53 rests on the recognition that the exiled community consists of both those who observe the servant's sufferings with horror and the servant himself. The symbol "Israel" is ambiguous in the biblical tradition generally and in the Second Isaiah in particular. In the Bible, Israel is portrayed as both faithful and rebellious, righteous and wicked. This ambivalence is reflected in the poetry of the Second Isaiah, which at times depicts the nation as chosen and beloved but also as a transgressor from the womb (Isa. 48:8) who is blind and deaf (Isa. 42:19, 43:8). There was no clear demarcation between righteous and rebellious Israel; rather there were two tendencies, two poles, two aspects. One of these aspects is symbolized by the servant. The servant terminology represents one side of the community, and that is Israel as the righteous and faithful follower of God (Kaufmann, 1970, 149–150).

Healthy, mature persons have a capacity to live with ambiguity (Rubin, 1975, 152–158). They know they are not perfect, but this knowledge does not paralyze them. It is evident, however, that ambiguity in Israel's collective awareness had become intolerable in the wake of the exile. The exilic community was at risk of forgetting any positive identity with Israel because it was overwhelmed with its self-knowledge as the punished and disobedient one. Moreover, the community could not renew its identity as God's servant without coping with its sense of injury and self-hatred. In Isaiah 53, the prophet calls on his audience to appreciate the destiny of the servant as one whom God will exalt and reward, but he can only do so by attempting to reframe the people's revulsion, their dissociation from their collective identity as one despised by God and rejected by men.

How does Isaiah 53 contend with the dissociative processes it describes? To answer this question, we need to have some idea about what emotional conflicts might underlie disesteem of the servant. I have already suggested that recalling the injuries of the exile was injurious to the community's self-esteem. This refusal to associate with the vocation of Israel as servant may be analyzed as a form of resistance born out of the fear of retraumatization (see Bacal & Newman, 1990, 261–262). But this resistance was also predicated on anger against God. The exiled community perceived its plight as unfair. They disputed the prophetic analysis that proclaimed that Jerusalem's destruction and exile were just retribution for the sins of the nation.

The Second Isaiah's position on this question is ambivalent. On the one hand, the violence of the exile is defended in trial disputations such as those in Isaiah 42:18–25 and 43:22–28. On the other hand, there is admission that the exile has been excessive. This is most notable in Isaiah 40:2: "Speak tenderly to Jerusalem and declare to her that her time of service is over, that her iniquity is pardoned; that she has received from the hand of YHWH double for all her sins" (adapted from RSV). Various scholars have sought to ward off any implication of injustice on the part of YHWH. A common tactic is to suppose that the word "double" in this context really means "equivalence" and that the proclamation of YHWH's forgiveness is commensurate with Jerusalem's punishment (for example, Whybray, 1987, 49–50; see the discussion in Baltzer, 2001, 52). But this attempt to exculpate YHWH will not do. The Hebrew word translated as "double" in Isaiah 40:2 means "twice as much" elsewhere in biblical and Rabbinic Hebrew. Behind the opening words of comfort in 40:1–2 lies the perception that

an innocent generation is now paying the price of the sins of its ancestors (North, 1964, 73; Phillips, 1982, 132).

Isaiah 53 addresses this situation by an innovative use of the imagery of vicarious atonement. The idea of vicarious atonement has two
references in the Hebrew Bible. First, it can refer to the fact that people
pay juridical penalties for the crimes of others. The execution of seven
sons of Saul for their father's infraction is an example of the juridical
application of vicarious atonement (2 Sam 21:1–9). Second, vicarious
atonement occurs through the concept of sacrificial substitution. For
example, Micah 6:7 reads, "Shall I give my first-born for my transgression, The fruit of my body for my sins?" This text suggests that
at one time in Israel, a father might contemplate offering his son as a
substitutionary offering to expiate sin (Kaufmann, 1970, 142–145).
Rituals for substitutionary offerings are found in Leviticus 4–5.

The juridical and cultic meanings of vicarious suffering come
together in Isaiah 53. It is clearly stated that the servant suffers on
account of the sins of others (v. 5). This is a juridical concept. But it is
also stated (v. 10) that the servant effects a cultic offering as a compensation for sin (Baltzer, 2001, 421). In both cases, the community's sufferings are revealed as having an expiatory significance.

Isaiah 53, therefore, offers to the community a process of rationalization whereby it can accept the offer of coming salvation without
denying the painfulness of its perceptions of the past. The narrative
reframes the perception that the suffering of the exile is unjust by
offering a new interpretation of the violence experienced by the exiles
as servant Israel. In fact, the servant continues to serve, even in the
midst of the exile, as a compensation for sin. But it is not the sins of
the past or the present that the exilic community's sufferings affect.
The superfluous violence of that experience has an atoning value that
will benefit future generations. This was YHWH's will. The result is
that servant Israel has a future with God, just as he had a past, which
gives an unrecognized dignity to the suffering of the second-generation
survivors of the exile. They are actually suffering so that others in the
future will not have to. Though they make their grave (figuratively
speaking) with rich Babylon (cf. Isa. 53:9), they will be the means
whereby future generations will prosper (Phillips, 1982, 132).

Vicarious Atonement and Empathy

Evaluation of the therapeutic effects of Isaiah 53 has mixed results.
The effects of its reframing exercise may not be entirely positive. It
can be debated whether the poem definitively addresses the problems

posed by PTSD among the exiles or simply sublimates those energies into a theological asset. The exiled community's sense of injustice and lack of entitlement were overridden by a new sense of time that tended to devalue those feelings by turning the present into an intermediate link between a sorrowful past and a glorious future.

Feminist analysis has rightly criticized imagery of sacrificial service for its abusive potential (Carlson Brown & Parker, 1990). The abused child or woman may embrace the identity of the saint chosen for martyrdom as a way of preserving a sense of value (Herman, 1997, 106). In this regard, we must be appropriately wary of the divine evaluation of the servant's self-offering, which is present in Isaiah 53:10, in that it sounds very much like the grandiosity of a victim in denial. Caution is required when taking such symbols as a model for dealing with suffering people. There is no doubt that such a perspective can bring meaning in difficult times, but it has the unfortunate side effect of arresting the perception that such affliction may be unjust. It was for this reason that Marx called religion "the opiate of the people" (Westphal, 1993, 137).

Nevertheless, the imagery of martyrdom is not the only place to find vicarious processes at work in Isaiah 53. The poem illustrates what Arlow describes as the ego-integration functions of mythology. Poets and prophets play a role similar to that of mythmakers in a particular community. They give words and form to works of art that function to externalize and address psychological needs. Myth, for example, plays a role in warding off feelings of guilt and anxiety. It also recommends a form of adaptation to reality and to the group in which the individual lives. The mythology of a particular culture or society, therefore, points the direction to the younger generation to the solution of various instinctual conflicts (Arlow, 1961, 375–380). Isaiah 53 offered a new myth of suffering to the exiles.

This new mythology was possible because the prophet was able to observe the conflicted identity of the exiles in a way that took the perspective of the community seriously. In other words, we can detect in Isaiah 53 a form of what Alice Miller calls "enlightened witness," the person who attends to the story of the trauma survivor and attests to the undeserved nature of the suffering (1993, 17). The prophet did not dispute the exiles' perception that it was excessive for an innocent generation to suffer the punishment meted out to their ancestors. By mirroring this belief and transforming it into a myth of vicarious suffering, the prophet built a bridge to his people that would allow them to take seriously his message of impending salvation.

Isaiah 53 worked in part because it communicated empathy between the two parties—a cardinal attribute in a working relationship between client and therapist, according to self-psychology. The ability of the patient to appropriate the insights gained in company with the therapist is a function of empathetic responsiveness on the part of the therapist (Bacal & Newman, 1990, 255–256). The prophet's sympathy with the exiles' perception of their plight led to a communication that allowed the community to increase its trust in the prophet's message of redemption.

Enlightened witness has connections with vicarious suffering. Observers of traumatic events can be injured by them. To become a witness to the suffering of another is to invite a vicarious experience of trauma and injury. In therapeutic circles, this sort of secondary injury is called vicarious traumatization or traumatic transference. Therapists working with victims of violence are simply told to expect this as part of the healing process. It is a function of the countertransference: the thoughts and feelings the therapist experiences in response to the client (Herman, 1997, 140–147).

The psychology of the countertransference has something to say about prophetic methodology. Abraham Heschel's classic description of the Israelite prophet begins by highlighting the prophet's sensitivity to evil (1969, 3–5). Feeling is central to the prophetic experience. For Heschel, the prophet discloses a divine pathos, not just a divine judgment: "An analysis of prophetic utterances shows that the fundamental experience of the prophet is a fellowship with the feelings of God, *a sympathy with the divine pathos.* . . . He lives not only his personal life, but also the life of God. The prophet hears God's voice and feels His heart" (1969, 26).

In biblical prophecy, countertransference occurs in two directions: from God to the prophet and from the people to the prophet. The prophet feels what God feels and also feels what the people could feel if they were truly aware (Brueggemann, 1978). As a prophet, the Second Isaiah experienced the self-loathing, the despair, and the constriction of the people. As a result, there was insight into the community's own dysfunctional belief system. The people were scapegoating themselves. In the Babylonian exile, the Second Isaiah observed a combination of extreme shame, guilt, grief, and inchoate rage. Israel had become appalling to itself, accounted as plagued, smitten, and afflicted by God (cf. Isa. 52:14, 53:2).

The community protected itself from witnessing its own pain by splitting itself off from its religious identity and growing hostile to it.

This process of dissociation made the symbol of servant Israel into a community scapegoat. The community chose to interpret the misfortune that came upon Israel as a mark of divine disfavor that justified their collective violence against it. All the marks of the scapegoating mechanism are visible in Isaiah 53: sacrificial expulsion, the violent removal of the innocent victim, and the healing that the community experiences because they have been able to channel their hostilities onto a common object of contempt (Goodhart, 2000, 210). There are parallels between the desire to disavow identity with the servant and disbelieve the prophet's message. As an enlightened witness, the prophet could feel these hostilities and name their unwarranted character.

Vicarious Processes in Isaiah 53

Recovery from PTSD involves reconstructing the trauma story and restoring the connection between the survivors and their community (Herman, 1997, 133). These concerns are visible in the poetry of the Second Isaiah in general and Isaiah 53 in particular. In the latter case, restorative power is conveyed through the myth of vicarious atonement and the empathetic witness to undeserved suffering that it represents.

The myth of vicarious atonement in Isaiah 53 is a function of various vicarious processes. Most evident is substitutionary atonement for the sins of others. But the symbolism in Isaiah 53 assumes other vicarious processes that can be associated with experiences of PTSD. First, the community addressed by the Second Isaiah vicariously suffered the shame of their ancestors, who lived through the destruction of Jerusalem and forced exile to Babylon. The exiles resented having to bear their parents' punishment, a resentment that resulted in hostility toward their collective identity as God's servant and disbelief in the message of salvation coming from God's servant, the prophet. Another vicarious process is connected with the prophet, who was one of the objects of the community's projected hostilities. The Second Isaiah, however, chose not to dissociate from this projected violence; instead he bore the risk of vicarious traumatization in order to act as an enlightened witness to the community's sense of undeserved suffering. Isaiah 53 is an expression of the prophet's enlightened witness. The exiles' sense of excess suffering is taken seriously but reframed as an asset instead of a liability.

In other words, the myth of vicarious atonement in Isaiah 53 was written not only in the context of a community that experienced trauma-induced difficulties but under their effects. As a member of that community, the prophet shared their symptoms as well as sought for their solution. Consequently, Isaiah 53 bridges the gap between the community and the prophet not only with concepts but also by communicating feeling. Behind Isaiah 53 one can detect empathy with the community's point of view. Communication of empathy with the exiles would have heightened their trust in Second Isaiah and the message of salvation they were being offered.

Isaiah 53 is a work of literature, nevertheless, not a therapeutic treatise. The poem appears to vacillate between validating the idea of sacrificial suffering and unveiling violent processes that blame the victim (Williams, 1991, 161–162). My account of the psychodynamics of Isaiah 53 has not resolved this contradiction. Its mythology of vicarious atonement afforded a culturally validated means for the community to reconnect with a disowned identity. At the same time, however, the poem seems to offer a grandiose model for understanding the community's debasement, a model that facilitates denial by subordinating present suffering to future gain. For this reason, Isaiah 53 offers a realistic portrayal of the experience of PTSD. It shows the typical traits of other works of literature (and dreams) that embody the basic conflict described by Herman in the quote that began this chapter. Literature written under the influence of trauma can both portray the violence and mask it at the same time (see Miller, 1993, 114–116). In that sense, perhaps the poem itself is a suffering servant: bearing the burden of violent processes while at the same time seeking to make them manifest.

References

Albertz, R. (1994). *A History of Israelite Religion in the Old Testament Period, vol. 2, From the Exile to the Maccabees.* Louisville: Westminster/John Knox.

American Psychiatric Association. (1994). *Diagnostic and Statistical Manual of Mental Disorders* (4th ed.). Washington, DC: American Psychiatric Association.

Arlow, J. (1961). Ego Psychology and the Study of Mythology. *Journal of the American Psychoanalytic Association, 9,* 371–393.

Bacal, H., & Newman, K. M. (1990). *Theories of Object Relations: Bridges to Self-Psychology.* New York: Columbia University Press.

Baltzer, K. (2001). *Deutero-Isaiah: A Commentary on Isaiah 40–55.* Minneapolis: Fortress.

Barré, M. L. (2000). Textual and Rhetorical-Critical Observations on the Last Servant Song (Isaiah 52:13–53:12). *Catholic Biblical Quarterly, 62,* 1–27.

Brueggemann, W. (1978). *The Prophetic Imagination.* Philadelphia: Fortress.

Carlson Brown, J., & Parker, R. (1990). For God So Loved the World? *Christianity, Patriarchy and Abuse: A Feminist Critique*, J. Carlson Brown & C. R. Bohn, eds. New York: Pilgrim, 1–30.

Clifford, R. J. (1992). Isaiah, Book of (Second Isaiah), *The Anchor Bible Dictionary*, vol. 3. New York: Doubleday, 490–501.

Clines, D. J. A. (1983). *I, He, We, and They. A Literary Approach to Isaiah 53.* Sheffield, UK: JSOT Press.

Dion, P. E. (1970). Les chants du serviteur de Yahweh et quelques passages apparentés d'Is 40–55: Un essai sur leurs limites précises et sur leurs origins respectives. *Biblica, 51*, 17–38.

Erkman, F. (1992). Support for Rohner's Parental Acceptance–Rejection Theory as a Psychological Abuse Theory in Turkey, *Innovations in Cross-Cultural Psychology: Selected Papers from the Tenth International Conference of the International Association for Cross-Cultural Psychology Held at Nara, Japan*, S. Iwawaki, Y. Kashima, & K. Leung, eds. Amsterdam: Swets & Zeitlinger, 384–395.

Girard, R. (1986). *The Scapegoat.* Baltimore: Johns Hopkins University Press.

Goodhart, S. (2000). "Al lo-chamas asah (although he had done no violence)": René Girard and the Innocent Victim, *Violence Renounced: René Girard, Biblical Studies, and Peacemaking*, W. M. Swartley, ed. Telford: Pandora, 200–217.

Gottwald, N. K. (1987). *The Hebrew Bible: A Socio-Literary Introduction.* Philadelphia: Fortress.

Gowan, D. E. (1998). *Theology of the Prophetic Books: The Death and Resurrection of Israel.* Louisville: Westminster/John Knox.

Herman, J. L. (1997). *Trauma and Recovery: The Aftermath of Violence—from Domestic Abuse to Political Terror.* New York: Basic Books.

Heschel, A. (1969). *The Prophets: An Introduction.* New York: Harper & Row.

Kaufmann, Y. (1970). *The Babylonian Captivity and Deutero-Isaiah.* New York: Union of American Hebrew Congregations.

Lemche, N. P. (1988). *Ancient Israel: A New History of Israelite Society.* Sheffield, UK: JSOT Press.

McBride, J. L., & Armstrong, G. (1995). The Spiritual Dynamics of Chronic Post-Traumatic Stress Disorder. *Journal of Religion and Health, 34*, 5–16.

McCann, I. L., & Pearlman, L. A. (1990). *Psychological Trauma and the Adult Survivor: Theory, Therapy, and Transformation.* New York: Brunner/Mazal.

McEvenue, S. (1997). Who Was the Second Isaiah? *Studies in the Book of Isaiah: W. A. M. Beuken Festschrift*, J. T. van Ruiten & M. Vervenne, eds. Louvain, Belgium: Louvain University Press, 213–222.

Meichenbaum, D. (1994). *A Clinical Handbook/ Practical Therapist Manual: For Assessing and Treating Adults with Post-Traumatic Stress Disorder (PTSD).* Waterloo, ON: Institute Press.

Miller, A. (1993). *Breaking Down the Wall of Silence: The Liberating Experience of Facing Painful Truth.* New York: Meridian.

Miller, J. M., & Hayes, J. H. (1986). *A History of Ancient Israel and Judah*. Philadelphia: Westminster.

Morrow, W. S. (2004). Comfort for Jerusalem: The Second Isaiah as Counselor to Refugees. *Biblical Theology Bulletin, 34.*

North, C. R. (1956). *The Suffering Servant in Deutero-Isaiah: An Historical and Critical Study* (2nd ed.). Oxford: Oxford University Press.

North, C. R. (1964). *The Second Isaiah: Introduction, Translation, and Commentary to Chapters 40–55*. Oxford: Clarendon Press.

Phillips, A. (1982). Double for All Her Sins. *Zeitschrift für die alttestamentliche Wissenschaft, 94,* 130–132.

Robinson, H. W. (1980). *Corporate Personality in Ancient Israel* (Rev. ed.). Philadelphia: Fortress.

Rogerson, J. W. (1992). Corporate Personality, *The Anchor Bible Dictionary,* vol. 1. New York: Doubleday, 1,156–1,157.

Rubin, T. I. (1975). *Compassion and Self-Hate: An Alternative to Despair*. New York: Ballentine.

Schoors, A. (1973). *I Am God Your Savior: A Form-Critical Study of the Main Genres in Is. 40–55*. Leiden: E. J. Brill.

Shay, J. (1994). *Achilles in Vietnam: Combat Trauma and the Undoing of Character*. New York: Scribner.

Shengold, L. (1989). *Soul Murder: The Effects of Childhood Abuse and Deprivation*. New York: Fawcett Columbine.

Stolper, M. W. (1992). Murashû, Archive of, *The Anchor Bible Dictionary,* vol. 4. New York: Doubleday, 927–928.

van der Veer, G. (1998). *Counselling and Therapy with Refugees and Victims of Trauma: Psychological Problems of Victims of War, Torture, and Repression* (2nd ed). Chichester, UK: John Wiley.

Westphal, M. (1993). *Suspicion and Faith: The Religious Uses of Modern Atheism*. Grand Rapids: Eerdmans.

Whybray, R. N. (1987). *Isaiah 40–66*. Grand Rapids: Eerdmans.

Williams, J. G. (1991). *The Bible, Violence and the Sacred: Liberation from the Myth of Sanctioned Violence*. New York: HarperSanFrancisco.

CHAPTER 10

FAMILY SYSTEMS PSYCHOLOGY AS HERMENEUTIC

Kamila Blessing

Family systems theory, first developed on a firm theoretical basis by psychiatrist Murray Bowen, is now more than a half century old. Bowen theory, as it is called, has filtered into standard training for clergy and lay religious leaders, and is now used to analyze and understand the functioning of congregations. Yet there is no systematic understanding of the relationship between family systems and the life of the community of faith, or between theory and the Bible. Because the salvation history of the Scriptures is the story of people—"the family of God"—we would expect Bowen theory to be applied to an analysis of biblical family systems. But this has not been realized.

This situation is the more astonishing because Bowen's own criterion for his theory was that it be a "common sense" description of everyday life. With a little reading, nearly anyone can apply Bowen theory, and anyone with a tutored knowledge of the Bible can apply it to interpretation. This stands in sharp contrast to the technical and specialized knowledge that is required, for instance, for interpretive use of psychodynamic theory.

In understanding family systems, Bowen refuses to ask the question "Why?" that is characteristic of psychoanalysis and other therapies. "Why?" demands inference of what may not be directly observable. Instead, Bowen asks "What? Where? How?" and "When?" and depends solely on observables for the answers. This makes Bowen theory highly adaptable to Bible interpretation because the Bible does not contain true *intra*psychic ("inside") information. It tells of external actions ("Jesus wept," and the onlookers' comment, "See how he loved him," John 11:35–36). It says that Saul was angry with David, feared him, and was jealous of the people's admiration of him (1 Sam. 19:8–9, 12, 29). It does not say, for instance, that behind these feelings were unresolved conflicts with a male relative from the past. To be sure, the Bible contains dreams and visions, but these are *texts about* these experiences—a formalized expression of the authority conveyed by a word from God, set down by a religious community. We can never get to the actual dreamers and visionaries to understand what was within their psyches.

Nevertheless, psychodynamic theory is not rejected as a hermeneutic. Bowen theory is its "child," coming as it did out of the experience of a psychoanalyst. Indeed, Bowen's analysis provides a way to "predict"—that is, to hypothesize—where an internal psychic event has occurred from the fact of an external event. So without reading into the text as such, we can understand the people in the text in greater depth. For instance, from Bowen theory, we know that families tend to form three-way relationships called "triangles" and that triangles have certain emotional dynamics. If the Bible tells us of a three-way familial relationship, we can infer, without compromising the text, that such dynamics are present.

Further, the text often includes the reader, as when John's Gospel remarks to the reader that the disciples did not yet understand what Jesus was saying (but we—John and the reader—do!).[1] So we may be able to use Bowen theory to infer certain dynamics within the triangle of the writer, the text/message, and the reader. Like reader-response criticism, Bowen hermeneutics provides a window into the depth of the writer's purpose and into the transmission of the Gospel that is occurring even at the moment of the reader's involvement with the text.

Considerations in Applying Bowen Theory

Another type of question poses itself: Why should we think that a modern theory is applicable to ancient peoples? Or to a modern religious "system" for that matter? Basic to Bowen theory is the concept that the attributes of the family-as-system are universal, across centuries, cultures, and languages. Further, religious "families" participate in many of the same dynamics as Bowen posits for the family system— particularly when the religious and family systems so thoroughly interpenetrate each other as they do in the Judaism and incipient Christianity of the Bible. This is not surprising, because Bowen himself discovered and incorporated into the theory the fact that society as a whole exhibits the same dynamics as the nuclear family.

What is really interesting is that the various documents of the Bible evidence a commonsense awareness of human nature analogous to that of Bowen theory. This awareness is reflected not only in the stories of the people but also in the writers themselves and in the human nature to which they appeal. That appeal in part takes the form of rhetorical technique, and more subtly (therefore the more forcefully), it takes the form of the psychological and spiritual relationships formed in the mind of the reader. Bowen theory can give us insight into the nature of that appeal and thus complement other kinds of knowledge about the text.

Bowen theory is a powerful tool for interpretation. However, there is one caution: in every case, our object is to correlate the psychological theory with the text by looking at each through the lens of the other. What we are *not* doing is psychologizing the text (explaining it away), claiming that Bowen was "doing religion," or claiming that the Bible's authors are "doing psychology." Above all, as we explore the human nature operating behind the texts, we in no way intend to mitigate the believer's conviction that the Holy Spirit is active in the events and teaching of the Bible, in its authors, or in its readers.

Bowen Theory and Other Hermeneutics

I have already mentioned one method of interpretation that has something in common with the family systems approach. Another is the sociological approach. This method attempts to flesh out the "present moment" of the text and its actors by inferring synchronic data from the information in the text. For instance, if the text speaks of a rabbi and disciples, sociological criticism makes use of the knowledge of the relationships between these social roles to fill out our knowledge of the text's meaning. This is often called "thick description" because in a sense it fattens the meaning. Knowing how social systems work in general, we can infer something more from the givens in the text than we otherwise would be able to do. Likewise, Bowen theory uses the thick description provided by our knowledge of the relationships among members of the family or religious systems of which the text speaks.

Bowen theory also makes use of chronologic data and has as its necessary companion the insights of historical criticism. The origin of the text, the needs of the community for which it was written, and ancient religious practices, for example, all set the table for our understanding of the text.

There is also a special relationship with reader-response criticism that views the reader's response to the text as vital to the interpretation of the text. Similarly, Bowen theory views the reader as part of a system composed of actors in the text, the storyteller, and the community of disciples over the ages. For instance, the parable of the Prodigal is so structured that the reader is prompted to respond negatively to the older brother who refused to celebrate the Prodigal's return—and positively to the Prodigal's decision to return to the father (and metaphorically, to the Father in heaven). The rhetoric aids the object of the Gospel, and that rhetoric uses the family system of the Prodigal as a spiritual family system for the reader.[2] This comparison then also gives family systems interpretation something in common with the rhetorical study characteristic of discourse analysis.

These older methods of interpretation contribute to the task of applying Bowen theory by showing us what is possible, what to look for, as we explore new interpretive techniques. The objective is to understand what and whom we see in the Scriptures. Jesus, Paul, and the other evangelists of the Bible did not just go against the popular model of religious behavior of their time. They also possessed astonishing facility to effect change in whole systems of religious behavior, and indeed to change the system itself. How did they do this? How does such change manifest itself in religious understanding and practice today? All of these questions are addressed by Bowen theory.

The Task

This chapter uses Bible texts to provide insight into the major aspects of Bowen theory. The companion chapter in volume 3 reverses this operation and seeks insight from Bowen theory into Bible texts, their effect on the reader, and the character of the Gospel message. In both, I focus on the principal elements of Bowen theory: (1) the *role of anxiety*, (2) combined with *differentiation of self* (the dominant factor in determining the health of a person's relationships), (3) *triangles* (the smallest basic unit of relationship), and (4) other system characteristics.[3] I begin with the concept of the system as it is used to describe family and other relationships.

We Are Connected: An Inductive Approach to the Family as System

The System

A few years ago a television commercial aired in which a woman was sitting and reading at a large and otherwise empty library table. A man sat down at the other end of the table but soon succumbed to the succession of "looks" the woman gave him. Clearly he was not welcome—no matter that it was a public place. He left. The announcer said, "This man has just lost a battle." I cannot remember what they were advertising, but I do remember feeling deeply intimidated by the stares of the woman, as if I myself were the intruder—and the situation was not even real.

We are all connected by what seems like empty air, but it is really thickly occupied by signals of all kinds—the "radiation" and "gravitational pull" from the various personalities in the situation. That connecting tissue contains much of the substance of our relationships, including our communication of love. It is also is the locus of much of our illness and social malfunctioning. To use another metaphor, we are all connected by an invisible web; when one person in it moves, all are moved in some way in a pattern that extends far out from that one. Of course, we are all moving at the same time, exerting physical and emotional influence on our entire network of relationships. This is what it means to be a system.

This attribute of human relationship is literally as old as Adam. In fact, it is a part of the "fall" of humankind that gets little or no attention. In Genesis 3, Adam and Eve ate of the forbidden fruit and, with their new self-awareness, realized that they were naked. They then made clothing for themselves out of fig leaves. But that was not enough to keep them from feeling shame. The Lord (portrayed as a human being) was walking in the garden in the cool of the evening and called out to the man, "Where are you?" Adam answered (Gen. 3:10 [NIV]): "I heard you in the garden, and I was afraid because I was naked; so I hid." Even God was astonished at Adam's answer. God asked, "Who told you that you were naked?"

Most people think only of God the Judge in this story, and it does describe what seems to be an inherently threatening situation. Up to this point, however, God had never judged, punished, or even chastised. He had told Adam and Eve they would die if they ate of a certain tree (Gen. 2:17), but that was a warning (as, "this is poisonous"). Apart from that tree, the whole garden was theirs. Besides, the animals were also naked, after their own fashion. Adam and Eve did not hide for fear of a punishment they had never seen.

They were afraid, it says, because they were naked. They felt self-conscious, unable to be seen—by anyone, including the God who made them and knew them better than they knew themselves. Like the man in the library, they were frozen by their emotional reaction, unable to face another's gaze. When God asked whether they had eaten of that tree, Adam responded by blaming the woman, who blamed the serpent. No one took responsibility for the behavior. In consequence, the text tells us, all future generations will reflect this disobedience to God and live in a lesser state.

What does this say about the first family? About us generally? According to Bowen, these attributes are evidence that a family or other social group is really a system, that is, that it functions as a unit in ways that go beyond the simple sum of the individuals in it. According to Bowen, "any relationship with balancing forces and counter forces in constant operation is a system" (1985a, 358–359). By "relationship" and "constant," he means that in some fashion, the family (or social group) maintains invisible boundaries around itself such that those within the boundaries function together over a substantial period of time. For instance, different families respond differently to stressors such as a job loss, marriage, or death. Each family has its own way of balancing emotion with coping, and of balancing both with engagement outside of the family boundaries.

This brings us to one of Bowen's chief reasons for departing from Freudian theory. According to Bowen, an important aspect of Freudian theory had not been taken to its logical conclusion in therapeutic practice. That is, that mental illness in one person is produced in relationship with others. Research into the origins of schizophrenia, already well acknowledged at Bowen's time, showed that schizophrenia develops over a number of generations, with a member of each generation more predisposed to illness by the previous generation. Bowen's extended study of the behavior of entire families, placed in the institutional setting, revealed that many normal aspects of emotional functioning are also a property of the family system as a whole. For instance, one of the most important predictors of adult differentiation of self is sibling position. The effect of sibling position must be located in the relationship per se.

Further, he found that the family system may include the client's belief-producing systems such as membership in a religious group.

Bowen therefore developed his theory and his therapeutic practice in relation to relationship—that is, to the system.

Anxiety and the Triangle

The most important influence on the family's health, according to Bowen, is the level of anxiety in the system. There are two kinds of anxiety: the prevailing (chronic) level in the family, and the increase and decrease with events that affect the group. Within the family, there are specific mechanisms for dealing with this anxiety. The most basic is the triangle. According to Bowen, triangles are the most stable interpsychic relationships (as a three-legged stool is more stable than a two-legged one). The "corners" of a triangle are not necessarily people. God or a religious group, for instance, may form one corner of the triangle. However, the corners always exert a controlling influence on the other relationships and on the person's sense of identity.

In the fall story, there is an obvious triangle: God, Adam, and Eve.[4] God created Adam and Eve and asked for obedience in one specific action—not eating of that one tree. After the two had both eaten, the triangle became painfully obvious: now they had to face their creator with their disobedience. One specific value of a triangle, however, is to displace stress to a more vulnerable third party, and this is exactly what Adam does when he blames Eve for their action. This is also what Eve does when she blames the serpent. Triangles may overlap, and here is another one: God, Eve, and the serpent. Eve was once pulled between the two of them, between good and evil, and now again she is pulled and tries to reject the evil one, but to no avail. For better or worse, the effect of disobedience is perpetuated to the generations of human beings to come. Thus we see the beginning of what Bowen calls multigenerational transmission—the transmission of the emotional characteristics of the family through generations yet unborn.

Differentiation: The Family of Samuel

The most basic determinant of how the individual will deal with stress is the level of differentiation. Adam and Eve each demonstrated "undifferentiated" responses; instead of taking responsibility for their actions, they reacted out of fear and shame, that is, out of emotion untempered by reason or conviction. Another example—the story of Hannah and the birth of Samuel—gives a more in-depth view of differentiation of self.

In 1 Samuel 1 we are told that Elkanah, the father-to-be of the prophet Samuel, had two wives, Hannah and Peninnah. Every year he took his wives and Peninnah's children to Shiloh to make sacrifices to the Lord. Receiving back his part of the sacrificial meat, he would give one portion to Peninnah and to each of her children. But he would give a double portion to Hannah—"because he loved her, and the Lord had closed her womb" (1 Sam. 1:5). In that time and culture, remaining childless was a wife's worst shame and considered a punishment from God. However, Hannah and her husband had a special bond, and he reassured her that their love should be enough. Peninnah, possibly jealous of that bond, always taunted Hannah until Hannah "wept and would not eat." The text says she was "downhearted" (1:7–8).

Imagine her feelings. Her stomach was tight, and she lost her appetite. Her face was "downcast" (v. 18), and in fact she went off by herself as soon as she could get away. This particular year was different, however. After the meal, she went to the shrine and prayed with all her heart that if the Lord would give her a son, she would dedicate the son to the service of the Lord for all his life. One of the priests saw her and accused her, in her distraught state, of being drunk. However, she explained her plea and the priest blessed her: "Go in peace, and may the God of Israel grant you what you have asked" (1:17). This was not just "have a good day." This was a prophecy, and it was evidence that the Lord has heard her prayer. Her whole countenance changed. She went back and ate, and "her face was no longer downcast."

What does this mean? She had to go back to the family for the journey home, and she knew she would be in close quarters with Peninnah again. But her head was held high, and her spirit was light and confident. No longer could the mere sight of Peninnah make her lose heart. Something within her had changed, healed. Later she discovered she was pregnant, and still later the child was born, a son, and still later he became a prophet in Israel at a time when there had been no prophet for many years. However, her intimidation was gone before she received the fulfillment of her prayer.

What happened? First, observe the triangle: Elkanah, Hannah, and Peninnah. Bowen allows us to infer that there was tension between the two wives, and also between Elkanah and Peninnah. Why? The text says Peninnah taunted Hannah "because the Lord had closed her [Hannah's] womb" (v. 6). In itself, that her rival did not have children was a (perverse) benefit to Peninnah. On the other hand, if her insecurity was with Elkanah, the taunting makes sense. It was not acceptable for Peninnah to vent her jealousy and anger on her husband, so she vented it on (displaced it to) the other wife. The second triangle, however, is the key to the development in the story—that of Elkanah, Hannah, and God. All of the action took place in and around God's house at Shiloh—on God's turf—and that tells us who was really in control of the situation.

Notice the undifferentiated responses of the two women, and the change in those interactions as the story progresses. Peninnah's taunting comes out of her emotions, apparently unchecked by reason. Hannah's response of emotional downcast, her inability to be consoled by her husband (1 Sam. 1:8, "Don't I mean more to you than ten sons?"—evidently he is not blaming her for having no children), and her inability to eat all point to the rule of raw emotion. This set of responses to each other was chronic (1:7: "This went on year after year"). Evidently there was a high ambient level of anxiety to begin with in this family, caused in part by the rivalry between the wives and in part by Hannah's barrenness. It seems there was no escape for Hannah from her misery—except this once when she went to pray.

At this point, another attribute of triangles can be seen: triangles can be pathogenic or therapeutic. Triangles are so stable that they can function to keep toxic behavior in place; they can also keep healthy development in place. The structure of the initial triangle of Elkanah–Peninnah–Hannah was apparently very effective in keeping Hannah's poor ability to cope in place. The overlapping triangle of God–Hannah–Elkanah was about to become the stronger element in the situation, however, and being a healthy triangle, it had the capacity to keep her new, healthier behavior in place.

Observe what happened when Hannah prayed and received the blessing. In that moment, the kind of response she would make changed. Bowen would say that one of two things occurred here: (1) if the rise in anxiety was sharp but momentary, she had become temporarily unable to cope but had rebounded; or (2) if the anxiety was chronic, the necessity posed by this moment of crisis had produced an overall increase in her level of differentiation.

Because we know that the anxiety was chronic (or at least recurring regularly), and no further emotional upset is reported, this change is most likely one toward greater differentiation. The healing she received was first seen in her ability to relate to other people, and only later was it seen in her conceiving a child. Look at the means of this change: she stopped relating primarily to Peninnah and to her own childlessness, and (out of her desperation) put relationship with God first. Acknowledging God in the triangle and hearing God's representative seal that new state with his blessing released her from the toxic triangle. Without in the least denying the miraculous nature of her conceiving, we may observe that the general lessening of anxiety was itself both a healing and a source of healing. Bowen says that in families and individuals who are subject to a high chronic state of anxiety, emotional and physical illness is common, whereas the less anxious system tends toward greater all-around health. So it is no coincidence that Hannah is able to conceive children after this fundamental change in her family relationships.

Bowen states that the level of differentiation of a child is strongly related to the level of differentiation of the parents at the time of conception and birth. Given Samuel's role as the most important leader and prophet of his time, it is likely that there is a further implication here. In the biblical salvation history schema, we see repeated the pattern of a barren woman bearing a child who ultimately brings the people of God further on that road between Eden and the heavenly city. It may be that Hannah could not bear and nurture a child who had the (differentiated) capacity to carry out such a mission until she had experienced this increase in her own differentiation.

Basics of Bowen Theory

As we have seen with Hannah, a person's degree of differentiation determines the degree of health in the person's relationships. In Bowen's terminology, *differentiation* refers to the balance between emotional and intellectual functioning. These two aspects of a person are said to be more "fused," or more "differentiated," from each other. Unlike the ego differentiation of Freud, Bowen's differentiation is characterized as a continuum. At a given time, any individual or group lies somewhere along this continuum. At the "low" end (fusion), emotion dominates everything the person does, and the sense of self is largely dependent on others. One of the characteristics of fusion— fugue, or emotional cutoff—is a flight from relationships, which, however, does not liberate the person. In fact, fugue actually perpetuates the unhealthy relationship. At the "high" end, the feeling system is balanced with the intellectual, the person has a strong sense of self, and relationships are governed by deliberate values and principles. The person may leave the family, but the leaving does not represent a flight. These aspects of the continuum are discussed further below. The continuum is represented in Table 10.1.

Bowen represents his theory as a continuum because in a given situation, if the anxiety in the system increases, the person's expressed

Table 10.1: The Differentiation Continuum

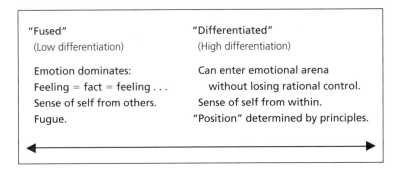

"Fused" (Low differentiation)	"Differentiated" (High differentiation)
Emotion dominates: Feeling = fact = feeling . . . Sense of self from others. Fugue.	Can enter emotional arena without losing rational control. Sense of self from within. "Position" determined by principles.

level of differentiation decreases relative to his original point on the continuum. That is, the person moves toward the "fused" end. Likewise, a decrease in anxiety moves the person to a more differentiated point, as Hannah did when the priest's blessing gave her hope of a child.

This process is also seen in a more global manifestation: over the long term, if high anxiety prevails in the system, the entire system "regresses" (moves toward the low end). If the anxiety is society-wide, the result may be what Bowen calls "societal regression." The entire society experiences a loss of contact with intellectually determined principles and increasingly makes emotionally determined decisions to allay the societal anxiety of the moment. For instance, the Great Depression was a time of societal anxiety; the initial reactionary attempt to balance the national budget had the character of an emotionally driven decision. Roosevelt's speech—we have "nothing to fear but fear itself"—was a superb example of a differentiated course correction in a dysfunctional societal system.

For Bowen, the object of therapy (one might think here, biblically, of "healing") is in large part to move a person, family, or group toward the high end of this continuum. Although such movement will be very limited, even a small change at the basic level will significantly impact the functional level, that is, the person's style and quality of life (Bowen 1985a, 371). It is consistent with Bowen theory that Hannah not only had her son but went on to have five more children and the social recognition and pride of place that accompanied motherhood in that culture. If indeed the taunts and the emotional dominance of Peninnah also ceased or lessened, it is more confirmation of Hannah's "move" on the continuum. It is interesting in this context that the object of the Gospel is to move a person to a different place in faith. Jesus speaks of this "place" thus: "I have come that they may have life, and have it to the full" (John 10:10). So here is another congruity between the text and Bowen theory.

Solid Self and Pseudo-Self

The differentiation continuum can be further articulated using Bowen's terminology of the pseudo-self and the solid self. When the person exists more toward the "fused" end of the continuum, the pseudo-self is more manifest; when the emotions and intellect are in healthy balance (on the "differentiated" end of the spectrum), the solid self is more prominent. The pseudo-self and the solid self are both aspects of every individual. Table 10.2 further articulates the character of the differentiation continuum.[5]

The person who is governed more by the solid self is more independent of the emotionality of others, even in highly charged situations, but is still free to participate in the emotional. Relationships tend to be constructive. This person's goals are determined by the self rather than by social pressure, a trait often characteristic of a leader in the community. The person who is governed more by the pseudo-self has a

Table 10.2: Comparison of Solid Self and Pseudo-Self

The pseudo-self	The solid self
1 It is a vast *assortment of principles, beliefs,* philosophies, and knowledge.	1 It is made up of *clearly defined beliefs,* opinions, convictions, and life principles.
2 These principles, beliefs, philosophies, and knowledge are acquired because it is required or *considered right by the group . . . acquired under pressure, they can be modified by emotional pressure . . .*	2 These are incorporated into self . . . by . . . *careful consideration* of the alternatives . . .
3 They are *random and inconsistent* with one another, without the individual's being aware of the discrepancy.	3 Each belief and life principle is *consistent* with all the others.
4 Self will become submerged in the group's identity in the event of a crisis or sudden increase in anxiety.	4 Self will take action on the principles even in situations of high anxiety and duress . . . one becomes *responsible for self* and for the consequences.

relative inability to deal with emotional closeness. For example, it is significant that when Samuel was weaned (at about age three), Hannah took him to the temple as promised and left him in God's service. In contrast, a "fused" person clings and substitutes emotional constraint for true intimacy. This kind of functioning tends to have a destructive effect on others.

Propagation of the Level of Differentiation

In any family, the group members who actually live together comprise the nuclear family; that group has a characteristic base level of anxiety and characteristic ways of dealing with changes in the level of anxiety. Further, the members of the nuclear family develop (in relation to each other) certain patterns that are expressed by two or three people together. Patterns include conflict, distancing (emotional or physical; fugue), over- or underfunctioning (as when a healthy child acts as the "perfect" child in response to a sick or misbehaving sibling), as well as the use of triangles to displace anxiety. A child's level of differentiation is a function of these family dynamics and is formed by what Bowen calls the "family projection process."[6]

The ultimate benefit of Bowen theory as a hermeneutic is the way in which it can provide insight into the perpetuation of the family of God by means that are not limited to the biological and emotional. This tells us something about the very nature of the Gospel message and something about ourselves as readers of it. In the following example from John 9, we read what is a family story twice over: it concerns a son, his parents, and a development in their relationship; and it concerns the family of God in the synagogue. The latter has a split in it: the "followers of Moses" as they call themselves, and those who "confess Jesus." Over both is the Father in heaven, the same God to whom both families are trying to be faithful.

Let us begin with the text of the healing that sets the larger story in motion, from John 9. The story takes place on the Sabbath (9:14).

[1] As he [Jesus] went along, he saw a man blind from birth. [2] His disciples asked him, "Rabbi, who sinned, this man or his parents, that he was born blind?" [3] "Neither this man nor his parents sinned," said Jesus, "but this happened so that the work of God might be displayed in his life. [4] As long as it is day, we must do the work of him who sent me. Night is coming, when no one can work. [5] While I am in the world, I am the light of the world." [6] Having said this, he spit on the ground, made some mud with the saliva, and put it on the man's eyes. [7] "Go," he told him, "wash

in the Pool of Siloam" [this word means Sent]. So the man went and washed, and came home seeing.

Jesus came upon a man who was blind from birth. The disciples asked Jesus who was the cause of the blindness—commonly taken to be punishment for sin—the man or his parents. The first triangle in the text is therefore Jesus–man–parents. But as Jesus responded, he made reference immediately to an overlapping triangle:

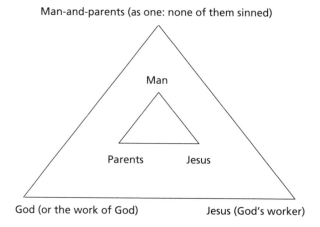

The overlapping triangles could be presented as two triangles that share a corner (Jesus), but Bowen talks about the emotional place of a significant other in the course of therapy/change (1985a, 344–345). The triangles are expressed in this way to show God's place in the perception of a first-century Jew, and as voiced by Jesus (vv. 3–4); God's place is so great as to overwhelm the importance of other relationships. The healing took place in the setting of this double family system. Two life-givers (the parents and God) are contrasted implicitly as the story unfolds.

In the course of invoking God's role, Jesus identified himself with God: "we must do the work of him who sent me" (v. 4). On that basis ("Having said this," v. 6), he spit and made mud, anointed the man's eyes, and told the man to wash in the pool of Siloam ("Sent").

The text states definitely that the man "came home seeing" (v. 7). We might say that the man's dysfunction was "displaced" onto Jesus. That is, with Jesus in the triangle (and within a triangle in which God reigns), the man no longer had to bear the weight of his affliction solely in relationship with his parents. Thus the psychological reality of displacement is congruent with the spiritual assertion of the text that Jesus in fact healed him. There is no reason to assume there was no true spiritual healing; in fact, it is likely that these various levels of a person's nature work together for therapeutic change.

The account of the healing is rehearsed in the story three times (vv. 11, 14, 15) and substantially repeated by allusion three times (vv. 21, 23, 27). If the reader is in doubt that Jesus is the light, and the source of light for this man, he must be blind. Implicitly, but by very clear and obvious writing technique, John has thus created yet another triangle:

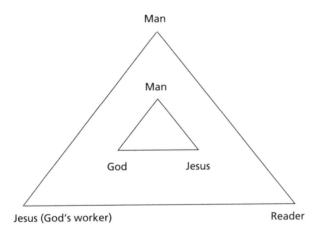

Scholars generally acknowledge that John used his rhetorical technique to involve the reader and to achieve a specific effect: the reader knows himself to be one of the "in" group, possessing the knowledge of the post-resurrection disciples. Does this configuration imply that the reader too may have his dysfunction displaced to Jesus? Can the new health that is implied be kept in place by such a therapeutic triangle? Such questions (in some form) are meant to come to mind when a person encounters such a story. It is an important part of the text and is furthered by the role of the differentiated versus the fused in the story.

Observe the manner in which Jesus answered the question about who sinned. It is reasoned and nondefensive. The question (which one sinned?) presupposed a certain kind of answer, and another leader might have felt impelled to make a choice and defend it. Jesus, however, had evidently thought this out earlier and was "coming from a different place," as we would say. Furthermore, by the end, the effect on the man in particular was doubly constructive: besides being able to see, he believed in and worshiped Jesus. Finally, as usual, Jesus made his "reference point" plain. The blindness was the key—not to the source of sin but to the work of God. A higher principle was involved and would govern Jesus' responses to the man now and to the Pharisees later (vv. 40–41).

The mention of the Sabbath is significant in this regard. Forty-six times in the Gospels—nine in John (two in this passage)—reference is made to Jesus' healing or otherwise "working" on the Sabbath. The import of this obvious affront to the Law of Moses (Keep the Sabbath holy . . .) is stated in Mark 2:28 and parallels "the Son of Man is Lord even of the Sabbath." This repeated theme is the mark of someone who has very deliberately set out a principle on which he will act and teach. Further, his is sound Pharisaic reasoning, namely, that the work of giving life and sustaining life is permitted, even required, by the Law. Hence this is no grandstanding but a theologically reflective pedagogy.

These attributes of Jesus' answers recur throughout the Gospels. They are reasoned and consistent; governed by a higher principle and reference point—the work of God; and constructive in their effects on other people. Further, Jesus takes responsibility for himself and for the consequences of his actions (cf. John 12:27 and similar passages). These are signs of the differentiated person. They contrast sharply with those of the parents and Jesus' opponents in the story.

The argument about the Sabbath provided the first "skirmish" in the Pharisees' reception of Jesus (vv. 13–17, as they examined the healed man). However, the undifferentiated responses began in earnest when the man's parents were called before "the Jews" (as they are called in vv. 18, 22; actually, everyone in the story is a Jew). The parents' statement—"Ask him; he is of age; he will speak for himself" (v. 21)—was hardly neutral, although it masqueraded as such. The text quickly reveals the emotionally driven cause of this answer, stating the fact twice: "His parents said this *because they were afraid of the Jews*, for already the Jews had decided that anyone who acknowledged that Jesus was the Christ would be put out of the synagogue. That was why his parents said, 'He is of age; ask him'" (vv. 22–23). At this moment, at least, they were manifesting fusion.[7] (It should be noted that the Greek word *Ioudaioi*, often unfortunately translated "Jews" in John, refers to the Judean authorities, not to the entire ethnic group of Jews, which would include Jesus, his disciples, and most of the community John was addressing.)

The threat of being thrown out of the synagogue has historical significance that bears on the interpretation of the text. Scholars generally believe that at the time of the writing of John, an urgent issue for the Jewish followers of Jesus was the fact that the nonbelievers were throwing them out of the synagogues. Up until that time, as we see in

Acts and some of the epistles, the believers (like Paul) were welcome to teach about Jesus in the synagogue. At this point, however, a new and fledgling community of God's people was being pushed out of the nest, as it were. They wondered whether God had rejected them, and John answers that worry in this story by assuring them of God's providence and Jesus' reward of healing and new life for those who believed in his name.

This is also the story of the birthing of a new "child" of God in the form of a new community "descendant" from (in Bible cosmology) God's original people. Paul talks about different birthings in Galatians, for example, and one of John's principal themes is the new birth—not only as Christians but as God's children (for example, John 1:12). Thus historical analysis of the passage, in tandem with family systems analysis, reveals that there are two family systems emerging from what was originally one. This situation is inherently threatening to those in charge of the whole original family, however, and this threat of expulsion is a systemic response to that anxiety.

Notice that the parents displaced their portion of the anxiety (fear) directly onto their son. The triangle is an unhealthy one.

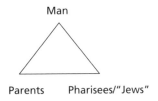

The man was made to feel the displaced anxiety immediately, and in fact he suffered the fate with which his parents had been threatened. This happened when "the Jews" called him a second time to account for his healing, and their anxiety over the situation manifested itself increasingly. His exchange with the Pharisees reflected this, as their responses to him became less differentiated. The text says,

> 28 They hurled insults at him and said, "You are this fellow's disciple! We are disciples of Moses! 29 We know that God spoke to Moses, but as for this fellow, we don't even know where he comes from." . . . 34 "You were steeped in sin at birth; how dare you lecture us!" And they threw him out.

The insults, the scorn ("we don't even know where he comes from"; "how dare you lecture us!"), and the extreme and angry action ("they threw him out") mark this as an unreasoned, destructive, and defensive response. They referred to God, but it was as far from Jesus' principled reference to the standard of holiness as it could be. As the man himself pointed out (vv. 30–33), their stance was also inconsistent with their rabbinic teaching. This is the opposite of the way Jesus responded to people, and it is fusion.

In contrast, in mid-insult—even under duress—the man maintains his straightforward and (here) rabbinically reasoned stance:

> [30] The man answered, "Now that is remarkable! You don't know where he comes from, yet he opened my eyes. [31] We know that God does not listen to sinners. He listens to the godly man who does his will. [32] Nobody has ever heard of opening the eyes of a man born blind. [33] If this man were not from God, he could do nothing."

Thus at the end of the story, the Pharisees' triangles are as follows:

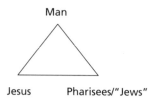

and implicitly:

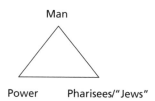

In the story, the Jesus who healed was a threat to the Pharisees' power; they displaced the resulting anxiety onto the man. The rule about throwing out those who confessed Jesus was meant (in Bowen's terms) to create the triangle that would keep their power, and presumably their relationships in the community, in place.

The man, however, was evidently no longer living primarily in the triangle with his parents but in the one with Jesus (based on 9:31–33); otherwise the reader will think his triangle came out of the blue.

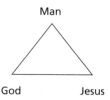

In effect, Jesus became the parent; he brought new life to the man, and not just any life. It was a life of (at least) psychological abundance because Jesus was the bearer of differentiation. The final verses of the story show that this was so. The man met Jesus, spoke with him, and committed himself to him, regardless of all social consequences: "Lord, I believe" (v. 38). This is a highly differentiated move; the man takes responsibility for himself and the consequences of his actions, and does not seem to care what others—even his parents—think. The final triangle is as shown (v. 37):

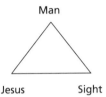

That of the Pharisees is signaled by vv. 40–41: "Jesus said, 'If you were blind, you would not be guilty of sin; but now that you claim you can see, your guilt remains.'"

All were held in place by their choice of a source of power—for the man, Jesus, and for the Pharisees, their control over the social and religious system.

Having come to the end of the surface story, we are not yet at the ultimate end. Another "story" has built quietly from the beginning of this text, reinforced by other, similar, rhetoric by the rest of this Gospel. We have said that the reader is included in the story—remember the first triangles. The reader has in fact really never been outside of it. As Jesus and his new follower (the man born blind) prove differentiated and we see the attributes of their responses, they become attractive—inviting, in fact. No one wants to identify with the Pharisees the way the author presents them. Consider the following triangle:

Pharisees

Jesus   Reader

and

Man born blind

Jesus   Reader

These two relationships (however mental) have developed as the story proceeds. Which is comfortable? Which creates tension, and which relieves it? Consider how unpalatable is the "fused" manner of the Pharisees as presented here. Consider also the role of the parents of the man born blind. Ultimately, they did not fulfill their role as life givers, in sharp contrast to God, who has given the man a whole new life. Further, there is the sense of being "inside"—presumed by the text to know, with the writer, that Jesus is the Son of God (the point of the Gospel). Then there is the powerful message of excommunication. The reader has come to identify with the man and to reject the way in which he was treated. The reader is propelled "out of the synagogue" with him, as it were—and into the triangle with the man and Jesus.

Moreover, though John would not have put it this way: following Jesus is presented as the differentiated thing to do. Following Jesus is not the action of a cult, and Jesus is not merely a charismatic leader; following him is something the healthy and reasoning person would choose, *even over his own biological and religious families.* This is a powerful message, and the entire aspect of it goes into the mind and heart without conscious effort. It plants its own seeds. It is the psychological facet of a powerful work of the Spirit in the reader.

All that has gone by is under the greater relationship with God, the one whose work has just been described with such concrete vitality. This is a therapeutic (life-giving) triangle that is meant to keep the reader within it for life:

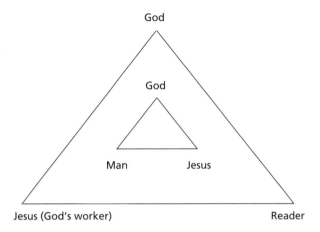

All of this has the effect of layering the invitations to follow Jesus. The Gospel begins and ends with explicit invitations to the reader to believe in the name of Jesus, and believing, to have life in his name (John 1:12, 20:31). The invitation is reinforced powerfully by the example of the story. Then, with still greater effect, the invitation is *incarnated* in the psychological and spiritual self of the reader: the system patterns in the story bring about a change in the reader that draws him into relationship with the healed man and with Christ. And this occurs regardless of the reader's time, place, or culture. The effect is similar to the way perfume is often sold—not just one bottle, but eau de parfum, packaged along with body lotion and body wash of the same scent. You are supposed to use all three at once, to "layer" the perfume. The same could be applied to this Gospel. The Bowen theoretical structures serve to bring this layering effect into the soul. And, of course, the theory serves to identify the ways in which the text accomplishes this sacred task.

Conclusion

Family systems theory is a powerful tool for understanding not only the content of the text, but the very nature of the message and of the reader's relationship with it. Although the theory was not intended to do so, it provides a view into the human aspect of the work of the Spirit. In fact, it might be said that with Bowen theory, the communion of saints is seen to operate as one system that crosses the boundaries of time, geography, and culture. The theory allows us to peek into the ways in which "mere words," in the Bible, help to birth and nurture this communion—in sum, to see the *text as communion*.

Notes

1. For instance, at John 2:20–22, 8:27, 10:6, 12:16.

2. An analysis of the Prodigal in this regard can be found in a companion chapter, "Differentiation in the Family of Faith: The Prodigal Son and Galatians 1–2," in vol. 3 of this set.

3. Because this treatment of Bowen's theory must be brief, the reader is referred to an article in which Bowen wrote that he had updated and summarized previous expositions of his theory (1985a). Bowen theory contains eight basic elements: differentiation; the nuclear family emotional system; the triangle; the family projection process; the effect of sibling position; multigenerational transmission; the emotional cutoff; and societal regression. There is not space to discuss all of them here, but I discuss the most important and refer to the others as they become relevant to our discussion. For a discussion of Bowen family dynamics for laypeople, a very good source is Gilbert (n.d.).

4. For the inclusion of God in the triangle and its application in therapy, see Jensen, 2003.

5. The comparison is a paraphrase of Bowen (1985a, 365).

6. In the family projection process, the family displaces anxiety differently to different children. For instance, the most vulnerable child (the youngest, the sick one, and so on) will become the focus of the family's anxiety, and that ultimately results in a greater overall anxiety in the child. The child is the symptom-bearer for the family, the "expresser"—but also will develop a lifestyle of greater neediness as time goes on. Different siblings will develop differently in this respect; sibling position is important in determining this. An "oldest," for instance, will often be very dependable and self-reliant, whereas a youngest may be more dependent on others. As this process continues, it becomes multigenerational transmission.

7. Leon Morris (1971), coming from a completely different hermeneutical point of view, makes the point about the parents' fusion and the displacement of their anxiety onto their son extraordinarily well. He writes: "The parents were evidently of a very different temper from that of their sturdily minded son. Their reply is characterized by timidity and a complete readiness to submit to the authority of their questioners [fusion]. . . . In saying 'ask him' they also put emphasis on 'him,' and they have the emphatic pronoun when they say '*he* shall speak. . . .' All this emphasis shows their determination not to get mixed up in the affair any more than they can help. . . . [What was surprising] was that they should manifest such an indecent concern for thrusting the matter back on their son [displacement], with their 'ask him,' and their 'he is of age,' and their 'he shall speak for himself.' It is plain that they discerned danger, and had no intention of being caught up in it with their son" (1971, 487).

References

Bowen, M., ed. (1985a). Theory in the Practice of Psychotherapy, *Family Therapy in Clinical Practice*. Northvale: Jason Aronson, 337–387.

Bowen, M., ed. (1985b). Toward the Differentiation of Self in One's Family of Origin, *Family Therapy in Clinical Practice*. Northvale: Jason Aronson, 529–547.

Gilbert, R. M. (n.d.). *Connecting with Our Children: Guiding Principles for Parents in a Troubled World*. New York: John Wiley.

Jensen, C. A. (2003). Toward Pastoral Counseling Integration: One Bowen-Oriented Approach. *Journal of Pastoral Care and Counseling, 57*(2), 117–129.

Morris, L. (1971). *The Gospel According to John*. Grand Rapids: William B. Eerdmans Publishing Company.

CHAPTER 11

A Romantic Psychologist Reads the Bible: Eugen Drewermann

Bernhard Lang

Around 1990, the German media newly discovered Eugen Drewermann, a Catholic theologian who quickly became one of the most widely quoted priests in his country. Currently, he appears to be more popular than, for instance, Hans Küng, another Catholic theologian with whom he shares the fate of being banned from teaching. Born in 1940, Drewermann served as a Catholic priest, received training in psychoanalysis, taught dogmatic theology at a Catholic seminary, and in 1991, after being challenged by ecclesiastical authorities and eventually banned from teaching, began a new career as an independent author, therapist, and lecturer living in Paderborn, Westphalia, the place of his former pastoral ministry and academic activity.

Drewermann's list of publications is almost overwhelming. About a quarter of his seventy-volume oeuvre is devoted to biblical exegesis. Between 1977 and 2003 he produced more than ten books of psychological interpretation of biblical texts, mostly weighty tomes running to more than five hundred pages. His first relevant work, titled *Structures of Evil* (*Strukturen des Bösen*), dates from 1977 and deals with Genesis 2–11 in three volumes; then followed bulky two-volume commentaries on Mark and Matthew, a two-volume work titled *Depth-Psychology and Exegesis* (*Tiefenpsychologie und Exegese*), and minor books on the Lukan birth narratives and the book of Tobit. His most recent contribution to psychological exegesis dates from 2003—a commentary on the Fourth Gospel, again in two volumes. During the past twenty-five years the author's interest shifted from the Old Testament to the New, and a closer look reveals another shift: from a more pronounced Freudian approach, characteristic of the author's early work in the 1970s, to one that can be described as eclectic with a strong Jungian and romantic emphasis. When Drewermann was around forty, he discovered the work of Carl Gustav Jung. He was at an age around which Jungians expect this sort of thing to happen, an age they call the "zenith of life," a moment of particular spiritual intensity and productivity.

The account that follows uses an example from Drewermann's mature work to introduce his method or, as specialists have it, his "hermeneutics"—his art of interpreting biblical texts. This presentation is followed by reflections on the two sources that inspire this exegesis, giving it its unique and uniquely interesting quality: Freudian psychoanalysis and the liberal-Jungian view of religion. Finally, I comment on Drewermann's wider theological program, which is also inspired by the liberal or, more properly, by the romantic tradition.[1]

Psychological Readings of Biblical Texts

Drewermann's book on the Lukan infancy narratives is one of the author's minor contributions to biblical exegesis, yet it may be his most outstanding exegetical exercise, for this small masterpiece reveals his distinctive approach particularly well. Published under the title *Discovering the God Child Within: A Spiritual Psychology of the Infancy of Jesus* (1994), it is one of the few books by Drewermann currently available in English.

How are we to understand the story of the birth of Christ? Drewermann asks in *Discovering the God Child Within*. What we have, Drewermann tells us, is clearly an account of the birth of one particular person in history, the first episode in the life of Jesus Christ. Christ's birth is a historical event, and the account takes the form of a historical narrative. However, a closer reading reveals that the biblical text does not simply echo a historical event but is actually inspired by a general mythical pattern. That pattern can be called the birth of the hero, a birth surrounded by a magical atmosphere and marked by divine intervention. This myth can profitably be illustrated from ancient Egyptian sources that speak of Pharaoh's supernatural conception and birth. When moving below the surface of the biblical text to explore its depths, we not only move from history to mythology but also from the one to the many: from the historical Jesus to a multiplicity of mythical heroes. Although this deeper level has left many traces in the biblical texts and reveals a basis much broader than concentration on the historical figure of Christ, Drewermann is still not quite satisfied. Below the myth, one can discover yet another level, that of a very widespread dream. In midlife, men and women frequently report dreams in which they are pregnant, give birth to a child, or simply hold an infant for whom they care. Such dreams are accompanied by positive feelings. Analysts agree that this kind of dream announces a new start in life, a new stage of personal development toward fulfillment or completion. In Drewermann's words:

> Over a longish period of psychotherapy people whose lives undergo a crucial transformation will almost always report of dreams in which they see themselves confronting the figure of a newborn child. One woman client of mine, for example, had all her life followed the model of her highly suicidal mother and responded to every imaginable conflict with extended death fantasies. In one dream she saw herself going through a barbed-wire enclosure that kept narrowing in front of her until it finally opened as if by herself. Behind the fence stood a woman who handed a foundling to her. For many weeks my patient felt deeply moved by this dream. "I'm experiencing something like a second birth," she said. "I'm leaving behind my childhood, which was like a concentration camp. I knew that things couldn't go on the way they had been up till now. But in the dream it looks as if I am allowed to really live again. . . . Somehow I myself was the child. (1994, 51)

Drewermann explains that "in the language of myth, fairy tales, and dreams the symbol of the *child* always stands for the basically religious permission to get a fresh start in life" (1994, 50). Moreover, "you must follow the image of the newborn child in the dream, or you will squander what may be the last chance to change your life" (1994, 50–51).

Drewermann's reading moves from the surface of the text down to ever-deeper levels that involve an increasing number of persons. The first level, which we may term the historical or surface level, concerns just one person: Jesus Christ. The second level, symbolically located below the surface, concerns kings or heroes in general, for the myth is much less specific than historical narration. The third level, subjacent to this, concerns or may concern everyone: thus we move from history to myth to anthropological reality.

Perhaps one more biblical example can help us understand Drewermann's approach, and in what follows I rely on my own, Drewermann-inspired exegetical work. In Genesis 2, the five enigmatic verses 10–14 explain that there were four rivers in Paradise: Pishon, Gihon, Tigris, and Euphrates. Commentators generally agree that the four rivers are to be identified as the Nile, the two rivers of Mesopotamia, and ancient Jerusalem's main source. But what is the meaning of this text?

Obviously, what we have here is a mythical text describing a mythical abundance of water. The very notion of Paradise implies rich and lush vegetation and therefore an inexhaustible supply of water. From the level of myth, we can easily ascend to the superior level, that of history. Here, we are outside Paradise and in real geography. Presumably the mythic description of Paradise dates from the Babylonian Exile or at any rate from a period in which Jews lived all over the Fertile Crescent and beyond: not only in Jerusalem, but also as the Mesopotamian and Egyptian Diaspora. Read in the concrete historical situation of their existence, the myth, for the Diaspora, has a very positive message: all over the world, the God of Israel provides abundantly for his beloved people. Paradise, or fragments thereof, can be found everywhere.

Again, we must look for another level, the one symbolically located below the myth. The anthropological structure concealed beneath the myth of paradisal abundance echoes the abundance experienced by the child in infancy. The mother is a child's true Paradise, whose breasts supply more than all necessary nourishment; in the child's fantasy, the two breasts become four—so that four rivers stand for the four breasts of a supermother. Outside Israel, this kind of fantasy is echoed in ancient Greek mythology and iconography, where multi-breasted Artemis is the divine nurse who never fails to satisfy all oral desires a baby might have.

As before, three levels can be discerned: the historical level of the real world and its promises to the Diaspora; the mythical level with its depiction of abundance in Paradise; and finally the ideal world of all of us—the world of early childhood in which all our desires, oral desires, were fulfilled. (This interpretation of the rivers of Paradise is my own, but it is accepted by Drewermann as adequately reflecting his approach.)

To summarize: the reading of the New Testament infancy narrative and the reading of part of the Paradise story proceed along similar lines. Although the two biblical texts belong to different literary types, the analyses fit the same general pattern of superimposed levels: a historical surface level, a mythical level, and an anthropological level, which may be represented thus: (a) history; (b) myth; and (c) human existence.

Drewermann has never sought to explain his methodology in a systematic way, so both his approach and the inspiration behind it remain concealed in the pages of his exegetical work. The three levels that I distinguish can serve as a guide to understanding Drewermann's approach, and the distinction of the various levels echoes a Freudian method of analysis.

The Freudian Inspiration

Although Jung's appreciation of archetypes is relevant at one point, Drewermann's methodological inspiration derives ultimately from Freud's *Interpretation of Dreams*—which does not come as a surprise, for Drewermann's psychological training was in neo-Freudian analysis. From Freud he learned that the analysis of dreams can also be applied to the interpretation of fictional texts, whether film, mythology, or fairy tale, and to stories included in the Bible. Often Drewermann analyzes complete biblical texts or portions of texts, for example, the deuterocanonical book of Tobit or the story of Jesus leaving his parents to stay in the Temple of Jerusalem. However, Freudian dream analysis also encouraged Drewermann to dissolve biblical texts into tiny components that have to be analyzed separately to reveal their own individual message. In Freud's words, "one cannot make the dream as a whole the object of one's attention, but only the individual components of its content. . . . [The analysis] is an interpretation in detail, not *en masse*; like this, it conceives the dream, from the outset, as something built up, as a conglomerate of psychic formations" (1938, 194). More important than the disarticulation or "deconstruction" of narrative surface structures is the recognition that texts, like dreams, may have and usually do have more than one single meaning.

The rule of multiple meanings in Freudian dream interpretation can best be explained on the basis of an example, and I have selected one found in Freud's own work. A young woman, Freud reports, related the following dream: "I arrange the center of a table with flowers for a birthday celebration" (1938, 382). The dream is accompanied by intense feelings of joy and happiness. What can be the meaning of this dream, reported by a young woman shortly before her wedding? Freud owes the report and interpretation to his friend Alfred Robitsek, who discovered three levels of meaning in this dream. At the first level, the dream simply represents fulfillment of the young woman's wish to have her own home. All dreams, according to Freud, are wish fulfillments. Robitsek does not stop his analysis at this point. Digging deeper, he discovers sexual symbolism. The table may stand for the marriage bed, for to be married means to share bed and table. And the flowers stand for the woman's genitals. Flowers, we are reminded, are plants' genital organs. In the dream, the young woman prepares herself for having intercourse with her husband, and she already looks forward to a child from this union—hence the association of the flowers and the birthday. Robitsek again digs deeper into the symbolism of arranging flowers and suggests a third meaning concealed in the dream. The manipulation of the flowers may echo infantile autoerotic sexuality or, more precisely, the joy and happiness derived from such activity. So we have here three levels of meaning: a surface meaning, a concealed erotic meaning, and a third, autoerotic meaning of the dream. They can be represented as three layers: (a) reality of the day; (b) concealed erotic reality; and (c) concealed echo from childhood.

One can easily see that Drewermann's interpretation of biblical texts shares certain features of Freudian dream analysis. Robitsek's Freudian dream analysis moves from the particular circumstances of the young woman longing for her own home to the erotic desires that are common to everyone. Drewermann moves from Christ's birth to an experience shared by some if not all human beings. They both move from the specific to the general, from the individual case to shared humanity. If Drewermann has made a contribution to biblical exegesis, I would locate it precisely at this point: he has convincingly demonstrated that traditional historical analysis can fruitfully be supplemented, and indeed balanced, by a wider anthropological approach that looks beyond mere history. Drewermann's critics have often argued that he shows little interest in the details of ancient times and places and moves all too easily out of history, using the biblical text as a mere springboard from which to jump into the soothing and motherly sea of archetypes. Regression to childhood and primordial unity rather than faith and historical events seem to bring salvation. As a Christian theologian, Drewermann may actually be justified in neglecting what others overemphasize. Jesus himself seems to have cared little about the particular political situation of his country. Unlike some of the Old Testament prophets, he is not an interpreter of particular historical events but, like the Old Testament sages, an interpreter of the human condition as such. Instead of referring to recent events, Jesus most often appealed to the timeless world of human experience or made observations about nature. "Consider the lilies of the field; they neither toil nor spin." Drewermann's project is not out of tune with a theology that emphasizes Christ the Galilean sage and teacher of universal truth (rather than, for instance, Christ the mystic, the charismatic leader, the miracle worker, or the apocalyptic prophet).

As a challenging psychological interpreter, Drewermann makes an effort to bring back to biblical studies the timeless world of human experience.

Although starting with a kind of Freudian analysis, Drewermann does not qualify as a full-fledged Freudian, however. He rejects Freud's pessimistic view of human reality as incompatible with a truly Christian and humanistic outlook. Once his analysis has arrived at its deepest level, he switches the code and turns to a Jungian and Eliadean interpretation of the human condition.

The Eliadean and Jungian Inspirations

One of the main characteristics of the deeper levels, the focus of Drewermann's biblical interpretation, is their ahistorical nature. The surface level, the story about the birth of Christ, seems to be a more or less straightforward account of the facts. But this level is of little relevance for Drewermann. He is interested in the myth and, ultimately, in the deep psychological layer that we have symbolically located below it—a level twice removed from history. Here we come across one of Drewermann's central ideas for which he is indebted to Eliade: the notion that "history" is of limited meaning for religious existence.

One of Mircea Eliade's most famous books, *Cosmos and History: The Myth of the Eternal Return* (1954), compares two notions of time and history, one characteristic of Western cultures and the other of non-European peoples. Eliade agrees with theological authors who stated that ancient Israel had abandoned pagan notions of cyclical time and thus developed the concept of linear, forward-moving history. This concept contributed to the emergence of a new culture, one that liberated humanity from the bondage of cyclical existence. History, in this view, does not repeat itself. Linear time and linear history were generally hailed as one of Israel's greatest gifts to the world. Unlike contemporaneous European and American theologians, Eliade was not enthusiastic about linear time. Instead, he sought to rehabilitate cyclical notions that he illustrates from several non-European sources, especially India. According to Eliade, modern Western humanity cannot escape from the "terror of history." Linear history, in the Western world, means wars and competition and an endless variety of unexpected forms of estrangement. Traditional civilizations defended themselves against this pattern by periodically abolishing their history through the repetition of the cosmogony, or by giving historical events a mythical meaning that was not only consoling but also coherent. As a romantic document, Eliade's *Cosmos and History* idealizes archaic and non-Western modes of thought that were implicitly recommended as an attractive alternative to the Western worldview.

In his early work *Structures of Evil*, Drewermann subscribed to the then current notion that the discovery of linear history was one of Israel's greatest intellectual achievements, indeed its greatest legacy to the Western world. Drewermann hailed Israel's discovery as an important contribution to setting humankind free from the bondage of nature (1977, xxix, 3:xxi–xl). Drewermann, in fact, equated history with freedom and culture, while he saw cyclical notions as being linked to nature. Under the impact of Eliade's work, however, Drewermann revised his earlier thought. Although it is impossible to describe this revision as a full-fledged conversion to the Eliadean view, Drewermann did make a step in this direction. In the revised edition of *Structures of Evil*, Drewermann included a new chapter that discusses the cyclical experience of time as belonging to humanity's primordial bliss (1981, 378–379). The second volume of *Depth-Psychology and Exegesis* also includes a long chapter on the meaning of time, and it is here that he suggests there should be a synthesis of cyclical and linear time, of myth and history, of the unconscious and the conscious mind (1984–1985, 2:596–635). Drewermann no longer accepts the unconditional appreciation of linear notions of time and history so characteristic of much of theological writing. His earlier fascination with linear time as the condition of human freedom has all but completely disappeared.

Although Drewermann's shift away from the historical dimension of the biblical text reflects his reading of Eliade, his interest in the child archetype is clearly indebted to Carl Gustav Jung's study "The Psychology of the Child Archetype." In a Jungian reading of the dream reported by Drewermann, the child dreamt about by one of his patients represents the "self." Jung defines the self as being larger than and superordinate to the conscious ego, because it embraces the conscious and the unconscious mind and therefore stands for the completeness of the human person. The early stages of someone's biographical development involve an emphasis on consciousness and ego, leading to the illusion that the ego is in full control. Later, a less ego-centric and more balanced view may and indeed should appear in a process Jung has termed "individuation." In the true "individual," the goal of this development, ego and self are no longer separated but form an indivisible unity. The child symbolizes the sacred image of a person's wholeness, and thus the dream announces the advent of "individuation."

Individuation restructures the personality. Having given birth to the "self," the person no longer revolves around the problematic ego but discovers a second, more important and sacred center in himself or herself, a center represented by the child. For Jung, as for Drewermann, individuation involves an increase in strength and optimism, a new lease on life. The child signifies future: "One of the essential features of the child archetype is its futurity. The child is potential future. Hence the occurrence of the child motif in the psychology of the individual signifies as a rule an anticipation of future developments" (Jung, 1991, 164: No. 278). So the child stands for a new, powerful start in life.

By now we have gone a long way toward understanding Drewermann's biblical interpretation. Thus far, however, our account has failed to point out the wider context in which Drewermann's biblical exegesis functions. Biblical interpretation, for him, is not an isolated activity; instead, it functions in the context of a wider theological agenda. In fact, it forms an integral part of a comprehensive theological project—that of a new romantic theology inspired by eighteenth- and nineteenth-century German romanticism.

The Wider Context: The Romantic Inspiration

In the 1970s and early 1980s, Drewermann developed his unique approach to understanding the Bible, religion, and what he considers the proper task of theology. This formative period encompassed two distinctive phases. The first phase is represented by the first edition of *Structures of Evil.* Published in 1977 and 1978, it shows Drewermann as a Freudian psychoanalyst and a follower of Sören Kierkegaard. Drewermann uses biblical texts to define anxiety (Angst) as the basic human predicament, and the implied message is that only the Church, with her traditional doctrines and means of grace, can free us from this situation.

After 1978, we can discern a gradual shift. Drewermann no longer presents traditional ecclesiastical doctrine as the answer to anxiety. Increasingly dissatisfied with Roman Catholicism and its oppressive ecclesiastical system, he comes to emphasize the soothing and liberating quality of the archetypal world unearthed in the exegetical process. One might say that Drewermann, then at the "zenith" of his life, became more of a Jungian analyst, although this is not the whole story. Drewermann came to embrace what is known as theological liberalism, and like all liberals, he rejects speculative theology, considers dogma an illegitimate mixture of religion and metaphysics (therefore secondary or dispensable), cherishes human freedom, is suspicious of ecclesiastical claims to authority, and finally, following Jesus, emphasizes the practical side of religion.

Jung is just one of a series of romantic authors whose work Drewermann discovers, appreciates, and increasingly uses to define the ways in which human existence is to be transformed and healed. The beginnings of his indebtedness to the liberal tradition and indeed to romanticism can be found in his series on fairy tales by the brothers Grimm, which he began to publish in 1981, and in the two volumes of *Depth-Psychology and Exegesis* of 1984 and 1985. It must be remembered that the Grimm brothers' fairy tales are a basic embodiment of the romantic temper and its optimism. "The fairy-story is optimistic, no matter how terrifyingly serious some features of the story may be," remarked the Freudian psychologist Bruno Bettelheim (1903–1990) in *The Uses of Enchantment: The Meaning and Importance of Fairy Tales* (1976, 37), and Drewermann agrees—to the point of being convinced that Grimm's *Nursery and Household Tales* and the Gospel stories are inspired by the same spirit and, albeit in different ways, convey the same message. In more recent publications such as *Faith in Freedom* (*Glauben in Freiheit*), Drewermann has maintained his interest in the romantic approach. Both critics and followers of Drewermann generally comment on psychoanalysis as the hallmark of this author's writing, and they are certainly not mistaken. If we are to understand Drewermann's work properly, however, we should take into account what I suggest we call the second source of his thinking: romanticism. Jungian and romantic influences inspired him to write his book on the Lukan infancy narratives (written in 1986; English translation, titled *Discovering the God Child Within*, 1994).

Two romantic authors are clearly among Drewermann's favorites: Schleiermacher and Novalis.

Schleiermacher

Friedrich Schleiermacher (1768–1834) ranks as one of the most important theologians of all times, and his book *On Religion: Speeches to Its Cultured Despisers* (1799/1996) can be said to embody the romantic vision of religion. The best way to explain Schleiermacher's view is to contrast it with eighteenth-century philosophical notions of "natural religion." Eighteenth-century deistic authors defined religion in terms of universally held basic doctrines: belief in God, belief in life after death, and belief in the postmortem punishment or reward for one's deeds. Schleiermacher did not accept this doctrinal notion of religion. For him, religion was an intense feeling of and taste for the infinite, rooted in a natural endowment or disposition. Far from being confined to a few gifted individuals, this disposition was regarded as present in every human being. It belongs to the very structure of the human spirit and represents its most noble faculty. Although life's circumstances may help this disposition to unfold to full consciousness or to prevent it from developing, Schleiermacher felt that all human beings were essentially religious. What the individual generally needed was stimulation from more advanced religious personalities.

Schleiermacher's notion of religiosity as a natural quality of the human mind is echoed in the work of another of Drewermann's favorite authorities: Mircea Eliade. Eliade is known for his interest in the archaic *homo religiosus*, whose mentality was characteristic of all non-Western peoples, and aspects of whose religiosity survive in Western nostalgic feelings about nature and in the longing for a perfect paradise. The very notion of *homo religiosus* derives from Schleiermacher, who in his *Speeches on Religion* coined the term *der religiöse Mensch*; translated into Latin as *homo religiosus*, this expression became one of Eliade's favorite technical terms. Because Schleiermacher's *religiöser Mensch* and Eliade's *homo religiosus* are the same person, we are justified to claim romantic ancestry for one of the most basic notions of Eliade's thought. Unsurprisingly, Drewermann occasionally uses the Eliadean term *homo religiosus* (Drewermann, 1984–1985, 2:635).

Religion for Schleiermacher, then, is deeply rooted in the human person. His analysis of particular historical religions such as Christianity, Judaism, and what he terms "natural religions" is ambivalent. On the one hand, he considers their historical particularity and even attempts a ranking (with Christianity being placed at the top of the list). On the other hand, he insists on the essential unity and compatibility of all particular religious expressions. This unity becomes apparent as soon as we consider not creedal abstractions but the original inspiration underlying them. In a way, the move from inner experience to outer expression, from spirit to word, is inevitable, but the move always involves a loss of authenticity. The gravest error is committed by those who, misunderstanding the process, replace the underlying living experiences with mere dead abstractions. Saint Paul's word applies here: "The letter kills, but the Spirit gives life" (2 Cor. 3:6). It is the romantic theologian's duty to rediscover and restore the original authenticity by reinventing the spirit, the original religious feeling. Unfortunately, it is the doctrinal, inauthentic form of religion that is the one most familiar to Schleiermacher's contemporaries, and it is for this reason that religion is despised by many intellectuals. In the Fourth Speech, Schleiermacher compares estranged forms of religion with authentic ones (1799/1996, 81).[2] Estranged religion is that imposed by the state—here Schleiermacher refers to the Protestant state church of the kingdom of Prussia. Estranged religion is creedal, doctrinal, and imposed; authentic religion realizes that official ecclesiastical doctrines are nothing but abstractions, signs, images, or symbols of certain basic and shared religious feelings that arise in the human soul. The relevant passage from Schleiermacher's speeches is actually quoted by Drewermann in *Depth-Psychology and Exegesis* (1984–1985, 1:73). He refers with approval to Schleiermacher's interpretation of religious language not as something alien to the human spirit but as something to be found inside the human mind and belonging to it. In this very context, Drewermann also quotes Novalis: "The way to all mysteries leads inwards. Eternity, with all its worlds, all past and future, is either within us or nowhere" (Drewermann, 1984–1985, 1:73; see Novalis, 1978, 2:233). This quotation brings us to another author: Friedrich von Hardenberg.

Novalis

Friedrich von Hardenberg (1772–1801), better known under his pen name Novalis, epitomizes early romantic poetry. Despite its poetic form and its largely fragmentary nature, Novalis's writing reveals a complete philosophy of history and human thought. This philosophy is based on the Platonic distinction between the ideal and the real worlds. The real world is the one in which we live: a world of appearances and estrangement. However, by intellectual intuition, we can glimpse the other, ideal world, which Novalis sometimes calls "die Welt des Märchens," the fairy-tale world (1978, 2:514). This is the superior and original world, in fact, the primordial world that was at the beginning. Fortunately, this world has not disappeared altogether; it is still with us. "It is due only to the weakness of our faculties that we cannot see ourselves in a world of fairies. All fairy-tales are nothing but dreams of that homely world which is everywhere and nowhere" (Novalis, 2:353). The poet's supreme task is to "poeticize" the world in which we live, and thus bring it closer to the ideal, fairy-tale world. "Poetry is the truly absolute reality. This is the kernel of my philosophy. The more poetic, the closer to truth" (2:420).

But what is poetry? Although Novalis thought, of course, of poetic literature, his notion of poetry was more complex. Poetry, for him, was both a worldview and a way of life. In either case, the prosaic approach to reality has to be overcome by a poeticizing, by transfiguration into another mode.

As a *worldview*, poetry expresses itself in human intellectual culture. Historiography, the natural sciences, and of course religion all have to be poeticized, that is, transformed by poetry and into poetry. Only the poet can look beyond appearances and mere facts into "real" reality. The genius-historian, for instance, is able to organize historical data into *Kunstgebilde*, that is, to describe historical facts so that they make sense and, at the same time, represent works of art (Novalis, 1978, 2:271). All conventional notions of scholarship eventually must give way to this new intuitive approach. As a *way of life*, poetry means heightened, transfigured existence, the mode of being known to and experienced even by prosaic people as soon as they step outside their everyday routine. Novalis refers to traveling, attending a wedding or baptism, and going to church as typical occasions for people to get a glimpse of poetic existence: "A Philistine reaches the highest degree of his poetic existence when he travels, attends a wedding, a baptism or a church service. It is here that his most daring desires are gratified and often surpassed" (2:263). On such occasions, people's normal lives give way to a higher, heightened, and celebratory existence in which they tap the transforming power of a higher, divine world. Under ideal circumstances, the faithful mutual love between a man and a woman transforms the life of both into "eternal poetry" (1:332).

A poetic fragment describes the project envisaged by Novalis:

When numbers, figures, no more hold the key
to solve the living creatures' mystery,
when those who kiss and sing have knowledge more
than all the deeply learned scholars' store . . .
And when in poesy and faërie
men read the world's eternal story,
then will a secret word oblige to flee
all of this mad perversity.

(Novalis, 1978, 1:395)[3]

The "mad perversity" also has to flee from religion. Religion, like everything else, has to be brought back to its primordial poetic truth. "Among the ancients," Novalis states, "religion was already in a certain measure what it should become with us, namely, practical poesy" (Novalis, 1978, 2:326). "In the beginning, poet and priest were one, and only later times have separated them. The true poet, however, has always remained a priest, just as the true priest has always remained a poet. And should not the future bring back the former state?" he confides to his notebook (Novalis, 1978, 2:255). The affinity of poetry and true religion and, what is more, their fusion, have become a common theme of many romantic authors. The French romantic historian and orientalist Ernest Renan echoes this sentiment quite well: "Le temps est venu où le christianisme doit cesser d'étre un dogme pour devenir une poétique" (1960, 1,530). The time has come for Christianity to cease being a doctrine in order to become a form of poetry.

The affinity of Drewermann's thought and that of Novalis is indeed striking. Drewermann occasionally refers to Novalis as an authority or to illustrate his thought (1984–1985, 1:73; 1993, 142–143 n. 14); he also quotes the poem "When numbers, figures, no more hold the key" (1989, 853 n. 35), cited earlier in Mabel Cotterell's elegant translation. Echoes of Novalis's thought abound in Drewermann's writing. In love—to quote but one first example—everyone is able to discover the "natural poetry of the heart," for to love means to lead a poetic existence (1994, 149). Drewermann frequently asserts the poetic nature of true religiosity and authentic religious discourse. Jesus, for him, is a poet, especially in the parables (1984–1985, 2:729) but also in the whole of his being (1989, 720; 1996, 236). "The central fact is, that Jesus has in some way lived as in a fairy tale or, rather, that he aimed at realizing the universal fairy tale of the Kingdom of God" (1996, 2:244): this statement may surprise those used to the language of biblical exegetes, but in terms of Novalis's philosophy, it sounds rather normal. According to Drewermann, the Christian priest must also be a poet, and a good sermon cannot but be poetic in nature (1987, 114). "In religion," Drewermann contends, "we can observe the goal of all romanticism, the living unity of faith and poetry"(1994, 17); it is to this goal that he wants to guide his readers, all of whom should be poets of their lives, not mere producers of literature (1996, 220). Drewermann's most detailed statement on poetry and religion can be found in the second volume of *Faith in Freedom*; the relevant chapter is subtitled "Of Poetry and Therapy" (1996, 214), a heading that can serve as a reminder of the two sources of Drewermann's thought: romanticism and psychoanalysis.

What Drewermann has learnt from Schleiermacher, Novalis, and Eliade combines to form a rudimentary theory of religion. According to this theory, religion is based on, and flows from, a disposition inherent in the human person. The human being has a longing for the infinite. As this taste develops, it needs the stimulation of concrete, historical religion as it is embodied in the Bible. For Drewermann, the Bible is a poetic rather than a dogmatic document. Turning to Eliade, Drewermann realized that nonbiblical and non-Western religious experience could help to avoid the one-sided reliance on certain biblical themes such as history. A truly romantic religious thinker must draw from a variety of sources to construct a universal and archetypal spirituality, to him the only adequate religion for contemporary humanity.

Notes

1. For more detailed presentations, see Lang (1994, 1995, 2001). Thus far, only one English source is available, Beier (2002).

2. The same set of ideas can be found in the work of Johann Gottfried Herder (1744–1803), another romantic theologian. Religion, according to Herder, "does not want to be doctrine. Doctrines separate and embitter. Religion unifies, for in all human hearts religion is but one" (1993, 92).

3. The translation is by Mabel Cotterell, in Flores (1960, 55). This crucial Novalis text is a poetic rendering of one of Romanticism's most elementary hopes—the hope that poetry will again be what it was among the ancient Greeks: the basis of all education. The Romantics hoped to create a poetry worthy of Homer and Hesiod. See the so-called "oldest program of a system of German idealism," an anonymous text dating from 1796 or 1797, which includes the line: "Poetry will acquire a higher dignity; it will be in the end what it was in the beginning—the teacher of humankind." Discovered by Franz Rosenzweig, this anonymous text was published in 1917; see Hegel (1971, 1:235–236).

References

Beier, M. (2002). *Analyzing a Violent God-Image: A Psychohistorical Introduction to the Work and Life of Eugen Drewermann.* Unpublished doctoral dissertation, Drew University.

Bettelheim, B. (1976). *The Uses of Enchantment: The Meaning and Importance of Fairy Tales.* London: Thames & Hudson.

Drewermann, E. (1977). *Strukturen des Bösen,* vol. 1. Paderborn: Schöningh.

Drewermann, E. (1981). *Strukturen des Bösen,* vol. 1 (3rd ed.). Paderborn: Schöningh.

Drewermann, E. (1984–1985). *Tiefenpsychologie und Exegese,* 2 vols. Olten: Walter-Verlag.

Drewermann, E. (1987). *Das Markusevangelium: Bilder der Erlösung,* vol. 1. Olten: Walter-Verlag.

Drewermann, E. (1989). *Kleriker: Psychogramm eines Ideals.* Olten: Walter-Verlag.

Drewermann, E. (1993). *Discovering the Royal Child Within: A Spiritual Psychology of "The Little Prince,"* Peter Heinegg, trans. New York: Crossroad.

Drewermann, E. (1994). *Discovering the God Child Within: A Spiritual Psychology of the Infancy of Jesus,* Peter Heinegg, trans. New York: Crossroad.

Drewermann, E. (1996). *Glauben in Freiheit,* vol. 2, *Jesus von Nazareth.* Zurich: Walter-Verlag.

Eliade, M. (1954). *Cosmos and History: The Myth of the Eternal Return.* Princeton: Princeton University Press.

Flores, A., ed. (1960). *An Anthology of German Poetry from Hölderlin to Rilke.* Garden City: Doubleday.

Freud, S. (1938). *The Basic Writings,* A. A. Brill, trans. New York: Modern Library.

Hegel, G. F. W. (1971). *Werke in 20 Bänden,* vol. 1. Frankfurt: Suhrkamp.

Herder, J. G. (1993). *Against Pure Reason: Writings on Religion, Language, and History,* Marcia Bunge, trans. Minneapolis: Fortress.

Jung, C. G. (1991). *The Archetypes and the Collective Unconscious,* R. F. C. Hull, trans., *Collected Works.* (Vol. 9.1). London: Routledge.

Lang, B. (1994). *Drewermann interprète de la Bible.* Paris: Cerf.

Lang, B. (1995). *Die Bibel neu entdecken: Drewermann als Leser der Bibel.* Munich: Kösel.

Lang, B. (2001). *Eugen Drewermann: Kleines Porträt eines Romantikers.* Paderborn: Universität.

Novalis. (1978). *Werke, Tagebücher und Briefe Friedrich von Hardenbergs,* Hans-Joachim Mähl & Richard Samuel, eds., vols. 1 and 2. Munich: Hanser.

Renan, E. (1960). *Oeuvres complètes,* Henriette Psichari, ed., vol. 9. Paris: Calmann-Lévy.

Schleiermacher, F. (1996). *On Religion: Speeches to Its Cultured Despisers,* Richard Crouter, trans. (2nd ed.). Cambridge: Cambridge University Press. (Original work published 1799)

CHAPTER 12

THE PSYCHOSYMBOLIC APPROACH TO BIBLICAL INTERPRETATION

Robert H. Neuwoehner

The psychosymbolic approach provides a framework within which a variety of literary, historical, comparative, psychological, and theological techniques may be brought together in a reflexive and holistic hermeneutic. In this chapter I describe the psychosymbolic process and then move on to a discussion of some of the psychological and philosophical theories that support it. The psychological discussion offers a preliminary formulation of a psychology of biblical inspiration, whereas the philosophical discussion suggests that psychosymbolic interpretation is best understood as a postmodern hermeneutic.

Psychosymbolic interpretation is an adaptation of C. G. Jung's method of clinical dream analysis for use with nonclinical materials. When we fix our analytical attentions on a text, there is no living, breathing client in the consulting room. Even the author of the text is inaccessible. This absence means that some of Jung's clinical techniques cannot be used to interpret texts. His most important analytical techniques, however, *can* be used outside the clinic.

When used as a method of applying Jung's core techniques to a text, psychosymbolic interpretation is a three-stage process. The first stage is to *read* the text; the second is to *amplify* the text's symbolic images; the third is to *interpret* the text. Reading the text is an exercise in literary criticism. Amplifying the images is an exercise in historical and comparative study. Interpreting the text involves using the psychological concepts of the Jungian model to describe what the symbolic meaning of the text might be. I describe the complexities involved in each stage of a psychosymbolic analysis later in the chapter; for now, a few general observations about the process are in order.

The fundamental question motivating a psychosymbolic analysis is: What is there about *this* text that gives it life for someone who reads or hears it in today's world? The psychosymbolic question is not "How did these elements get into the text at hand?" but rather, "Given the elements present in the text, how might we understand what is being said, suggested, or implied?" In other words, a psychosymbolic interpretation seeks to bring to the fore the possibilities for meaning that a text might offer to a contemporary reader.

Psychosymbolic interpretation acknowledges the uniqueness of each individual's engagement with a text. Each reader brings a unique set of presuppositions and interests to an encounter with a text. Each also brings a *different* set of presuppositions and interests to each successive encounter. If we accept the suggestion that a meaningful "text" comes into existence only when an audience encounters a set of material signs or symbols—when a reader encounters the words on a page, for example—then not only will the text be different for each reader but also different for the "same" reader each time it is engaged (see Moore, 1989, 121).

Like any reading, therefore, psychosymbolic interpretation offers only limited, even biased, readings. The bias of a psychosymbolic reading, however, is in some ways limited by the text-centered orientation of the analytical techniques employed. On the one hand, the psychosymbolic interpreter perceives as selectively as any other critic or reader. On the other hand, the objective signs and symbols that make up the physical text can always be seen alongside and behind these selective perceptions. The "words on the page" thus act both as a control of sorts and as an invitation to interpreters to engage in dialogue.

When such an interpretation becomes psychological, it also becomes most explicitly one of a number of quasi-allegorical, critical paraphrases available to readers of the text under consideration. A psychosymbolic interpretation, therefore, makes no claim to exclusive validity. Rather, it is but one voice among many. Some of these voices will be telling psychosymbolic stories, some will be telling other interpretive stories. It is hoped that this choir of multiple voices will blend in a complex contrapuntal texture.

To say that psychosymbolic interpretation is only one voice in a polyphonic choir of biblical critics is not, however, entirely accurate. It

is true that the biblical studies guild is characterized today by a pleth-
ora of apparently competing methodological approaches. This fact,
however, points to one of the more attractive features of psychosymbolic interpretation, namely, that it offers a way to bring a number of
these apparently exclusive critical approaches together in a relatively
comprehensive and integrated interpretive paradigm. Taking a second
look at the steps involved in carrying out a psychosymbolic analysis of
a biblical text allows us not only to identify the major methodological
approaches that can be used, or adapted for use, within the psychosymbolic framework, but also to locate psychosymbolic interpretation
in the biblical guild's current methodological discourse.

Reading the Text

The work of reading—or "listening to"—the text is essentially an
exercise in literary exegesis. At this stage of the analysis, therefore, a
variety of critical approaches may be used effectively. At one end of the
spectrum of possibilities is the traditional, grammatical exegesis of
the text (with reference to the Hebrew, Aramaic, or Greek underlying
the translation); at the other are the postmodern literary-critical readings. In fact, it is often best to bring several literary-critical methods
into conversation with each other as a way of being sure we are seeing
and hearing clearly. The basic question at this stage of the process is:
What is the text before me saying?

In most if not all cases, the basic question of what a text says can be
addressed effectively through a literary analysis of its narrative structure and dynamics. Focusing on the events, characters, and settings
described by the text, we can develop a fundamental understanding of
what the story being told is about (see Powell, 1990, 23). By paying
close attention to point of view, narrative patterns, figures of speech,
and rhetorical devices, we come to understand *how* the story is being
told (see Powell, 1990, 23–34). The aim of this analysis is to bring the
elements of the narrative into clear focus and identify the ones that
seem to be most important to the story. These central elements or
images provide the material for the amplification stage of the interpretive process.

The analytical techniques I describe here are essentially the same
as the core techniques of narrative criticism. "Narrative criticism,"
Stephen Moore observes, "is a story-preoccupied gospel criticism"—
which means "most of all" that it is "preoccupied with plot and character" (1989, 14). Plot and character, however, are inseparable: "Charac-

ters are defined in and through the plot, by what they do and . . . say.
The plot in turn comes into view as characters act and interact" (15).
Thus, in hopes of getting a solid grip on the text at hand, a narrative
critic—like a good investigative reporter—seeks a clear understanding of the Who? What? When? Where? and Why? of the story by
analyzing the interplay of forces and characters, events and settings
present in the narrative.

To say that narrative criticism is preoccupied with story elements
to the exclusion of all else, however, would be misleading. Narrative
critics analyze not only the *content* of a narrative but also its *rhetoric*—
not only its *story* but also its *discourse* (Powell, 1990, 23; Moore, 1989,
43–45). A narrative's elements of discourse—including such things as
simile, metaphor, symbolism, irony, repetition, comparison, inclusion,
and intercalation (Powell, 1990, 23–34)—add shape and definition
both to its plot developments and its characterizations. Thus, if we
hope to develop a satisfying understanding of a narrative, we have to
read its content and *listen* to its rhetoric.

Yet because biblical critics usually focus on episodes or pericopes
rather than entire books—and sometimes work with texts that are not
typically thought to be narratives—the literary techniques of narrative criticism must often be modified slightly when they are used in
biblical interpretation. With its concern for plot and character, story
elements and discourse elements, and content and rhetoric, narrative
criticism (technically speaking) offers a way to analyze the structure
and dynamics of literary works in their entirety. Fortunately, its analytical questions can be used effectively in the exegesis of individual
pericopes (Powell, 1990, 103–105). When working with smaller sub-
units of a larger narrative, some elements of the plot or character
development or patterns of association will not be visible within the
chosen pericope. From a psychosymbolic perspective this means that
consideration of these "extrinsic" elements will become part of the
amplification stage of the analysis. When we are dealing with a text
that does not seem to tell a story—a Pauline epistle, for example—
asking narrative questions, examining the "narrative" patterns, rhetorical devices, and stylistic techniques used by the voice in the text,
and identifying and defining the metaphors and figurative dimensions
of its language can help us hear the accents and modulations that mark
the important images in the text.

Because *reading the text* is fundamentally a literary critical task, it is
important to keep in mind that the traditional questions of text,
source, and redaction criticism are not taken up at this stage of the

psychosymbolic process. The historical inquiries pursued by these critical methods will be of interest when it comes time to amplify the images read in the text. Moreover, the more "historically oriented" speculations that may emerge from narrative criticism—suggestions about a text's real author, for example, or the author's intent, or the original audience—are not of immediate interest in a psychosymbolic analysis. Instead, psychosymbolic interpretation is interested in the text rather than the author and aims at facilitating readings by readers in today's world rather than trying to get inside the mind of a hypothetical historical reader.

Amplifying the Images

The aim of the first stage of psychosymbolic interpretation, thus, can be said to be the construction of a "critical" text out of the "original" text. The construction of this "new" text makes use of materials brought forward by the literary critical reading. Characterizations, plot dynamics, symbolic images, and metaphors are often particularly valuable during this construction project. Once it is in place, the new text serves as a foundation for the interpretive constructions produced by the remaining stages of the psychosymbolic analysis.

The first interpretive construction to take shape on the foundation laid down by the reading process is an amplified text. The construction process at this stage involves using various techniques of association to amplify the key images of the critically constructed text. This second stage is, therefore, a process of constructing a more elaborate text—but it is a construction resting securely on the foundation set in place by the preliminary stage of critical, constructive reading.

Amplification, then, is a process of construction through association. During the amplification process, each of the key images of the critical text becomes the focus for a series of investigations that may include philological, historical, sociological, anthropological, and comparative studies. The goal of the process is to identify and explore the depths of meaning associated with the various images.

It is at this stage that the biblical guild's traditional methods of historical-critical inquiry can be useful. Word studies, for example, can help us explore, survey, and map the fields of meaning and symbolic resonance that constellate around the narrative's key elements of story and rhetoric. This kind of philological exploration can be particularly useful when we are working with names, because the name of a character or a place often has a semantic significance that extends far beyond its basic naming function. In the book of Judges, for example, chapters 4 and 5 are devoted to the story of Deborah. She is identified as the woman (or wife) of Lapidoth (Judg. 4:4). Because Deborah in Hebrew means "bee," her name conjures up associations with the divine Great Mother of the ancient Mediterranean, a figure who was often linked with bees. Moreover, because Lapidoth can be understood as an abstract noun, it may not be the name of her husband. Instead it may offer a description of Deborah, the bee, as a woman of brilliance or radiance. Thus, amplification of Deborah's name allows us to see a prophetess and judge who is not just a wife but rather a powerfully numinous figure, perhaps even a manifestation of the Great Mother.

Historical studies and social scientific analyses provide additional means for uncovering important nuances of plot and characterization. Knowing something of the Zeitgeist and cultural milieu surrounding the text, understanding some of the political and social forces at play in its environment, and examining some of the historical developments and traditions associated with its story can suggest significant connotations of meaning that would not otherwise be available to a naïve reader. If we recognize, within the context of first-century Mediterranean culture, the implications of openhanded and backhanded blows to the face (the first implying the equality of the parties, the second used by a master to strike a slave), we begin to see the famous injunction to turn the other cheek in a whole new light. Now the act becomes a radical challenge, daring a "superior" to treat an "inferior" as a social equal.

It can also be useful to examine the ways in which the text being studied may be linked to other biblical texts and to extra-biblical texts. Tracing lines of intra- and intertextuality enlarges the text's images by bringing into view new facets of association and allusion in the semantic constellations that surround them. At the same time, this type of literary amplification also enriches our ability to understand the surplus of meaning these symbolic expressions open up. The lofty "Bread of Life" discourse in John 6 is an excellent example here. Not only does the image of bread bring to mind a wide range of biblical associations, but the text of the discourse includes references to other passages of Scripture, which develop a constellation of meaning based on associations of the bread of life with manna, the Israelites in the wilderness, the Torah, Lady Wisdom, and even Demeter, the great Hellenistic goddess of grain.

It should be clear, on the basis of what I have said so far, that comparative studies form the heart of the amplification process. A comparative approach is both appropriate and necessary because the unconscious depths of the psyche do not appear to be bound by either space or time. The recognition of this unbound quality of the unconscious is not only an expression of Jung's insistence that the unconscious is truly unknown; it is also a logical extension of Jung's acausal connecting principle and Erich Neumann's theory of unitary reality (a philosophical elaboration of the principle of synchronicity).

In theory, therefore, the comparative net used in the amplification process may be cast into any region of the world and any era of human history. The intuitive and imaginative range of the process is limited only by Jung's "rule" for comparative associations in amplification. In fact, it is the application of this rule that differentiates Jung's method of amplification from the psychoanalytic method of free association. The rule itself is really quite simple: each successive association must be linked more or less directly to the original image. Free association, on the other hand, is a theoretically infinite progression, a series of associations in which an association gives rise to another association, which may give rise to another association, and so on and on in a process that carries you farther and farther away from your point of origin in an ever-receding meander. The associative constellation produced by amplification, however, is more like a star burst with a set of rays emanating from a center point.

The limited amount of control exercised on the practice of amplification by this rule of "centered association" leaves the process relatively unbounded. The amplification process is not a search for historical influences; nor is it an attempt to trace paths of cultural diffusion or a quest for literary sources. Instead, it is an exercise aimed at bringing out and specifying as fully as possible the range of symbolic expressions that are available to the reader engaging the images of the text here and now. By amplifying the central and important images identified in the process of reading, we construct a new text that brings into view significantly more of the surplus of meaning available in the "possible world" that lies "in front of" the text (see Ricoeur, 1976, 53–57, 87, 89–95). If we can see the images clearly enough, if we can hear their voices distinctly enough, perhaps we will be able to understand what the story is saying and what it means.

Because the amplified text provides an expanded view of the text's symbolic materials and their patterns of association, we find ourselves at the threshold of the second of Paul Ricoeur's dialectics of interpretation. Reading and amplifying have moved our interpretive efforts from a naïve, pre-critical understanding of the text into highly

nuanced analytical explanations of the text in terms of its key components. The process of amplification has, in fact, taken us a step or two
beyond the usual limits of critical insight into a more intuitive realm
where the move from explanation to comprehension and appropriation becomes possible. It is at this point that our encounter with the
text has the potential to become a life-transforming event (see Ricoeur,
1976, 71–95).

Interpreting the Text

What we cannot lose sight of, however, is the fact that the relationship between explanation and comprehension is indeed a dialectic.
The intuitive possibilities and revelations made available through the
amplification process must remain in conversation with the analytical
foundations upon which they are built. In other words, the dialectic of
the second, post-critical naïveté requires that the event of appropriation give way, once again, to explanation. The task of the interpretation phase of a psychosymbolic analysis is, therefore, to develop a psychologically meaningful explanation of the symbolic expressions given
voice in the images of the amplified text. Because there are a number
of distinct psychological theories that could serve to govern one's
decisions concerning what is psychologically meaningful, I reiterate
that psychosymbolic interpretation is grounded in Jungian psychology. Thus, it can be said that this final stage of the interpretive process amounts to an exercise in "translation" through which yet
another text is constructed, this one written in the language of analytical psychology.

Describing the end-product of psychosymbolic interpretation as
a new text constructed through translation seems to condemn the
method by implying it is an unscientific and biased reversion to
allegory—that is, by implying it is a reversion to a method of explanation that relies on a series of apparently arbitrary associations,
which equate key terms from the text with terms from the interpreter's
own analytical vocabulary. This charge is true only to the extent that
the psychological language used to explain the amplified text is held
out as the last word or ultimate meaning of the text. If, however, we
recognize that the psychological interpretation is but another mode of
symbolic expression, its language will remain open and resist reduc-
tions to simple allegorical equations.

Psychosymbolic interpretation, then, culminates in the "translation"
of the symbolic language of the amplified text into a psychological

language whose basic vocabulary is drawn from Jungian theory. The most familiar aspects of Jung's model of the psyche are the structural concepts known as the collective unconscious and archetypes. What is not as commonly recognized is that the Jungian model actually presents a carefully balanced set of theoretical constructs that describes both consciousness and the unconscious. Another feature of Jung's model that is not typically acknowledged is the fact that it includes not one but two collective dimensions. In addition to the familiar collective *unconscious*, Jung also recognized the influences of collective *consciousness*.

The Jungian model, therefore, describes the structure and dynamics of the psyche in terms of a two-dimensional matrix. One dimension is marked at its poles by consciousness and the unconscious; the other differentiates between individual and collective phenomena in a continuum that runs from collective to individual to collective. Thus, Jung's structural matrix gives us a model of psychic "space" with four realms: collective consciousness, individual (or ego) consciousness, the individual (or personal) unconscious, and the collective unconscious.

The conscious side of Jung's structural model is focused on the ego-complex, which functions as the organizing center of identity and consciousness. Ego-consciousness interacts with the collective dimensions of consciousness through the mediating functions provided by the archetypal complex Jung called the persona. This side of Jung's model is thus characterized by a continuum that extends from collective consciousness through the persona to the individuality of ego-consciousness.

The unconscious side of the Jungian model can be conceived as a mirror image of the conscious side. The archetypal complex Jung called the shadow is in many respects an unconscious alter-ego that holds together personal elements of the psyche that are not acceptable as components of the ego-complex. The archetypal pattern that mediates between the personal and collective dimensions of the unconscious—the unconscious analog of the persona—is the contra-sexual complex that Jung called the anima in men and the animus in women. The unconscious continuum in Jung's model thus runs from the personal shadow through the contra-sexual complex (anima/animus) to the collective or transpersonal dimension of the unconscious psyche.

The *quinta essentia*, or fifth element, in the Jungian model is the archetypal complex Jung labeled the self. Jung's conceptualization of the self is fundamentally paradoxical. On the one hand, the self is the essence of individuality that stands at the very center of each person's psyche. When seen in this aspect, the self can be thought of as occupying the center point between the ego (and consciousness) and the shadow (and the unconscious). On the other hand, the self is the archetypal complex that encompasses the totality of the psyche. As a complex of totality, therefore, the self is not only the essence of one's individuality but also (and simultaneously) the quintessence of transpersonal collectivity.

The paradoxical nature of the self as a theoretical construct points to an aspect of the Jungian model that is seldom acknowledged: this is a *radically open* and fundamentally transpersonal model of the psyche. By postulating a collective dimension of consciousness, Jung opened his model of the psyche outward toward the transpersonal domains of culture and society. By constructing a theory of the collective unconscious, Jung recognized that the inward boundaries of the psyche are ultimately impossible to fix. Because the unconscious is in fact and by definition unknown, what we "know" of the unconscious is only what we can deduce or infer from certain peculiar manifestations that intrude into consciousness. The unconscious itself remains *un*-conscious.

Nevertheless, material from the unconscious does, in fact, intrude into consciousness. The psyche, according to Jung, is a system whose innate tendency is to attempt to correct any imbalances that may develop in its functioning. In order for the psyche's self-regulating mechanisms to operate, consciousness and the unconscious must be able to interact. Practically speaking, this means that consciousness must be able to gain access to unconscious material. The meeting of conscious and unconscious contents is described, through an analogy with mathematics, as the transcendent function. As Jung explains, "there is nothing mysterious or metaphysical about the term 'transcendent function.' It means a psychological function comparable in its way to a mathematical function of the same name, which is a function of real and imaginary numbers. The psychological 'transcendent function' arises from the union of conscious and unconscious contents" (1969, par. 131). The transcendent function is what allows one "to bring conscious and unconscious together and so arrive at a new attitude" (par. 146). It describes a process in which unconscious material is given form (or formulated) in a symbolic image whose meaning is meant to be understood by ego-consciousness.

The transcendent function is thus the mechanism of personal transformation and psychological growth. "Consciousness is continually widened through the confrontation with previously unconscious contents," Jung declares, "or—to be more accurate—[it] could be widened if it took the trouble to integrate them" (par. 193). Psycho-symbolic interpretation, then, is a way to facilitate the process of trans-formation made possible by the transcendent function. The reader's conscious and unconscious are brought into contact through reading and amplifying the text. Conscious understanding is encouraged by advancing psychological interpretations.

In addition to its potential for facilitating personal transformation through "transcendent" encounters with archetypally symbolic texts, the psychosymbolic interpretation of biblical texts also has potentially significant implications for our understanding of the psyche. During the interpretation process, the symbolic language of the amplified bib-lical text is "translated" into the language of analytical psychology. This act of translation, however, is not simply a process of confirming Jungian theory. In any translation process there is always the possi-bility of confronting untranslatable terms. The process of psychosym-bolic interpretation, therefore, must remain open to the possibility that the data uncovered in the engagement with the biblical text may demand a reconsideration or modification of the psychological theo-ries brought into the encounter.

Thus, the act of translating the language of the amplified text into psychological language not only constructs a new "psychological" text but also brings the Bible into a constructive dialogue with psycholog-ical theory. As we have seen, the conversation between the two has enormous potential for transformation. First of all, it can transform our understanding of the Bible—by constructing amplified, symbolic texts for us to appropriate. Moreover, the conversation has the poten-tial to transform our understanding of the structure and dynamics of the psyche—by constructing an enlarged psychological "meta-text." Finally, the psychosymbolic conversation can transform our lives—by constructing an "expanded self."

The Psychology of Inspiration

Up to this point, I have focused on describing the process of psycho-symbolic interpretation, considering some of the critical methods the process is able to integrate, and reflecting on the transformative potential of the approach. Two key questions remain, however. Is this approach appropriate for interpreting biblical texts, and is it valid? I address the first question by looking at how biblical texts were com-posed. Then, in the last section, I address the validity of psychosym-bolic interpretation by means of a more philosophical analysis.

The key to recognizing the appropriateness of the psychosymbolic approach lies in developing an understanding of how inspiration and artistic creativity relate to the processes of biblical composition. Once again, Jungian theory provides the essential framework. As I indicated earlier, Jung developed a model of the psyche that is radically open. Not only did he recognize collective dimensions in both the outer (conscious) and the inner (unconscious) reaches of the psyche but he also insisted that the boundaries of the unconscious are unknown and impossible to fix with any certainty.

The radical nature of Jung's theoretical thinking did not stop there, however. Jung also proposed a principle that implies the interconnectedness of the inner and outer dimensions of reality. This principle is, of course, *synchronicity*, Jung's famous "acausal connecting principle." The synchronicity principle was used by Jung to account for both meaningful personal coincidences (for example, the familiar story of the beetle appearing at his window at a crucial moment during a difficult analytical session focused on a patient's dream of an Egyptian scarab) and the constellations of events and images that define historical epochs (for example, his analysis of the correlation between the astrological age of Pisces and the fish symbolism of the Christian era).

Although Jung himself did not work out the implications of the synchronicity principle in a sustained or detailed fashion, Erich Neumann elaborated it into a theory of unitary reality. Neumann mounts a psychologically grounded epistemological argument in support of an ontological theory of unified reality, which sees inner and outer, subject and object, as inextricably bound into a multidimensional but unified field (Neumann, 1989, 3–62). One of the most significant aspects of this theory is the explicit recognition that consciousness is a "specifically restricted field of knowledge" (Neumann, 9), which Neumann characterizes as a "cognitive system whose emphasis is on clarity and discrimination" (13). The deep unconscious, however, is a cognitive system of an entirely different character. "I find myself compelled," Neumann says, "to regard the separation of inner and outer as principally invalid for the archetypal sphere. . . . While the archetypal images emerge within the realm of the psychic personality, their corresponding reality is a field outside" (24).

Unitary reality is transpersonal; "its presence can be detected prior to and outside of the human dimension" (66). At the same time, unitary reality lies at the heart of our being: "At the deepest level of all, we ourselves merge insensibly into the unitary reality" (116). Thus, Neumann observes,

psychic images are "mundane" . . . they relate to the real world. Archetypes, for example . . . do not represent an "inner psychic" reality which
can be isolated from the real world. . . . The two sides are tailored to each
other and are interdependent, so that what our conscious minds describe
as "world" and "psyche" are not simply two aspects of the one reality but
two manifestations of the same oneness which are interdependent. . . .
there is no psyche without a world and no world without a psyche.
(1989, 67–68)

Because of the interdependent unity of the world and the psyche, the
evocation and expression of an archetype require an "indispensable"
conjunction of an outer "world factor" and an inner "psychic factor"
(Neumann, 1989, 82). The experience of such a conjunction is, in turn,
"always connected with the experience of a meaningful fate" (1989, 56).
Thus, manifestations of unitary reality are not only fundamentally
paradoxical but also profoundly numinous: "Even when the unitary
reality manifests itself in an archetypally conditioned human encounter, a transpersonal element will intervene, spontaneously, as it were,
and bring with it a symbolism that is universal and cosmic" (121).

With your head reeling from the attempt to grasp these visions of
synchronicity and unitary reality, you might well be asking yourself:
Why bother? Why are these theories important for understanding the
Bible? These psychological insights are important because of what
they can tell us about the process of literary creation. In essence, Jung
and Neumann have provided us with the foundations for a psychological theory of inspiration.

Jung, in his essays on art and literature (1966), distinguishes
between two types of artistic creation. The first could be called
"inspired" because the work of art seems to have a life of its own. The
second could be called "intentional" because the will of the artist seems
to hold the dominant position in the creative process (Jung, 1966,
pars. 108–109). Jung argues that the unconscious is the true guiding
factor in both types of creativity. When the unconscious is dominant
in the process, it produces "explicit symbols" in inspired creations;
when the artist's creative ego seems to be in control, the unconscious
produces "hidden symbols." In either case, the creative process acts like
"a living thing implanted in the human psyche" (par. 115). In other
words, Jung points out that the creative process is like an autonomous
complex with "a kind of innate drive that seizes a human being and
makes him [or her] its instrument" (par. 157).

Jung's understanding of the creative process expresses in psychological terms what is commonly known about creativity: the creative

process is not ultimately controlled by the artist or author. The creative person, says Neumann, is one who is "closer to" the unconscious, the archetypal realm, and the unitary reality (1989, 101); one "in whom the connection between ego and self is alive in a special way" (52). This connection between the artist's ego and the collective unconscious, however, is not really a two-way street. It is the unconscious, not the will of the artist or author, that has the upper hand. Neumann describes the situation of the creative person with compelling clarity:

> It is part of the paradox inherent in . . . the unitary reality that, although it manifests itself in and through creative [people], it cannot be "known" by him [or her]. [The creative person] does not grasp it, he [or she] is seized and possessed by it, and even when he [or she] helps to fashion and develop, with the full cooperation of [the] conscious mind, an experience which is intuitive or which gradually takes possession of him [or her], the primary fact that he [or she] has been overwhelmed is always a significant element in the situation.
>
> What we are referring to here is not simply the relative autonomy of the creative process, which always partakes of the nature of grace and the origin of which . . . can never be manufactured or brought about by an arbitrary act of the ego. The fascination by which the ego is seized and possessed and by means of which the human personality becomes the instrument of the transpersonal is always identical with a state of being emotionally overwhelmed. (Neumann, 1989, 103–104)

Creative inspiration, then, is an experience of coming into contact with, perhaps even being overpowered by, a mysterious and numinous force. Because creativity is a relatively autonomous process and is based on fantasy, it is able to bring archetypal patterns into manifest expression. Archetypal images appear, according to Jung, "wherever creative fantasy is freely expressed" (1966, par. 127). Archetypes, however, are not simply the "products" of fantasy; they are also the guiding spirits of the intellect, the "regulators and stimulators of creative fantasy-activity" (Jung, 1969, pars. 403, 406). Thus, "however different the experiences of artists may be, and in whatever different ways these experiences may appear to them and through them, their creativity always represents a breakthrough in which the dimension of the purely personal opens out into that realm of the intrinsic essence of things which constitutes the suprapersonal background of reality" (Neumann, 1989, 160).

How great a step is it from these characterizations of the creative process to the theological notion of a divinely inspired biblical text? Clearly, for the committed theologian and the person of faith, it is an unimaginably great leap. From a psychological perspective, however, it is no step at all. For once you venture across the threshold of consciousness into the unconscious, the unknown and ultimately unknowable realm of unitary reality, all ontological and metaphysical claims become equally untenable. Thus, "ordinary" inspiration is psychologically indistinguishable from "divine" inspiration, and biblical texts are indistinguishable from other forms of literature—they are all creative "products" of the psyche. The Muses, then, are sisters of the Paraclete.

However you choose to understand the inspiration of biblical texts—whether you see them as divinely inspired or "only" as products of an "ordinary" process of literary creation, whether you believe they are collective compositions or the works of individual writers—one fact remains inescapable: the psyche is the medium through which the texts have come to be. In other words, the creative (and/or divine) breakthroughs made manifest in biblical texts have all passed through the "filter" of the human psyche. A key function of the psyche as a filtering medium for breakthroughs from the transpersonal is to transform "unformed dynamic energies . . . into that form which possesses a direction toward consciousness" (Neumann, 1989, 41). The forms that this transformation process produces are *symbols*. Jung says: "Symbols, like dreams, are natural products, but they do not only occur in dreams. They can appear in any number of psychic manifestations: there are symbolic thoughts and feelings, symbolic acts and situations, and it often looks as if not only the unconscious but even inanimate objects were concurring in the arrangement of symbolic patterns" (1954, par. 480).

Once "dynamic energies" become manifest in symbols, intuitive breakthroughs become possible for anyone who comes into contact with the "texts" carrying the symbols. In order to understand artistic or literary texts, therefore, one must be able to "speak" the language of the unconscious, the transpersonal language of symbols.

A Postmodern Hermeneutic

Because biblical texts are (at least in part) creative products of the psyche in which symbols give expression to material emerging from the collective "depths" of the unconscious, it seems entirely appropriate to use the psychosymbolic approach in their interpretation. In order to indicate the validity of the approach, I place psychosymbolic interpretation within the context of the theoretical discourse now current among biblical scholars.

Psychosymbolic interpretation is an integrative, psychological, reflexive, and holistic approach that shares a number of important values and assumptions with the realm of contemporary academic discourse somewhat oxymoronically called postmodernism. Indeed, because psychosymbolic interpretation is also a hermeneutic method, it can be described as a postmodern hermeneutic. But what does such an ostentatious classification really mean? To address this question, I sketch an overview of the more important characteristics of both postmodernism and hermeneutics.

According to the Bible and Culture Collective, the postmodern perspective emerges from a transformed awareness of our locations in modern culture (Bible and Culture Collective, 1995, 1–15). This transformed self-awareness gives rise to the affirmation of a potentially radical set of countercultural values. The key characteristic of the postmodern transformation of awareness is its radical reflexivity. The postmodern attitude demands that we be not only self-conscious but also self-critical. This critical, postmodern self-awareness is then brought to bear on our theories, our methods of interpretation, our ethics, ideologies, psychological dynamics, social relations, and our manipulations of power. The values affirmed as a result of such a postmodern self-criticism exalt difference over identity, diversity over conformity, democracy over hegemonic domination.

At its heart, A. K. M. Adam insists, postmodernism is a "movement of resistance" (1995, 1). There is no privileged starting point, there is no all-encompassing theory, and there are no value-neutral or ideology-free claims in the postmodern resistance (5). "Radical hermeneutics is a sustained effort to write from below, without celestial, transcendental justifications," John Caputo declares (1987, 272). He then goes on to proclaim what Stephen Moore calls a "postmodern creed" (1989, 174): "I reject all forms of privileged positions above the flux. . . . I write . . . from below, and I ask all who do otherwise how they acquired their elevated position" (Caputo, 1987, 279).

Indeed, because it is an antifoundational and demystifying movement that resists totalities (Adam, 1995, 61–70), postmodern interpretation is not only deconstructive and political but also transgressive, multidisciplinary, and often undisciplined. Adam suggests that these transgressive interpretations may be seen as "the positive face of deconstruction: while deconstruction chastens our efforts to ascertain anything about a text, transgressive readers assert audacious 'versions' of texts: *in*versions, *extra*versions, *con*versions, *per*versions, *contra*versions, *di*versions, *trans*versions, *sub*versions. . . . [Postmodern readers]

deliberately flout the discursive rules that have separated various theoretical domains in order to produce disruptive interpretive effects"
(1995, 61).

Postmodern interpretation is an approach that often constructs
interpretive *bricolages* "from the various materials at hand" (62).

In addition to suggesting the reflexiveness, inclusiveness, trans-
gressiveness, and playfulness of the postmodern (*keine*) *Weltanschaung*,
these descriptions of the principal trajectories of postmodernism issue
a call for biblical studies to turn away from the traditional historical-
critical interest in reconstructing the past. "The postmodern has to do
with transformation in the local ways we understand ourselves" (Bible
and Culture Collective, 1995, 9). In this context, "local" indicates the
postmodern rejection of universals in favor of the here and now of
the present. Thus, if we adopt a postmodern approach, we will be focusing our efforts on reading texts in radical ways with the hope of transforming ourselves and the communities in which we live.

Consideration of the postmodern emphasis on interpreting texts in
order to effect transformations in the present leads us rather naturally
to the topic of hermeneutics. With its countercultural values and
transgressive attitudes, the postmodern approach constructs (or "de-
constructs") a transformed understanding of texts. In other words, the
postmodern resistance has a dominating hermeneutic interest: a desire
to approach the goal of understanding a text through explorations of
the ways in which texts are created and received.

One of my claims is that the psychosymbolic approach not only
shares the reflexive and holistic qualities of postmodern approaches
(which are holistic both in the sense of being inclusive of diversity and
in the sense of teasing out the "holes" in texts) but also pursues goals
that make it a hermeneutic method. Peter Homans, focusing especially
on Jung's theory of archetypes and archetypal interpretation, describes
Jungian psychology as "a psychological hermeneutic of religious
images" (1969, 348). His analysis demonstrates that this Jungian
hermeneutic has significant affinities with the hermeneutics of both
Rudolf Bultmann and Paul Ricoeur (Homans, 1969, 350–352), two
dominant figures in biblical hermeneutics during the past fifty years.
The following brief review of their thinking will make it easier to understand the hermeneutic dimension of psychosymbolic interpretation.

Bultmann was not only one of the pioneers of form criticism but also
an influential practitioner of the history-of-religions method. Most of
all, however, his interpretive work was committed to the process he
called demythologizing. During the cultural crisis that emerged in the

aftermath of World War I, Bultmann was one of several Protestant theologians who were instrumental in shifting the focus of interpretive activity away from the questions of historical reconstruction and toward the question of meaning and understanding for contemporary readers of the Christian Testament. The interpretive task for these "theological exegetes" came to be seen as the attempt to bring out the spiritual essence from within or behind the historically conditioned text (Kümmel, 1972, 363–369). For Bultmann, this spiritual essence came into view as the mythical and fantastic elements were stripped away from the biblical narratives. Through this process of demythologizing, the proclamation of good news contained in the texts would be revealed in a form that was not handicapped or obscured by the pseudo-scandal of mythological language. Once the demythologized kerygma was brought into view, Bultmann fully expected the reader's encounter with the text to bring about an existential crisis of faith. Thus, Bultmann's hermeneutics were grounded in modern historical criticism but aimed at theological and existential transformation.

Ricoeur introduces another shift in our understanding of the hermeneutic task by drawing attention to the fact that in the process of demythologization, "another language replaces the language of myth and hence calls for a new kind of interpretation" (1974, 395). Arguing that Bultmann seems to have had little interest in this fact or its implications, Ricoeur insists on establishing the hermeneutic task on a different foundation. He rejects not only the historical orientation of hermeneutics but also the assumption that there is an independent, objective text (Ricoeur, 1974, 397; 1976, 22–23). Instead, Ricoeur erects his hermeneutics on linguistics and a literary theory of discourse (1976).

For Ricoeur, the absence of a truly objective text leads to the necessity of developing a new way of entering into and engaging the paradox of the hermeneutic circle. The traditional way of describing this paradox of interpretation is to speak of the impossibility not only of understanding a part without understanding the whole but also of understanding the whole without understanding its parts. Ricoeur's first move is to reformulate the paradox in terms of belief and understanding: "to understand the text, it is necessary to believe what the text announces . . . but what the text announces . . . is given nowhere but in the text. . . . it is necessary to understand the text in order to believe" (1974, 390).

Working from within this circle of paradox, Ricoeur develops a dialectical model of the interpretative process that takes the hermeneutic task beyond a semantic exegesis focused on understanding the objective references of a text and toward a moment of understanding and appropriation (1974, 397–398; 1976). To speak as if there is only a single moment of appropriation, however, obscures Ricoeur's recognition of the "surplus of meaning" to be found in metaphor and symbol (1976, 45–69). This awareness of the surplus of meaning makes Ricoeurian hermeneutics a living enterprise that remains forever open to new encounters.

What, then, are the fundamental characteristics of a postmodern hermeneutic? The postmodern designation suggests an approach that values self-reflective subjectivity over an unachievable quest for objectivity—one that welcomes a pluralistic and multivocal discourse in place of a violent hierarchy of exclusivism. It implies an approach that functions with a holistic epistemology, one that transgresses the limits of a one-sided rationalism and acknowledges the importance of feelings, and one that calls for replacing the traditional historical interest in original authors and audiences with a focus on the effects that texts can have on contemporary readers and reading communities. A postmodern approach becomes a hermeneutic when it focuses attention on the life-transforming nature of appropriation and understanding. On the other hand, a hermeneutic such as Ricoeur's theory of interpretation reveals its postmodern character in its recognition of the "trans-rational" in the surplus of meaning, in its awareness of the pluralistic subjectivity contained in the paradox of the hermeneutic circle, and in its focus on meaning as an event entered into by contemporary readers in their encounters with a textual discourse.

Psychosymbolic interpretation, therefore, may be classified as a postmodern hermeneutic if it puts into practice a set of values and assumptions analogous to or consistent with those listed earlier. It does, in fact, work with such a set of values and assumptions. Because it is a psychological method, psychosymbolic interpretation is fundamentally reflexive and radically conscious of its inescapable subjectivity—the psyche, after all, can only view itself reflexively. The psychosymbolic approach operates with a holistic epistemology based not only on Jung's fourfold model of conscious functioning (i.e., his theory of psychological types) but also on his understanding of the transcendent function and the synchronicity principle. These theoretical constructs give value to the rational functions of thought and feeling, to the nonrational functions of intuition and sensation, to the creative interactions of consciousness and the unconscious, and to the inextricably unified nature of inner and outer reality. These same theoretical foundations also demand that we reject hegemonic systems of domination in favor of a pluralistic and democratic acceptance of differences.

From the methodological point of view, psychosymbolic interpretation is not only psychological, reflexive, and holistic; it is also integrative. Its foundations in Jungian theory provide the psychosymbolic approach with a critical awareness of and profound appreciation for the inexhaustible multivocality of the symbolic life. As a result, the psychosymbolic process brings literary, historical, and social scientific methods together in a meaningfully coordinated, analytical (and sometimes playful) interpretive effort that not only focuses on the possibilities for meaning available to contemporary readers but also strives to open up opportunities for entering into the transforming experience of understanding and appropriation.

References

Adam, A. K. M. (1995). *What Is Postmodern Biblical Criticism?* Minneapolis: Fortress.

Bible and Culture Collective. (1995). *The Postmodern Bible*, E. A. Castelli, S. D. Moore, & R. M. Schwartz, eds. New Haven: Yale University Press.

Caputo, J. D. (1987). *Radical Hermeneutics: Repetition, Deconstruction, and the Hermeneutic Project.* Bloomington: Indiana University Press.

Homans, P. (1969). Psychology and Hermeneutics: Jung's Contribution. *Zygon*, 4(4), 333–355.

Jung, C. G. (1954). *The Symbolic Life: Miscellaneous Writings, The Collected Works of C. G. Jung*, R. F. C. Hull, trans. (Vol. 18). Princeton: Princeton University Press.

Jung, C. G. (1966). *The Spirit in Man, Art, and Literature, The Collected Works of C. G. Jung*, R. F. C. Hull, trans. (Vol. 15). Princeton: Princeton University Press.

Jung, C. G. (1969). *The Structure and Dynamics of the Psyche* (2nd ed.), *The Collected Works of C. G. Jung*, R. F. C. Hull, trans. (Vol. 8). Princeton: Princeton University Press.

Kümmel, W. G. (1972). *The New Testament: The History of the Investigation of Its Problems*, S. McLean Gilmour & H. C. Kee, trans. Nashville: Abingdon.

Moore, S. D. (1989). *Literary Criticism and the Gospels: The Theoretical Challenge.* New Haven: Yale University Press.

Neumann, E. (1989). *The Place of Creation: Six Essays, Essays of Erich Neumann*, H. Nagel, E. Rolfe, J. van Heurck, & K. Winston, trans., vol. 3. Bollingen Series 61. Princeton: Princeton University Press.

Powell, M. A. (1990). *What Is Narrative Criticism?* Minneapolis: Fortress.

Ricoeur, P. (1974). Preface to Bultmann, P. McCormick, trans., *The Conflict of Interpretations: Essays in Hermeneutics,* Don Ihde, ed. Evanston: Northwestern University Press, 381–401.

Ricoeur, P. (1976). *Interpretation Theory: Discourse and the Surplus of Meaning.* Fort Worth: Texas Christian University Press.

CHAPTER 13

JEWISH AND CHRISTIAN MESSIANISM: THE PSYCHOANALYTIC APPROACH OF HEINZ KOHUT

Ithamar Gruenwald

When viewed from thematic and historical points of view, discussion of the subject of messianism in the days of early Christianity and in rabbinic writings up to the Middle Ages cannot be conducted in the framework of a common nominator or denominator. I believe that not only the nominators but also the denominators are too diversified to render a coherent picture of the subject, both in terms of its linear historical development and in essential matters of structure and context. Furthermore, one should bear in mind that theological considerations often color the scholarly discussion of the subject. Too much seems to be at stake when issues concerning historical fulfillment surface in messianic contexts and terms of reference. The reasons are too obvious to mention here. Even a direct dialogue on this issue can hardly hide the nuances in terminology and concepts emerging from the differing perspectives and motivations.

Many of the scholarly discussions of the subject of messianism are conducted across two boundaries: the first between Christianity and Judaism, and the second, on the Judaic side, between group-oriented messianism and more widely spread rabbinic messianism. These discussions are often trapped in stereotypes, and what looks to me even graver, they force the dialogue into contextual constraints that are more confusing than clarifying. In this respect, it is common to find that a certain messianic passage plays Christian tunes to one scholar whose ears are attuned to Christian modalities, whereas another scholar, wearing Judaic glasses, sees in the same passage yet another example of Jewish messianic hopes.[1] On Judaic and Christian grounds, then, the differences are always radiating contextual considerations, which often reflect theological interests if not undisguised biases and prejudices.

This chapter suggests taking an altogether different path from the one found in many scholarly and theological studies of the subject. It discusses the subject of messianism in the context of its plurality and diversity of expressions and from the point of view of an underlying psychoanalytic paradigm. This concerns messianism in both its Judaic and Christian frameworks. In both cases, the psychoanalytic point of view followed and developed in this essay has its clinical and theoretical foundations in the work of Heinz Kohut and his school (Kohut, 1971, 1977; Greenberg & Mitchell, 1983). To the best of my knowledge, this point of view has not been explored before in the context of messianism and in its relevance to the scholarly assessment of the subject. I believe that in taking up the subject from this angle, those interested in messianism and in its scholarly evaluation will find new insights suggested to them. The main advantage of the present approach is in its suggesting a coherent and integrated platform for the discussion of the historical development of the subject matter and in its underlying diversity. Because psychoanalytic paradigms and not historical considerations are here viewed as the common cultural frame of motivations, messianism is likely to appear in a new light, addressing psychological needs rather than historical necessity.

I make a few preliminary observations, most of which concern the psychoanalytic premises I consider relevant to accomplishing the present project. Before doing so, however, I refer the reader to the complexity of the subject matter and to its embedded diversity.

Exposition

When speaking of Jewish and Christian messianism, I use the plural form, *messianisms*, because it makes better sense than does the singular. A careful study of the sources shows that there were several types of messianism in Judaism in the same way that there certainly were several concepts and configurations of messianism in early Christianity. In this respect, the title of the collection of studies *Judaisms and Their Messiahs* (Neusner et al., 1987) gives a good idea of the problems involved in the subject, although the volume does not draw the kind of conclusions drawn in this chapter. One of my conclusions concerns functional matters, that is, the diversity of ways in which the first Christians wished to bring about, and thereby to define, their relationship to the various Judaic groups of the time. Here, a variety of matters—beliefs, social structuring, and modes of religious practice—played a significant role. Because, as we now know (Collins, 1995, 1 n. 1), there was hardly a uniform kind of messianism in Judaism, there can be no uniform mode of describing the nature of the parting of the ways, on messianic grounds, between the new and the old religion (Dunn, 1991). In terms of a general outline, though, we may distinguish between two kinds of separating positions. One was developed by Paul and the other by "pastoral" writers of the New Testament and postcanonical writings. In these writings, messianism crystallized mainly in theological terms of reference and as a theological issue. Another form of messianism unfolded in the four Gospels, three of which are labeled "synoptic." In the Gospels, messianism shows a pivotal interest in biographical, historical, and ritual matters. The theological and historical narratives in the New Testament do not readily converge. They certainly do not gather under the unifying canopy of a uniform kind of "Christian messianism."

One way of explaining this factor is that because there was no single, homogeneous, normative kind of Judaism in the early Christian era, no single, perfectly integrated, and homogeneous type of messianic reaction could build up against it. In any event, it is interesting that the books marking the beginning of the new creed show that there was no single kind of Christianity. For that matter, the new creed, which by logical standards should have striven to present a consensus with a clear and unambiguous voice vis-à-vis the rest of the religio-cultural world of the time, shows a remarkable degree of inner diversity. This diversity is not just a matter of literary transmission and historical perception of past events, as several scholars have suggested (Koester, 1982).

Having in mind similar phenomena in the Judaic world of that time, we have to acquaint ourselves with a mode of understanding in which a prolific output of writings does not necessarily strive to give expression to identical perceptions of the same religious events, sensibilities, and processes. On the contrary, people in the ancient world were as much prone as we moderns are to allow parallel versions, establishing a rich palette of relevant reports. As to what has ultimately become the normative and mainstream report, under what circumstances, and serving which purposes are open questions whose solution often takes the risk of scholarly speculation. In this sense, the early phases of

Christianity are no exception to the rule. Thus, one may argue that the dogmatic decisions that were taken in later centuries when the Church held its first synods did not solve differences in the narrative traditions but in the manner the new creed was enacted. Clearly, these decisions were not motivated by a desire to reinforce an already existing kind of homogeneity. On the contrary, they attempted to solve an endemic tendency within the early Church to manipulate diversity and schismatic splitting, in an ongoing effort to win power and hegemony by exploiting the differences.

If one focuses attention on the synoptic Gospels (Matthew, Mark, and Luke), one cannot avoid the conclusion that, with all the similarity that prevails between them, the presence of a nonnegligible number of differences makes sweeping conclusions based on comparative similarities a tricky subject. In fact, the term *synoptic* is not necessarily the best choice, in this case. Furthermore, when we add the Gospel of John to the list of materials to be considered for assessing historical comparability, matters become even more complicated than they look at first glance. Just compare how each of the Gospels introduces the subject of Jesus. Matthew begins with the family tree of Jesus. Mark makes the baptism in the Jordan his starting point. Luke starts with the scene in the Temple, where the coming birth of John the Baptist is proclaimed. And John has an altogether different beginning, the implications of which are discussed at some length later in the chapter. Even Paul, whose writings preceded those of the Gospels, does not show a perfectly coordinated view in this respect. One would expect the author whose name is most connected with the endeavor of establishing the theology of the nascent Church to show a persistent attempt at achieving a straight line of argumentation from beginning to end. Instead, one finds Paul engaging in long chains of deliberation that hardly meet at an appointed end. In short, these examples alert the reader to the weight that the New Testament has to carry in terms of its inner diversity and documentary profusion.

There are good reasons to believe that Paul was motivated by a desire to create a theologically coherent doctrine of the role that Jesus played in his own lifetime and in the lives of those who were expected to follow him on their way to righteousness and personal and communal redemption. However, in developing his ideas, Paul was faced with many issues that required addressing immediate problems and in many cases could be applied only on an ad hoc basis. Consequently, his theological thrust sometimes projects the impression of drafts that required an expert editor to make the arguments stick together. On a more principial level, the Gospels show a similar trend or tendency. The Gospel writers can still be heard saying that, with all its theological thrust, the Pauline oeuvre did not dictate the shaping of the Christian event. There was still a need to supply the biographical dimension in order to supplement the theological one. However, substantial disagreement over key issues, matters of historical sequence, narratival perception, and literary formulation created the sharp edges that threatened to tear the documents asunder in spite of their apparent desire to coordinate their messages, align the information, and create cohesive convergence. In this respect, Paul constitutes one voice that adds to the other ones competing for hegemony in the New Testament.

For instance, when reading the Letter of James and the one to the Hebrews, two out of several examples, one realizes the existence of altogether different worldviews from the ones maintained by Paul, on the one hand, and the Gospels, on the other. They too address central issues that relate to Israelite history, the Law, the Temple, and, very specifically, the role of a messianic figure. Even when we, for the sake of argument, ignore the information contained in the extra-canonical (Elliott, 1993) and apostolic writings, there is still much in the New Testament itself that makes the beginning of Christianity a kaleidoscopic event with many focal points and shaping configurations. All this bears heavily on the various ways in which Christianity showed its opposition to the diverse forms of the Judaisms of the time. Most relevant in this respect are the various forms of messianism, those that crystallized in the apocryphal literature and in the Qumran writings, and those reflected in the early rabbinic literature.

In this respect, the processes involved in what is called the Parting of the Ways crystallized as a multilayered phenomenon too. Here too, the plural form, *partings*, does a better service than the singular. Accordingly, the various ways in which the messianic factor is introduced in early Christianity depend on the manner in which several questions are answered. These questions are (1) How did Christianity begin? (2) How did Jesus begin his mission? (3) How do the various writings of the New Testament view the nature of the messianic functions of Jesus? (4) What was the role of John the Baptist in shaping the messianic message of Christianity? In short, what kind of position did the Christian forms of messianism take over against their counterparts in Judaism? Even more succinctly, what made Jesus the kind of Messiah the first Christians were taught to think he was?

I wish to push the last question a little further. Did Christianity originally crystallize as a new kind of messianism, or as a new kind of religious orientation in which various modes of Judaic messianism played an important role? Keep in mind the fact that although the word *mashiah* is a Hebrew one, the messianic factor is not uniquely Judaic. There are messianic figures in other religions and cultures of the ancient world.[2] However, the Judaic form of the messianic idea, whether on the level of political resistance or spiritual redemption as it developed in the Land of Israel, was certainly the most relevant one to the shaping of the figure of Jesus and to the manner in which he is described in the Gospels.[3] Furthermore, as several New Testament scholars have pointed out, Paul's center of interest was not necessarily the messianic one. There is a noteworthy gap between the sacrificial redeemer figure as depicted in Paul and the more messianic, hence, royal-Davidic, figure as depicted in the Synoptic Gospels. Other New Testament writings focus on other aspects in the messianic configuration of Jesus, chief among them being the enigmatic term "Son of Man," where one would have expected the otherwise prevalent term "Son of God."

Kohut: A New Lens for Seeing Sacred Scripture

This is the point to make a turn and outline the main road this chapter explores. My aim is to suggest new answers to some of the questions I've just asked. I also wish to explore other areas on the map, mostly those hitherto unfrequented by scholars of Judaic studies and Christian origins. As indicated, I believe that psychoanalysis suggests the vantage points from which old as well as new questions and answers will help us understand and coherently assess this subject matter. The reader will soon become acquainted with my way of thinking and of the manner in which I make it relevant to the discussion of messianism. I believe that, consequently, the reader will soon be convinced of the advantage of the new approach.

My discussion takes up the subject from a line of considerations not usually applied in the study of religion in general, and of early Christianity in particular. It is connected with what is technically known as the psychology or the psychoanalysis of the self/self-object relationship. The uninformed reader needs a detailed introduction to the subject, before its relevance to the discussion of messianism becomes evident. As I mentioned earlier, the psychological theory, which I consider relevant to the present discussion, is associated with the name of the American psychoanalyst Heinz Kohut and his school. Because I have no professional training in this area of studies, I owe the reader a word of explanation. During the academic year 2001, the Program in Religion Studies at Tel Aviv University co-sponsored a conference with the School of Psychotherapy at the same university on the subject Hate and Hating Persons. In that framework, I gave a lecture, coordinated with Ra`anan Kulka, one of the leading psychoanalysts in Israel, on religious texts (biblical and Qabbalistic) that allegedly take up the subject of God's responsibility for the existence and prevalence of evil among humans. Another conference, held a year later and devoted to the subject Perversion and the Culture of Deception, gave me another opportunity to coordinate my observations, this time with another psychoanalyst, Sara Kolker. She gave a lecture on sexual perversion as manifested in acts of inappropriate gazing on naked males and their sex organs. My lecture was on the nature of inappropriately procuring mystical visions of God and the danger that was involved in such visions. The major example discussed in my paper came from the rabbinic story of the four who entered paradise, three of whom were described as inappropriately gazing and therefore suffering destructive consequences. Only one, Rabbi Aqiva, entered and came out safely. Significantly, in his case, the language of gazing is dropped.

In the academic year 2002–2003, I co-taught with Ra`anan Kulka a graduate seminar titled "Religion and Psychoanalysis." All these activities stimulated in me a new line of thinking: instead of subjecting religion and religious texts to psychoanalytic scrutiny and assessment (and, quite frequently, judgmental criticism), I suggested viewing religious texts as providing patterns of thinking and behavior that are paradigmatically relevant to the understanding of psychoanalytic positions. I felt assured in my taking this path—that is, concentrating on the more philosophical aspects of psychoanalysis—because I worked with psychoanalytic clinicians who could always place me back on the correct track. Admittedly, I allowed myself a degree of freedom, which those engaged in clinical treatment were somewhat reluctant to adopt. However, the dialogue always was a productive one and stimulated further thinking, investigation, and insight.

Following Heinz Kohut's psychology of the self/self-object, one may argue that God figures as an idealized provider of empathy. This empathy manifests as grace, benevolence, life-giving energy, and the ability to survive. In other words, God positions himself as the grandiose self-object of all humans in need of a self/self-object relationship. Obviously, this observation requires a comment, particularly in the context of the subject of messianism. We shall immediately see how this observation is connected to the subject. However, before we move in this direction, a few more remarks are due about the notion of the psychoanalysis of self/self-object relationship. From the very moment of its birth, the infant identifies objects that are at hand to position themselves to him as self-objects. That is to say, they are objects that provide the needed empathy, which sustains the infant's life and self. Self-objects supply the needs of the self to function healthily, that is, cohesively and creatively. In other words, empathy is the generic term used for anything that at any specific moment has the ability to awaken, in the self, psychic (and consequently physical) processes that the self uses for its preservation and survival. Psychic life is sustained, or helped along, by many "objects," whether physical, emotional, or intellectual. They all are instrumental in, and essential to, establishing a self that enjoys, or benefits from, the existence of a cosmos that is empathically full and that, as a result, is cohesively held together.

According to the prevalent view among psychoanalysts of the Kohut school, there is a certain degree of intentionality in the manner in which these objects position themselves as self-objects. They express the specific aim of gratifying, in an empathic manner, the special needs that they identify in the self. Their effectiveness in achieving this goal is measured by various factors, such as the timing of their addressing particular needs, and the manner and the intensity with which they do so. Whether it is the mother's breast, her voice, her touch, or her caressing gestures, words, and tones—all of these are "objects" that function as self-objects. The infant almost instinctively identifies these self-objects in its mother. This is the source of the special relationship between mother and child. The mother's capacity, or incapacity, to satisfy these needs for an empathic type of relationship is a crucial factor in the child's development.

The infant often serves as the self-object by satisfying certain needs in the mother. A fluctuating kind of relationship in which mutuality plays an important role frequently exists between the object and the self-object. This point is of pivotal importance for the ensuing discussion. Of course the fluctuating mutuality does not exist when inanimate objects are the self-objects. However, if we think in terms that make no distinctions between animate and inanimate objects, the latter ones may still be engaged in relationship that evolves in empathic mutuality. The inanimate nature of certain self-objects makes them transcend their inanimateness. In terms of normative religion, this is the gateway to fetishism.

In short, then, the empathy that marks the self/self-object relationship establishes the cohesion, security, wholeness, and particularly the energy and creativity that the self needs for its ability to live a full and healthy life. In the words of Kohut (speaking of the completion of an analysis), the self reaches a point at "which ambitions, skills, and ideals form an unbroken continuum that permits joyful creative activity" (1977, 63). Being deprived of this interplay of self/self-object-factors in infancy and later on in life can cause many things. Chief among them are a chronic lack of self-esteem and the inability to live a normal and healthy life. Deprivation and mutilation of empathic processes are also likely to impede healthy developmental processes in children and the inability in grownups to create and maintain normal social contacts. In other cases, pleasure seeking rather than living a full, productive, creative, and procreative life may be the result of a life in which the child or the person in question experienced a mutilated self/self-object relationship.

Simply put, children and grownups need relationships in which empathy plays a major role. People and objects can position themselves as self-objects, that is, as objects that serve people's need for empathy. A refusal to address these empathic needs and the inability to benefit from their fulfillment are likely to produce in the self negative feelings such as alienation and failure. They may also lead to perversion and aggression. When the self loses its cohesion, it undergoes mutilation, fragmentation, and even destruction.

Self-Psychology and Messianism

What has all this to do with messianism? In the discussion that follows I try to give coherent answers to this question. I focus on how the psychoanalytic approach helps in understanding central issues in the area of Jewish and Christian messianism and begin with a few comments on the place God has in this system. If empathy and self-object are the main issue, then God is the metaphysical provider of empathy. I use the term *metaphysical* in the sense that depicts God as embodying all the possible modes of serving empathic needs to an endless number of people, on an endless number of occasions, and for an endless number of purposes. Using the word *metaphysical*, in this case, also means the absolute guarantee that there is an ultimate, irremovable being whose presence is his readiness to be there at all times, under all circumstances, and to everyone who needs a self/self-object relationship. More specifically, God positions himself as a self-object to every human being in need of a grandiose, idealized, and omnipresent self-object. People believing in God are confident that he will never fail or forsake them. They believe that he will never refuse to fulfill their requests.

We shall see that any kind of rejection or denial on the part of God creates a state of crisis in which God too is involved. The whole cosmos, including the one that involves God, collapses. To use a modern expression, if he is not always there, the quantum essence of his being and of all that depends on it dissipates. In a deep sense, there is no world without the empathy that God stands for. This statement may sound like a religious one, however, it is here taken to signify a philosophical realization and from a psychological point of view a default kind of existence. In principle, there is no limit to God's capacity to address in an empathic manner any need of any self. His role as an omnipotent father and, in certain cases, as an ever-present mother who cares makes this clear.[4]

According to the psychoanalysis of the self/self-object relationship, there are three stages, which are not necessarily successive or progressive, in which this relationship is established. The first stage, or form, is mirroring. The self sees itself mirrored in the self-object. Mirroring, in this case, means that the self considers itself worthy of establishing the kind of relationship that makes the transmission and the reception of empathy possible. Sayings such as "I am nice and you love me" are typical of this stage. In being mirrored in another self, the self recognizes the object that is ready to be the empathy-transmitting self-object. The self is confident that the self-object responds to its needs. This response is the essence of empathy. The second stage is idealization. Sayings such as "You are perfect, and I am part of you" are typical of this stage. Idealization, in this case, means that the self views the self-object as a grandiose and elated type of entity. Idealization reflects the endeavor on the part of the self to create a merger with a figure greater than the self.

In many cases, God and other divine beings enter this zone of idealized self-objects. In accepting this idealized status, they enter the phase in which their relationship with the idealizing selves crystallizes in empathy. Empathy, in this case, means that the self is affirmed by what the idealized self-object offers. The third phase is twinship. In this phase, which in many respects is the most relevant one to the present discussion, the self and the self-object totally merge. Practically speaking, distinctions are no longer maintained between the self and its self-object. Likeness, expressed in an absolute merging of motivations and goals, is the very essence of this kind of self/self-object relationship.

These three stages should be clearly distinguished from the notion of projection, so common in the psychological interpretation of behavior and, therefore in the psychological interpretation of religion. The self-object is simply, and in the case of God it is always, "there" and does not depend on any act of projection initiated by a "self." Projection is the reverse process of assumed empathy. It projects out of the self and imposes the characteristics of the self upon another self, whether animate or inanimate, without assuming, or even expecting, empathic reciprocation. Empathy, however, is absorbed by the self. Its source is in what the self views its self-object to be, that is, as an object, whether animate or inanimate, that has this status by virtue of its ability to provide empathy. The self-object is not generated by the self, although in certain cases, I believe, the self is active in shaping the manner in which the self-object operates.

As we have seen, empathy establishes a unique kind of a life-generating, and hence life-preserving, relationship. Among other things, it entails the fluctuations of reciprocity. In projection, the self creates entities that are a replica of its own image. It positions these entities "out there" in the phenomenal world, shaping its qualities in its own image. In many cases, projection is limited to the second stage in the self/self-object types of relationship, namely, the idealization of the grandiose. In this case it is the grandiose self that is projected. Before the process begins, that is, before a projected replica has been shaped or created, no real relationship can begin between the self and the projected self. In the empathic relationship, something different happens. The self-object does not depend on the self either to create it or to express a specifically formulated desire to benefit from its willingness to impart empathy. It is "there" to enact its functioning position, when it meets a self in need of its "self-objecthood." In short, projection does not necessarily entail an empathic function that in many cases is independent of what the self does or wishes to gain.

God as Self-Object

God figures in religion as the ultimate and in psychoanalytic terms as grandiose and idealized, as a self-object of human beings. God is seen as unceasingly addressing the full range of human needs. Collectively speaking, people expect God to be infinitely benevolent in supplying the endless varieties of empathic positions and needs of any conceivable self. In his metaphysical presence God is infinite, which in psychoanalytic terms, and not only in them, means that he is more grandiose than any other grandiose being, and conceivably more readily given to empathic relationships than any other self-object.

To draw a fuller and more dialectic picture, however, requires one to note the other side of these observations. In religious terms, God is too grandiose for commensurately addressing ordinary human needs. In many cases, humans are unable to receive the full intensity of God's empathy. In this respect, it is interesting to follow the dialogue when Moses asks God if he might see God's glory and God responds to this request:

> And the Lord said to Moses: "This very thing that you have spoken I will do; for you have found favour in my sight, and I know you by name." Moses said: "Please, show me your glory." And he [God] said: "I will make all my goodness pass before you, and will proclaim my name, YHWH, before you. And I will be gracious to whom I will be gracious, and I will show mercy on whom I will show mercy." And he [God] said: "You cannot see my face, for man shall not see my face and live. . . . And you shall see my back, but my face shall not be seen. (Exod. 33:17–23 [RSV])

It is interesting to note that in this passage God, to use the terms of the present study, concedes to position himself as a self-object, as requested by Moses. God does not act as self-object before Moses asks him to act in this capacity. In other words, there is a certain initiative that the self takes to make the self-object exert empathy. This notion is not commonly accepted among clinicians of the Heinz Kohut school. In their view, the self is utterly passive in the process. All the initiative, if there is any, comes from the self-object. However, in the more philosophical approach adopted here, I venture into a more relaxed attitude than the one that clinicians think ought to prevail in the clinical situation. Thus I believe that texts that show the self takes an initiative in establishing the self/self-object relationship have a paradigmatic significance in stating factual evidence. In this respect, the request on the part of Moses does not lose its relevance to the psychoanalytic discourse. On the contrary, it presents a case, even an option, that needs to be taken into consideration in terms of psychoanalytic theory.

There is, however, more in this biblical passage than we have just observed. At one point Moses interchanges roles with God; the self becomes a self-object and vice versa. God's words "for you have found favour in my sight" may be interpreted as saying that Moses is, even temporarily, God's self-object. Moses asks God to be his self-object, "Show me your glory," and God concedes because "you have found favour in my sight." As we have seen, this is a typical situation of the self/self-object relationship. The self and the self-object often interchange roles, that is, there is a marked degree of fluctuation in the kind of relationship established between them: a mutuality, a reciprocation.

God accepts the request in most empathic terms: "I will make all my goodness pass before you." However, God adds a clear point, which creates a conditional stance. Because his capacity as self-object transcends human needs and human capability of absorbing his empathy, a limit is enforced: "You shall see my back, but my face shall not be seen."

The medieval Jewish philosopher Maimonides (1135–1204) gives this idea a philosophical-theological expression. Interestingly, it paradigmatically speaks the language of the self/self-object psychology:

> What was it that Moses wanted to comprehend . . . ? He sought to have so clear an apprehension of the truth of God's existence that the knowledge might be like that which one possesses of a human being, whose face one has seen and whose image is imprinted on the mind and whom, therefore, the mind distinguishes from other men. . . . God replied that it is beyond the mental capacity of a human creature, composed of body and soul, to obtain in this regard clear knowledge of the truth. The Almighty, however, imparted to Moses, what has been vouchsafed to no man before or since. (Mishneh Torah, Hilkhot Yesodei Ha-Torah 1:10)

The dialogue to which Maimonides refers explicates matters that *initially* did not address issues relevant to the psychology of the self/self-object relationship. However, the foundational line of the conversation paradigmatically speaks the language of this psychology. If we replace "truth" with "empathy," everything falls into place in terms of the psychological attitudes discussed in this chapter. What I stress, once again, is the fact that Moses initiates the positioning of God in God's role as self-object. Furthermore, God responds positively. However, God sets certain limits so that he can function as self-object vis-à-vis human beings without propelling counterproductive side effects.

To sum up this part of the discussion, and before turning to messianism, one may say that the Kohut school offers a reasonable explanation for the prevalence of religion in human culture. Religion offers a psychoanalytically understandable answer to the question why so many people at all times turn to a god. He functions as the ever present and almighty provider of empathy. Speaking the language of quantum theory, God is the quantum of empathy. Because there is always someone, somewhere, who needs him for something, his existence is indelible.

Evolution of God as Self-Object

We have now to address issues that reflect substantial changes in God's position as self-object. These changes lead the way to the introduction of messianism, particularly in its mediatory functions. In the Hebrew Scripture, God is a speaking God. He tells people what to do and what to avoid, and he conducts dialogues with humans, mostly in a prophetic context. In the New Testament, however, God's voice is rarely if ever heard. He may say something through the Holy Spirit, declaring, for instance, the divine "sonship" of Jesus, either in the Baptism scene or in that of the Transfiguration. God is neither speaking nor engaging in any verbal dialogue with any of the people who play a major role in the New Testament.[5] In other words, the New Testament lacks the kind of prophetic dimension that the Hebrew Scriptures have. This concerns the Pentateuch and the Prophets alike. There are, however, several books in the Hebrew Scripture (parts of Deuteronomy, the Psalms, the Song of Songs, Esther, and Proverbs are notable examples to this effect) that lack the direct speech of God. At times, the inclusion of some of these books in the Hebrew canon was subject to repeated questioning (Mishnah tractate Yadayim 3:5). In the final resort, though, their inclusion was justified by a newly formalized principle, namely, the inspiration caused by the Spirit of the Holy One, the *Ruach Ha-Qodesh* (Babylonian Talmud Megilah 7/a).

Speaking of the silence of God in the New Testament, one may argue that the New Testament fulfills in real life the word of God in the Hebrew Scripture. In other words, the New Testament is a live prolongation of the word of God as it was spoken in the Hebrew Scripture. The Christian way of handling this difference speaks of one axis. One of its ends marks the phase of speaking, the other the phase of fulfillment. Everything that had to be said was said; the time of fulfillment has come. In practice, this is the approach that characterizes the rabbinic sages. For the sages, the word of Scripture had to be interpreted according to the changing circumstances and hermeneutic acumen developed in every generation. In principle, the Christian position was almost the same, although it related to historical events and less to the ritual.

In the Hebrew Scriptures, God created the world using his speech in a detailed manner for every single act of creation. Then he issued commands to humans, telling them what they should do and what they should avoid doing. However, his word did not always prevail. When it came to matters of showing obedience, humankind often chose the opposite way, namely, that of disobedience. Ultimately, God regretted that he had created man and decided to annul the work of creation. The words "And the Lord was sorry that he had made man on the earth, and it grieved him to his heart" (Gen. 6:6) convey several notions on a variety of levels. In a sense, these words reflect a notion of failure. First God expelled Adam and Eve from the Garden of Eden. Then he brought the total destruction of the deluge. Then he scattered the people who had built the Temple-Tower of Babylon. Finally, at much later times, he destroyed the First and the Second Temple, sending the People of Israel into their exilic existence.

In historical and theological perspectives, this is a unique situation, and it calls for commenting. How can a God, who admits his failure, function as the grandiose self-object of the people addressed by him in Scripture? In many respects, the speaking God of the Hebrew Scripture found himself in the position of an enfeebled self-object. His speech led to disaster and ended in failure. A god who rejects his own creation faces a serious problem not only on the level of his role as the metaphysical self-object. In the terms used here, those people whom God had hoped would see in him the ultimate source of empathy no longer showed interest in or concern for what he could offer them.

At an interesting juncture in the history of the People of Israel, toward the end of Samuel's office, they even made an explicit request that God anoint a king for them. Given the circumstances, the request as formulated by the people sounds utterly reasonable. However, God was dissatisfied with it, telling Samuel that the request reflected the people's desire to replace the divine sovereign with an earthly one. God says: "they have rejected *me* from being king over them" (1 Sam. 8:7). It may not be altogether accidental then that when Samuel speaks to the people before his death, he says, "testify against me before the Lord and before the anointed one [the Hebrew word is *mashiah*]" (1 Sam. 12:3). This is the first occurrence of the term *mashiah* referring to a royal sovereign. Its occurrence comes right after God realizes that the people no longer like him and therefore have requested a royal substitute. In other words, in the eyes of God, the mashiah is a substitute, and he is not a very successful one. The history of kingship in ancient Israel in no way accumulated points of success to change this situation.

Even King David, whose lineage was expected to lead to the future messiah, did not reach a high score as the ideal king. In fact, the question of leadership in ancient Israel has to be viewed in a wider spectrum than is often the case. Most of the leaders of ancient Israel are presented in a critical light. Moses, Aaron, Saul, David, and Solomon are all described as leaders who at one point or another committed sins or displeased God. Many of the ideal figures in ancient Israel, if not all of them, showed basic flaws through their behavior. This situation radically changed in the New Testament. Jesus and Paul, to give two prominent examples, show no blemish in their career. Their flawless behavior is a remarkable fact when compared with the kind of leadership known from ancient Israel. The explanation of this change shows that the speaking presence of God fades away in the period between the cessation of prophecy in ancient Israel and the rise of Christianity. As noted earlier, God does not speak in the New Testament, and his distance allows for a lesser degree of judgmental interference and a wider range for assessing potentials of human excellence. The depth of this change and the impact it had on the minds of the people concerned cannot be underrated, especially if we keep in mind what this meant in terms of the prevalence of divine empathy.

Apocalyptic Messianism: Second Temple Judaism

In the days of the Second Temple (mid-fifth century B.C.E.–70 C.E.), matters radically changed in a number of essential ways. We cannot enter here into a full-scale discussion of every aspect of these changes, their reasons, and implications. However, in the second century B.C.E., already before the Maccabean Revolt (164 B.C.E.), a new set of ideas and ideologies had transformed Judaism from within, preparing the way for the dawn of the rabbinic period on the one hand and the birth of Christianity on the other. More than just historical coincidence may account for the fact that both events happened in temporal proximity to the destruction of the Second Temple. Although the need for redemption had long existed before this catastrophe shattered Jewish life, it became emphatically clear that new paths had to be found that would guarantee the prolongation of processes involved in procuring divine empathy.

Apocalypticism embodied one of the major road maps to these processes. It provided a historical scheme, valid for all times, in which eras, events, and everything else were viewed as pre-planned at the time of the creation of the world. In the words used in one of the Qumran documents, the new era fulfilled the words of the scriptural prophets as "the last preordained end" unfolding in accordance with "the wondrous secrets of God [*razei el*]" (Pesher Habakkuk, col. 7, lines 7–8). Because the historical scheme was initially bound to the work of creation, nature was included in the plan; the historical events had cosmological implications (1 Enoch 1–5). Cosmic, in this respect, also meant political changes on a scale that was often likened to a cosmic upheaval (Nickelsburg, 2001, 146). In apocalypticism, one could find various charts as to how matters were going to evolve and thus prepare the way for the future in the form of a new beginning (Isa. 66:22). Among other things, apocalypticism created the scenario for the mundane king of Israel to be transformed into a messianic redeemer. In certain cases (i.e., the Testament of Levi and in some of the Qumran writings) the messiah was a priestly figure. In other ones, two messiahs, one monarchic and one priestly, are mentioned. In short, various documents played their respective roles in shaping the ideal figure of this messiah. In rabbinic writings, we find the idea that the warrior-messiah of the house of Joseph will usher in the days of the messiah of the house of David. There are good reasons to believe that in certain Christian circles, John the Baptist had a similar role, ushering in the figure of the Davidic messiah.

Apocalypticism is often discussed in the framework of the crisis of prophecy. What did this crisis signify? In the first place, it signified the separation, even rift, between the speaking God and his people. Dialogue *is* the quintessence of prophecy. In many respects, it is also the epitome of empathy. Consequently, the cessation of speech signifies the total collapse of the empathic relationship between the People of Israel and their God. What caused this rift? Several factors suggest themselves as plausible answers. However, we seek a paradigmatic one that shows neither theological interests nor ideological concerns but that takes us in the psychological direction. I give this direction precedence because of the changes that had happened in the life of the people, after the destruction of the First Temple, and their relationship to God marked, in an essential manner, a crisis in self/self-object relationship. This crisis was clearly enhanced by the introduction of Iranian, Babylonian, and Hellenistic ideas into the Judaic world, whether in the Land of Israel or in the Diaspora.

In principle, I would say that a god who tells people what to do and enforces a punitive system on those deviating from his decrees cannot easily and under all conditions position himself as a source of empathy to his people. To fulfill his empathic roles, this god would do better if he showed to his people a different face, one that, in Pauline terms, does not depend on attaining righteousness through obedience to the binding force of the law of the Torah. The position taken by the Psalmists, and for that matter by the authors of Isaiah 40–66 and the Qumran *Hodayyot*, shows a general concern for the laws of God, although no specific ritual and laws are mentioned. In this respect, the requests and expectations of the person in need of finding consolation and help in divine empathy come from a position that is quite often enfranchised by factors such as obedience to the law and unblemished ethical accomplishments. In my view, then, the kind of conclusions Paul draws with regard to the Torah is already prefigured in Scripture and then in apocalypticism.

The legal aspects of Torah play a remarkably small role in apocalypticism, of which the first five chapters in 1 Enoch are a good example. The subject of these chapters is the revelation on Mount Sinai. However, what is revealed is not the Decalogue but something that establishes a general ethical code. It admonishes the readers to draw conclusions from "Nature's obedience and humanity's disobedience" (Nickelsburg, 2001, 152–158). As many have already noted, the Torah plays no role in the book of Enoch and in other apocalyptic writings.[6] As noted earlier, the information one can draw from the non-Pentateuchal writings in ancient Judaism with regard to the existence of Torah and its contents is not very exciting. To give a striking example, in at least three places in the book of Psalms (chaps. 78, 105, 136) the poets concerned tell about the great events and miracles connected with the exodus from Egypt and the walk in the Sinai Desert. However, the giving of the Torah is not mentioned in any of these historical summaries, as if it had been a non-event.

From a psychoanalytic point of view, the breaking point between God and his disobedient human creation did not start with the giving of the Torah on Mount Sinai (Gal. 4:25). Even the event in the Garden of Eden, which in Paul's terminology is the original sin (Rom. 5:12–14), does not start the process of troubles. If one sets psychoanalytic parameters to the present discussion, then the creation of man in the *tselem* (image or likeness) of God is the starting point of all trouble in that the scriptural story can be interpreted as saying that in designing man as the *tselem* of God, God indulged in an act of projection. We have seen that projection is the opposite of the self-object experience. It leaves little room for empathy and therefore ejects the story from the context of the self/self-object relationship. In other words, the manner in which man was created initially excluded him from the potential position of the self-object of God. His position as the projection of God was the trap in which the human condition found itself, being deprived of the dramatic potential for empathic redemption.

In order to maintain an empathic relationship and make it fully realizable, one has to leave open a wide door leading onto the stage on which the independent existence of the self-object may be fully realized. The self-object is an entity completely independent of the self. Creating the self-object in the image of the self is exactly the reverse of what the psychoanalysis of the self/self-object relationship conceives of as the conditions needed for a healthy empathic relationship. Thus the first crisis between God and man—on the level of the self/self-object relationship—did not happen, as many think, when Adam disobeyed God's order not to eat from the tree of the knowledge of good and evil. It happened with the very act of the creation of man as God's *tselem*, that is, as an act of projection. This act excludes the crucial possibility of establishing a true and standing self/self-object relationship of empathy. Nothing was changing for the better, in this respect, when another story (in Gen. 2) replaced the story in Genesis 1. How then could matters be brought to a point of radical change?

Paul and Christian Messianism

The answer is split in two and concerns man and God alike. In the Pauline understanding of the issue, the "old man in us" had to be crucified with Jesus (Rom. 6:6). A new man—internal (Rom. 7:22) and spiritual (1 Cor. 2:15)—had to become part of the new creation (2 Cor. 5:17). In short, man is likely to undergo resurrection and receive a new body (1 Cor. 15:35–53), a subject that has received intensive attention in New Testament theology and scholarship. The subject likewise creates an interesting link between messianism and the issue of the self/self-object relationship. As I noted earlier, the issue was missed in the Genesis story but was taken up and received a new approach in the writings of Paul. The second part of the answer is that a new kind of God had to be established in the minds of people. This subject has received less attention than has the subject of the new man. Furthermore, one cannot avoid commenting that a somewhat provocative element may sneak into the discussion of the second subject. In all likelihood, the shift in both cases occurred in the last centuries before the rise of Christianity and the destruction of the Temple. We cannot enter here a detailed discussion of the various aspects of these processes. However, a few aspects of this shift are relevant to the understanding of the perspective from which we view the present discussion.

The main point I wish to make here is that many of the writings included in the intertestamental or Second Temple literature reconstruct the history of ancient Israel in a manner that showed the voice of God gradually fading away from its audible presence as heard, comparably speaking, in the Hebrew Scripture. The book of Daniel paradigmatically serves as our example of this phenomenon. Daniel sees God in his appearance, or manifestation, as the Ancient of Days. It should be noted that this God is seen but not heard. Instead, an angel speaks to Daniel, explaining to him the nature of the vision and its historical implications. In principle, the book of Jubilees shows a similar trend. For instance, in its version of the creation of the world, God speaks only once. Furthermore, although in the book of Genesis God tells Abraham to leave his home, in the book of Jubilees the angel says that he was speaking to Abraham on that occasion. The angel simply says that the order given to Abraham to go to the land of Canaan "was sent to him by my hand" (Jubilees 12:22). As far as humans are concerned, God's voice is also muted in the book of Enoch. The only case in which God speaks to a human being, in the book of Enoch, is when he replies to the appeal of the fallen angels, which Enoch presents to God. In a somewhat long address, God rejects the angels' appeal, although the subject is not, as it is in the Hebrew Scripture, the divine decrees to man but a reply to the request of the fallen angels.

This is not to say that, in other cases in the apocalyptic literature, God is not present behind the scene (if we may say so). However, there are many other examples in which one would expect God to speak but an angel acts as a substitute emissary. In many respects, then, one of the major features of the apocalyptic literature in the intertestamental corpus is this fading away of the voice of God. The subject still requires a more detailed analysis than can be given to it here. However, when in a number of places in the Temple Scroll the third-person form of speech used in the scriptural references to God changes into the first person, this change evidently signals a dramatic attempt at reversing the ongoing trend toward God's voicelessness.

In my view, the increase in the presence of angels in the reading of the revelatory tradition of ancient Israel as it is retold in the literature of the intertestamental period and the complementary amplification of their voice are two of the most significant preambles to the development of the messianic idea in Judaism, and consequently in Christianity. What establishes the connection between the creation of the first man in the *tselem* of God and Christian messianism? The question deserves a more detailed answer than I give it here. Paul uses the notion of *tselem* (in Greek, *eikonos*; the same word used in the Septuagint version of Gen 1:26–27) and relates it to "his son" (Rom. 8:29), in other words, to Jesus, the Christian messiah. Clearly, this process bypasses the notion of projection, because filial relationship always crystallizes in a matrix that, in healthy cases, calls forth empathy.

In this connection, we view the opening passages of each of the Gospels as a story that wishes to usher in a new version of the "beginning"—that is, in a context not specifically related to the Genesis story. The synoptic Gospels present their respective versions of a new beginning, although, as indicated, not in connection with the creation of the world. Each Gospel tells its own story, thus giving different accounts of the "beginning." The following example comes from the Gospel of John: "In the beginning was the Word, and the Word was with God, and the Word was God. He was in the beginning with God; all things were made through him, and without him was not anything made that was made. In him was life, and the life was the light of men. The light shines in the darkness, and the darkness has not overcome it" (John 1:5).

These familiar words require some elucidation of their relevance to the psychoanalytic discussion proposed here. They clearly echo the opening verses in the book of Genesis.[7] However, although the book of Genesis quotes every single word that God said in connection with the creation of the world, the Gospel of John speaks about the preexistential presence of the Word. I would refer to this presence of the Word (*Logos*) as a metaphysical notion. At this early stage, it lacks any specificity—even with regard to its unfolding in the figure of Jesus. In any event, God does not functionally relate to the work of creation as a process that involved specifically articulated verbal expressions.

How do I interpret this fact? I think that the Gospel of John intentionally places the Logos before the act of creation. When we think of what the book of Genesis postulates in this matter, the Gospel of John constitutes a radical change in manner that the word of God is used. In the book of Genesis, the act of creation begins with the word of God. In the Gospel of John, however, the Word preexists the work of creation. Furthermore, the Word has no instrumental role in the creation of the world. Furthermore, the Word is not envisioned in any process-of-stages situation relating to the detailed stages of the creation. Everything comes into being through the Word and in it, but the Gospel of John refrains from saying anything specific about the manner in which the Word acted or was active in the process of creation. In fact, the manner in which the Gospel of John relates to it strengthens the metaphysical position of the Word. In the terms used earlier, the Word potentially awaits its historical time of realization. This moment begins when the Word becomes the ultimate self-object, the messiah.

The messianic configuration of the Word has speech functions mostly in connection with its miraculous powers to heal and to affect people to choose a new, redemptive, way of life. When Jesus is quoted as saying to Martha concerning her brother Lazarus, "I am the resurrection and the life; he who believes in me, though he die, yet shall he live, and whoever lives and believes in me shall never die. Do you believe this?" (John 11:25–26), he quintessentially gives expression to the purest and strongest form of empathy. In this respect, Jesus changes the discourse of God. It focuses on the power of empathic belief. In the terms used by Paul, the Nomos formerly spoke the language of God, and it did so in a manner that always left humans in a situation of guilt. Whether one obeyed the word of God in Scripture or disobeyed it made, at least in Paul's view, no real difference. In the terms used in the present discussion, the reason was that God situated himself in a position of projection vis-à-vis man, whereas Jesus, in whatever theological conception he manifested, could position himself as man's empathic self-object.

The manner in which God addressed his people with admonitions and decrees left little room for the crystallization of empathic positions. It constantly put humans in conflictual situations in which the central axis was marked by dilemmas—obedience and disobedience. However, a Christian could grow up without necessarily engaging in punitive discourse. Thus, Jesus was able to concentrate on his function as a self-object, who almost unconditionally addressed the needs of the humans who approached him. This does not mean that Jesus preached the abrogation of law and order. On the contrary, his teachings and sayings as they are recorded in the Gospels tell the story of intensive mental concentration and austere self-discipline. No healer of the kind Jesus was could be an absent-minded person, leading a frivolous life. After all, practicing magic requires a high degree of self-discipline and psychic concentration. What caused a problem, from a Judaic point of view, was the fact that Jesus replaced the healing functions and capacity of God. These divinely ordained healing functions are not unconditional: "If you will diligently hearken to the voice of the Lord your God, and do that which is right in his eyes, and give heed to his commandments and keep all his statues, I will put none of the diseases upon you which I put upon the Egyptians; for I am the Lord, your healer" (Exod. 15:26). In sharp contrast, Jesus speaks a completely different language: "Daughter, your faith has made you well; go in peace, and be healed of your disease" (Mark 5:34).

Jesus replaced God in a new capacity: that of the unconditional pro-

vider of empathy. If this position is read in the context of his redemptive, that is, his messianic mission and proclamation, then Christianity
epitomizes a radically changed religious mind-set and experience.
Jesus strove to empathically ease the existential troubles of people.
Whether the image used in each case was that of the Lamb or of the
suffering servant of God, the effect was the same—an empathic relief
of the burden that marked the human condition. In other words, the
novelty of the Christian position in contrast to its Judaic counterpart
was mainly lying in its concept of what a grandiose human being—a
messianic figure—could accomplish. The notion of the Word and of
its being placed as an antecedent to the act of creation is yet another
image that early Christianity developed. Because the Word is no part
of the creative process, it easily takes on a role as a redeeming factor.
Anything not contaminated, for example, by mundane materiality can
take on a redeeming function.

This brings us to the message—particularly as given in some of the
writings found at Nag Hammadi— that Gnosticism wished to spread
in the Christian world. Various Gnostic writings describe the divine
redeemer as forcing his way through the eons, with the evil angels,
who represent the evil God of Israel, trying to block his way. The
Father of Truth, who is also called Incorruptibility or Incomprehen-
sibility, still reaches a few, the *Gnostikoi*, who listen to his message of
self-knowledge. They are redeemed. This is what John says: "The true
light that enlightens every man . . . But to all who received him, who
believed in his name, he gave power to become children of God" (John
1:9, 12). Those familiar with the Gnostic texts from Nag Hammadi
will easily recognize sayings like these. One of the texts from Nag
Hammadi says, "now the Word [the Coptic text uses the Greek word
Logos] that is superior to all beings was sent for this purpose alone:
that he might proclaim the unknown" (*On the Origins of the World* 125,
14–15). Or, as the Valentinian Gospel of Truth says, "the gospel of
truth is joy for those who have received from the Father of Truth the
grace of knowing him, through the power of the Word that came forth
from the Pleroma" (1:16). In any event, the words "to give power to
become children of God" are the epitome of the empathic language
that we highlight in this chapter. The same may be said of the words
"the true light that enlightens every man." Once again the Gospel of
Truth offers an interesting parallel: "Jesus, the Christ, enlightened
those who were in darkness through oblivion. He enlightened them;
he showed [them] a way; and the way is the truth which he taught
them" (18, 16–20; cf. 1 Cor. 2:1–8).

Conclusion

We have followed a line of thinking that, on psychoanalytic grounds, makes sense of Christianity vis-à-vis Judaism in that it argues that the Christian messiah, the godlike human being, took upon himself the empathic role previously maintained by God. We have even argued that, because of its existence in the flesh, the Word has an improved capacity for showing empathy. More succinctly expressed, one may say that from a Christian perspective, the Word in its human configuration is more adequate than God is for addressing human needs. To cut a long story short, the human–divine messiah may be viewed as the ideal substitute for the empathic position that the divine used to occupy in the Hebrew Scripture. Who can give better expression to divine empathy than a human being who acts as the sacrificial redeemer on behalf of the people to whom he has shown empathy?

The process of distancing Judaism from the immediate speech dimension of God had an enormous impact on the formation of the rabbinic discourse after the destruction of the Second Temple in that the hermeneutic stances of the Mishnaic and Talmudic sages replaced the spoken word of God. God does not speak *in* Mishnah, but he speaks *through* the Halakhic deliberations of the rabbis in Mishnah. Furthermore, there are a number of sayings in rabbinic literature declaring the cessation of prophecy in the days of the "Last Prophets"— Haggai, Zachariah, and Malachi (Tosefta tractate Sotah 13:3 and parallels). Furthermore, any intervention of a divine voice from heaven in favor of taking a certain Halakhic decision is declared void.[8] But this takes us off the main track of our discussion. I referred to these instances to show that the process of bracketing off the direct speech of God is a long and a wide-ranging one. It is interesting, in this connection, to note that Maimonides argues in *The Guide of the Perplexed* that the whole notion of a speaking God should be understood in a manner that removes an anthropomorphic understanding of the scriptural texts. Speech in Maimonides' understanding stands for an expression of will and planned intention (pt. 1, chap. 65).

Messianism unfolds in various ways. Gershom Scholem pointed out two polarized directions—one restorative, in which the messiah restores the glory of the Eden-like past, the other utopian, in which the messiah ushers in a completely new world order (1971, 1–48). Other scholars have pointed out the national aspects of messianism, and yet other ones indicated the more individual or personal aspects of (Collins, 1995, 1 n. 1). Personal messianism always shows a tendency toward interiorizing the messianic process or realizing its dynamics on a spiritual level. Christian messianism often operates on the personal level. Reading the Gospels, one can see how Jesus redeems the individual person before a fully fledged Christian messianism spreads its wings to include a wider range of people and nations. However, when Paul speaks of the "internal man" that Christianity awakens, a decisive step is taken in the direction of interiorizing the messianic events or process. Although messianism plays an important role in Qabbalah and Hasidism, the major text of the Qabbalists, the book of Zohar has very little to say on the subject. Messianic ideas are discussed only in one part of the Zohar, "The Great Assembly" (*Idra Rabba*). Rabbi Shimon bar Yohai, the Tannaitic sage to whom the book of Zohar is attributed, is the messianic figure in this part of the Zohar (Liebes, 1993, 1–84).

Messianism, however, found its way to the headlines of Jewish mysticism (Idel, 1998). In fact, the messianic matrix adds an important dimension to the realization of the mystical experience in Judaism. The terms of reference that developed within later Qabbalistic circles, particularly in post-Renaissance times, embed messianism or messianic ideas in a cosmic context. A key notion in Qabbalah, in this respect, is the redemption of the worlds (in Hebrew, *tiqqun ha-ʿolamot*), that is to say, a mystical drive is always present in the minds of the mystics. It motivates their mystical endeavors to bring about radical changes of order both in the metaphysical realms as conceived in the Qabbalah and the Sefirot, and in the physical world. The physical world mostly concerns the existence of the People of Israel among the nations. One may argue that Qabbalah had an interesting answer to give to the Pauline notion of the redemption from original sin. For Paul, this event had serious anthropological consequences. Since the fatal moment in the Garden of Eden, humankind finds itself living in a state of an irremovable sin. Paul argues that all the attempts made by God, speaking through the Torah (in Paul, *Nomos*), to point a way of justification and atonement failed. Instead, the Christ event suggested itself in its sacrificial dimensions as the major instrument of justification and hence acquired its redeeming functions. How does this come into effect? The crucifixion is a sacrificial event that epitomizes death. Death relieves human beings from sin and suffering. Mentally, then, every Christian is given a chance to ritually participate in the death event of Jesus. Through this act, a redemptive process comes into effect. What can be more empathic than a redemptive process?

In connection with the psychoanalytic point of view, the mode of

empathy that comes into effect in the participation in the death of
Jesus belongs in the category of twinship. Twinship is the third type of
self/self-object relationship discussed earlier. In twinship, a complete
merger-event, or fusion, occurs between the self and its self-object. In
many cases, this may involve total immersion in situations that
involve death. In this respect, one has to mention also the Christian
ritual of Baptism.[9] On the ritual level, twinship is here enacted either
in the Eucharist or in the mystical belief uniting the Christian believer
with the sacrificial death of Jesus (Gruenwald, 2003, chap. 6). In any
event, only a radical case like the messianic one incorporates the
power to transform realities in the manner described in this chapter.

Clearly, the two ends of the axis discussed here are the silencing of
the voice of God, on the one hand, and the substitution of this voice
either by a messianic figure or by a hermeneutic revival, which is the
result of a new reading of the scriptural texts.[10] In both cases, hermeneutics paved the way to the historical realities of messianism as it did
to the Halakhic way of life as developed in rabbinic Judaism. The new
reading of Scripture, as suggested in different ways and for different
purposes in the New Testament and in the Midrashic documents of
Talmudic times, has its clear precedents in the writings of the intertestamental period, the apocalypticism and the Qumran documents
included. The new reading of Scripture amounts to a new positioning
of the scriptural text vis-à-vis the reader. God's words, which had
long ceased to be audible entities, became legible realities with everything that such a change implied. Christian messianism suggested
another level of realization—that of fulfilling—with regard to the
scriptural texts. It evolved in Midrashic stances, which in the eyes of
the New Testament writers easily translated into the historical realities connected with the life of Jesus.

In other words, we now move into a phase in which not the spoken
but the written text of Scripture presents itself as a potential self-
object. This process has a notable advantage. It rescues the spoken
word from the redundancy of unfulfilled messages, also known as
either the crisis of prophecy or the arbitrariness of disobedience. The
spoken texts of God live on in their being constantly opened for new
contextual realizations, either in theological or historical hermeneutics. The texts are viewed as readily offering themselves to situations
in which constant changes affect their spectra of signification. The
reader is always able to see in them self-objects that continue to do
for him what the word of God, and his revelatory speech, used to
do to the people who had originally heard the word. Both in the

messianic situation and in the hermeneutic elaborations of the rabbis, life-generating processes were set in motion that influenced the behavior of the people concerned in a manner that showed they were convinced their lives were full and worth living.

Finally, we come again to Qabbalah. The fatal event in the Garden of Eden had destructive consequences in the world of the ten Sefirot. Briefly, the Sefirot are divine entities that have emanated from God and thus continue to contain divine essences and potencies. When Adam and his wife sinned, they caused a fatal breach in the world of the Sefirot. The male entity incorporated in the sixth Sefirah, Tif'eret (Glory), was separated from its feminine counterpart, incorporated in the tenth Sefirah, Malkhut (Kingdom). In the psychoanalytic terms used here, something happened in the world of the Sefirot that disrupted their capacity to act in full empathy. One may say that sexual twinship in the Sefirotic world embodied the ideal form of empathy. The ideal form here implies the prevalence of the same kind of empathic twinship in the mundane world. Since the occurrence of the tragic event in the Garden of Eden, nothing could operate in the upper and lower worlds in the manner it had worked before. In the Qabbalistic view, then, every human action, particularly the good deeds, contribute to repairing this breach in the world of the Sefirot. However, a final, and irreversible, repair, the Tiqqun, can come into effect only when messianic conditions begin to prevail. The Tiqqun of the Sefirot has messianic significance. Once it has happened, it signifies the resumption of the undisturbed flow of divine grace. In our terms of reference, the overflow of empathic compassion will reach everyone who wishes to receive it and deserves to do so. In other words, the appearance of the messiah marks the dawn of the empathic relationship between the divine and the human. He will redeem humankind from its misery, as expressed in lack or deficiency in empathic relationships. However, the extent to which he will reverse the process in which the voice of God will be restored to its pristine place and role in the life of the people is one of the issues that constitute the speculations of various messianic theologies.

Notes

1. Thus, the passage quoted in Collins (1995, 1) from the Testament of Judah 24, may resonate Christian themes. However, it may equally reflect a kind of messianism growing on Judaic soil that is not as familiar to us as we often think. What is absolutely Christian and what is typical Judaic even in

the Gospel tradition are interesting questions that, in my view, deserve a fresh reconsideration. This chapter, however, suggests a line of thinking—a psychoanalytic one—that makes the needed distinctions less relevant than they are usually taken to mean.

2. See, for example, Eddy (1961).

3. In this respect I find recent speculations about the cynic prototype of Jesus somewhat farfetched. See Betz (1998).

4. The motherly configuration of God is an interesting subject from a psychological point of view. In Christianity, Mary has, or takes upon herself, the motherly role of the deity. In Judaism, the subject is of a more complex nature. Suffice it here to say that the feminine aspect of the deity is amply highlighted in Qabbalah.

5. Obviously this excludes such events as described in Acts 2 and 4, where people are described as speaking "in languages" or in "the holy spirit." See also Acts 10:44–47.

6. Ezra 4 is an interesting exception to this rule. There is no shortage of scholarly discussion of this subject. However, I wish to draw attention, in this connection, to Davies (1952).

7. Paul, in Philippians 4:15, uses the phrase "the beginning of the gospel." He refers to the beginning of his traveling from Asia Minor to Rome. Dunn (1998, 164–169), discusses the importance of the term *Euangelion* in Paul.

8. This is the view of Rabbi Yehosh'a. He says, "one should not pay attention to what a *bat qol* (a Halakhic-oriented oracular voice) says" (Bav. Berakhot 52b, and parallels).

9. See Dunn (1998, 442–459). Dunn's discussion is particularly relevant to my discussion because he is fully aware of the mystical implication of the rite.

10. In this connection it is interesting to read Paul's discussion—in Rom. 11—of the question "has God rejected his people?"

References

Betz, H. D. (1998). Jesus and the Cynics: Survey and Analysis of a Hypothesis, *Antike und Christentum: Gesammelte Aufsätze*, vol. 4. Tübingen: Mohr Siebeck, 32–56.

Collins, J. J. (1995). *The Scepter and the Star: The Messiahs of the Dead Sea Scrolls and Other Ancient Literature*. New York: Doubleday.

Davies, W. D. (1952). *Torah in the Messianic Age and/or the Age to Come*. Philadelphia: Society of Biblical Literature.

Dunn, J. D. G. (1991). *The Parting of the Ways: Between Christianity and Judaism and Their Significance for the Character of Christianity*. London: SCM Press.

Dunn, J. D. G. (1998). *The Theology of Paul the Apostle*. Edinburgh: T&T Clark.

Eddy, S. K. (1961). *The King Is Dead: Studies in the Near Eastern Resistance to Hellenism*. Lincoln: University of Nebraska Press.

Elliott, J. K., ed. (1993). *The Apocryphal New Testament*. Oxford: Clarendon Press.

Greenberg, J. R., & Mitchell, S. A. (1983). *Object Relations in Psychoanalytic Theory*. Cambridge: Harvard University Press.

Gruenwald, I. (2003). *Ritual and Ritual Theory in Ancient Judaism*. Boston: Brill.

Idel, M. (1998). *Messianic Mystics*. New Haven: Yale University Press.

Koester, H. (1982). *Introduction to the New Testament*. New York: Walter de Gruyter.

Kohut, H. (1971). *The Analysis of the Self*. Madison: International Universities Press.

Kohut, H. (1977). *The Restoration of the Self*. Madison: International Universities Press.

Liebes, Y. (1993). *Studies in the Zohar*. Albany: State University of New York Press.

Neusner, J., Green, W. S., et al., eds. (1987). *Judaisms and Their Messiahs*. Cambridge: Cambridge University Press.

Nickelsburg, G. W. E. (2001). *1 Enoch/ 1*. Minneapolis: Fortress.

Scholem, G. (1971). *The Messianic Idea in Judaism*. New York: Schocken Books.

CHAPTER 14

THE BIBLE AND PSYCHOLOGY:
AN INTERDISCIPLINARY PILGRIMAGE

J. Harold Ellens

The authors of the chapters in this volume have discussed at length the interface of the discrete disciplines of psychology and biblical studies. They have outlined various principles relevant to the interdisciplinary enterprise of relating these sciences and set forth a variety of important ideas for the illumination of psychological models with biblical perspectives as well as for the employment of psychology as a new perspective in which to see the biblical text, offering new depths of understanding. Now, in bringing this volume to a summary conclusion, I set forth two basic claims.

First, the relationship of psychology and the Bible is less a matter of integration of the two into each other's framework, scientifically or intuitively, and more a matter of the kind of interface between them that affords the mutual illumination of the two phenomena, knowing that these are two sources of insight and information in which truth is revealed about us, and therefore, presumably, about God who created, sustains, and heals us.

Second, biblical interpretation, as text analysis, cultural understanding, literary-historical appreciation, and theology formation, is an enterprise upon which all the tools of human inquiry must be brought to bear in order to distill from the text the full range of cognitive and affective import that it carries and offers the inquirer. Among these tools are historical criticism, literary criticism, form criticism, redaction criticism, textual criticism proper, and social scientific criticism.

I emphasize here how and why the science and models of psychology can be employed as a lens through which to see any text in fresh ways with productive results and new dimensions of insight. I illustrate this point by describing to some degree my personal odyssey in the pursuit of this interface of sciences and their applications during my forty years of work in both clinical psychology and scientific theology.

Somewhat more than a half century ago, movements arose in both the conservative and progressive branches of American Christianity that sought to explore the interface of psychology and biblical interpretation. The Pastoral Psychology movement with its journal titled *Pastoral Psychology* and the Christian Association for Psychological Studies with its *CAPS Bulletin* and the *Journal of Psychology and Christianity* were just two of those formal enterprises. From the outset it was the clear intent of the founders that the Christian scholars should explore in a systematic way the manner in which our understanding of religious texts could be illumined by our growing scientific knowledge about what came to be known as "the living human document," a human being. The assumption behind that concern was the conviction that the more we know about human psychology, the more we can understand the real story in our religious texts. It was clear from the earliest publications of these movements that in this enterprise was an assumption that texts can produce psycho-spiritual health or pathology and that psycho-spiritual health and pathology can enhance or distort our reading of religious texts.

It was not the concern of the founders to drag the psychologically aware community, or indeed any part of the communities of faith and science, into the questionable processes of mysticism, subjective Pietism, parapsychology, spiritism, or the occult. Indeed, it was very much the opposite: to explore why it seemed to be at least heuristically and perhaps even empirically evident that texts can be constructive or toxic.

So there was an implication at the center of this charter that if we could understand the relationship between psychology and biblical studies, we would be able to discern better how religious faith interfaces with human health. Then we would also see how the dynamics of human health and illness illumine the messages in the text of the Bible. In retrospect, that seems to have been a fruitful set of objectives and intuitive assumptions. These have become the focus of inquiry for a wider world of scholarship today. In any case, it was largely that two-sided trajectory that became the channel for my personal and scholarly quest for the majority of my life and work.

Exposition

When I came to the position of executive director of the Christian Association for Psychological Studies in 1974, the scene was verdant in both the Evangelical and the Progressive or mainline Christian communities, with a luxuriant growth of models for exploring and conceptualizing the relationship between the Bible and psychology. On the one hand, such Evangelical psychologists as H. Newton Malony, John Carter, Bruce Narramore, and others were beginning to write on these issues. On the other hand, such Progressive scholars as Seward Hiltner, Don Browning, James Lapsley, LeRoy Aden, Colin Brown, Wayne Oates, Liston Mills, and others were producing a spate of sturdy volumes treating the interface of psychology, the Bible, and religious experience.

There were two interesting negative characteristics in that phase of the inquiry which I have tried to heal. The first was that the Evangelical community did not speak to or read the works of the Progressive, then referred to as the liberal, community. Neither did the mainline scholars read the Evangelicals or conduct dialogue with them. The second problem was that the Evangelicals generally came to this inquiry into the relationship between the Bible and psychology from the side of scientific psychology, having been trained primarily as professional psychologists, mostly at the doctoral level. On the other hand, the Progressives came to the inquiry from the side of scientific theology, having been trained primarily as professional theologians teaching in pastoral care departments at seminaries. Therefore, the Evangelicals did not trust the Progressives because they thought they did not know scientific psychology and were working mainly with an intuitive popularization of the field. The Progressives did not trust the Evangelicals because they thought they did not know scientific theology and were working mainly with an intuitive and primitive Sunday school religion, or the dogmatic categories and language of fundamentalism.

They were both in error, of course. Actually scholars such as Seward Hiltner, Don Browning, Peter Homans, and the like were heavily trained in psychoanalytic and psychodynamic psychology. Moreover, Professor Malony is an ordained Methodist minister with a standard theological education who spent most of his teaching life addressing the issue the Evangelicals called the integration of psychology and spirituality. His Evangelical colleagues were mostly well-informed persons who, even if they had little formal theological training, were biblically and spiritually reasonably well informed and at least consummately honest. Moreover, it must be said for the Evangelicals that they began to read the work of and take seriously the dialogue with the Progressives before the latter began to take them seriously. Today, it seems to me, the dialogue between the two communities runs on apace so that the names, Evangelical and Progressive, that once distinguished them are becoming less and less useful at the academic, clinical, and research levels.

There was, however, a central problem in the framework within which the Evangelical community generally tended to conceptualize the relationship between the Bible and psychology, and in the language used to express that relationship. Evangelical scholars have tended even to this time to describe the problem as that of the *integration* of biblical studies and psychology. To think of the issue as one of integration suggests that the two components to be integrated in a unified model are in some way inherently disparate. Both biblical studies and psychology are scientific and academic disciplines. Moreover, they have their subject matter in common, namely, the living human document and textual documents that interpret and are interpreted by that living human document, the human person.

There is a difference, of course, between the science of biblical studies and that of psychology. Each has its own universe of discourse, each its own paradigms, arena of inquiry, database, objectives, and controls within the framework of scientific inquiry. Both depend on empirical and heuristic data and methods. Each has its own forming and informing history. Each depends on theory formation that must respond with integrity to the scientific constraints on theory development and testing, and each must respond with integrity to its respective database.

The word *integration* remains problematic for me because it suggests a model in which two disparate entities, psychology and biblical studies, essentially alien to each other, must be lined up or force-fitted to each other in order to ensure responsible work in the helping professions or in biblical exegesis. My perception has been consistently that what we really have always sought in the quest to understand the relationship between the scientific disciplines of psychology and biblical studies is an *interface* of mutual illumination. This I argued with some vigor in my Finch Lectures in 1980 and in *God's Grace and Human Health* (1982, 19–36, 94–115). The question whether *integration* or *interface of mutual illumination* is the better term is an epistemological problem on the theoretical science level, a structural problem on the applied science level, and a problem of psychodynamic consonance or dissonance on the experience level.

There is also a philosophical problem that may be implied in the integration paradigm and that for many Evangelicals lurks only slightly below the surface of conscious thought, namely, that the truth value of data produced by psychology has a lesser valence than the truth value of the insights of biblical studies, the message of the text of the Bible. To put it simply, there may be the assumption or claim that the truth of the Bible is more truthful than the truth of psychology. I have vigorously contested this position, as have the scholars from the Progressive community generally, largely on the philosophical grounds that God reveals himself in nature and in grace, in Scripture and in creation, in faith and work—and with equal valence, because all truth is God's truth, and he does not speak with a forked tongue.

The Reformed tradition, for example, in which I have always stood, consistently has held out for the notion of God's two books: the created universe and the Bible. Under the rubrics of this rich tradition, scientific inquiry into biblical studies, as well as theology and spirituality, stood on equal footing with scientific inquiry into the natural and social sciences, and vice versa.

Perhaps there is a second theological problem implied in the integration model, namely, the notion that the revelation in creation is not merely different in value from that of religious Scripture but that what we see through the text of the Bible and what we see through the science of psychology represent two radically different realms of ontological reality, namely, the worlds of the natural and of the supernatural. These terms have become largely nonfunctional in the thought world of the Progressive community, although there has been an increase in such terminology as "material versus transcendant worlds" and the like, as the positivism of Enlightenment thinking has come under fire in recent decades.

The insights of the postmodern era regarding the difficulty of achieving a valueless scientific objectivity are crucial here, namely, the realization that all scientific theory development is born, in the first place, out of assumptions that are to some degree driven or shaped by one's religious, theological, or value-laden predisposition. All the data one acquires, therefore, are not strictly speaking empirical data or objective rationality but rather the formulations of "Reason Within the Bounds of Religion" (Wolterstorff, 1976). It must be added that our inherent lack of absolute objectivity is shaped equally by our psychological predispositions, archetypes, and unconscious value judgments.

A Model of Mutual Scientific Illumination

To speak of a model of interface between two scientific enterprises that offers them mutual illumination is to suggest what I have called a perspectival model. There are three principles, I think, that such a model must reflect if it is to be a thorough-going expression of scientific and exegetical integrity.

First, biblical studies and psychology are both sciences in their own right, stand legitimately on their own foundations, and read carefully are two equivalent sources of illumining truth; hence they are two equivalent subjects of scientific study. They are not alien in any inherent sense. When they seem at odds, paradoxical, or disparate in some way, it must always be because of a dysfunction on one of three counts. Perhaps we have failed to read the Bible well enough or we have failed to investigate the science of psychology thoroughly enough; or we have distorted our search for truth in either field by dogmatism or some other distorting factor; or we have drawn erroneous conclusions in either of those investigations and not allowed the two scientific disciplines to illumine each other adequately. Wherever truth is found it is truth, God's truth, having equal warrant with all other truth. Some truth may have greater weight than other truth in a specific situation, but there is no difference in its warrant or valence as *truth* (Ellens, 1982, 24). If you have just been hit by a car and are bleeding from the jugular, the truth about blood pressure and arterial closure may be significantly more important at that moment than biblical exegesis. There are undoubtedly other circumstances in which the opposite is the case. At any rate, truth is truth, regardless of who finds it, where, or how.

Egbert Schuurman, at the time a professor of philosophy at Eindhoven Institute of Technology and lecturer at the Free University of Amsterdam, published *Technology and the Future: A Philosophical Challenge* (1980b) and *Reflections of the Technological Society* (1980a). These volumes were only slightly preceded by the work of the distinguished Benedictine priest Stanley L. Jaki, *The Road of Science and the Ways to God* (1978) and *Cosmos and Creator* (1984). In these seminal works the authors developed the claim that, given the nature of human mind and personality, it is imperative to recognize that the mutual illumination of all scientific disciplines is essential to a full-orbed and honest achievement in any of them.

Second, the criterion of soundness in theory development or operational application of the illumination the sciences of psychology and biblical studies bring to each other is not the effectiveness with which our psychological insights fit into our religious worldviews, or our spiritual insights fit our psychological worldviews, but rather whether they make discernible claims on each other in a way that either requires modification of the other or makes the thoroughgoing understanding of the other plainer or more evident. Perhaps one could say that it has to do with the way in which the one enlarges or resolves problems in the internal coherence of the other. Psychological data, insights, paradigms, or worldviews may be helpful in illumining a biblical text by enlarging the perception of the internal coherence of the text, resolving problems in the coherence of the text, or disturbing the supposed coherence of the text in a way that leads to an enlarged understanding of what the coherent message of the text is. Textual data, insights, paradigms, or worldviews may be helpful in illumining the internal coherence or lack thereof in the living human document, namely, the patient in the clinical process, in a way that will discernibly enhance the healing progress of that patient. Or such biblical textual illumination may resolve problems or impasses in the process of the therapy. It may even disturb the presumed progress only to lay bare deeper needs, coherence, or incoherence in the living human document (Gerkin, 1984). Similarly, biblical light may illumine the process of theoretical work in psychology, enhancing the understanding of the living human document about which that science is concerned to take accurate account.

Third, the responsible function of the perspectival model of interface providing mutual illumination between the psychological and biblical sciences requires an incarnational posture on the part of the scientist or practitioner. That is, for the illumination to take place, the person who brings the lights of psychology to the biblical text or those of textual interpretation to the living human document must believe that each respective science has legitimate light to bring to bear and that that light is the light of truth incarnated in the understanding possessed by the scholar. This implies that the scholar perceives herself or himself as a midwife of the truth, not merely a manipulator of insights or data.

A Formal Model of Scientific Interface

The biblical story is a paradigm of the human psychological odyssey. However literally or mythically we conceive of that paradigm, the biblical narrative and the life of the human psyche cut across each other at such substantive levels as to effect the description and definition of both. Presumably the only thing we can know about the meaning and content of the biblical text is what we can understand through the perceptions and projections of the human person. So we are heavily dependent on the cognitive and affective processes of human beings' ways of knowing. Thus to understand a text requires the employment of a warrantable anthropology and therefore, a sound psychology. Conversely, to employ a proper psychology in the pursuit of truth also requires a useful and warrantable anthropology and therefore, I claim, a sound science of biblical studies.

Psychology and biblical studies are thus inevitably interlinked, regardless of what the immediate focus or concern of either is. Hence, whether we are exploring the biblical text or the living human document, the mutual illumination of psychology and biblical studies is imperative because a properly enlightened anthropology is required for both. Moreover, the mutual illumination undoubtedly takes place precisely in the anthropology that is forming or functioning in each of the two disciplines. Because both disciplines deal with the psycho-spiritual domains, neither of these can ignore the other or it is not adequately serious about itself.

So one must come at each of these two disciplines with an eye to the other. This is likely to be true regarding the science that explores any other facet of the cosmos, of course. Biblical studies are barren without a comprehensive appreciation of the experiences of the inner human self, the psyche; psychology is barren unless it comprehends the dynamics of human spirituality. The natural and social sciences must inquire finally of biblical studies, and the field of biblical studies must listen to the natural and social sciences in order to make sense of itself.

Psychology and biblical studies exercise the stewardship of their mandates by collecting data, formulating theories for accounting for the data, and applying the interpreted data to operational concerns in their respective disciplines. Theory development in this process depends on the perspective from which one comes to the scientific enterprise. This means that behind the theory development and data collection or interpretation is a philosophical assumption, a belief regarding the nature and function of reality (cf. Wolterstorff, 1976).

There are four levels at which scientific and operational disciplines interface. These are the levels of (1) theory development, (2) research methodology, (3) database development, and (4) operational application (clinical operations for psychology and textual analysis for biblical studies).

These categories do not differ in their scientific function from one discipline to the next. The crucial issue regarding the interface and mutual illumination that psychology and biblical studies afford each other in this model is the recognition that each of these disciplines comes to the work at each of the four levels with its own independent parlance, prerogatives, perspectives, and purposes, but all encounter each other at each level of the model in the anthropology that is functioning or forming at that level in the mind and worldview of the scientist.

In fact, one can go a step farther and demonstrate that it is in the personality theory that is functioning or forming in that anthropology that the interface and mutual illumination take place.

It is in the notion of the nature and function of the human person who does science, experiences conceptualization of aspects and functions of the cosmos, and relates to the biblical text that the various disciplines meet to bring their illuminating insights to bear on all the others. From this base of common interest in the nature and function of the human person, biblical studies and psychology can prove to be mutually illuminating enterprises.

Our anthropology, properly illumined, affords us our understanding of how the text speaks to us. In sum, therefore, I see biblical studies and psychology as different perspectives or frames of reference, with differing fields of discourse, dealing with the same subject matter, namely, the function of the living human document, which is always implied in the textual documents of the Bible. Thus the illumination that psychology can bring to biblical studies is the light it offers about the nature and function of the living human document as author, context, initial audience, interpreter, subsequent audience, and object of the text. The illumination biblical studies can bring to psychology is the light it offers about the nature and function of the scriptural text as context, in the sense of author or modifier, audience, and interpreter of the living human document.

Conclusion

It is clear that psychology and biblical studies are thrown inextricably together. Psychology has been able to develop a number of standardized paradigms for understanding the living human document, and these paradigms have proven useful cross-culturally. Therefore, it may be assumed that they are also applicable cross-generationally and over millennia. That is, our current models for understanding human beings are likely to be applicable when we use them to view persons from a thousand years ago or from biblical times, provided we can secure a substantial amount of information about those persons.

We might be able, for example, to note that Tertullian was a lawyer by training and that he was meticulously preoccupied with the precise and subtle nuances of the meaning of words and expressions, that he tolerated no variance or margin of flexibility in the denotation or connotation of the words he used in formulating his early Christian creedal statements, that he was inordinately legalistic in his theological and church political notions, and that when the church of North Africa moved toward vesting its authority in the bishops and their Apostolic Succession, he left the Orthodox Church for the Montanists (Jackson & Gilmore, 1950, 305–308). Having noted these things and presumably having developed a similar but more extended body of knowledge about Tertullian, his history, and function, we could successfully employ our diagnostic categories of today, with their implied psychological models, for understanding the living human document and draw appropriate conclusions regarding Tertullian's health and pathology. We might conclude, for example, that he was suffering from at least a mild case of compulsivity and paranoia. In such a case, it would be important to have made this psychological assessment in order to understand what he wrote, intended, and meant by his theological works, and how we should take them, and perhaps even how seriously we should take them.

Similarly, it is possible today to bring the insights and models of psychology to bear on a biblical text, assessing the nature and function of the author, of the implied or stated intended audience, of the real audiences in the church's history who interpreted the text, together with their interpretations, and thus assess the reasons, healthy or pathological, for the constructs that were expressed in the text and in subsequent uses of it. That is to say, in addition to all the other text-critical paradigms that are legitimately applied to the text of Scripture, surely we must apply the paradigms for understanding how humans function, what they tend to say, why they say what they say the way they say it, and what messages mean as seen through standardized psychological paradigms when applied in a given context. Psychology is another lens through which it is possible to see any text and understand dimensions of it and the way it reflects the living human documents behind it, which could not be understood if one did not employ this lens.

References

Ellens, J. H. (1982). *God's Grace and Human Health*. Nashville: Abingdon.

Gerkin, C. V. (1984). *The Living Human Document*. Nashville: Abingdon.

Jaki, S. L. (1978). *The Road of Science and the Ways to God*. Chicago: University of Chicago Press.

Jaki, S. L. (1984). *Cosmos and Creator*. Chicago: University of Chicago Press.

Jackson, S. M., & Gilmore, G. W., eds. (1950). *The New Schaff–Herzog Encyclopedia of Religious Knowledge*, vol. 11. Grand Rapids: Baker.

Schuurman, E. (1980a). *Reflections of the Technological Society*. Toronto: Wedge.

Schuurman, E. (1980b). *Technology and the Future: A Philosophical Challenge*. New York: Radix.

Wolterstorff, N. (1976). *Reason within the Bounds of Religion*. Grand Rapids: Eerdmans.

GLOSSARY

Active imagination: A Jungian technique of exploring levels of meaning in a dream image by expressing that image in new forms, for example, poetry, art, dance, or clay. Jung had observed that "often the hands know how to solve a riddle with which the intellect has wrestled in vain" (Jung, 1953–1978, 8:86).

Amplification: A Jungian technique of dream interpretation that consists of introducing parallels to dream images from folklore, mythology, the history of religions, and personal history, toward the end of finding associations that will assist in the conscious clarification of the dream images.

Analytic psychology: The phrase Jung chose for his psychological approach in distinction from the term *psychoanalysis* used by Freud and *individual psychology* used by Adler.

Anima/animus: Latin for "soul," "person," "life," or "mind." Jung adopted these terms to refer to the unconscious archetypal depiction of the opposite gender. *Anima* refers to the image of the feminine in the masculine psyche; *animus* is the image of the masculine in the feminine psyche. Because these images are unconscious, they can be projected on members of the opposite sex, producing "love at first sight."

Archetype/archetypal image: Jungian psychology speaks of a pattern-making tendency of the collective psyche to portray mainstay human experiences, conditions, and life crises with a glossary of typical images that recur recognizably in slightly different garb in the literature and lore of cultures around the world, past and present. Although this patterning tendency is unconscious, and therefore cannot be directly observed, it can be seen at work in the "archetypal images" it produces in its "stories." These include trans-culturally recurrent figures such as the primordial garden, the divine child, the trickster, the golden age, the wise old man, the suffering servant, the patriarch, the virgin mother, the stages of history, and so on.

Behaviorism: A school of psychology, associated for decades with B. F. Skinner, that holds that the only proper subjects for psychological inquiry are the facts of human and animal behavior and animals and their conditioning. Behaviorism regarded the mind, the psyche, and the soul as inaccessible to psychological inquiry.

Biblical criticism: The art of the scholarly study of biblical texts that emerged in its modern form in the mid-nineteenth century. Until the 1960s, the enterprise involved the diachronic examination of Scripture from the standpoint of the historical, archaeological, literary, and theological critic. Since the 1960s, synchronic forms of biblical criticism have developed that include, among others, rhetorical, feminist, canonical, ideological, social scientific, and psychological criticism.

Canon: Within the field of biblical studies, the word *canon* refers to the collection of writings officially approved by a religious body. For Judaism the canon consists of the Hebrew Scriptures (Old Testament), and for Christianity the Old and New Testaments.

Cognitive dissonance: The discomfort that comes with the tension that can emerge out of a discrepancy between the realities of one's world and one's expectations, or between what we know and what we do. The condition can lead to paralysis of action, or it can serve as motivator to take steps to reduce the inconsistency.

Cognitive psychology: The fundamental assumption of cognitive psychology is that fears, complexes, and generally negative emotions can be traced to faulty ideas, distorted perceptions, and destructive attitudes or cognitions. The therapeutic goal of cognitive psychology is to change cognition and to examine the way in which the client construes reality.

Collective unconscious: In Jung's psychology the collective unconscious (or *objective unconscious*), in distinction from the personal unconscious, represents the deepest and broadest level of the unconscious, an inherited function common to the human race. It is the origin of the primordial archetypal images that are the common heritage of humankind.

Complex: Jung coined this term to refer to a psychologically significant entity on which an individual has focused a near-addictive amount of energy and feeling.

Cura animarum: A medieval ecclesiastical phrase meaning "the care or cure of souls" that has been used to define the mission of the church. It is also regarded in some therapeutic circles as the goal of psychology.

Defense mechanism: Also called *ego-defense mechanisms*, these are strategies, often unconscious and neurotic, for defending the self from unpleasant persons or situations. They include the strategies of displacement, denial, repression, suppression, compulsive behavior, transference, sublimation, projection, and reaction formation. In modern psychoanalytic theory they differ from the conscious "coping mechanisms" that a mature person employs to meet threatening circumstances (Hunter, 1990, 269 [E. M. Pattison]).

Demythologization: The term was introduced by New Testament scholar Rudolf Bultmann in the 1950s as a tactic for getting behind the literal meaning of biblical myths to their originating intent and existential relevance.

Displacement: A defense mechanism of redirecting one's defensive or belligerent feelings from the person who "deserves" them to a less threatening person who does not, like the man who barks at his wife at home rather than at the offending boss at work.

Dissociation: The psychological description of an unconscious defense mechanism of the splitting off from consciousness of certain uncomfortable, threatening, or disturbing realities in one's life, resulting in the possibility of memory loss, depression, or even multiple personality.

Exegesis: Derived from a Greek word that means "to lead out," it is used by scholars and literary critics to refer to the scholarly process of "leading out" the meaning of a text, focusing on the meaning of the words in their original historic context and within the framework of the world in which they were written. Exegesis is often described as the art of discerning "what the text said."

Feminist criticism: A school of biblical scholarship that studies Scripture with an eye to the role, valuation, and treatment of women. Three branches have developed: one that focuses on what is perceived as

the incorrigibly androcentric and patriarchal character of the
Bible; a second that focuses on those voices in the Bible that oppose
human oppression, including the oppression of women; a third that
seeks to bring to light the significant role of women in biblical culture, despite a perceived male-dominated tendency to dismiss it as
unimportant.

Form criticism: A branch of biblical criticism originating in the 1920s
aimed originally at studying the "forms" in which the oral traditions
behind the Gospels were preserved and transmitted (for example,
miracle stories, parables, sayings). In time, it was conceived more
broadly as the study of the form or genre of biblical writings and
their constituent parts, mindful of the different kinds of meanings
and "truths" each conveys and the different functions each is
designed to serve (for example, myth, legend, fable, law, psalm prophetic utterance, epistle, gospel, and apocalypse).

Hellenistic Judaism: The vast population of Jews living in the Mediterranean world between the second century B.C.E. and the second
century A.D. who spoke Greek, produced the Greek translation of
the Hebrew Bible, and developed a literature that incorporated
Greek philosophical learning. A good example is Philo Judaeus of
Alexandria.

Hermeneutics: Derived from a Greek root that means "interpretation,"
the term is used currently to refer to the study of the meaning trans-
acted in the exchange between a text and a reader. It is often
described as the art of determining "what the text says," with
emphasis on the meaning(s) it can convey or catalyze for a present-
day reader and on the meaning that the reader brings to the text.

Hermeneutics of suspicion: A phrase introduced by Paul Ricoeur that
endorsed the need to read alerted to the ulterior motives, special
interests, and ideologies that might be operative in the text being
read.

Heuristic: Derived from the Greek root "to find," it refers to an idea or
method that is employed toward the end of finding or teasing out
further discoveries.

Humanistic psychology: A movement within psychology in the second
half of the twentieth century that provided an option to psychoanalytic and behaviorist psychologies in its emphasis on human subjectivity, human potential, and strategies for self-improvement.

Ideological criticism: A branch of biblical studies that seeks to uncover
ideologies (for example, racial, ethnic, class, social, political, gender-

oriented) implicit in particular biblical authors, biblical texts, and biblical readers and interpretations.

Individuation: A Jungian term for the goal of the life process of becoming the "individual" one uniquely is, through a lifelong process of integrating the psychic components in one's life, and bringing the unconscious to fuller consciousness.

Logia: Greek for "sayings." A technical phrase in New Testament studies referring to the "sayings" of Jesus preserved in oral and literary tradition.

Myth: A foundational story within a culture that provides an interpretation of "how things are." Distinct from fables, which aim at providing moral examples, and legends, which enhance national figures of the past, the myth provides a "storied" introduction to a culture's understanding of physical, metaphysical, cultural, social, familial, personal, and cosmic realities and their meaning.

Neurosis/neurotic: A clinically imprecise term for emotional, behavioral, or cognitive disturbance that is distressing but not totally incapacitating for an individual. With respect to the cause of neurosis, Freud observed that behind a neurosis there is often concealed all the natural and necessary suffering the patient has been unwilling to bear. Karen Horney defined *neurotic anxiety* as a pathological, dysfunction-generating state in which anxiety is disproportionate to reality.

Pathogenic: Producing illness, disease, or dysfunction, physical or psychological.

Persona: A term popularized in Jungian psychology to refer to the face or "mask" one selects consciously or unconsciously as part of the task of adapting to and presenting oneself to the world. Jung commented, "one could say, with a little exaggeration, that the persona is that which in reality one is not, but which oneself as well as others think one is" (Jung, 1963, 397).

Personal unconscious: A Jungian phrase for that part of the unconscious that derives from personal experience of the individual, as opposed to a collective unconscious common to the species.

Post-traumatic stress disorder: "An anxiety disorder characterized by a pattern of symptoms attributable to the experience of a traumatic event. The symptoms of PTSD include (1) re-experiencing the traumatic event, (2) emotional numbing, and (3) any of a variety of autonomic, cognitive or behavioral symptoms" (Hunter, 1990, 931 [N. C. Brown]).

Projection: "A defense mechanism in which one unconsciously attributes one's own unacceptable feelings, desire, thoughts, and impulses to another person. This removes the responsibility for unacceptable qualities or feelings from oneself, thus protecting the ego. An example is a husband who is barely able to control his anger toward his spouse and subsequently becomes suspicious that *she* is angry" (Hunter, 1990, 960 [J. Estelle]).

Psyche: A term used in classical and biblical Greek to refer to the vital force, life, breath, true self, or soul; ultimately adopted in psychoanalytic tradition to refer to the totality of the psychic processes, conscious and unconscious, including affect, perception, cognition, conation, intuition, imagination, rationality, and spirituality, among others.

Psychodynamics: A term that means literally the "power of the psyche," referring to any "psychological theory or therapeutic method that explains and approaches psychological processes in terms of motives and drives" (Hunter, 1990, 989 [M. A. Woltersdorf]). It is also used currently to refer to the dynamic interactive psychic factors at work in human relations, whether in real time or as portrayed and expressed in art and literature.

Psychological biblical criticism: A branch of biblical studies that applies psychological and psychoanalytic insight to the study of the Bible, its origins, its content, its interpretation, and the history of its effects.

Psychologizing: The practice of explaining the essence or origin of events, persons, or entities (for example, art, religion, politics) in exclusively psychological terms.

Q: A code word in New Testament studies to refer to a collection of traditional sayings of Jesus that appear in the Gospels of Matthew and Luke but not in Mark or John. The collection includes the Lord's Prayer and the Sermon on the Mount, among many other "logia" or "sayings" of Jesus. The letter *Q* is an abbreviation of the German word *Quelle* for "source." It is believed that Matthew's sources include the Gospel of Mark, Q, and Matthew's own special material (or M). Luke's sources include the Gospel of Mark, Q, and Luke's own special material (or L).

Reader-response criticism: A branch of literary and biblical criticism that focuses on reading as an act of "construction" and on the role of the reader's values, responses, and attitudes in the process.

Redaction criticism: A branch of biblical studies that examines the effect of biblical authors on their texts, with respect to the principles of organization, selection of materials, interpretive cues, written and oral sources, vocabulary, and points of view they have enlisted or employed in creating and shaping their texts.

Repression: One of several defense mechanisms that consists of excluding unwanted memories, thoughts, or concerns from conscious awareness; living in denial.

Rhetorical criticism: A branch of literary and biblical criticism that focuses on the rhetorical or "persuasive" character, design, and function of a text or text unit within the original rhetorical context of its writing. Rhetoric has been defined as "that quality of discourse by which a speaker or writer seeks to accomplish his purposes." Accordingly rhetorical critics examine the rhetorical literary units, the rhetorical situation or problem, devices of style, and the writer's objective in context (Coggins & Houlden, 1990, 599–600 [J. I. H. McDonald]).

Self: Jungian psychology uses this term to refer to the archetype of the individuated person. This view of self, usually achieved in the second half of life, displaces the personal ego as the center of one's conscious life.

Self psychology: Psychologies that place the self at the center of personality and make the growth or actualization of the self the primary goal of life in general and of psychotherapy and counseling in particular (Hunter, 1990, 1137 [P. C. Vitz]). Representative "self psychologists" include Alfred Adler, Erich Fromm, Carl Rogers, Abraham Maslow, Rollo May, and Heinz Kohut. Kohut's psychology offers a positive perspective on narcissism (Wulff, 1991, 353).

Sitz im Leben: A phrase originating in German biblical scholarship to refer to the "life-setting" (lit., "seat in life") of a biblical text or event. Thus one might speak of the *Sitz im Leben* of John's Gospel, that is, the historical and cultural circumstances of the author of the Gospel and his community at the time the Gospel was being written.

Social scientific criticism: In its broadest sense, social scientific criticism "applies methods and theories to biblical texts in an attempt to reconstruct the social worlds behind these texts . . . while simultaneously illuminating the lives of the people living in these worlds" (Hayes, 1999, 2:478 [N. Steinberg]).

Superego: The part of the psyche in Freudian psychology that represents the introjection of societal, religious, and/or familial values,

obligations, and obsessions that exercise unconscious inner authority in an individual's thoughts, values, and decisions.

Textual criticism: One of the earliest of biblical critical disciplines, dating to the sixteenth century. It began with the recognition that we
do not have the original Hebrew or Greek "autograph" text of any
biblical book but only centuries of handwritten copies. Furthermore, although the copies largely agree with one another, close
inspection reveals that no copy agrees with any other copy in every
detail. The task of textual criticism is to devise scholarly techniques
for deciding which of the variant readings are corruptions and
which are most likely the original.

Unconscious: "That part of the mind or psyche containing information
that has never been conscious, or that was once conscious but is no
longer" (Hunter, 1990, 1290 [H. Coward]). Jung defined the contents of the unconscious as including "everything of which I know,
but of which I am not at the moment thinking, everything of which
I was once conscious but have now forgotten; everything perceived
by my senses, but not noted by my conscious mind; everything
which, involuntarily and without paying attention to it, I feel, think,
remember, want, and do; all the future things that are taking shape
in me and will sometime come to consciousness" (Jung, 1963, 401).

References

Coggins, R. J., & Houlden, J. L. (1990). *A Dictionary of Biblical Interpretation.*
Philadelphia: Trinity Press International.

Hayes, J. H., ed. (1999). *Dictionary of Biblical Interpretation.* Nashville:
Abingdon.

Hunter, R., ed. (1990). *Dictionary of Pastoral Care and Counseling.* Nashville:
Abingdon.

Jung, C. G. (1953–1978). *The Collected Works of C. G. Jung.* Princeton: Princeton University Press.

Jung, C. G. (1963). *Memories, Dreams, Reflections.* New York: Vintage Books.

Wulff, D. (1991). *Psychology of Religion: Classic and Contemporary Views.* New
York: John Wiley.

INDEX

About the Contributors

PAUL N. ANDERSON is professor of biblical and Quaker studies and chair of the Department of Religious Studies at George Fox University, where he has served since 1989, other than a year as a visiting professor at Yale Divinity School (1998–1999). He is author of *The Christology of the Fourth Gospel: Its Unity and Disunity in the Light of John 6* (1996) and *Navigating the Living Waters of the Gospel of John: On Wading with Children and Swimming with Elephants* (2000). In addition, he has written many essays on biblical and Quaker themes and is editor of *Quaker Religious Thought*. He serves on the steering committee of the Psychology and Biblical Studies Section of the Society of Biblical Literature and teaches the New Testament Interpretation course in the PsyD program of George Fox University. His PhD in New Testament is from Glasgow University (1989), his MDiv is from the Earlham School of Religion (1981), and his BA in psychology and BA in Christian ministries are from Malone College (1978).

ANTHONY BASH serves as honorary fellow in theology and director of Studies in New Testament in the Department of Humanities on the faculty of the University of Hull, England. His fields of specialization include New Testament studies, biblical studies, and the use of social sciences in biblical studies. He has recently written one of the first articles to be published in the *Journal for the Study in the New Testament* on the application of psychological models to biblical interpretation, "The Interpretation of 2 Corinthians 10–13" (2001).

LYN M. BECHTEL received her PhD in biblical studies from Drew University prior to her appointment as visiting associate professor of Hebrew Bible at Drew Theological School and associate professor of Hebrew Bible at Moravian Theological Seminary. Her areas of specialization include the books of Genesis and Job, psychoanalytic theory and the Hebrew Bible, feminist interpretation of the Hebrew Bible, and the biblical experience of shame and shaming. Her publications include "Shame as a Sanction of Social Control in Biblical Israel: Judicial, Political, and Social Shaming" (*Journal of the Study of the Old Testament*, 1991) and "Genesis 2.4b–3.24: A Myth about Human Maturation" (*Journal for the Study of Old Testament*, 1995).

KAMILA BLESSING is an Episcopal priest of twenty years' standing and an "intentional interim" specializing in the health and healing of congregations. She has graduate training in family systems therapy, a PhD in information systems (studying the "people systems" in organizations and their communication) from the University of Pittsburgh, and a PhD in New Testament from Duke University. Her research in New Testament includes the applications of systems theories to Bible interpretation as well as the role of narrative in the maintenance of religious identity groups. Her publications include "Murray Bowen's Family Systems Theory as Bible Hermeneutic using the Family of the Prodigal, Luke 15:11–32" (*Journal of Psychology and Christianity*, 2000) and "The 'Confusion Technique' of Milton Erickson as Hermeneutic for Biblical Parables" (*Journal of Psychology and Christianity*, 2002).

SCHUYLER BROWN received his BA in classical languages from Harvard University in 1952, and as a member of the Jesuit order in the 1950s and 1960s, Brown received licentiates in philosophy (1957), theology (1964), and biblical studies (1969). He received his DrTheol from the University of Münster (Westphalia) in 1969. His academic appointments have included teaching positions at Woodstock College, General Theological Seminary in New York City, the University of London, and as professor of New Testament at the University of Toronto (St. Michael's College). He has served as a lecturer at the Jung Institute in Zurich and in the Training Program of the Ontario Association of Jungian Analysts. His wife, Margaret Eileen Meredith, is a graduate of the Jung Institute in Zurich and a practicing Jungian analyst in Toronto. Brown's publications include *The Origins of Christianity: A Historical Introduction to the New Testament* (1984; rev. ed., 1993) and *Text and Psyche: Experiencing Scripture Today* (1998, 2002).

MARTIN J. BUSS, professor of religion at Emory University, received a BD and a ThM from Princeton Theological Seminary in 1954 and 1955 and a PhD from Yale University in 1958. He has taught in the Department of Religion at Emory University from 1959 until the present, with a specialization in Hebrew Bible. He has examined this literature from a number of perspectives: anthropological, sociological, psychological, and philosophical. His first essay dealing with a psychological approach to the Hebrew Bible was "Self-Theory and Theology" (*Journal of Religion*, 1965).

DONALD CAPPS, psychologist of religion, is William Hart Felmeth Professor of Pastoral Theology at Princeton Theological Seminary. In 1989 he was awarded an honorary doctorate from the University of Uppsala, Sweden, in recognition of the importance of his publications. He served as president of the Society for the Scientific Study of Religion from 1990 to 1992. Among his many significant books are *Men, Religion, and Melancholia: James, Otto, Jung and Erikson and Freud* (1997); *The Freudians on Religion: A Reader* (2001); *Social Phobia: Alleviating Anxiety in an Age of Self-Promotion* (1999); and *Jesus: A Psychological Biography* (2000). He also authored *The Child's Song: The Religious Abuse of Children* (1995).

JAMES H. CHARLESWORTH is the George L. Collord Professor of New Testament Language and Literature as well as editor and director of the Princeton Theological Seminary Dead Sea Scrolls Project at Princeton University. He received his PhD from Duke University and has advanced degrees or study at Edinburgh, the École Biblique de Jerusalem, the Hebrew University, the University of Tübingen, and elsewhere. Charlesworth is editor of the *Old Testament Pseudepigrapha* and *The Dead Sea Scrolls* (the Princeton critical edition and translation). He has written or edited more than sixty-five books and completed the first in-depth study of serpent symbolism in antiquity and the Bible. He introduced the term "Jesus research" into the study of the historical Jesus.

HAL CHILDS is psychotherapist and clinical director at the California Counseling Institute, San Francisco. He holds the degrees of MDiv, MA, and PhD. He is closely affiliated with the work of the Guild for Psychological Studies in San Francisco. His field of specialization is New Testament interpretation and depth psychology, as is amply demonstrated in his trail-blazing doctoral dissertation, now published as *The Myth of the Historical Jesus and the Evolution of Consciousness* (2000).

DERECK DASCHKE received his MA and PhD in Divinity from the University of Chicago Divinity School and is presently assistant professor of philosophy and religion at Truman State University, Kirksville, Missouri. His fields of interest include religion and culture, psychology and religion, religion and health, new religious movements, and apocalypticism and millennialism. His publications include "Mourning the End of Time: Apocalypses as Texts of Cultural Loss" in *Millennialism from the Hebrew Bible to the Present*, edited by Leonard J. Greenspoon and Ronald A. Simpkins (2002) and "Desolate among Them: Loss, Fantasy, and Recovery in the Book of Ezekiel" (*American Imago*, 1999).

CHARLES T. DAVIS III studied at Emory University with Dr. Norman Perrin, graduating with BD and PhD degrees after special study at the University of Heidelberg. Although specializing in New Testament studies, he has also published articles and book reviews in the fields of American religion, computers and the humanities, philosophy, and Buddhist studies. He is the author of *Speaking of Jesus* and currently serves as professor of philosophy and religion at Appalachian State University in Boone, North Carolina, where he teaches biblical literature, Islam, and seminars on symbols and healing.

J. HAROLD ELLENS is a research scholar at the University of Michigan, Department of Near Eastern Studies. He is a retired Presbyterian theologian and ordained minister, a retired U.S. Army colonel, and a retired professor of philosophy, theology, and psychology. He has authored, coauthored, or edited 104 books and 165 professional journal articles. He served fifteen years as executive director of the Christian Association for Psychological Studies and as founding editor and editor in chief of the *Journal of Psychology and Christianity*. He holds a PhD from Wayne State University in the psychology of human communication, a PhD from the University of Michigan in biblical and Near Eastern studies, and master's degrees from Calvin Theological Seminary, Princeton Theological Seminary, and the University of Michigan. His publications include *God's Grace and Human Health* (1982) *Jesus as Son of Man, the Literary Character: A Progression of Images* (2003), *The Destructive Power of Religion, Violence in Judaism, Christianity, and Islam* (2004), and *Psychotheology: Key Issues* (1987) as well as chapters in *Moral Obligation and the Military*, *Baker Encyclopedia of Psychology*, and *Abingdon Dictionary of Pastoral Care*.

JAMES W. FOWLER is Professor of Theology and Human Development at Emory University in Atlanta and lecturer at Candler School of Theology. He was formerly on the faculty of Harvard University. He is currently the director of the Center for Faith Development and one of its primary research project directors. His prolific publications list includes such notable works as *Stages of Faith*; *Life-Maps*; *To See the Kingdom: The Theological Vision of H. Richard Niebuhr*; and *Becoming Adult, Becoming Christian, Adult Development and Christian Faith*. Professor Fowler is one of the great developmental theorists and researchers of the late twentieth and early twenty-first century.

DAVID G. GARBER JR., a PhD candidate at Emory University, is currently completing his dissertation, titled "Trauma, Memory, and Survival in Ezekiel 1–24." After receiving a BA in religious studies from Baylor University, he completed master of divinity and master of theology degrees from Princeton Theological Seminary. For the past two years, he has served as an adjunct professor at the McAfee School of Theology of Mercer University, Macon, Georgia, teaching courses in Hebrew Bible and biblical languages.

ITHAMAR GRUENWALD has served on the faculty of Tel Aviv University since 1967 in the Department of Jewish Philosophy and Program in Religious Studies. He has also been affiliated on a visiting basis as fellow with the Institute for Advanced Studies, Hebrew University; guest professor at the Revell Graduate School, Yeshiva University, New York; Martin Buber Guest Professor at the J. W. Goethe Universität, Frankfurt; and fellow at the Institute for Advanced Studies in Religion, University of Chicago. He has participated as chair and member of various committees of the Council for Higher Education in Israel. His publications include *Apocalyptic and Merkavah Mysticism* (1980), *From Apocalypticism to Gnosticism* (1988), and *Rituals and Ritual Theory in Ancient Israel* (2003).

DAVID JOBLING recently retired as professor of Hebrew Scriptures at St. Andrews College, Saskatoon, Canada, a post he had held since 1978. A native of England, he received his MA from Cambridge University and his PhD from Union Theological Seminary, New York City. He is the author of *The Sense of Biblical Narrative* (2 volumes) and of *1 Samuel* (Berit Olam series). As a member of the Bible and Culture Collective he coauthored *The Postmodern Bible* and coedited *The Postmodern Bible Reader*. He is a former general editor of the journal *Semeia* and a past president of the Canadian Society of Biblical Studies.

D. ANDREW KILLE received his PhD from the Graduate Theological Union in Berkeley in psychological biblical criticism. He is the author of *Psychological Biblical Criticism: Genesis 3 as a Test Case* (2001). As a former pastor, he teaches psychology and spirituality in the San Francisco Bay Area and is principal consultant for Revdak Consulting. He has served as co-chair of the Psychology and Biblical Studies Section of the Society of Biblical Literature and on the steering committee of the Person, Culture, and Religion Group of the American Academy of Religion.

ANDRÉ LACOCQUE is emeritus professor of Hebrew Scriptures at the Chicago Theological Seminary and emeritus director of its doctoral Center for Jewish–Christian Studies. He received his PhD and ThD from the University of Strasburg and honorary degrees from the University of Chicago and the University of Brussels. He is a longstanding member of the American Academy of Religion and the Chicago Society of Biblical Research, and he served as president of the Middle West Region of the Society of Biblical Literature (1973–1975). His publications include *Jonah, a Psycho-Religious Approach to the Prophet* (with Pierre-E. Lacocque, 1990) and *Thinking Biblically* (with Paul Ricoeur, 1998), which has been translated into Spanish, French, Portuguese, Italian, Polish, Hungarian, and Rumanian, with additional translations in progress in Greek and Korean. In 2001, colleagues published a Festschrift in his honor: *The Honeycomb of the Word: Interpreting the Primary Testament with André LaCocque*, edited by W. Dow Edgerton.

BERNHARD LANG received the degree of DTheol from the University of Tübingen and the DHabil from the University of Freiburg. He serves on the Faculty of Arts and Humanities at the University of Paderborn, Germany. He also holds the position of honorary professor of religious studies at the University of St. Andrews, U.K. His fields of specialization include biblical studies, the cultural history of the biblical world, history of Christian spirituality, and the anthropology and theory of religion. His major publications include *Drewermann, interprète la Bible* (1994); *Heaven: A History* (2nd ed., 2001, with many translations); *Sacred Games: A History of Christian Worship* (1997); and *The Hebrew God: Portrait of an Ancient Deity* (2002).

JILL L. McNISH received her JD from Rutgers University, and MDiv and a PhD in psychology and religion from Union Theological Seminary, New York City. Her field of specialization is the interface between psychology, theology, and spirituality. She is currently working in the Blanton-Peale Institute Pastoral Studies Program, New York City, and is engaged in interim ministry with the Episcopal Diocese of Newark. She is author of *Transforming Shame: A Pastoral Response* (2004) and "Uses of Theories of Depth Psychology in Ordained Ministry and the Institutional Church"(*Journal of Pastoral Care*, 2002).

PETRI MERENLAHTI received his PhD from the University of Helsinki and is currently working as research fellow in its Department of Biblical Studies. His field of specialization is narrative criticism of the New Testament and Gospels, with special interest in the Gospel of Mark. He has been a regular participant in the national programs of the Psychology and Biblical Studies Section of the Society of Biblical Literature. His publications include *Poetics for the Gospels? Rethinking Narrative Criticism* (2002).

DAN MERKUR received his PhD from the University of Stockholm and is currently in private practice as a psychoanalytic psychotherapist. He is affiliated with the Department for the Study of Religion, University of Toronto, and enrolled as a candidate at the Toronto Institute for Contemporary Psychoanalysis. His field of specialization is comparative religions. His publications include "'And He Trusted in Yahweh': The Transformation of Abram in Gen 12–13 and 15" (*Journal of Psychology of Religion*, 1995–1996) and *Mystical Moments and Unitive Thinking* (1999).

DAVID L. MILLER holds a BD degree from Bethany Theological Seminary (1960) and a PhD from Drew University (1963). Until 1999 he was the Watson-Ledden Professor of Religion at Syracuse University (New York), and until 2003 he served as a core faculty person at Pacifica Graduate Institute in Santa Barbara. He specializes in the fields of religion and literature, and psychology and mythology, and is the author of four books—*Christs: Archetypal Images in Christian Theology* (1981); *Three Faces of God* (1987); *Hells and Holy Ghosts: A Theopoetics of Christian Belief* (1989); and *Gods and Games: Toward a Theology of Play* (1970)—as well as the editor of the book *Jung and the Interpretation of the Bible* (1995).

JOHN MILLER holds a ThD from the University of Basel and is professor emeritus of religious studies at Conrad Grebel College, University of Waterloo, Ontario. He was cofounder and co-chair of the Historical Jesus Section in the Society of Biblical Literature. He also served as director of Psychiatric Rehabilitation Services at Chicago State Hospital. His writings include *The Origins of the Bible: Rethinking Canon History* (1994); *Biblical Faith and Fathering* (1989); and *Jesus at Thirty: A Psychological and Historical Portrait* (1997).

DIETER MITTERNACHT holds the MDiv, MTheol, MPhil, and DTheol degrees and is currently researcher and lecturer at Lund University in Sweden. He also serves as visiting lecturer at the Swedish Agricultural University and as fellow of the Swedish Council of Research with the research project Social Cognition and Strategies of Persuasion in Pauline Letters. His fields of specialization include Pauline studies, texts and communication (rhetoric and epistolography in antiquity), early Christian identity, and sociopsychological approaches to exegesis. He is also a specialist on the ancient synagogue, participating as a fellow of the research project The Ancient Synagogue: Birthplace for Two World Religions. His publications include "By Works of The Law No One Shall Be Justified" (1988) and *Forum für Sprachlose: Eine kommunikationspsychologische und epistolär-rhetorische Untersuchung des Galaterbriefs* (1999). He has coedited *The Synagogue of Ancient Ostia and the Jews of Rome: Interdisciplinary Studies* (2001).

WILLIAM MORROW received his PhD from the University of Toronto; currently he is associate professor of Hebrew and Hebrew Scriptures at Queen's Theological College and the Department of Religious Studies, Queen's University, Kingston, Ontario. He is the author of *Scribing the Center: Organization and Redaction in Deuteronomy 14:1–17:1* (1995) and various articles related to the composition of biblical law. His publications in the area of psychological biblical criticism include "Toxic Religion and the Daughters of Job" (*Studies in Religion*, 1998).

ROBERT H. NEUWOEHNER earned his doctorate through the University of Denver and Iliff School of Theology joint PhD program in religious and theological studies, where he concentrated his research on the feminine symbolism in the Gospel of John. He has presented papers at national and regional meetings of the American Academy of Religion and the Society of Biblical Literature, and he recently published a psychosymbolic interpretation of John 20:14–18 in the Jungian journal *Psychological Perspectives*. Drawing on thirty years of work with Jungian theory, he has begun developing and offering seminars and workshops to provide "education for the second half of life."

MICHAEL WILLETT NEWHEART is associate professor of New Testament language and literature at Howard University School of Divinity, where he has taught since 1991. He holds a PhD from Southern Baptist Theological Seminary and is the author of *Wisdom Christology in the Fourth Gospel* (1992) and *Word and Soul: A Psychological, Literary, and Cultural Reading of the Fourth Gospel* (2001) as well as numerous articles on the psychological and literary interpretation of the New Testament.

ILONA N. RASHKOW is professor of Judaic studies, women's studies, and comparative literature at the State University of New York, Stony Brook. She has also been the visiting chair in Judaic studies at the University of Alabama. Among her publications are *Upon the Dark Places: Sexism and Anti-Semitism in English Renaissance Bible Translation* (1990); *The Phallacy of Genesis* (1993); and *Taboo or Not Taboo: Human Sexuality and the Hebrew Bible* (2000). Her areas of interest include psychoanalytic literary theory as applied to the Hebrew Bible and, more generally, as applied to Judaic studies, religious studies, feminist literary criticism, and women's studies.

WAYNE G. ROLLINS is professor emeritus of biblical studies at Assumption College, Worcester, Massachusetts, and adjunct professor of Scripture at Hartford Seminary, Hartford, Connecticut. He has also taught at Princeton University and Wellesley College and served as visiting professor at Mount Holyoke College, Yale College, College of the Holy Cross, and Colgate Rochester Divinity School. His writings include *The Gospels: Portraits of Christ* (1964); *Jung and the Bible* (1983); *Soul and Psyche: The Bible in Psychological Perspective* (1999); and numerous articles on psychology and biblical studies. He received his BD from Yale Divinity School and his PhD in New Testament studies from Yale University. He served as president of the New England section of the American Academy of Religion (1984–1985) and is the founder and past chair (1990–2000) of the Society of Biblical Literature Section on Psychology and Biblical Studies.

JOHN SCHMITT is associate professor in the Department of Theology at Marquette University. His special interests lie in the field of monastic and interfaith studies. His publications include, as coauthor,

The Prophets II, volume 7 of *The Storyteller's Companion to the Bible* (1995); "Samaria in the Books of the Eighth Century Prophets" in *The Pitcher Is Broken: Memorial Essays for Goesta W. Ahlstroem*, edited by Steven W. Holloway and Lowell K. Handy (1996); and "The City as Woman in Isaiah 1–39" in *Writing and Reading the Scroll of Isaiah: Studies in an Interpretive Tradition* (1997).

KARI SYREENI received his doctor of theology from the University of Helsinki, Finland, and is professor of New Testament studies at the University of Uppsala, Sweden. His special research interests include the Gospels, New Testament hermeneutics, psychological exegesis, and the Bible and modern literature. His publications include *The Making of the Sermon on the Mount: A Procedural Analysis on Matthew's Redactional Activity. Part I: Methodology and Compositional Analysis* (1987); "Separation and Identity: Aspects of the Symbolic World of Matt. 6:1–18" (*New Testament Studies*, 1994); Metaphorical Appropriation: (Post-) Modern Biblical Hermeneutic and the Theory of Metaphor" (*Literature and Theology*, 1995); and a forthcoming work, *In Memory of Jesus: Grief Work in the Gospels.*

RALPH L. UNDERWOOD, BD, MTh, MA, PhD, is emeritus professor of pastoral care at Austin Presbyterian Theological Seminary, Austin, Texas. He has been a member of the faculty there since 1978. He retired at the end of 2001. Before teaching at Austin Seminary he was director of the Wholistic Health Center in Woodridge, Illinois. His terminal degree is from the University of Chicago Divinity School in religion and psychological studies. A United Methodist minister, he was ordained in 1961. In addition to his article cited in the note of his chapter, his relevant publications are *Pastoral Care and the Means of Grace* (1993) and "Scripture: The Substance of Pastoral Care" (*Quarterly Review*, 1991).

ANDRIES G. VAN AARDE, DD, PhD, is on the faculty of theology and professor of New Testament at the University of Pretoria, South Africa. He is a member of the Context Group and the Jesus Seminar and co-chair of the Matthew Seminar of the International Society of New Testament Studies. His publications include *Fatherless in Galilee: Jesus as Child of God* (2001); "Jesus as Fatherless Child" in *The Social Setting of Jesus and the Gospels*, edited by W. Stegemann, B. J. Malina, and G. Theissen (2002); "Jesus and Perseus in Graeco-Roman Literature" (*Acta Patristica et Byzantina*, 2000); and "Jesus' Father: The Quest for the Historical Joseph" (*HTS Theological Studies*, 1998).

WALTER WINK is professor of biblical interpretation at Auburn Theological Seminary in New York City. Previously he was a parish minister and taught at Union Theological Seminary in New York City. In 1989 and 1990, he was a peace fellow at the United States Institute of Peace. His most recent book is *The Human Being: The Enigma of the Son of the Man* (2001). He is author of *The Powers*; and a trilogy, *Naming the Powers: The Language of Power in the New Testament* (1984), *Unmasking the Powers: The Invisible Forces That Determine Human Existence* (1986), and *Engaging the Powers: Discernment and Resistance in a World of Domination* (1992). *Engaging the Powers* received three Religious Book of the Year awards for 1993, from Pax Christi, the Academy of Parish Clergy, and the Midwestern Independent Publishers Association. His other works include *Jesus and Nonviolence* (2003); *The Powers That Be* (1998); and *When the Powers Fall: Reconciliation in the Healing of Nations* (1998). He has published more than 250 journal articles.

About the Series Editor
and Advisers

J. HAROLD ELLENS is a Research Scholar at the University of Michigan, Department of Near Eastern Studies. He is a retired Presbyterian theologian and ordained minister, a retired U.S. Army Colonel, and a retired Professor of Philosophy, Theology and Psychology. He has authored, coauthored, and/or edited 104 books and 165 professional journal articles. He served fifteen years as Executive Director of the Christian Association for Psychological Studies, and as Founding Editor and Editor-in-Chief of the *Journal of Psychology and Christianity*. He holds a PhD from Wayne State University in the Psychology of Human Communication, a PhD from the University of Michigan in Biblical and Near Eastern Studies, and master's degrees from Calvin Theological Seminary, Princeton Theological Seminary, and the University of Michigan. He was born in Michigan, grew up in a Dutch-German immigrant community, and determined at age seven to enter the Christian Ministry as a means to help his people with the great amount of suffering he perceived all around him. His life's work has focused on the interface of psychology and religion.

ARCHBISHOP DESMOND TUTU is best known for his contribution to the cause of racial justice in South Africa, a contribution for which he was recognized with the Nobel Peace Prize in 1984. Archbishop Tutu has been an ordained priest since 1960. Among his many accomplishments are being named the first black General Secretary of the South African Council of Churches and serving as Archbishop of Cape Town. Once a high school teacher in South Africa, he has also taught theology in college and holds honorary degrees from universities including Harvard, Oxford, Columbia, and Kent State. He has been awarded the Order for Meritorious Service presented by President Nelson Mandela, the Archbishop of Canterbury's Award for outstanding service to the Anglican community, the Family of Man Gold Medal Award, and the Martin Luther King Jr. Non-Violent Peace Award. The publications Archbishop Tutu authored, coauthored, or made contributions to include *No Future Without Forgiveness* (2000), *Crying in the Wilderness* (1986), and *Rainbow People of God: The Making of a Peaceful Revolution* (1996).

LEROY H. ADEN is Professor Emeritus of Pastoral Theology at the Lutheran Theological Seminary in Philadelphia, Pennsylvania. He taught full-time at the seminary from 1967 to 1994 and part-time from 1994 to 2001. He served as Visiting Lecturer at Princeton Theological Seminary, Princeton, New Jersey, on a regular basis. In 2002 he coauthored *Preaching God's Compassion: Comforting Those Who Suffer* with Robert G. Hughes. Previously, he edited four books in a Psychology and Christianity series with J. Harold Ellens and David G. Benner. He served on the Board of Directors of the Christian Association for Psychological Studies for six years.

DONALD CAPPS, Psychologist of Religion, is William Hart Felmeth Professor of Pastoral Theology at Princeton Theological Seminary. In 1989 he was awarded an honorary doctorate from the University of Uppsala, Sweden, in recognition of the importance of his publications. He served as president of the Society for the Scientific Study of Religion from 1990 to 1992. Among his many significant books are *Men, Religion and Melancholia: James, Otto, Jung and Erikson and Freud*; and *The Freudians on Religion: A Reader*; and *Social Phobia: Alleviating Anxiety in an Age of Self-Promotion*; and *Jesus: A Psychological Biography*. He also authored *The Child's Song: The Religious Abuse of Children*.

ZENON LOTUFO JR. is a Presbyterian minister (Independent Presbyterian Church of Brazil), a philosopher, and a psychotherapist, specialized in Transactional Analysis. He has lectured both to undergraduate and graduate courses in universities in São Paulo, Brazil. He coordinates the course of specialization in Pastoral Psychology of the Christian Psychologists and Psychiatrists Association. He is the author of the books *Relações Humanas* [Human Relations]; *Disfunções no Comportamento Organizacional* [Dysfunctions in Organizational Behavior]; and coauthor of *O Potencial Humano* [Human Potential]. He has also authored numerous journal articles.

DIRK ODENDAAL is South African; he was born in what is now called the Province of the Eastern Cape. He spent much of his youth in the Transkei in the town of Umtata, where his parents were teachers at a seminary. He trained as a minister at the Stellenbosch Seminary for the Dutch Reformed Church and was ordained in 1983 in the Dutch Reformed Church in Southern Africa. He transferred to East London in 1988 to minister to members of the Uniting Reformed Church in Southern Africa in one of the huge suburbs for Xhosa speaking people. He received his doctorate (DLitt) in 1992 at the University of Port Elizabeth in Semitic Languages. At present, he is enrolled in a master's course in Counseling Psychology at Rhodes University.

WAYNE G. ROLLINS is Adjunct Professor of Scripture at the Hartford Seminary and Professor Emeritus of Theology at Assumption College, Worcester, Massachusetts, where he served as Director of the Ecumenical Institute and Graduate Program of Religious Studies. He has also taught on the faculties of Princeton University and Wellesley College, with visiting lectureships at Yale College, The College of the Holy Cross, Mt. Holyoke, and Colgate–Rochester Divinity School. An ordained minister in the United Church of Christ, he received the BD, MA, and PhD degrees from Yale University, with post-graduate study at Cambridge University (U.K.), Harvard University, and the Graduate Theological Union in Berkeley, California. His writings include numerous articles and three books: *The Gospels: Portraits of Christ; Jung and the Bible;* and, most recently, *Soul and Psyche: The Bible in Psychological Perspective.* He is the founding chair of the Psychology and Biblical Studies Section of the Society of Biblical Literature, an international organization of biblical scholars.